Canada and the Changing Arctic

**Franklyn Griffiths, Rob Huebert,
and P. Whitney Lackenbauer**
Forewords by Bill Graham and
Hugh Segal

Canada and the Changing Arctic

Sovereignty, Security, and Stewardship

**WILFRID LAURIER
UNIVERSITY PRESS**

We acknowledge the support of the Canada Council for the Arts for our publishing program. We acknowledge the financial support of the Government of Canada through the Canada Book Fund for our publishing activities.

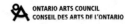

Library and Archives Canada Cataloguing in Publication

Griffiths, Franklyn, 1935–
    Canada and the changing Arctic : sovereignty, security, and stewardship / Franklyn Griffiths, Rob Huebert, and P. Whitney Lackenbauer.

Includes bibliographical references and index.
Issued also in electronic format.
ISBN 978-1-55458-338-6

    1. Canada, Northern—Strategic aspects. 2. Arctic regions—Strategic aspects. 3. Canada, Northern—Military policy. 4. Canada, Northern—Government policy. 5. Canada—Boundaries—Arctic regions. I. Huebert, Robert N. (Robert Neil), 1960– II. Lackenbauer, P. Whitney III. Title.

FC191.G75 2011   341.4'209719   C2011-904876-0

Type of computer file: Electronic monograph.
Issued also in print format.
ISBN 978-1-55458-413-0 (PDF). —ISBN 978-1-55458-414-7 (EPUB)

    1. Canada, Northern—Strategic aspects. 2. Arctic regions—Strategic aspects. 3. Canada, Northern—Military policy. 4. Canada, Northern—Government policy. 5. Canada—Boundaries—Arctic regions. I. Huebert, Robert N. (Robert Neil), 1960– II. Lackenbauer, P. Whitney III. Title.

FC191.G75 2011a   341.4'209719   C2011-904877-9

Cover design by Blakeley Words+Pictures. Cover photograph by Master Corporal Kevin Paul/DND. http://www.airforce.forces.gc.ca/v2/netpub/index-eng.asp?rid=7598-IS2008-3138. Text design by Catharine Bonas-Taylor.

© 2011 Wilfrid Laurier University Press
Waterloo, Ontario, Canada
www.wlupress.wlu.ca

This book is printed on FSC recycled paper and is certified Ecologo. It is made from 100% post-consumer fibre, processed chlorine free, and manufactured using biogas energy.

Printed in Canada

Contents

List of Maps   vii

List of Figures   ix

Foreword / *Hugh Segal, Senator*   xi

Foreword / *Bill Graham, former Minister of Foreign Affairs and of National Defence*   xv

Acknowledgments   xxiii

List of Acronyms   xxvii

1 **Introduction**   1

2 **Canadian Arctic Sovereignty and Security in a Transforming Circumpolar World** / Rob Huebert   13
   Understanding Sovereignty and Security   14
   Canadian Concepts of Arctic Sovereignty and Security   19
   The Changing Arctic   25
   Conclusion   59

3 **From Polar Race to Polar Saga: An Integrated Strategy for Canada and the Circumpolar World** / P. Whitney Lackenbauer   69
   Background   72
   Defence   93
   Diplomacy   118
   Development   146
   Conclusion   161

4 Towards a Canadian Arctic Strategy / Franklyn Griffiths 181
The Arctic as an Arena 183
Arctic Strategy for Canada 195
Domestic Sources of Stewardship 211
Recommendations 218

5 Sovereignty, Security, and Stewardship: An Update /
P. Whitney Lackenbauer 227
Canada's Northern Strategy 227
The Emerging Arctic Security Regime? 228

Appendix: *Statement on Canada's Arctic Foreign Policy: Exercising
Sovereignty and Promoting Canada's Northern Strategy Abroad,*
August 2010 / *Department of Foreign Affairs and International Trade* 255
Introduction 255
Exercising Sovereignty 257
Promoting Economic and Social Development 261
Protecting the Arctic Environment 265
Improving and Devolving Governance 270
The Way Forward 271
Conclusion 273

Bibliography 275
Index 303

List of Maps

Map 1 Circumpolar world   xxx

Map 2-1 Arctic Ocean marine routes   20

Map 2-2 US Geological Survey Circum-Arctic Resource Appraisal of undiscovered oil and gas   30

Map 2-3 Maritime jurisdictions and boundaries in the Arctic Region   40

Map 3-1 Inuit Nunaat   72

Map 3-2 Canadian Arctic islands and mainland baselines   79

Map 3-3 Northern Canada Vessel Traffic Services (NORDREG) zone   115

Map 3-4 Hans Island   120

Map 3-5 Beaufort Sea: US and Canadian claims   125

Map 3-6 Arctic peoples subdivided according to language families   135

Map 3-7 Resource knowledge: oil and gas   151

Map 3-8 Modern treaties in the North   155

Map 4 Potential intercontinental shipping routes   182

List of Figures

2-1 Maritime zones of Canada   15

2-2 USCGS *Polar Sea* in Beaufort Sea, 2009   35

2-3 RadarSat-2, launched 2007   37

2-4 Russian *Yamal* nuclear-powered icebreaker   44

2-5 CF-18 Hornet with Russian Tu-95 "Bear" bomber, 2007   51

2-6 CC-138 Twin Otter with Canadian Rangers on patrol, 2008   53

2-7 HMCS *Montreal* and iceberg in Strathcona Sound   61

3-1 Canadian Ranger with army personnel in Penguin, 1954   74

3-2 Global Business Network Future Arctic Marine Navigation Matrix, 2008   91

3-3 Stephen Harper at opening ceremony for Operation Lancaster, 2006   95

3-4 Canadian Rangers at briefing, Cumberland Peninsula area, Baffin Island, 2004   100

3-5 CC-177 Globemaster at Alert, Nunavut, on Operation Nunalivut, 2010   105

3-6 Canadian officials during Operation Nanook 09 in Frobisher Bay   108

3-7 Co-chairs at meeting of Arctic Security Working Group, Yellowknife, 2009   109

3-8   CCGS *Henry Larsen* in Strathcona Sound during Operation
Nanook 10   111

3-9   Ships in formation on Labrador Sea during Operation Nanook,
2010   117

3-10 Icebreakers on research expedition in Canadian Basin, Arctic Ocean,
2010   124

3-11 Ministers of foreign affairs meet in Chelsea, Quebec, 2010   133

3-12 Duane Smith at Social Development Working Group of Arctic
Council   137

3-13 Mary Simon responds to official apology for residential schools,
2008   144

3-14 Stephen Harper in Tuktoyaktuk, 2010   153

3-15 Scientist Luke Copland on Ayles Ice Shelf, Ellesmere Island,
2008   159

5-1   Ceremony marking conclusion of Operation Nunavilut, Alert,
2010   229

5-2   Canadian Ranger instructs soldiers near Resolute during Operation
Nanook, 2010   231

5-3   Signing of Canada–Denmark memorandum of understanding on
Arctic defence, 2010   236

5-4   Arctic Ocean Foreign Ministers' Meeting in Chelsea, Quebec,
2010   241

5-5   Arctic Council Ministerial Meeting, Norway, 2009   243

Foreword

Hugh Segal

It is rare that a territory seen by so few can be emotionally, spiritually, and personally so compellingly important to so many. Yet that is a modest and understated description of the relationship between Canadians and their Arctic region and territories. It is a passionate, possessive, patriotic, and nationalistic relationship second only to our embrace of hockey. It is not yet jingoistic, which is a good thing. But it is also prone, as is often the case with visions seen from a great distance, to substantive and dangerous distortion. To suggest that the relationship is simply geo-strategic, or narrowly territorial, or militaristic, or simply about the oil and gas, is to oversimplify. Because the relationship between Canadians and the Arctic is about all of the above and a highly romantic quality, understanding the dynamics of the romance, its sustainability and attendant risks, is not only constructive but actually vital to the kind of public, defence, and foreign policies essential to maintaining the relationship at its optimum clarity and balance.

The political, environmental, and international law prospectus for the Arctic is complex, as are the instruments available for Canada and Canadians to secure our interests. *Canada and the Changing Arctic* is essentially a careful unpacking of the challenges that are most germane to Canada's Arctic purposes and of the instruments available to deal with them. It is very reflective of Canada's history and the postwar growth and aspirations, which strongly shaped who we are today through events and clarion calls in the 1950s and 1960s, that Mike Pearson's universal health insurance is totemic for many and that John Diefenbaker's "northern vision" of "roads to resources" is as totemic for others. And in fact, in a way that confounds sterile assumptions dividing right from left, many of the same people had their sense of Canadian identity imprinted by both.

That another Canadian prime minister from the West should, half a century later, re-engage both the symbolism and the promise of the Arctic and make substantive policy announcements and yearly visits part of three election campaigns and his regular schedule, speaks to the enduring impact of the Arctic challenge on Canadians. That vote-rich southern Ontario or the B.C. Lower Mainland remains interested in this issue and attracted to coherent policy for the North underlines the seminal roll the North plays in people's sense of what Canada is and who we are as Canadians.

Some may view Prime Minister Harper's championing of a northern policy as shrewd political strategy. That may or may not be true. My own sense is that it also reflects an Ontario-born reflective and intuitive political leader rooted in the political culture of the West whose own sense of Canada has always been shaped not only by a clear affection for hockey but also by the Arctic reality of our national identity. It is a reality, after all, that agitates no inter-regional animosity, language tension, or beggar-thy-neighbour confederal friction. Prime ministers avoid engaging this kind of challenge at their peril. Deciding for the right reasons to articulate a nation's hopes and core elements of identity is what prime ministers at their best do well. The present focus on diverse aspects of Arctic policy, and on the instruments to achieve that policy, whether already available or to be designed, not only in this book but also in a growing cottage industry at think tanks, in the private sector, at universities and foundations, and within the First Nation Arctic family, owes much to Prime Minister Harper's determined thematic coherence on the challenge of the North.

For Canada and Canadians this is a defining issue, for it embraces every aspect of our way ahead. Sovereignty, not as an end state but as an instrument for the national and public interest, is a vital issue. Fundamental components of this are real military capacity, procedures, training, and location. Working alliances with former Cold War enemies matter, as does how we manage them on this issue. Hydrographic competence and acuity join climate change policy impacts as defining subforces that will contribute heavily to how our northern prospects are sustained and evaluated.

This book helps us through the maze by offering *realpolitik* analysis as well as helpful instrumental precision around issues such as the law of the sea, defensible perimeters, and joint environmental protection priorities. And, as is often the case when a bright and intellectually honest light is shone on assumptions and fears, the paths to a rational way ahead appear less murky and less risky and the supportive policy choices necessary to clear those paths begin to emerge. *Canada and the Changing Arctic* sheds a measure of helpful light, not unlike a candle in the dark, on the true import of Arctic policy choices. Indian Affairs and Northern Development, Foreign Affairs, and the Department of National Defence should make this monograph compulsory reading for all of their staff who have present or potential responsibilities for Arctic policy and delivery issues. It is one of my great joys that in the initiating work I did to assist the Canadian International Council over three years ago to stand up its peer-reviewed research program, I was able, with Bill Graham, Janice Stein, John English, Jim Balsillie, Pierre Marc Johnson, Douglas Gould, Jennifer Jeffs, Tamara Zur, Jodi Whyte, Don Macnamara, Eddie Goldenberg, and others, to work with this book's co-authors in what was one of the first new peer-reviewed and CIC-sponsored strategic research projects of the newly created council. That the academic research committee of the CIC would have chosen established and younger scholars of the compelling depth and skill of the three co-authors to work on the Arctic reflects the importance of research to policy development that is well founded and based on a competent understanding of the variables—the underlining of which is a key goal of the CIC and its antecedent organizations, the Canadian Institute for International Affairs (CIIA) and the Canadian Institute for Strategic Studies (CISS).

The Arctic is Canadian identity writ large. Foreign diplomats who serve in Canada often remark that in all their travels while stationed here, they never really understood the full measure of Canada and Canadians until the Arctic tour that Foreign Affairs Canada and DND arranged for them during their time here. This book helps all of us who care about realizing the full potential of our country, internationally, domestically, economically, and in a way that is environmentally responsible, better understand some of the choices relating to the Arctic that need to be better appreciated. One need not agree with all the analyses or conclusions to admire the integrity, thinking, balance, and insight that fuel this book. Every romance needs engagement and reflection. Our romance with the Arctic requires nothing less.

Foreword

Bill Graham

When Professor Huebert asked me to contribute an introduction to this collection of essays by some of Canada's foremost experts on Arctic matters, I wondered what I could add to their informed reflections on these issues, which Canadians must understand if they are to meet the challenges presented by that important but neglected region. On reflection, I thought it might be helpful for me to contribute a somewhat different perspective on the impact of Arctic concerns: that of my experience as a parliamentarian from urban Canada. So I offer these observations in the modest hope they might contribute to an understanding of the political climate in which recent decisions that have influenced the shape of Canadian Arctic policy were made, for good or ill.

There has always been somewhat of a disconnect between political rhetoric about the importance of the Arctic in Canada's identity as a northern nation and the resources we have provided to turn that rhetoric into reality. This dichotomy was brought home to me when I was Chair of Parliament's Standing Committee on Foreign Affairs and International Trade (SCFAIT).

In 1996, SCFAIT members conducted extensive travel and research in the Arctic (including Russia and Norway), hearing expert witnesses and Arctic residents, both on their home ground and in Ottawa. Our report issued in the spring of 1997, *Canada and the Circumpolar World*, discussed issues of sovereignty and security, international cooperation, the environment, and sustainable development. Its recommendations largely still ring true, and many of them are found among the prescriptions offered by the contributors to this collection.

The report did not use the term "global warming," but it emphasized the impact of climate change and accompanying environmental damage on the Arctic; the resulting changes to the Inuit way of life; increased access to mineral and other resources; and the impact of retreating Arctic ice on Canadian claims and geopolitical realities in the region. It called for significant investments in Arctic science and research—a recommendation that arose from recognition that the Russian mapping of the continental seabed required a similar Canadian engagement. We also urged more northern education and increased defence capabilities. As we know, the government of the day first had been preoccupied with restoring Canada's fiscal integrity, and when that was restored it focused on health, scientific research, and university financing (the Millennium Scholarships). So, as had often happened before, those recommendations that cost money to implement went largely unimplemented.

One thing the report did accomplish was to improve the understanding in Parliament of the role played by the northern peoples themselves in Arctic governance and stewardship of the land. This was reflected in work done by other members of SCFAIT, such as Reform Party MP Charlie Penson, and by the members of Charles Caccia's House of Commons Environment Committee, as well as complementary interparliamentary bodies such as the Conference of Parliamentarians of the Arctic Region (CPAR), in which Clifford Lincoln was very active.

SCFAIT's work impressed upon me the extent to which modern technology has enabled Canada's northern peoples to pool resources and coordinate activities with the neighbouring peoples of Alaska, Russia, and northern Norway. High-speed Internet has linked facilities such as the Aurora Research Institute and Yukon College, allowing northern residents and visiting researchers to share their experiences and knowledge as well as the results of their work on the ground. This in turn enriches their capacity to design and implement local solutions to their problems—something I came to appreciate when I was Foreign Minister and saw the unique role that northern peoples can play in institutions like the Arctic Council.

Perhaps surprisingly, one institution of government that has become publicly identified with the Arctic in recent years is the office of Governor General. Adrienne Clarkson and John Ralston Saul travelled widely in the region, bringing Arctic concerns to the attention of southern Canadians and emphasizing Canada's northern identity in their travels abroad. More recently, they drew attention to Arctic issues by holding the Lafontaine–Baldwin Lecture in Iqaluit. And Michaëlle Jean's meal of raw seal meat at an Inuit community event was welcomed by many Canadians who were aware of the fragile state of Aboriginal life in the Arctic and the role that the Inuit and other northern peoples play in the stewardship of its renewable resources. Her gesture was, for many, a riposte to what many perceive as the hypocrisy of European parliamentarians who profess deep concern for Aboriginal peoples but who condemn the seal hunt and other fur-gathering activities that sustain their existence.

As Foreign Minister, I had direct exposure to issues of Canadian sovereignty, particularly the question of whether the Northwest Passage is an international passage or part of our internal waters. There is an extensive literature on this question, to which this book adds. Something that has always puzzled me—and apparently Professor Huebert—is the American insistence that the passage be treated as international waters, an insistence recently reinforced in a National Security Directive by the outgoing Bush administration.

I can understand American concerns about a precedent that might affect the Malacca Strait or other contested waters of interest to the US Navy. But it would seem to be in the interest of the United States that the passage be regarded as Canadian. The United States, as a friend and ally, would have virtually unrestricted passage, subject to environmental controls from which we and they would both benefit. Similar arrangements could meet the EU's interest in free commercial use, while less benign powers would be denied the right of unrestricted free passage. We are familiar with Russia's claims in the region and its interest in its resources, but it may be that China's recent interest in the area, seen in light of its worldwide resource acquisition policy and its development of Arctic research and a blue water navy with icebreaker capacity, would mandate American and European support of the Canadian position.

Another preoccupation of the Department of Foreign Affairs when I was its minister was the question of how Arctic sovereignty could be exercised effectively. It seemed to me then—and even more now—that many Arctic issues demand a multilateral approach, or "cooperative stewardship," as described by Professor Griffiths in his contribution. This holds even for what might seem like purely national concerns, as we learned in the case of the deteriorating Russian nuclear fleet in Murmansk: an immediate problem for the Russians, to be sure, but one for us as well should a disaster occur; radioactive activity in the sea does not respect national borders. This, of course, was one of our motivations in signing on to the project for removing Russian chemical and nuclear wastes, agreed on at the Kananaskis G-8 summit.

One institution essential to multilateral cooperation in the Arctic is the Arctic Council. When I was minister, the Americans paid little attention to the council, reflecting the Bush administration's general hostility toward international institutions that it saw as impinging on American sovereignty. Members such as Norway and Canada, however, treated it as important. For example, it enabled us to engage in scientific research without problematic political overtones. Indeed, scientists with the Arctic Council conducted much of the initial research into the effects of climate change in the Arctic. While there has been politically driven reluctance in some quarters to endorse policies that flow from that research, it has done much to establish the facts on which policy makers must rely.

Unlike any other international institution of which I know, the Arctic Council has the additional advantage of providing a formal role for the Aboriginal peoples who populate the Arctic. In my experience, the participation of the Inuit Tapirisat of Canada (now Inuit Tapiriit Kanatami) and the Athabaska nations, to give two examples, brought insight into events on the ground as well as practical solutions. In addition, Canadian members gained a truly circumpolar perspective by sharing experiences and best practices with their Aboriginal counterparts in the other Arctic countries.

Underlying all claims to Arctic sovereignty is the United Nations Convention on the Law of the Sea, which Canada signed in 1982 but did not ratify until 2003 because of domestic opposition, which was largely centred on the North Atlantic fishery. As a professor of international law, I had often lamented in class our failure to ratify the very convention we had inspired and helped draft. When I pointed out to Prime Minister Jean Chrétien the importance of the treaty for our claims in the Arctic, he agreed to take it once again to Cabinet, and this time we got approval. So it was with considerable personal satisfaction that in November of 2003, I signed the instrument of ratification, in the presence of Alan Beesley, our principal negotiator and one of the fathers of the convention. In fact, it was almost twenty-one years to the day that he and the Honourable Allan MacEachen signed the treaty on behalf of Canada. Russia's recent effort to extend its claims to the continental shelf based on the treaty confirms the wisdom of our action; even the Americans now recognize that if they are to protect their rights in the Arctic they will have to do so under the treaty, and they are slowly moving towards ratification.

As Minister of National Defence, I was more deeply involved in the Arctic than I expected to be when Prime Minister Paul Martin appointed me. In fact, the Department of National Defence has major responsibilities in the North, including the infrastructure for responding to events that in the southern provinces are the responsibility of provincial governments. For example, the department is responsible for search and rescue throughout the North, not just offshore, as it is in southern Canada. In that context, it was sometimes argued that, given the relatively small number of Arctic incidents compared to those in the south, it would be more efficient to locate the materiel for our search and rescue capability at bases in Trenton, Cold Lake, or elsewhere in the south, deploying it to the North when necessary. I was strongly of the view that we needed an actual physical presence there, because our absence would only confirm to northerners our basic lack of interest in their requirements.

Northern search and rescue was one activity on which I worked with my Russian counterpart, Sergei Ivanov, when we met in Moscow. In fact, there is a long-standing tradition of discreet, non-politicized—"under the radar," so to speak—cooperation among Canada, Russia, and the United States on search and rescue, a model for other areas of circumpolar cooperation. The present government—wisely in my view—has turned to the Arctic Council as the appropriate forum for drawing up a multilateral arrangement for Arctic search and rescue, and this could well serve as a template for further cooperation of this nature in other fields.

The DND no longer maintains the Arctic presence it had during the Cold War, with the DEW line and forward staging bases for CF-18s. But it retains an active presence through exercises and the Canadian Rangers, who serve as a visible symbol of Canadian sovereignty. It is quite an experience to participate in exercises with the Rangers and to see how proudly and professionally they carry out their functions. Finding a cost-effective way to train other reserve troops for northern activities, however, remains a formidable challenge.

Equally challenging, in fiscal terms, are some of the present government's proposals for a permanent naval presence in the Arctic. In my view, most of these proposals are unlikely to survive the Finance Department's hostile gaze, and in fact some of the more expensive proposals made in the 2006 election have already been shelved, including one for a permanent base with nine hundred personnel. In the near future, at least, we will continue to rely on Radarsat and the stepped-up use of UAVs for Arctic surveillance to give us an active presence. Indeed, a recent report for the DND has recommended relying on drones to enforce Arctic sovereignty, rather than the fighter jets the government proposed to buy. It remains to be seen whether there will be effective complementary instruments.

As recent Arctic operations such as *Nanook* have emphasized, the future needs of the North can only be met by a holistic, multidepartmental approach that recognizes we are more in need of policing and environmental protection than of classic military measures. You need only ask just what nation's ships an armed Canadian vessel would fire upon to realize that we need different assets and policy approaches than we did only a few years ago. As ice melts and much of the Far North becomes more accessible, this will only become more evident. Today in Tuktoyaktuk, for example, visiting cruise ships and the importation of drugs are displacing previous challenges.

In July 2005, I had occasion to visit our northernmost base at Alert. At the height of the Cold War, hundreds of personnel were stationed at Alert, monitoring Soviet communications across the pole. It is now a shadow of its Cold War self, with one or two technicians and just enough DND personnel to maintain the base, with all the information that's gathered funnelled south for analysis. While I was at Alert, I could not resist the temptation to visit Hans Island, even though the initiative was not popular with Foreign Affairs, to plant a Canadian flag as one more assertion of our sovereignty against that of Denmark. This is an unusual and very limited territorial dispute, since we have agreed on the boundary from a point 1 km north of the island and 1 km south, so determining who owns Hans Island does not have a significant territorial impact. There is an important point of principle, though it is certainly one that will be resolved without a military confrontation between us and our Danish allies. Indeed, at a subsequent conference of NATO defence ministers, my Danish colleague good-naturedly asked me to take a Danish flag on my next trip to the island so "it would save him the trouble of having to go there." More recently, our ships have taken part in joint exercises with the Danish navy in the North, all without any impact on our respective claims to this uninhabited rock about the size of a football field.

To me, the Hans Island episode symbolizes much about the political process. It received a lot of attention on the Internet in its time, dramatizing a "conflict" that is quite limited, involving as it does minimal territorial claims.

The press of the day recognized my gesture for what it was. An editorial in the *Toronto Star* observed: "Despite the inevitable jokes about Hans Island, there was a serious underlying reason for Graham's visit." The same view was reflected in the *National Post*, which, while it wanted "to applaud Mr. Graham's Nordic jaunt," went on to observe that "much more was needed to keep … our northern lands under Canadian control." Meanwhile, the dispute between ourselves and the Americans over the North Slope in the Western Arctic, which is of inestimable importance, is largely ignored today even through there is a freeze on the issuing of exploration licences in the area. As Professor Huebert puts it in his contribution, "the ultimate question facing Canada is the level of control of its Arctic borders." This border issue and the question of the Northwest Passage pit us against our closest ally, with enormous potential resource and environmental consequences.

In some of its recent statements and policy positions, the present government has indicated a renewed interest in the Arctic. To some extent, this began under the Martin government, which formed a special Cabinet committee to examine Arctic issues under the chairmanship of Andy Scott. This initiative ended, of course, with the electoral defeat of January 2006. But the Martin government did take some concrete steps, such as the first *Narwhal* operation, which recognized that northern issues are not just about sovereignty and defence but also involve the environment, law enforcement, and other questions, which together require a holistic approach and close interdepartmental cooperation.

Mr. Harper's government has increased these activities considerably, and while there has been some criticism of his much-publicized Arctic "photo ops," it is precisely these photo ops that draw attention to the Arctic. And program initiatives like those described in this book mark significant advances in our investment in the region. Meanwhile, technological advances such as the Radarsat and the use of UAVs do provide us with new vehicles for enforcing our sovereignty.

My hope is that this book's scholarly assessment of Arctic realities and needs will inspire this government and future ones to make the investments needed to bring this one-third of Canada's land mass properly within our national scope. I also hope these studies will find a wider audience and thus inform Canadian opinion, so that it will demand more of our political masters, and so that the realities of future government action will come closer to the political rhetoric than has often been the case until now.

Acknowledgments

First and foremost, we thank the Canadian International Council (CIC) for granting us research fellowships to pursue these studies in 2008–9. Tamara Zur, Jordan Dupuis, Frances Cation, and Laura Sunderland organized speaking engagements, edited drafts, and supported us in myriad other ways. Hugh Segal and Bill Graham supported us during our fellowship year and graciously agreed to write forewords to this book. Jennifer Jeffs, the new executive director of the CIC, supported our plans to publish our studies with WLU Press and provided a generous subvention to make this book possible. Our thanks as well to David Bercuson, director of the Centre for Military and Strategic Studies at the University of Calgary, and Terry Copp, director of the Laurier Centre for Military Strategic and Disarmament Studies, for supporting research programs on Arctic security and providing funds that made the publication of this book possible. Rob Huebert and Whitney Lackenbauer would also like to thank ArcticNet for its generous funding for their project on the evolving Arctic security environment that has facilitated their ongoing research. Peter Kikkert offered valuable comments that helped us frame the introduction, as did two anonymous reviewers. Lisa Beiler assisted with last-minute updates to the bibliography. At WLU Press, Ryan Chynces was instrumental in guiding us through the publication process quickly and efficiently.

Franklyn Griffiths

The author wishes to express his gratitude to the Canadian International Council for its generous support of the work that went into this study. Thanks go also to the many officials and private analysts who gave freely of their knowledge and opinions in interviews that contributed markedly to whatever is of value here. Special acknowledgment is due to three individuals whose views on an early version of this paper were of singular value: Hans Corell, former Legal Counsel to the United Nations; Professor Willy Østreng, Scientific Director of the Centre for Advanced Studies, Norwegian Academy of Sciences and Letters, Oslo; and Oran R. Young, Professor at the Bren School of Environmental Science and Management, University of California at Santa Barbara. Much obliged to all three, the author frees them of responsibility for any errors of commission or omission in what follows.

Rob Huebert

This study represents the culmination of research that I have been conducting since the end of the 1980s on the issue of Canadian Arctic sovereignty and security. It is therefore with sincere gratitude that I acknowledge the support of the Canadian International Council in awarding me one of their first fellowships to address this very important issue. I also wish to thank the CIC for awarding fellowships to my friends and colleagues, Franklyn Griffiths and Whitney Lackenbauer, to support their work in examining Arctic issues. Since the three of us seldom agree on issues related to the Arctic, the intellectual wrestling that we have engaged in has allowed me to focus and refine my own thinking on the subject.

Within the CIC, I wish to extend my thanks and gratitude to Tamara Zur, Frances Cation, and Jordan Dupuis, who have, with the utmost professionalism and courtesy, performed an outstanding job in keeping me on schedule and providing administrative help. I would also like to thank the anonymous reviewer for her/his helpful comments and to acknowledge the leadership shown by Senator Hugh Segal in guiding the "Arctic group," as well as the encouragement that Denis Stairs and David Bercuson gave me to apply for the CIC fellowship. Thanks also to the Canadian Defence and Foreign Affairs Institute for their support of my work on the evolving Arctic security environment that informs this study.

My most profound appreciation goes to my wife, Shabnam, and our three children, Ben, Ethan, and Kishan, and my mother, Sophie Huebert. They are my most important inspirations in my work and my life, and their unwavering support was absolutely necessary for me to complete my commitments for the fellowship. While I know that none of them like my absences when I need to leave home, I also know that they all understand why I need to do it!

P. Whitney Lackenbauer

Thanks to the civil servants, politicians, Canadian Forces personnel, and northern residents who agreed to interviews or spoke informally with me over the past several years.

Rob Huebert has been generous in his guidance and encouragement, even where we do not see eye to eye. Ken Coates, Bill Morrison, and Greg Poelzer shared ideas as we co-authored *Arctic Front: Defending Canada's Far North.* Careful readers will see in this document where I disagree with the observations and conclusions we drew collectively ("majority rules") in that book. Captain (Navy) Jamie Cotter and Lieutenant Colonel Paul Dittmann, both of whom I had the privilege to supervise while they were completing their Masters of Defence Studies papers through Canadian Forces College, shared research and ideas. Research assistants Lisa Beiler, Andrew Ottaway, and Matthew Willis were instrumental in gathering information and discussing ideas, for which I am grateful. Peter Kikkert was particularly helpful in sharing his important research and insights based upon interviews with northern stakeholders. Reviewer David Haglund and CIC copy editor Frances Cation also helped strengthen my arguments.

I wrote the introduction and conclusions to this book as a Fulbright Scholar at the School for Advanced International Studies, Johns Hopkins University, in Washington, DC, in the fall of 2010. Thanks to the Fulbright program for supporting dedicated research and writing time, as well as the Social Sciences and Humanities Research Council of Canada and ArcticNet for funding further research on Arctic security over the past two years. Thanks also to my three sons—Harrison, Rendall, and Pierce—for enduring my frequent absences as I headed "down north."

Last and never least, Jennifer Arthur-Lackenbauer forced me to clarify my ideas and to resist my temptation, as a historian, to qualify every statement. My contributions to this book, like everything I write, are a product of our partnership, but I claim full responsibility for all errors herein.

Acronyms

3-D	defence-development-diplomacy
AAC	Arctic Athabaskan Council
ACAC	Arctic Council Advisory Committee
ACIA	Arctic Climate Impact Assessment
ACND	Advisory Committee on Northern Development
AEPS	Arctic Environmental Protection Strategy
AGC	Auditor General of Canada
AIP	air-independent propulsion
AIS	Arctic Identification System
AMAP	Arctic Monitoring and Assessment Program
AOPSs	Arctic offshore patrol ships
ASAT	anti-satellite attack technology
ASWG	Arctic Security Working Group (formerly ASIWG/Arctic Security Intergovernmental Working Group)
AU	assessment unit
AWPPA	Arctic Waters Pollution Prevention Act
BP	British Petroleum
BPA	Basic Principles Agreement
C4ISR	command, control, communications, computers, intelligence, surveillance, and reconnaissance
CAFF	Conservation of Arctic Flora and Fauna
CARA	Circum-Arctic Resource Appraisal
CARC	Canadian Arctic Resources Committee

CBC Canadian Broadcasting Corporation
CCG Canadian Coast Guard
CF Canadian Forces
CFNA Canadian Forces Northern Area
CLCS Commission on Limits of the Continental Shelf
CMS Chief of the Maritime Staff
CMSS Centre for Military and Strategic Studies, University of Calgary
CSCE Conference on Security and Cooperation in Europe
DEW Distant Early Warning
DEXAF Department of External Affairs
DFAIT Department of Foreign Affairs and International Trade
DFO Department of Fisheries and Oceans
DND Department of National Defence
DRDC Defence Research and Development Canada
EC European Commission
EEZ exclusive economic zone
EU European Union
GBN Global Business Network
HCSCFAIT House of Commons Standing Committee on Foreign Affairs
and International Trade
IASC International Arctic Science Committee
ICC Inuit Circumpolar Council
IMO International Maritime Organization
INAC Department of Indian and Northern Affairs Canada
IPO indigenous people's organization
IPS *International Policy Statement*
ISR intelligence, surveillance, and reconnaissance
ITK Inuit Tapiriit Kanatami
JTFN Joint Task Force North
LAC Library and Archives Canada
LCMSDS Laurier Centre for Military Strategic and Disarmament
Studies, Wilfrid Laurier University
LNG liquefied natural gas
MCDV Maritime Coastal Defence Vessel
MELAW Marine and Environmental Law Institute, Dalhousie Law
School
MMBOE million barrels of oil equivalent
MP Member of Parliament
MSOC Marine Security Operations Centres Project
n.m. nautical mile

NATO North Atlantic Treaty Organization
NDFP *Northern Dimension of Canada's Foreign Policy*
NMC Nunavut Marine Council
NNF Nanisivik Naval Facility
NORAD North American Aerospace Defence Command
NORDREG Northern Canada Vessel Traffic Services
NORPLOY Northern Deployment (Canadian Maritime Forces)
NSERC Natural Sciences and Engineering Research Council of Canada
NSR Northern Sea Route (Northeast Passage)
NTI Nunavut Tunggavik Inc.
NWP Northwest Passage
NWT Northwest Territories
OSPAR Convention for the Protection of the Marine Environment of the North-East Atlantic
PAIR Pre-Arrival Information Report
PAME Protection of the Arctic Marine Environment
PM Prime Minister
PMO Prime Minister's Office
PMO-A Senior Official in the PMO
RAIPON Russian Association of Indigenous Peoples of the North
RG Record Group
RCMP Royal Canadian Mounted Police
SAOs senior Arctic officials
SAR search and rescue
SCPA Standing Committee on Public Accounts
SS-A Secretary of State for the Arctic
SSCFO Standing Senate Committee on Fisheries and Oceans
SSCNSD Standing Senate Committee on National Security and Defence
SSHRC Social Sciences and Humanities Research Council of Canada
UArctic University of the Arctic
UAV unmanned aerial vehicle
UBC University of British Columbia
UNCLOS United Nations Convention on the Law of the Sea
UNEP United Nations Environment Programme
UNFCC United Nations Framework on Climate Change
UV ultraviolet
WDGF Walter & Duncan Gordon Foundation

Map 1   Circumpolar world, 2007–8.
Source: Natural Resources Canada

1

Introduction

Canada's far North is a fundamental part of Canada—it is part of our heritage, our future and our identity as a country. The North is undergoing rapid changes, from the impacts of climate change to the growth of Northern and Aboriginal governments and institutions. At the same time, domestic and international interest in the Arctic region is rising. This growing interest underscores the importance of Canada to exert effective leadership both at home and abroad in order to promote a prosperous and stable region responsive to Canadian interests and values.

—Canada's Northern Strategy: Our North, Our Heritage,
Our Future, *July 2009*

The Arctic is front page news in Canada and around the world. Mixed messages from journalists, academics, and government representatives predict both conflict and cooperation in the region. On the one hand, talk abounds of "a new Cold War" brewing, tied to a "race for resources," an international scramble to claim the riches of a newly accessible region, and the buildup of military capabilities designed for Arctic operations. On the other hand, the governments of the Arctic coastal states suggest an era of enhanced cooperation rooted in international law, respect for sovereign rights, and responsible stewardship.

There is a lively debate in Canada about what these developments mean for the future of our Arctic and the circumpolar world more generally.

Although Canadians supposedly eschew conflict and prefer to seek consensus on issues, competing viewpoints help clarify core issues and stimulate discussion about opportunities and constraints. The three authors of this volume—two political scientists and one historian—share several assumptions about the Arctic. We also differ in our assessments of what is happening in the Arctic, what Canada's priorities should be, and how Canada can best position itself to play a leadership role in the circumpolar world.

Franklyn Griffiths dates his engagement with Arctic policy matters to the intrusive Northwest Passage voyages of the US supertanker *Manhattan* in 1969 and 1970. In retrospect, he became an ardent Canadian Arctic sovereigntist and stayed that way well into the 1980s even as Canadian interest in the Arctic dissipated. On 13 June 1985 his influential *Globe and Mail* editorial comment was the catalyst for an outpouring of public concern about the transit of the Northwest Passage by the US icebreaker *Polar Sea*. Subsequently, however, as Canadian Arctic interest declined again, he began to question "sovereigntism" as a basis for the constancy of southerners in their approach not only to the Canadian Arctic but also to the region beyond, a region in which the need for environmental preservation loomed ever larger. As co-chair of the Arctic Council Panel into the early 1990s, he also began to see the Arctic from an indigenous peoples' as well as a southern perspective. The panel's report, which he thought through and wrote, laid much of the intellectual foundation for the Arctic Council that was finally established by the regional states in 1996. Pan-Arctic governance being his prime concern, he subsequently objected to those—his colleague Rob Huebert chief among them—who interpreted climate change principally as a sovereignty-on-thinning-ice threat to Canadian control over commercial shipping in the Northwest Passage. Instead, in his view, Canada's problem was and remains one of cooperative stewardship in which a confident people—not one needlessly fearful of its Arctic possessions—comes forward as a first mover for locally informed regional governance that not only polices but also respects and cares for the natural environment and all living things in it.

Rob Huebert began analyzing Arctic issues in the late 1980s. His first major project critically examined the Canadian response to the voyage of the *Polar Sea* and what this meant for the creation of Canada's Arctic foreign and defence policy. By the 1990s he observed that the state-centric, military-focused conceptualization of security that dominated during the Cold War had been transformed by a recent focus on environmental concerns and "human security" in the region. By the start of the new millennium, he was predicting that climate change and new geo-strategic imperatives would fundamentally transform the circumpolar world. His articles highlighted the sources of existing and potential conflicts for Canada in the Arctic by focusing on sovereignty and on boundary disputes between Canada and its immediate neighbours. He predicted that as the Arctic became more accessible through the impacts of climate change, the Canadian position regarding the Northwest Passage would come under increasing challenge from international actors. The media took interest in his assertions that an increased volume of foreign shipping and, consequently, a sovereignty challenge were likely and required sovereignty-affirming action by the federal government. These ideas were refined to emphasize the need for Canadian *control* in the region to safeguard its national interests. Huebert's studies have emphasized the need to understand what is happening in the Canadian North and to be able to respond to foreign challenges. His concerns have focused on Canada's security and military requirements.

Over the past decade, P. Whitney Lackenbauer (who studied under Huebert as a graduate student at the University of Calgary from 1998 to 2003) has critically re-examined the history of Canada's engagement with the circumpolar world. His initial work focused on the Canadian Rangers: members of the Canadian Forces Reserves who serve as Canada's "eyes and ears" in remote areas. In his view, the Rangers represent an example of how the military has successfully integrated the promotion of national security and sovereignty agendas with community-based activities and local management. It represents a practical partnership rather than shallow "consultation," and it promotes cooperation, communal and individual empowerment, and improved cross-cultural understanding. His ongoing participant observation fieldwork throughout the North, which began in 2002, has complemented his extensive archival research on Canada's official policies and practices since 1945. His particular attention to the Rangers' grassroots perspectives on sovereignty and security emphasizes the importance of *relationships* and the need to explicitly marry defence with diplomatic and development agendas to produce an integrated and sustainable Arctic strategy.

In January 2002, all three authors presented at a large conference in Ottawa on the "Thinning Ice" theme, organized by the Canadian Arctic Resources Committee, the Canadian Polar Commission, and the Centre for Military and Strategic Studies. Rob Huebert outlined his arguments about why Canadian sovereignty was on "thinning ice" and how the federal government had to make substantial investments in enforcement and surveillance. Although Griffiths had argued for increased spending on Arctic sovereignty in previous years, he now challenged the idea that melting sea ice would lead to increased international shipping, new challenges to Canada's exclusive jurisdiction, and new needs to invest in the defence of sovereignty.

He questioned the sovereignty-on-thinning-ice thesis and warned against the tendency for Canadian governments to formulate Arctic policies in reaction to "crises." In his paper, Lackenbauer focused on the need to balance military and community interests, suggesting that Northerners' priorities had to be acknowledged on a local level and accommodated in strategic planning.

These perspectives attracted increased national attention as media interest in the Arctic grew sharply in the middle of the decade. First came the escalation of the dispute between Canada and Demark over Hans Island. The Danes sent naval vessels to the island in 2002 and 2003. Canada responded in 2005 with an inukshuk-raising and flag-planting visit by a small group of Canadian Rangers and other land force personnel, followed by a highly publicized visit by the Minister of National Defence, Bill Graham. The media began alluding to Canada's 1995 "Turbot War" with the Spanish and even to a domino-theory effect, the suggestion being that if Canada lost Hans Island its other Arctic islands might succumb to a similar fate. Although Canada and Denmark soon restored the dispute to a diplomatic track, Hans Island remains a touchstone for popular misunderstandings of the sovereignty issues that Canada faces in the North.

The Arctic Council's seminal *Arctic Climate Impact Assessment* report, released in November 2004, revealed stunning ice and snow reductions across the region. Popular concerns about the implications for Canada, and particularly its control over the Northwest Passage, grew apace. The Paul Martin Liberals' 2005 *International Policy Statement* identified the importance of the Arctic and revealed growing political will to improve surveillance and control over this part of Canada. Prior to falling, the Martin government was in the final stages of completing a domestic Arctic policy. Along with the *International Policy Statement*, this revealed how senior decision makers were elevating concerns about Arctic sovereignty and security to a new level.

During the 2005–6 federal election campaign, Stephen Harper made Arctic sovereignty and security a core issue in his platform. After he became prime minister, he made annual trips to the Arctic and committed to invest significantly in improving Canada's security infrastructure. The political importance that he placed on the Arctic, as one of his primary legacy projects, generated significant debate about how Canada can best protect and project its national interests in the region.

All three authors were selected in a national competition as Canadian International Council research fellows for 2008–9 to critically examine Arctic issues and to each produce a "white paper" guiding Canadian Arctic policy. The results of their research form the core of this book. The scholars submitted preliminary directional papers at the beginning of June 2008 and participated in a CIC conference in Toronto that month. The authors' initial thoughts were published as an issue of *Behind the Headlines*, which also featured commentaries by then Nunavut premier Paul Okalik and international lawyer Suzanne Lalonde. The authors submitted the first drafts of their White Papers to the CIC in the fall of 2008, discussed their findings during national speaking tours, and debated their core ideas in a March 2009 national videoconference. They submitted their revised papers to the CIC in April 2009. Griffiths's was released in June, and those by Huebert and Lackenbauer the following month.

This book places their papers in dialogue with one another. In the first section, "Canadian Arctic Sovereignty and Security in a Transforming Circumpolar World," Huebert argues that control of the Arctic will yield significant benefit to the country wielding this control. He expects that Canada will need to deal with challenges to its Arctic in the future. Even non-Arctic states such as China, Japan, and South Korea have become active in the region. Competing claims vary relating to issues from resource exploitation and development, to division of the Arctic seabed, to the right of transit through the Northwest Passage. As various actors advance their claims, the potential exists for a serious challenge to Canada's sovereignty and security in its Arctic. Huebert lays out what he sees as the essential steps that the Canadian government must take to assert *control* over the region, enforce its claims, and cooperate better with its Arctic neighbours to develop an international framework that will serve as a guideline for rules of engagement.

In the second section, Lackenbauer suggests a different emphasis, with Canada reining in its alarmist rhetoric about alleged sovereignty and security threats. He argues that there is no "Arctic race" and that solutions to boundary disputes will be negotiated, not won or lost through military posturing. In his assessment, the "use it or lose it" message that has underpinned the Harper government's "call to arms" is erroneous and limiting. To devise a more confident and constructive Arctic strategy, Canada needs to marry its defence and resource development agenda with stronger diplomatic and social dimensions. A 3-D (defence–diplomacy–development) approach that recognizes the possibility for international cooperation, fixates less on potential "sovereignty loss," and encourages sustainable socio-economic development will place Canada in a better position to seize opportunities and become a world leader in circumpolar affairs. He suggests that the problems in the Arctic cannot be resolved by a return to Cold War rhetoric and a reactive, crisis-based mentality, which will preclude Canada from seizing opportunities in collaboration with northern residents. Canadians must recognize with confidence that Canadian arctic sovereignty is not in serious jeopardy, thanks to quiet diplomacy that has historically balanced continental security priorities with national interests. What Canada can anticipate and should seek is not an "Arctic race" but an "Arctic Saga," predicated on a greater demand for resources and trade coupled with more stable governance. This saga could be attained by focusing on sustainable development, constructive circumpolar engagement, and reasonable investments in defence, without sacrificing either sovereignty or security.

Griffiths, in the third and final section "Toward a Canadian Arctic Strategy," describes how climate change, the prospect of easier access and transit, and the expectation of long-term growth in the global demand for oil and gas have evoked unprecedented interest from the world at large and particularly the eight nations of the region: Canada, Denmark/Greenland, Finland, Iceland, Norway, the Russian Federation, Sweden, and the United States. While the strategic significance of the Arctic is increasing rapidly, Canada continues to have no strategy for the region in its entirety.

Griffiths details such a strategy, one that strives to channel the unfolding story of the region in a direction that mutes conflict and that enables all to exercise due care in the exploitation and enjoyment of a shared natural environment. It is his view that, without in any way stinting on the need to ensure sovereign possession, a Canadian Arctic strategy ought to strive for cooperative stewardship throughout the region. In this regard, he explores three main themes: *elevation* to the highest political level, *engagement* of the United States and the Russian Federation, and *invigoration* of the Arctic Council (as a forum for coordinating and supporting collective action). Given that the prerequisites for region-wide cooperation are in short supply, Canada will have to help create them by elevating Arctic international relations from the official to the highest political level, by engaging first the United States and then the Russian Federation in a strategy of stewardship, and by invigorating regional governance through the Arctic Council. In all of this, he urges the prime minister to take personal responsibility not only for Canada's northern development but also for Canada's future as an Arctic nation among other nations of the region and indeed non-Arctic nations as well.

The conclusions, written by Whitney Lackenbauer, discuss the government's Northern Strategy unveiled in July 2009, as well as subsequent domestic and international developments related to the Arctic, including the release of the *Statement on Canada's Arctic Foreign Policy* in August 2010 (which is included as an Appendix). Rather than trying to arrive at a "consensus" on what should be done, the authors invite ongoing debate among Canadians as to what we should be doing in our own front yard—and the region beyond—in an era of rapid change.

There are various points of convergence in the three chapters. All authors assert that the *status quo* is unacceptable and that Canada needs a much stronger and clearer Arctic strategy. Policy makers must not only interpret changes in the region but also adjust to them, and political rhetoric does not signify action. The Arctic is no longer a region that requires broad and sweeping policy pronouncements but little else; decision makers must deliver on successive commitments to "do something" to respond to challenges and seize opportunities. As this book shows, that "something" ranges from improving the means and instruments of control to creating new understandings and implementations of stewardship in the region. Good governance demands that Canadian officials prepare now and spend now to ensure that Canadian Arctic policy is not reactive and *ad hoc*, but is well-developed and supported by adequate resources so that Canadian interests and values are protected and promoted.

The authors also agree on the need for a more multilateral and regional approach to Arctic affairs. In particular, they recommend that Canada better engage the United States, Russia, and the Europeans. The normative bases for their respective viewpoints, however, are different. All three intimate that there is *possible* danger of an extraregional conflict moving into the Arctic; but Huebert sees this as more *probable* than Lackenbauer and Griffiths. Huebert's analysis (which he identifies as a realist viewpoint) equates sovereignty and security with control and emphasizes the need for military capabilities to respond to external threats. Lackenbauer and Griffiths have more faith that Canada's sovereignty is secure and that shared interests among the circumpolar states portend a future of cooperation. Lackenbauer blends a constructivist analysis of Canada's policy making with normative faith in international law and bilateral or multilateral mechanisms to resolve disputes. Like Griffiths in earlier works, Lackenbauer suggests that government *securitization* of the Arctic agenda promotes an alarmist "crisis-based mentality" that overemphasizes divergent interests, downplays common interests, and limits cooperation. Griffiths offers a strong internationalist message, one that calls for the voluntary coordination of basic principles of Arctic international relations— coordination that would encompass arms control provisions, regional confidence-building measures, and reciprocal pledges to refrain from "incidents with confrontation potential." While he disavows the need or prospects for a comprehensive Arctic treaty (something that Huebert has called for elsewhere, albeit only among the Arctic states), he is the strongest proponent of engagement—specifically of non-Arctic states—and is adamant that the Arctic states must tie their regional interests into global processes.

All of the authors in their chapters, as well as in other publications, support investments in Canadian Forces to operate in the Arctic. Their rationales for these investments, however, reveal salient differences in interpretation and threat assessment. Huebert's assertion that Canada has found itself in the initial stages of an Arctic "arms race" guides his argument that Canada must invest in more robust defence capabilities and a stronger CF presence or it will increasingly lose control over activities in its Arctic waters. Control is sovereignty, thus sovereignty requires defence capabilities to ensure control.

Lackenbauer urges the government to fulfill its existing defence promises, justifying each expenditure on the basis of its contributions to a "whole of government" strategy in which the CF plays a supporting role. He questions the common refrain that Canada needs more "boots on the ground" to enhance or preserve our sovereignty; he also justifies his support for previous defence announcements by reasoning that the military possesses a unique suite of skills and capabilities that are essential for Canada to respond to emergencies in the region. Huebert's emphasis is on the need for military capabilities (specifically, maritime and aerospace assets) to defend rights against assertive neighbours; Lackenbauer's is on exercising custodial responsibilities. Although they come to the conclusion from two different perspectives, they agree that improved surveillance and domain awareness are vital. As to Griffiths, he underlines the need, through cooperative stewardship on non-military or civil issues, to channel Arctic international relations away from conflict and toward greater civility.

Another point of disagreement relates to the role of history in framing expectations. Huebert contends that we are entering a new era of the Arctic in which Canadians can no longer count on the vast distances and extreme climatic conditions to keep the outside world away from their North. As climate change fundamentally transforms the entire region and new technologies combine to allow for easier access, Canada faces a drastically changing sovereignty and security environment in which previous experiences will not be a reliable guide for decision making. At best, history reveals Canada's limited capacity to protect its sovereignty and security in the region and explains why other nations have openly sought to advance their Arctic claims—often at the expense of Canada's position. Lackenbauer, by contrast, suggests that the past not only paints a more benign portrait of bilateral cooperation than Huebert allows, but also reveals a trend toward increasingly positive relations with our circumpolar neighbours. By tracing back Griffiths's idea of a bilateral "agreement to disagree" to the aftermath of the Second World War, Lackenbauer suggests that Canada has devised a responsible strategy that has yielded as strong a sovereignty position as international law allows and that avoids placing us in a "lose–lose" situation vis-à-vis the United States. Lackenbauer, like Huebert and Griffiths, laments the checkered history of Canada's interests in the region, a history that has been driven by intermittent Arctic "crises" that have failed to sustain strategic investment. For this reason, he shares Griffiths's insistence on the need for a new, confident strategic message that does not rely on Canadians' primordial fear of sovereignty loss.

Bilateral relations with the United States factor heavily in all three chapters, as they do in political and public debates more generally. Huebert hopes to advance our "challenging" relationship with the United States in areas of common interest; but he also emphasizes the need to minimize if not resolve disputes over boundaries and sovereignty—namely, the Beaufort Sea and the Northwest Passage. Regarding the latter, however, he does not specify how a long-standing legal impasse might be overcome. Griffiths continues to promote "agreement to disagree" over the status of the passage and urges the Canadian government to consider innovative forms of governance over it. Specifically, he outlines his case for establishing a regime under which the internal waters of the archipelago would be governed as though they were an international strait. Lackenbauer supports this idea and similarly concludes that informal arrangements and voluntary compliance are more feasible than prolonged negotiations of the sort that are unlikely to solve a core legal disagreement between two close friends and allies.

Lackenbauer also supports the official view that boundary disputes with our neighbours are well managed and that the threat to Canadian sovereignty and security has been overblown. While Huebert points to the need to resolve these disputes, which serve as ongoing stressors on circumpolar relations, Lackenbauer sees no immediate need to do so as long as they are managed diplomatically.

All three authors note that successive governments have dedicated substantial resources to ensure that the science behind the Canadian extended continental shelf claim is well established by the time it is submitted to the UN commission in 2013. While Griffiths and Lackenbauer acknowledge that national interests are at play and that boundary issues will require negotiations, neither anticipates armed conflict. Lackenbauer in particular notes that all the circumpolar nations share an interest in having boundary delimitation processes unfold according to international law. Huebert is less certain of a sanguine outcome, reminding readers that the legal framework for determining extended continental shelves does not include a mechanism for arbitrating disputes, something that is left to the states themselves. The Americans have not acceded to the UNCLOS, and thus have left in the air when they will submit their official claim. Furthermore, if Canada's claim overlaps with that of Russia, this may test the two countries' pledges made at Ilulissat in 2008 to peacefully and cooperatively resolve such differences. Given the nationalist fervour in both countries on Arctic sovereignty issues, compromise may prove difficult.

The authors also remind readers that Canada's relations extend beyond our western Arctic neighbour. All speak to Canada's need to engage with Russia in a constructive manner, given that nation's obvious interests in the region. While Lackenbauer and Griffiths emphasize common Russian and Canadian interests in development and environmental issues, Huebert highlights the need for defensive alliances to mitigate Russian aggressiveness. (Ironically, Huebert holds up the Barents Sea as a theatre of friction between Norway and Russia, while Griffiths cites it as an example of cooperation.)

Huebert also identifies the increasing assertiveness of Iceland, Denmark, Finland, Sweden, and Norway in pursuing their Arctic policies, as well as the growing activism of non-Arctic states such as China, Japan, and South Korea. As these various actors advance their claims, they pose potential challenges to Canada's sovereignty and security in the region. Although Lackenbauer acknowledges European references that disagree with Canada's position on the Northwest Passage, he argues that "this does not preclude a working relationship with the Europeans on other issues." Similarly, he urges decision makers to continue to enhance bilateral relations with Russia, despite the mixed messages they are sending, and to avoid holding Arctic cooperation hostage to global developments. Griffiths goes even further in promoting circumpolar collaboration and regional stewardship. In his view, this must accommodate new forces in world politics such as the European Union and China by bringing them directly into the Arctic dialogue. While subregional agreements will continue to produce "fragmented incrementalism," Griffiths urges the Arctic-8 to adopt a multilateral and region-wide approach to Arctic affairs that promotes a pan-Arctic vision and a regional practice of cooperative stewardship that is integrated with a global strategy (a theme that Lackenbauer echoes in the context of climate change).

All of the authors support enhanced mechanisms for international governance, but they emphasize different levels and issue areas. Huebert's main message is that Canada must assert control over its Arctic, but he recognizes that Canada cannot act in isolation. Accordingly, he promotes frameworks to protect the Arctic and to strengthen cooperation through the Arctic Council. He sees potential for coordination in search and rescue, prevention of environmental pollution, fisheries management, regulation of tourism, and mandatory shipping regulations. Huebert still insists, however, that any measures must safeguard Canadian interests and sovereignty. Lackenbauer also argues that Canada should take a leading role in promoting the activities of the Arctic Council, and he is the most ardent champion of the UN Convention on the

Law of the Sea as a framework for resolving sovereignty issues in the Arctic Basin. Whereas Huebert and Griffiths criticize the Arctic coastal states (the Arctic-5) for holding "exclusionary" meetings that do not include the other three Arctic states or the Permanent Participants, Lackenbauer suggests that such meetings are appropriate for discussing issues that are specific to the rights and responsibilities of the Arctic-5 under state-based international legal frameworks. Griffiths makes the most sustained case for a reinvigorated Arctic Council—"the central forum for pan-Arctic collaboration"—which he hopes will eventually achieve mandatory compliance with "agreed principles and rules." This intersects with an ongoing international debate on the future of the Arctic Council and regional governance, a debate that is discussed in the concluding chapter.

The timeliness of this debate is obvious. Canada will resume the chairpersonship of the Arctic Council in 2013, and this will provide an opportunity for leadership in terms of improving the central instrument of Arctic governance. This will not be easy, nor will it be without controversy. The council will need to make decisions on who is allowed to join it and under what conditions. Griffiths and Huebert want to reform the Arctic Council, with Griffiths advocating the end of current observer status and its replacement with a new "third-tier" in which non-Arctic states could engage the council as consultative parties with speaking rights. These states, however, would need to pay into an Arctic fund, providing financial assistance in exchange for permanent capacity as participants. Griffiths promotes extension of Permanent Observer status to the European Union and various non-Arctic states; Lackenbauer is more supportive of the Arctic Council's "soft law" approach and raises concerns about expanding the council in light of those raised by the Permanent Participants. All agree, however, that the Arctic Council needs to find ways to address its chronic lack of resources and should create a Permanent Secretariat.

All three authors identify the importance of domestic governance and decision making in promoting sovereignty, security, and stewardship. Lackenbauer in particular outlines a "whole of government" approach, which Huebert also mentions. Huebert places an obvious emphasis on defence, Griffiths on diplomacy, and Lackenbauer on a broad defence–diplomacy–development approach. Both Lackenbauer and Griffiths highlight the need for locally informed governance in which northern voices are central to the dialogue about their interests as residents and stewards of this unique environment.

The authors also articulate the need for political leadership on the Arctic file. Lamenting the inwardness of Canadian policy, Griffiths is the most vocal in arguing that the Arctic be elevated from the bureaucratic to the highest political level in Canada. By extension, he and Huebert propose that the prime minister lead some kind of committee or high-level Cabinet group on Arctic affairs. Griffiths recommends that the Prime Minister's Office oversee internal government decision making, with a new Secretary of State for the Arctic coordinating policies with provincial and territorial governments and representing Canada in international negotiations. Huebert also believes that the prime minister should anchor an all-encompassing Arctic policy, and he recommends that the federal leader chair a special Cabinet committee devoted to the region that will help sustain popular attention. While Lackenbauer sees the Arctic as an opportunity for the prime minister to carve out a legacy in nation building, he focuses on how to make the bureaucracy more effective and representative. To improve Northern participation in agenda setting and decision making, he recommends a range of new institutions, including an Arctic Canada Council, an interdepartmental Advisory Committee on Northern Security and Stewardship, and Inuit marine councils forming a Canadian Arctic Marine Environment Working Group. He ends, however, with a plea that the government change Canada's official motto to include its third ocean explicitly in the national mind.

All three authors acknowledge the uncertainty that is implicit in constructing future scenarios for the Arctic. Canadian policy makers obviously anticipate issues such as the chairpersonship of the Arctic Council, the submission of the claim for the extended continental shelf, and the resolution of the Beaufort Sea boundary dispute; but there will also be issues that erupt without prior notice. Certain predictions can be made in regard to their broad nature and identity, yet it is difficult to know with any certainty when they will occur or what they will look like. These would include new issues/crises brought about by climate change, resource development, or international political actions. Griffiths and Lackenbauer are adamant that Canada must seek a "polar saga." Huebert shares a similar hope but also cautions that an alternative future—that of a "polar race"—cannot be dismissed.

The Arctic is changing in ways that were unimaginable just a few years ago. No one knows with certainty where this will all lead, but the changing Arctic offers both challenges and opportunities for Canada. It will require foresight, critical thinking, and debate to ensure that Canadian interests and values are ultimately served, protected, and promoted. The authors hope that the arguments laid out in the following chapters stimulate an ongoing dialogue about what strategies Canada should embrace to navigate this exciting new era of the Arctic.

2

Canadian Arctic Sovereignty and Security in a Transforming Circumpolar World

Rob Huebert

The core objective of this chapter is to achieve an understanding of Canadian Arctic sovereignty and security in the context of a fundamentally changing Arctic. First, it will examine sovereignty and security. It will then examine the forces that are transforming the very fabric of the Arctic—specifically climate change, resource development, and geopolitical forces.

The Arctic is undergoing change at a startling pace, one that has astonished Canadians and the world. It is impossible to pick up a newspaper or to turn on the TV without learning about a new development that has ramifications for the Canadian North. Inevitably any discussion about the Canadian North usually begins with a discussion about "protecting" Arctic sovereignty. Sovereignty is an issue that always attracts the attention of the media and decision makers as well as Canadians in general. One only has to suggest that Canada is "losing" its Arctic sovereignty for a firestorm of heated debates to erupt. It is an interesting era for the Canadian Arctic and for Canadians.

Canadian Arctic policy is faced with some of the most intriguing and complex challenges in its history. Never before has the very nature of the Canadian Arctic region been altered by such a widespread set of factors. Perhaps the greatest current challenge for Canada is the worldwide realization that the Arctic is melting so that it is more accessible than ever before. Consequently, Canada must prepare for the outside world's entry into the Arctic. With international challenges to Canadian control of the region now emerging, Canada can no longer afford to ignore its Arctic.

Understanding Sovereignty and Security

Sovereignty

At the heart of the definition of sovereignty is its evolution as a legal term used to explain or define the means by which sovereigns, such as kings or queens, had control over their subjects. Sovereignty emerged as a term for understanding the rights and responsibilities that leaders had regarding their land. As the feudal period evolved into the modern state, this concept also evolved. Sovereignty became the theoretical cornerstone of the international legal state system.[1]

There are three main elements of sovereignty: a defined territory; an existing governance system; and a people within the defined territory. In order for a state to have "sovereignty," it must have each of these elements.[2] A state must have a functioning government system that is able to make final decisions that are enforced upon the people within its geographic territory. Each of these variables may appear to be straightforward, but the reality is that all three are difficult to achieve within the Arctic. Thus any question of whether or not a state has sovereignty tends to be bound in determining the degree to which these variables are fulfilled.

The most common problem with determining the existence of sovereignty tends to be associated with the existence of an accepted governance system. The sovereignty of a state is said to be threatened when parties compete to govern. In such cases, until one side is defeated, either militarily or politically, or a negotiated settlement is reached whereby the competing bodies agree to share power as a single entity, there is no one sovereign body. The process for determining sovereignty is complicated by the fact that even after the competition for power is internally settled, the international community must also accept the new governing body.

In the Canadian Arctic there is no question about the existence of an accepted governance system. This system may be evolving as power devolves to the territories, but as long as this is done on a peaceful basis, all sovereign states have the right to allocate their powers to political subunits within their borders. Within the borders of the Canadian Arctic, the northern Canadian population has completely accepted the government's right to govern. Thus the federal government does not diminish the sovereignty of the Canadian state by transferring powers to its three northern territories: the Northwest Territories, Nunavut, and Yukon.

This transfer leads to the issues surrounding the second variable of sovereignty, which requires that a people be contained within the defined geography of a state. Consequently, there is no sovereignty in a case where there is no local population, such as Antarctica. But there are no limits to how small a population can be. The Canadian Arctic contains a small number of individuals, but enough of them to give Canada sovereignty over all of the land territory of its Arctic. The only land area in Canada where Canada's sovereignty is challenged is Hans Island, a small, uninhabited island.

The third variable—defined boundaries—has the greatest relevance for the discussion of Canadian Arctic sovereignty. For a boundary to have validity, the international community needs to agree on it. The number of states that need to agree before a boundary is said to be accepted remains unclear.

The growing complexity of ocean boundaries is extremely pertinent to sovereignty in the Arctic. A move within existing international law created new maritime zones of control. The UN Convention on the Law of the Sea (UNCLOS), which was finalized in 1982 and came into force in 1994, codified existing customary international law and created several new maritime zones.[3] In general, the farther that the zone moves out from the land territory of the state, the less control the state has over activities within the zone. Thus the first main zone—the territorial sea—gives the coastal state almost complete control over all activities within it. The one important exception is that the state cannot interfere in the innocent passage of foreign vessels in these waters. Moving farther from shore, the Exclusive Economic Zone (EEZ) extends 200 nautical miles from the coastline of the state. The coastal state has control over all living and non-living resources in this zone. Therefore, only the coastal state can fish, drill for oil or gas, or grant permission to a foreign state or organization. However, in the EEZ, the coastal state has limited control over international shipping that is not engaged in resource exploitation.

UNCLOS also creates a third zone of control. A state can extend its control over the ocean soil and subsurface beyond the EEZ if it can show that it has an extended continental shelf. If a state can prove that it meets the criteria

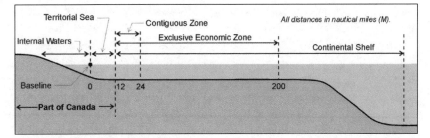

Figure 2-1 Maritime zones of Canada.
Source: Canadian Council of Land Surveyors

required for a continental shelf, and if this shelf extends beyond 200 nautical miles, then a state can claim control of the seabed and its resources for an additional 150 nautical miles and under certain circumstances even beyond that. A state with this zone has control of all activities that occur on or beneath the seabed. This control is currently understood to mean that the state has authority over activities such as oil and gas development. However, the state has no control over activities in the water column. Thus it cannot have power over shipping, fishing, or even scientific research.

There are two other maritime zones that depend on geography and history. If a state has a body of water that directly joins two other international bodies of water, and this body of water has been used in the past by international shipping, then the joining body of water, or strait, is used for international navigation. The coastal state has the right of control of all activity within this international strait except international shipping, for all foreign vessels enjoy the right of transit passage. This control specifically allows all vessels to travel in their normal mode of transportation. Thus submarines remain submerged as they transit an international strait.

Internal waters are the last maritime zone of significance for the Arctic. Bodies of water such as lakes and rivers that lie entirely within the land mass of a state normally fall into this category. The host state enjoys complete control over these waters, including the right to allow or forbid foreign shipping. There may be a small number of instances where a state may designate a specific body of water that lies outside its land boundaries as internal waters. Generally these exceptions occur where there has been historical acceptance of treating them like a lake or a river: this designation was codified by UNCLOS as "historical bays." Some countries, however, such as Canada, have attempted to extend this designation beyond bays. This is primarily through the drawing of straight baselines around a fringe of islands in the vicinity of the coast. The waters within the enclosed space then become internal waters over which the state exercises total sovereignty. This leads to one last important point. Whereas the state had complete sovereignty over internal waters, it has sovereign right over all of the resources of the EEZ but only the resources on the soil and subsoil of the resources in the extended continental shelf.

A challenge to Canadian Arctic sovereignty must involve a dispute with one of the three elements of sovereignty. There is no challenge to the Canadian governance system, and there is an identifiable population that completely accepts the authority of the Canadian government. Thus, the element of sovereignty that is challenged is the recognition of Canada's borders, specifically its Arctic maritime borders. The ultimate question facing Canada is its determination and control of its Arctic borders.

Security

The concept of security has undergone a transformation in both theoretical and practical terms since the end of the Cold War. Historically, security was framed in a context that focused on the military ability of a state to either defend itself against the military actions of other states or to enforce its will on another state. If a state was powerful enough, it acted alone. If it was not, it would develop alliances with other states. The critical element of security was the ability of states to utilize their economic capabilities to build militaries that could both enforce and protect their will.[4] Thus the use of deadly force was the ultimate means of providing for the security of the state. Security depended on victory in war.

The development of nuclear weapons changed the nature of security in that the deterrence of nuclear war rather than the actual waging of war became the ultimate security objective of states during the Cold War period. This was paradoxical, however, in that as to avoid war, it was necessary to prepare for war. Security was linked to the ability to build a nuclear weapon capability sufficient enough to deter the opposing side from attacking. National security was still viewed as the core responsibility of the state, one that could be achieved only by developing military force (either potential or actual).

As the Cold War came to an end, the consensus on the nature of security was challenged. First, the end of the Cold War ended the nuclear balance that had threatened the existence of the entire international system. With the collapse of the Soviet Union, the core military rivalry with the United States ended and the need for military forces appeared to dramatically diminish. But at the same time, debates began to develop among analysts over the meaning of security. Many began to question whether the traditional definition of security, with its focus on the military and the state, remained valid. Perhaps the best-known challenge came from those who argued that an expanded conceptualization of security was needed. This led to the development of the concept of human security.[5]

Human security was an attempt to move security away from state-based analysis. This movement was due in part to the recognition that in many instances the state was the *cause* of insecurity of some or all of its peoples. For example, in repressive regimes such as Pinochet's military dictatorship in Chile or the Khmer Rouge in Cambodia, the state threatened the security of its citizens.

The movement from defensive military use to the construction of international norms and institutions, such as treaties and agreements, supported this new concept of human security and created an environment wherein the affected parties could enjoy security. Efforts were made to construct international means of bringing justice to those who suffered at the hands of the state. A strong effort was made to create means for outlawing the construction and use of weapons systems, such as anti-personnel land mines, as well means for eliminating those that were already deployed.

A second and related challenge to traditional security began in the 1990s. During this decade some academics and policy makers began examining the dangers posed by environmental degradation as the best indicator of the need to expand the concept of security.[6] The physical security of an individual in Bangladesh or the Seychelles who loses his or her home due to rising sea levels from melting ice caps as a result of climate change was just as tenuous as that of someone in a war zone. The argument to extend the meaning of security beyond its traditional understanding gained ground. Supporters of this position pointed to the physical dangers that pollution and environmental degradation posed to the well-being of people both within and beyond the state. Here, as in the case of human security, greater security did not come from military action; rather, it came from international cooperation at the individual *and* state levels. Conceptual extensions of security, similar to advances made by environmental security specialists, have further extended the term "security" to include economic security, cultural security, and so on. The major defining element of these efforts is that they usually attempt to expand the definition of security beyond a focus on the state and the military.

The debate over the meaning of security continues today. Some argue that a continued reliance on a traditional understanding of security is not just wrong in an academic sense; it is also dangerous, for it misleads policy decision making. Others maintain that while the focus on military security may not be politically expedient, the state's primary responsibility is the security and well-being of its citizens.

Having briefly reviewed the manner in which sovereignty and security are understood, what conclusions can we reach prior to discussing Canadian Arctic sovereignty and security? In terms of sovereignty, the issues both complex and simple. If Canadian Arctic sovereignty is threatened, the Canadian government does not have control over a specific geographic territory. Stripped of all rhetoric and emotion that normally surrounds this issue, sovereignty becomes about controlling the actions of others within the boundaries claimed by the Canadian government. From this perspective, Canada's challenge lies in the maritime nature of the boundaries of the area in dispute. International laws pertaining to maritime sovereignty are different from those for sovereignty over a land mass. Specifically, UNCLOS clearly establishes the various degrees of control over maritime zones, the rule of thumb being that the farther away from the coastline they are, the less control the coastal state enjoys.

The most important question that follows from the exercise of sovereignty is, "Why exercise it in the first place?" What do states gain by pursuing and then defending national sovereignty? Once again, when we strip away the normal rhetoric that surrounds this issue, we find that the answer is *security*. States defend their sovereignty mainly in order to secure their core interests and values in a specific region. Traditionally, this was done through military force. But as the previous review makes clear, it is now recognized that some threats to a state's security cannot be addressed by military action. Instead, in some instances—such as relating to environmental security—it is necessary to go beyond traditional answers. Nevertheless, the underlying point is that whatever those steps are to be, they are undertaken with the objective of protecting the security of the state's citizens.

In the context of this discussion, the Canadian government attempts to defend Canadian Arctic sovereignty for the purpose of protecting the security of its citizens as well as the security of the core values and interests of Canadians. The meaning of this will be examined in the following section.

Canadian Concepts of Arctic Sovereignty and Security

Throughout much of the Cold War, the effort to have policy reflect the terms "Arctic sovereignty" and "Arctic security" was frustrated by the tendency of Canadian policy makers, media, and academics to assume that the two terms were separate and distinct. During the Cold War, Arctic security became associated with defence against the Soviet Union. Canada left the maritime dimensions of Arctic security entirely in American hands while allowing its southern neighbour to pay for much of its aerospace security. Arctic sovereignty was associated with diplomatic disputes with the United States and with reacting to American actions that were perceived to threaten Canada's claim over the region, in particular the waterways of the North. In this manner Arctic security and Arctic sovereignty were viewed as separate policy concerns.

However, as previously discussed, sovereignty and security are interconnected and cannot and should not be separated. This is specifically true in the Canadian Arctic. As argued in the previous section, the concept of sovereignty comes down to the issue of *control* within a specific geographic area by a specific body. Within Canada, Arctic sovereignty can be understood in the context of the Canadian government's ability to control what happens in the area that it defines as its Arctic region.

The issue of Canadian Arctic sovereignty is, however, complicated by the region's maritime dimension. Within the international law of the sea, the right to make final decisions about what activities occur within its maritime zones

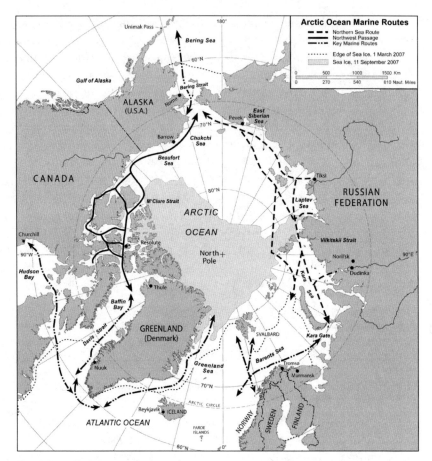

Map 2-1 Arctic Ocean marine routes.
Source: Dr. Lawson W. Brigham, University of Alaska Fairbanks

is not absolute; rather, it is modified by the waterway's nature. Simply put, there are rules that increasingly reduce a state's power the farther one ventures beyond its coastline. With the exception of Denmark's assertion of ownership of Hans Island, no other actors in the international system challenge Canada's right to control its Arctic land mass. However, international challenges do emerge over Canada's claim to its Arctic maritime space. The United States disagrees on the boundary dividing the Beaufort Sea. Likewise, Denmark disagrees on division of the Lincoln Sea (though only in two small regions). Canada may also disagree with the United States, Russia, and Denmark about its anticipated claim over its continental shelf boundaries in the Arctic Ocean. Canada's best-known Arctic sovereignty issue relates to the control of international maritime traffic in the Northwest Passage. Canada claims that the waterways comprising this Arctic passage are internal waters and, it follows, that the Canadian government has the right to control who can enter those waters and under what conditions. The American and the EU position is that these waters are part of an international strait, which means that Canada does not have final, authoritative decision-making power over the Northwest Passage. The United States and the EU both assert that the international community—in this case through the International Maritime Organization (IMO)—makes the final decisions and that Canada does not have control over international shipping in the Northwest Passage.

Ultimately, whether it is dividing the Arctic Ocean seabed, determining the boundaries of Canadian sections of the Beaufort and Lincoln Seas, or maintaining shipping in the Northwest Passage, the issue is control. What are the Arctic maritime boundaries that Canada can control? And what can it do within these boundaries?

This is where the issue of Arctic security connects with Arctic sovereignty. If sovereignty is about control, what is the reason for this control? If the pursuit of Canadian Arctic sovereignty is only about Canadian decision makers having personal satisfaction from some sense of control, then it is not worth much effort or expense. But if sovereignty is being pursued for the purpose of protecting the security, safety, and well-being of Canadians, then not only is it worth the effort, but it is an absolute necessity.

The core issue of Canadian Arctic sovereignty is *control;* the core issue of Canadian Arctic security is about responding to *threats.* The threats to Canadian Arctic security are nebulous, multi-dimensional, and evolving. Throughout the Cold War, Arctic security was associated only with the threat posed by the Soviet Union to the national survival of Canada and the United States. Soon after the Cold War ended and concerns about traditional threats to national security receded, scientists discovered that the Canadian Arctic was the end location for a wide number of pollutants that originated elsewhere around the globe (including seemingly improbable sources such as India and the Philippines). The environmental migration of transboundary pollutants such as persistent organic pollutants (e.g., pesticides and fertilizers) into the North was negatively affecting the health of Northern Canadians, who eat large amounts of local foods in which those pollutants come to be concentrated.[7] It was soon realized that the environmental security of the Canadian North needed protection. Obviously, the means for achieving this security would be different from those required for protection against the Soviet threat. But it was still a type of security from a threat that was coming from beyond Canadian boundaries.

Threats to the law and order of the Canadian North are arising. Recently, foreign criminal elements have been making unauthorized entries into the Canadian Arctic. In the summer of 2007, a group allegedly associated with the Norwegian Hells Angels made it as far as Cambridge Bay on a small boat.[8] Other threats in the Canadian Arctic involve economic, societal, and cultural issues. It also appears that traditional security threats are re-emerging now that each Arctic nation has begun rebuilding its northern military capabilities.

In effect, Canadian policy makers need to protect Canadian Arctic sovereignty in order to provide for Canadian Arctic security. The Canadian government needs to exert control over its North so that it can take action to protect against a wide number of threats that will be coming more and more from beyond Canadian northern boundaries. As it is impossible to protect Canadian Arctic security without protecting its Arctic sovereignty, and vice versa, the two concepts are completely interlinked.

Who Is Protected?

One of the most difficult questions to answer is who is to be protected and how best they are to be protected. The Canadian North is not a homogenous region; rather, it is one that supports multiple interests and values, not all of which are similar or complement one another. Furthermore, the events that transform the North have an impact *all* Canadians. While those who call the North home—particularly the northern Aboriginal peoples—have a special interest in the region, all Canadians are affected by what happens in the Arctic. How does one balance these different interests?

The specific challenges that Northern Canadians face complicate the picture. The North has one of the youngest populations in the country. At the same time, the provision of governmental services in this region lags behind the rest of the country. Education and health care do not match what is provided to southern Canadians. Thus a changing North offers both challenges and opportunities for Northerners. Climate change in combination with globalization may spell the end of traditional ways of life for many of the younger people. However, resource development may offer employment opportunities to a young population in a region where there is a dire need for new sources of employment. These new projects will contribute to the economic security of the region. But at the same time, these opportunities may result in serious problems. It is already known that megaprojects often result in serious social problems such as drug and alcohol abuse. Increasing suicide rates are also often associated with societies in transition. Improvements in the economic security of the region may come at the cost of societal security.

Policy makers need to understand how the factors affecting the North are affecting the people. In short, protecting Canada's Arctic sovereignty and security must be tied to the domestic needs of Canadians. Without this link to these needs, policy effort loses its meaning and becomes an empty gesture of nationalism. It may make Canadians "feel good" to protect the North against "the foreigners," but it does not afford any real protection for our interests and values, unless this link is understood.

Why Is This Protection Needed?

Why does the Canadian Arctic now need to be better controlled by Canadian decision makers and Canadians? Why is the existing status quo no longer acceptable? Multiple factors are transforming the North into a more accessible region of the world. Southern Canadians will be arriving in the North in increasing numbers to reap the benefits of a changing Arctic, which will further impact the Arctic region. But at the same time, this accessibility will enable non-Canadian actors to arrive on the scene and increasingly affect the Arctic region. Thus Canadian policy makers face a situation of developing complexity brought about by factors beyond Canada's borders.

The ongoing transformation of the North makes a moving target of the effort to come to terms with this issue of protection and control in the Canadian Arctic. At this time, we simply do not know who will come to the Arctic and what they will do there. Furthermore, the factors reshaping the North do not proceed in a linear, progressive manner. Instead, events occur at a rapidly increasing rate that defies prediction. The task of protection and control is further complicated by the fact that the duration of these changes is unknown. It is not known if or when the impact of climate change will stop. It is also uncertain how the resources of the North will be exploited, to what level this exploitation will occur, and who will exploit the resources. The oft-quoted figure that the Arctic contains 13 percent of undiscovered world oil resources and 30 percent of world gas resources is only a sophisticated estimate by the US Geological Survey.[9] It may be less, but it could also be more.

The geopolitical reality is developing in ways that are confounding to all states that border the region. The main issue in the context of geopolitics is the realization that UNCLOS allows most of the Arctic nations to claim the majority of the Arctic Ocean seabed. Under the terms of Article 76, states that believe they have a continental shelf first need to conduct the science to determine whether this belief has merit.[10] They then need to submit their findings to a UN commission that will pass judgment on the merits of their studies. Then it is the states' responsibility to peacefully resolve any overlaps they may have with neighbouring states that also claim an extended continental shelf.

Even though this section of UNCLOS was negotiated during the 1970s and the convention was finalized in 1982, it was not until the late 1990s that most Arctic nations realized how much potential this article had when it came to their claims to much of the Arctic Ocean seabed. This has given rise to an explosion of activity by the Arctic states as they prepare their claims. The Russians have already submitted their claim; Canada and Denmark will follow, in 2013 and 2014 respectively. Because it has not ratified the convention, the United States remains outside the process officially, though it is preparing its claim *un*officially.

The United States and Russia are two of the most important actors in the Arctic region. The United States is the sole remaining superpower, but when it comes to the Arctic it acts more like a "reluctant" power, refusing to take its circumpolar responsibilities seriously. It has consistently blocked efforts by Canada and other circumpolar states to create new forms of Arctic governance. For example, it only agreed to join the Arctic Council after the proposed powers of that body were substantially reduced. The Russians have staged a comeback in terms of their Arctic policies, fuelled by rising revenues from their oil and gas exports. This revenue increase in turn has encouraged the Russians to become more assertive as they move to consolidate and expand the development of their oil and gas resources in their Arctic region.

The Danes are also beginning to assert their power in the North. Denmark is an Arctic state by virtue of its control over Greenland. It currently cooperates with both Canada and the United States to determine both the limits and the potential of oil and gas exploration within its maritime territory. The Danes have also actively attempted to derail any efforts to develop a comprehensive Arctic treaty. Officially their position is that the existing framework is adequate for the development of Arctic relations. Unofficially, it may be that they are more concerned that an international Arctic treaty as it evolves could affect the development of their oil and gas reserves off Greenland, or perhaps force them to take a harder stance against the fishers of Greenland and the Faeroes Islands, who allegedly are increasingly entering Canadian waters illegally.

Meanwhile, the Norwegians are focusing their foreign and defence policy on the Arctic. They are in the process of building a naval capability that can operate in the North. They are also looking to develop oil and gas reserves in their claimed Arctic with positive anticipation, but they are more concerned about the expected increase in Russian offshore activity.

These are the foreign and defence policies of the main Arctic states as they existed in 2008. It should be clear that all of the countries involved are attempting to understand and prepare for the new Arctic age. However, it should also be apparent that the issue of the geopolitical North is a moving and developing target. While all of the main Arctic states are aware that the North is evolving into a much more important region, they are not entirely certain how that is happening. For example, while the long-term impact of climate change is understood as leading to the eventual melting of the Arctic ice cover, when this will occur is still being debated. Likewise, the regional variations in the melting process are not fully understood. There is even less understanding as to how the various forces of change interact. No one is investigating the impact that the development and use of Arctic oil and gas resources will have on the processes of climate change. As the ice melts and as it becomes easier to access these resources, their utilization will probably create a cycle that generates more greenhouse gases, thereby further increasing global temperatures. Yet there is little knowledge about how such a relationship would develop.

This discussion has focused solely on the actions of the main Arctic states. It is becoming increasingly apparent that the Arctic is becoming an area of interest for non-Arctic states as well. In particular, Asian interests in the region are growing. South Korean shipyards are increasingly entering the market to build ice-capable vessels. The Japanese are investing heavily in the study of Arctic gas hydrates off the coast of Canada as an energy source. The Chinese are also increasing their investment in polar research and have begun to deploy their large Arctic research vessel, the *Xue Long,* to the Arctic. In addition, Japan, South Korea, and China are attempting to join the Arctic Council as permanent observers[11]—perhaps the most explicit indication of their intent to become Arctic players.

The Changing Arctic

This chapter's title refers to the Arctic's *transforming.* That word was selected intentionally in order to highlight the coming challenges that Canada faces in its Arctic region. The Arctic is changing fundamentally. At least three unique and extremely powerful forces are driving this transformation: climate change, resource development, and geopolitical transformation. Any one of these factors by itself would result in a serious transformation of the Arctic. The reality that three such forces are at work only underlines the magnitude of the changes that are now occurring in the Canadian Arctic.

Climate Change

Climate change is warming the Arctic at a considerable rate, and this has garnered the attention of the Arctic states' leaders, their publics, and the world. As recently as the 1990s, few people had heard about climate change, let alone understood its magnitude. Among the many changes taking place in the Arctic, the most important is the melting of sea ice, which is receding at an accelerated and unprecedented rate.

The melting sea ice means that Canadian Arctic waters will be more open and therefore more accessible. This accessibility has led most observers to predict the entry of a broader array of interests into the region. The Canadian government's ability to control what happens in its Arctic region will be tested as these newcomers enter the Canadian Arctic, for they will seek to exploit and benefit from a more accessible Arctic. Thus the melting sea ice will be at the root of the challenges to Canadian Arctic sovereignty and security.

The expected impact of climate change is being hotly debated. Scientists studying the issue have repeatedly been taken aback by the rapid rate of change. The 2004 Arctic Climate Impact Assessment (ACIA), which utilized the research of the world's leading scientists, predicted that the polar ice cap would be completely melted by the end of the twenty-first century.[12] In 2009, only five years later, the most common prediction was that this would occur by 2030. Some analysts consider even this prediction too conservative. In December 2008, David Barber, one of Canada's leading Arctic experts, predicted that the Canadian Arctic will be ice-free for most of its summer by 2015.[13]

Regardless of when the ice will melt, two important elements must be stressed. First the processes that are leading to the melt are accelerating. While they are not fully understood, it is broadly recognized they are becoming more pronounced, and that recognition underlies the information emerging from the current studies. This suggests that the Arctic will be physically transformed even more rapidly than previously thought.

So what is happening? The ACIA study remains the definitive work on the subject, although it will soon require an update. This report had been commissioned by the Arctic's multilateral body, the Arctic Council, to determine what was happening when it became clear that processes not yet understood were physically transforming the entire Arctic region. In 2000 the Arctic Council directed two of its working groups, the Arctic Monitoring and Assessment Program (AMAP) and Conservation of Arctic Flora and Fauna (CAFF), along with the International Arctic Science Committee (IASC), to undertake an extensive and exhaustive study of the impact of climate change on the Arctic. After four years, the ACIA released its findings, which were both troubling and overwhelming. Perhaps the most important finding of the ACIA relates to the problem's magnitude. Its assessment had brought together the world's leading experts, who produced a peer-reviewed scientific document as well as a more concise summary document. The key findings for the Arctic marine environment are as follows:[14]

1) The Arctic climate is now warming rapidly and greater changes are projected. Annual average Arctic temperatures have increased at almost twice
   the rate of the rest of the world over the past few decades. Increasing pre-
   cipitation, shorter and warmer winters, and substantial decreases in ice
   and snow cover will likely persist for centuries. Unexpected and larger
   shifts and fluctuations are possible.

2) Arctic warming and its consequences have worldwide implications. These
   include the melting of highly reflective snow and ice cover, which will in
   turn lead to a greater warming of the planet; an increase in glacial melt
   and river runoff, which will result in rising sea levels; and the possible
   slowing of the world's ocean current circulation system.

3) Animal species' diversities, ranges, and distribution will change. Reduction in sea ice will drastically shrink marine habitats for species such as
   polar bears, ice-habiting seals, and some seabirds. Species' ranges will
   shift northward, bringing new species to the Arctic and limiting some
   already present. Some marine fisheries will become more productive,
   while freshwater fisheries are likely to decline.

4) Many coastal communities and facilities will face increasing exposure to
   storms. Severe coastal erosion will continue to be a problem as rising sea
   levels and reduction of sea ice allow for higher waves and storm surges to
   reach the shore. Some coastlines will face increased permafrost melt,
   adding to their vulnerability. Risk of flooding in coastal wetlands may
   increase. Some communities are already facing significant threats to their
   coastlines.

5) Reduced sea ice is very likely to increase marine transport and access to
   resources. Continued reduction of sea ice is likely to lengthen the navigation season and increase marine access to the Arctic's marine
   resources. Reduced sea ice is likely to increase offshore oil and gas extraction projects. Sovereignty, security, and safety issues, as well as social, cultural, and environmental concerns, are likely to arise as marine access
   increases.

6) Thawing ground will disrupt transportation, buildings, and other infrastructure. Transportation and industry on land, including oil and gas
   extraction, will increasingly be disrupted as the ice roads and tundra begin
   to freeze later and melt earlier in the year. This could mean a greater shift
   toward marine transport. As frozen ground thaws, many buildings, roads,
   and so forth will become destabilized, causing a need for substantial maintenance and rebuilding. Permafrost degradation will impact natural
   ecosystems as a result of the collapsing of ground surfaces, the draining
   of lakes, the deterioration of wetlands, and the toppling of trees.

7) Indigenous communities are facing major economic and cultural impacts. Many indigenous peoples depend on food sources that are now threatened. Changes in species' ranges and availability and in access to these species, and perceived and real changes in travel safety because of changing ice and weather conditions, will create serious challenges to human health and food security.

8) Elevated ultraviolet (UV) radiation levels will affect people, plants, and animals. The stratospheric ozone layer over the Arctic is not expected to improve for at least a few decades, largely due to the effect of greenhouse gases on stratospheric temperatures. The current generation of Arctic young people is likely to receive a lifetime dose of UV that is 30 percent higher than any prior generation. Elevated UV can disrupt photosynthesis in plants and have detrimental effects on the early life stages of fish and amphibians. Risks to some Arctic ecosystems are likely as the largest increases in UV exposure occurs in spring, when sensitive species are most vulnerable.

9) Multiple influences interact to cause impacts on people and ecosystems. Changes in climate are occurring in the context of many other stresses, including chemical pollution, overfishing, land use changes, habitat fragmentation, human population increases, and economic changes. These multiple stresses can combine to amplify impacts on human and ecosystem health and well-being. In many cases the total impact is greater than the sum of its parts.

This study had its limitations; one was its scale. The report made assessments of the *entire* Arctic rather than specific areas of the Arctic. It subsequently became apparent that the changes occurring in the Arctic vary with local conditions. Thus the original observation that the ice is receding has been tempered by the recognition that it recedes at different rates throughout the Arctic. Specifically, the Russian side of the Arctic has experienced the greatest rate of ice decline, followed by the central Arctic and then the Northwest Passage.[15] The passage's slower melting rate is due to a series of geophysical forces, which include prevailing ocean currents and the locations of the many islands of the Arctic Archipelago. However, while it may lag behind the other regions, it is still melting.

Historically, the extreme climate and extensive ice cover prevented the outside world from entering the Canadian Arctic. This is changing now that the Arctic is melting. As its ice cover diminishes, the Arctic is becoming more accessible, which in turn will make it easier for the world to come. But while accessibility is becoming greater, that is not necessarily a reason to arrive. The outside world needs a reason to take advantage of the improved accessibility. The second set of forces causing change in the Arctic relate to the world's reason for coming there: resource development.

Resource Development

Notwithstanding the melting, the Arctic will remain a unique and dangerous place to operate in. Regardless of the warming climate, the earth's tilt means that for significant periods of time, the Arctic will remain in darkness. This darkness alone complicates any activities that will be undertaken in the region. Related to this is the reality that unless the overall temperature of the earth reaches levels at which more southern latitudes are literally baking, some ice will re-form during the Arctic winters. So while the Arctic Ocean will be ice-free in the summer months, it will never be completely ice-free the year round, as is the case with the other oceans.

So if that is the case, why come north? The reason is that melting sea ice allows for greater accessibility to and exploitation of the Arctic's marine resources. In terms of oil and gas, the Arctic is estimated to contain approximately 25 percent of the world's remaining undiscovered oil and gas deposits. A study by the US Geological Survey—the most commonly cited such study—suggests that 13 percent of the world's oil and 30 percent of its natural gas is to be found in the Arctic. If that is so, the Arctic is the world's last major source of oil and gas.[16]

The potential riches of the Arctic continue substantially beyond oil and gas. There is growing recognition that another source of energy, known as gas hydrates, is found in Arctic waters. In very deep or very cold (or both) ocean waters, scientists have discovered a jelly-like substance that is a source of gas. These gas hydrates appear to be created as a result of the solidification of natural gas as it rises through the ocean bottom. While the quantity of this gas in the Arctic is unclear at this time, it seems very promising. In Canada and the United States, the Japanese are funding research to explore the use of gas hydrates as an energy source.[17] Currently there are no economical means of recovering these resources and bringing them to the surface for exploitation, but work is progressing. Gas hydrates may prove to be an important source of future energy and, therefore, an exploitable Arctic resource once the necessary technologies are developed.

By 2011 the predominant view of resource development in the Canadian Arctic was that its potential was both vast and uncertain. It is increasingly apparent that the Arctic is indeed a treasure trove of resources. But until the beginning of the 2000s, the market prices for most of these resources did not make their exploitation viable. But since the beginning

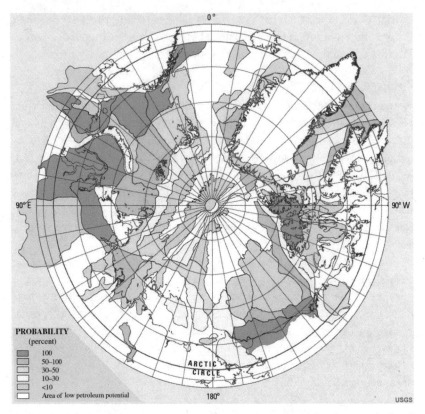

Map 2-2 US Geological Survey Circum-Arctic Resource Appraisal of undiscovered oil and gas.
Assessment units (AUs) in the Circum-Arctic Resource Appraisal (CARA), colour-coded by assessed probability of the presence of at least one undiscovered oil and/or gas field with recoverable resources greater than 50 million barrels of oil equivalent (MMBOE). Probabilities for AUs are based on the entire area of the AU, including any parts south of the Arctic Circle. Source: US Geological Survey

of the new millennium, there has been a generally steady rise in most commodity prices; there have also been improvements in the technologies that would allow for their extraction.

The validity of the estimates of the resource deposits must be determined through actual drilling, but North American oil and gas companies have already accepted the potential of these resources. In 2007, Exxon and several of its partners made a successful bid of over $585 million for a five-year exploration program in the Mackenzie Delta and Beaufort Sea.[18] As much as this figure astonished observers, British Petroleum (BP) shocked the industry the following year when it made a successful bid of $1.2 billion for a five-year exploration program in the same region.[19]

In addition, several land-based projects are now under way. One of the world's largest deposits of iron ore has been discovered in Mary River on Baffin Island, and plans are now in place to develop this site. It is anticipated that by taking advantage of new technologies for building ice-capable ships, it will be possible to ship the product during much of the year in ice-reinforced bulk carriers.[20]

On the other side of the Yukon–Alaska border, Shell since 2007 has been attempting to launch a $44 million exploration program. It has been held up by a court challenge filed by a coalition of community and environmental groups. In November 2008 the United States Court of Appeal for the Ninth Circuit ruled that the US federal government has not required strong enough environmental standards. This ruling meant that Shell could not proceed. Then in a surprise move, the court voided its own decision. Shell then proceeded with its offshore exploration program.[21]

The economic collapse of 2008 may affect Arctic resource exploration because it has affected the entire global economic system. At the time that Shell's exploration projects were being developed, the price of oil had been constantly increasing, eventually peaking at about $147 per barrel. The expectation at the time was that the price of oil would continue to increase. Although it has not been publicly confirmed, many analysts suggest that for Arctic oil to be profitable, the price of oil must be at least $80 per barrel.[22] The sudden reversal of world economic fortunes has seen the price drop to $40 per barrel; only recently has it begun to rise again, to $90 to $100 per barrel by the summer of 2011. Oil and gas companies have made no public statements as to whether the current price of oil will affect their exploration efforts in the North American Arctic. Statements by the Russians that they may slow the development of their northern resources have yet to be confirmed.

Even if the Arctic projects are put on hold in the foreseeable future, there is little doubt that they will eventually go forward. Given China's growth in the past decade and the growth that India is expected to experience in the coming years, these states' demands for oil alone will likely aid in the recovery of the price of oil. When that occurs, the North will become one of the main areas of new oil resource exploration and development. Thus the question is not whether oil and gas will be developed in the Arctic, but when.

New technologies for resource development are further facilitating changes in the Arctic. Non-Arctic states have entered the region and assumed leadership in advancing new technologies for use in the Arctic. The best-known example is the construction of ice-capable commercial vessels. Historically, Finnish and Russian companies have been the leaders in designing and building ice-capable vessels; today, they are being challenged increasingly by South Korean companies, which have invested heavily in building those ships.

Samsung Heavy Industry is building a number of medium-sized oil tankers weighing between 70,000 and 120,000 tons. These are being purchased for use in Russia's northern waters. Besides hulls designed to operate in up to 1.5-metre-thick ice, these tankers will have a new propulsion system known as Azipod, which will enable them to operate in both ice-covered waters and ice-free seas. In the ice-strengthened hulls of these ships, The South Koreans are installing a propeller that can rotate 360 degrees—known as Azipods. This rotation allows Samsung to place a regular bow on the front of the vessel and an ice-breaking bow on the stern of the vessel. In open-water conditions, these vessels operate as a normal tanker would. But when they are in ice-covered waters, they turn their propeller around and go "backwards." This latter con-figuration enables the ship to break the ice as it moves forward. Normally, ships that are designed to operate in ice possess characteristics that make oper-ating in ice-free waters problematic. Among other factors, the design of a bow needed to break through ice does not allow the ship to operate well in high waves. Historically, ships designed for operation in ice have not handled well on the open seas; conversely, ships that have been designed for the open sea have not been able to operate in ice. These new South Korean ships are ideal, then, to carry oil from ice-covered northern waters to southern ports, where the oil can be transferred to larger tankers or to pipelines. However, it is also possible for these ships to sail to other more distant ports. One of the first voyages made by one of these tankers carried a load of oil from a northern Russian field to Come By Chance, Newfoundland.[23]

There are no plans to use these vessels in Canadian or American waters because no offshore fields are currently in production. A second issue is that the North American side of the Arctic has thicker ice and a higher percentage of multi-year ice. Samsung officials admit that their design works best in freshly formed (first-year ice). However, it seems entirely possible that as the ice retreats and as production begins, such vessels could be used on the North American side of the Arctic Ocean.

Tankers would give the industry added flexibility in meeting new market demand, for they would provide Canadian producers with the opportunity to ship oil directly to Asian markets. But the use of these vessels could pose prob-lems for Canada. Canada could face an intensification of the dispute about con-trol of the Northwest Passage if the Americans were to use these tankers to ship oil from their side of the Arctic to European or eastern American markets. If the Americans were to use such vessels, it is unlikely that they would ask the Canadian government for permission to transit the passage since they insist that the passage is an international strait. On the other hand, Canada would not face this issue if the terminals for providing the oil were on the Canadian side of the border, for Canada would have sovereign control over any resource development on this side.

The current ship construction is of ice-capable oil tankers, but not of natural gas carriers. Several South Korean companies are developing plans to build natural gas carriers, but this is still in the planning stages. Given their ability to design and build ice-capable oil tankers, it is likely that the South Koreans will be equally successful in building gas carriers. The problem is how to liquefy natural gas in order to transport it. The Russians are also investigating this problem and have considered the construction of a nuclear-powered floating terminal that could be used to liquefy the gas on site. Even if they succeed, it is unclear whether Canada will consider using similar technology. In Canada, the ongoing resistance to nuclear power may lead to reluctance to adopt this technology. In this situation the gas would probably have to be shipped by pipeline to southern markets, in which case a pipeline through the Mackenzie Valley may be needed. If Canada is willing to invest in this nuclear-powered technology, then the Mackenzie pipeline may not be needed, for the gas from offshore sites could be loaded directly onboard the new ice-capable gas carriers.

It is necessary to remember that all of this remains speculative due to the uncertainty that surrounds almost all aspects of northern resource development. The quantity of oil and gas in the Canadian Arctic is unknown; the technology to exploit these resources is in a state of rapid development; which resources are usable and when they will even be used is a further unknown. Resource exploration and development is further complicated by sliding commodity prices, which demonstrate that it is impossible to expect regularity in the market.

Where does this leave the issue of Canadian Arctic sovereignty and security? The pursuit of resources will be the incentive for outside interests to enter the Canadian Arctic. However, international law gives Canada the sovereign right to control the development of these resources. UNCLOS gives coastal states the sovereign right to control the resources within two hundred miles of their coastline. Thus the Canadian government has the right to control all shipping that comes into Canadian Arctic waters for the purposes of resources, if it chooses to do so. The challenge is to control vessels that want to use Canadian Arctic waters as a passage. If Canada loses its dispute with the Americans and Europeans as to the international legal status of the Northwest Passage, they will not be able to unilaterally control those vessels. On the other hand, if the Canadian position that these waters are internal Canadian waters perseveres, it will be able to control that shipping.

As the Arctic's resources are developed, Canada will need to continue strengthening its ability to enforce its rules in the Arctic. Canada has the right to control all economic activity on its Arctic lands and in its Arctic Ocean, with the exception of Arctic shipping to a distance of two hundred nautical miles from its coastline. But having the right to do so and having the ability are two separate things. In order for Canada to actually control economic activity in its Arctic, the Canadian government will have to act to improve its ability to know what is happening in the North as well as its ability to control any activity that takes place there.

While successive Canadian governments have recognized the need to protect Canadian security and sovereignty in the region, they generally have been unwilling to allocate the funds to acquire the necessary assets.[24] At the end of the Second World War, the Canadian government recognized the importance of the Arctic to its security. German forces had set up secret weather stations in northern regions (including northern Labrador) to provide weather information for their submarine forces. The Japanese were perceived to be a threat to Alaska and Yukon and even to the Canadian West Coast. However, it was only when the Cold War erupted that the Canadian government became deeply concerned about its Arctic security. This became one of the government's most critical concerns as the Soviets developed nuclear-tipped weapon systems capable of crossing the Arctic region to hit North American targets. At the same time, the Canadian government became equally concerned about American efforts to improve North American Arctic security on Canadian territory. However, when faced with two possible choices—pay the full cost of the system to defend itself, or accept American assistance and risk American intrusion in the Canadian North—the government decided to accept American aid. As it turned out, once the various radar systems such as the Distant Early Warning (DEW) Line were built, the Americans were content to turn over the new infrastructure to Canada's control even though they had paid for the bulk of its construction.[25]

In 1969, American action reignited Canadian Arctic sovereignty concerns. Following the discovery of a very large oil field in northern Alaska in 1968, the Americans considered the possibility of shipping the oil to southern American markets via the Northwest Passage.[26] The Americans argued that the passage was an international strait and therefore they did not need Canadian permission to go through it. The Canadian position was that the waters were internal waters and therefore under Canadian control, thus requiring Canadian permission. In the name of good relations with the United States, the Canadian government granted "permission" to the American voyages even though it had not been sought, and even provided icebreaker assistance. As a result of the American voyage, the Trudeau government passed the Arctic Waters Pollution Prevention Act and embarked on an international campaign

Figure 2-2   The USCGS *Polar Sea* in the Beaufort Sea, 2009.
Source: United States Coast Guard

to gain acceptance for its position regarding the legal status of the Northwest Passage.[27] However, little effort was made to improve the Canadian government's ability to act in the North because the immediate threat from the Americans ended when they decided to build a pipeline running north to south across Alaska instead of shipping it by tanker. Once this threat ceased, there seemed little likelihood that any other non-Canadians would come into the Canadian North.

The next sovereignty dispute arose in 1985 when an American icebreaker transited the Northwest Passage without asking for Canadian permission,[28] creating a crisis in Canadian–American Arctic relations. The American purpose for the voyage was not to test Canadian claims but to meet a NATO requirement to provide an icebreaker escort to resupply a military base in Thule, Greenland. When the American icebreaker that normally undertook this resupply broke down, the United States asked Canada if its forces could take on this mission on short notice, but this proved impossible. The American icebreaker *Polar Sea* was sent through the Panama Canal to Thule. It then needed to return to Alaska as quickly as possible. In order to do so, it sailed through the Northwest Passage on its return voyage. Prior to the voyage an interim agreement had been reached to allow the voyage to occur, but the agreement fell through after editorials were published about the forthcoming voyage.[29]

To counter criticism that it was bowing to the Americans, the Canadian government cancelled the agreement. Nevertheless, it granted permission to the Americans even though they had not sought Canadian permission in the first place. Once again, following the crisis the Mulroney government promised a wide range of actions to address Canada's weaknesses in the Arctic region. Ultimately, it implemented the promises that did not involve spending money. Canada successfully negotiated an agreement with the Americans for future icebreaker transits. Any future transit by American icebreakers would be preceded by a request for consent, which was expected to be given.[30] Canada also established straight baselines around its Arctic islands to mark its territory clearly. However, it did not build a new Polar 8 Class icebreaker as it had promised, nor did it provide its armed forces with any new Arctic capabilities such as the proposed nuclear-powered submarines.[31]

As the Cold War ended, both the Mulroney government and the subsequent Chrétien government saw an opportunity to improve circumpolar relations.[32] In a 1989 speech in Leningrad, Mulroney suggested that the time had come to create a multilateral body that would bring together the Arctic states to improve cooperation between former enemies. Neither the Americans nor the Soviets accepted the initial effort to create this council, so it went nowhere. Instead, Canada joined forces with Finland to create the Arctic Environmental Protection Strategy (AEPS), which was an agreement to examine the emerging circumpolar environmental problems discovered by scientists. This was less ambitious than the plans for the council; however, Canadian officials viewed it as offering the best means for improving cooperation. Canada, though, never lost sight of its goal of creating an Arctic Council and eventually, in 1996, succeeded in transforming the AEPS into the Arctic Council.

The Americans remained unconvinced about the Arctic Council. Canada eventually persuaded them to join it, albeit reluctantly. The price paid for persuading the Americans to join was their determination to keep the council as weak as possible. Canadian officials were unable to give the Arctic Council the powers they believed it needed to serve an effective forum for the circumpolar world.

The end of the Cold War coincided with American resistance to creating and strengthening multilateral Arctic bodies. The Canadian government around this time allowed its existing physical Arctic capabilities to further atrophy, and it made little effort to pursue diplomatic initiatives about the Arctic. Not until the end of the 1990s did it began to reverse this inaction. This sea change began under the Martin government; the Harper government that took its place has increasingly recognized the significance of maintaining a strong presence in the Arctic and has vigorously begun to improve Canada's northern abilities.

With respect to the issue of knowing who is in the Arctic and what is happening there, the current Harper government is improving Canada's northern surveillance by increasing its expenditures on research. Northern Watch is a research program dedicated to developing a Canadian built and designed system that will provide surveillance of the Arctic subsurface, surface, and airspace. It is not yet operational, and it is not clear when the government will make a decision on funding an operational version of the system.

Canadians scientists have also developed a more advanced program of satellite imagery systems designed to provide space-based surveillance of surface vessels in the Arctic. The first satellite, RadarSat-1, had been designed primarily as an ice-detection observation system. However, it soon became apparent that it could also be used to "see" large vessels. The recently launched RadarSat-2 has better resolution and is expected to be able to detect smaller vessels. At the lower end of the technology spectrum, the Martin and Harper governments increased the size of the Rangers units based in the North and also improved their training. The Rangers are a northern militia unit whose primary task is to provide surveillance in the North at the local level. The

Figure 2-3 RadarSat-2, launched by MacDonald, Dettwiler and Associates Ltd. in December 2007, integrates commercial satellite data into defence and intelligence systems.
Source: Canadian Space Agency

Rangers are volunteers comprised primarily of indigenous people and are particularly skilled observers who can live off the land. All of these initiatives will enable the Canadian government to know who is in its Arctic region and what they are doing, which is the first step in controlling activity in the Canadian North.

Once the Canadian government knows who is there and what is happening there, it must be able to control those people and their activities. To that end, the Martin and Harper governments recognized that it was necessary to increase Canada's enforcement capability in the Arctic. Since 2002, both governments have increased the number of military exercises in the North. The Harper government has made a series of promises to considerably expand Canada's northern capability, including these: six to eight Arctic offshore patrol vessels that will be able to sail in first-year ice that is up to 1 metre thick; a replacement for the Coast Guard's largest and oldest icebreaker, the *Louis St. Laurent*; the construction of a deep-water replenishment site at Nanisivik; new replenishment vessels that will have the capability to operate in first-year ice for the naval forces; new long-range patrol aircraft to replace the Aurora (CF-140); and a training base in Resolute. If these promises are implemented, Canada will have significantly improved its ability to control activity in its Arctic. However, most of these commitments have not yet moved from promise to reality. There are now signs that the government is backtracking on some of its promises. The program to build the new replenishment vessels, for instance, was postponed after domestic builders submitted bids that were too high for the government. It remains uncertain what will happen with this program. Likewise, there has been little public discussion of when construction of the Arctic offshore patrol vessels or the icebreaker will begin. While plans are still being developed for both the icebreaker and the AOPVs as of 2011, neither has yet been sent to tender.

Canada needs to act on these programs. When commodity prices rebound, with the ice continuing to melt, more foreign nationals will come to the Canadian North to explore and develop Arctic marine resources. Canada will need to ensure that they know Canadian rules and laws and will follow them. For that to happen, the Canadian government will have to be able to control the activity of these foreign nationals.

Geopolitical Change

As if climate change and resource development were not sufficient forces to drive change, the geopolitical forces that have re-emerged since the end of the Cold War are literally redrawing the map of the Arctic. New international laws have allowed the Arctic nations to extend their control over the Arctic seabed.

It is possible that almost all of the Arctic Ocean's seabed may come under the control of one of the Arctic states. Second, most Arctic nations are beginning to strengthen the ability of their armed forces and coast guards to operate in the North. Third, non-Arctic states have begun to show interest in Arctic operations. The net effect of these factors is a growing international recognition of the importance of the Arctic, concurrent with increasing international action in the region.

The media are reporting more and more regularly about a race for resources in the Arctic, with repeated references to efforts to "carve" up the Arctic. The reality is that there is no division of the Arctic—yet. Currently, the five states with coastlines on the Arctic Ocean are about to extend their control so that it includes the seabeds extending from their respective continental shelves. Central to this extension is rights to the minerals and oil and gas reserves that may be found on and in these extensions. Canada's extension may give it one of the largest new territories in the Arctic.

This extension is occurring under the terms of UNCLOS. This convention is one of the most complex and comprehensive of all international treaties and has received almost universal agreement. So far (as of August 2011), 162 states and international bodies have ratified or acceded to the treaty. The negotiations began in 1973 and concluded in 1982. It required sixty ratifications before it came into force, which happened in 1996. Much of UNCLOS was a codification of existing customary international law. But it also introduced new means of ocean governance. At the centre of these efforts was the creation of new zones of control over ocean space. Prior to the convention, international law only recognized the right of a state to extend control of its adjacent ocean space to a distance of twelve nautical miles. As discussed earlier in this chapter, UNCLOS has created different zones of control. Specifically, the convention gives coastal states control of resources up to a distance of two hundred nautical miles in an area called the EEZ.

Under the terms of Article 76, a state that sits on an extension of the continental shelf that goes beyond 200 nautical miles can also claim control of the resources on the soil and subsoil for an additional distance of 150 nautical miles, and in certain instances even beyond this. Unlike the EEZ, which all coastal states can claim, states must prove they have an extended continental shelf. They have ten years to engage in the research necessary to do this. At that point they must submit their findings to an international body named the Commission on Limits of the Continental Shelf (CLCS). This body reviews and passes judgment on the technical and scientific merits of the country's submission. If the CLCS accepts the submission and if the state's neighbours have submitted overlapping claims, the dispute must be resolved at that stage. The

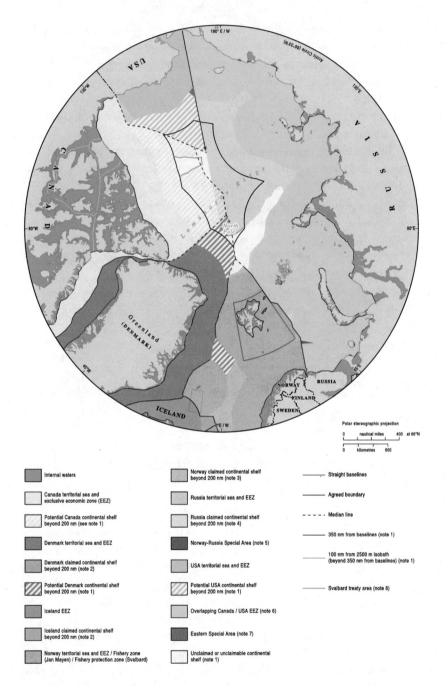

Map 2-3   Maritime jurisdictions and boundaries in the Arctic Region.
Source: International Boundaries Research Unit, Durham University, UK

convention provides that all such disputes must be resolved peacefully and also provides a variety of means for achieving resolution. Article 280 of Section XV of the convention allows the state parties to a dispute to use "any peaceful means of their own choice," to resolve a dispute caused by the convention. The overlapping claims thus created by Article 76 will be such a dispute.

The parties to such a dispute can also use Article 284 of Section XV of the convention, which allows for a conciliation process established in Annex V of the convention. If neither of these processes is acceptable, Article 287 requires the parties to the dispute to select from four options: 1(a) the International Tribunal for the Law of the Sea; 1(b) the International Court of Justice; 1(c) an arbitral tribunal constituted in accordance with Annex VII of the convention; or 1(d) a special arbitral tribunal constituted under Annex VIII of the convention. If the parties are unable to agree on the specific means of settlement, option 1(d) is to be employed. The five Arctic states that are making continental shelf claims, which were agreed upon in June 2008 in a meeting held in Ilulissat, Greenland, will have to resolve any differences peacefully and through the mechanisms established by the UNCLOS.[33] However, as will be discussed in following section, the United States is not yet a party to the convention, so it remains uncertain how these countries will be able to use the mechanisms created by the convention. It is hoped that the Americans will soon accede to the treaty; if they do not, it is unclear what can be done to include their participation.

Almost the entire Arctic Ocean may be an extension of the continental shelves of the North American and Eurasian land masses. Canada, Denmark (for Greenland), Russia, and the United States are all engaged in research programs to determine the extent of their continental shelves. Russia submitted a claim in 2001,[34] and on completing its review of this claim, the CLCS asked the Russians to provide more data to support it.

The four Arctic nations that can claim an extended continental shelf in the Arctic Ocean—Russia, Denmark (for Greenland), the United States, and Canada—are taking this process very seriously, as is clear from their current level of effort. The Russians ratified the convention on 12 March 1997, the Danes on 16 November 2003, and the Canadians on 7 November 2003. The Norwegians ratified the Convention on 24 June 1996 and also claim a northern extended continental shelf, albeit farther south than the other four.[35] Norway has already submitted its claim to the CLCS.[36]

The United States has neither signed nor ratified the treaty. Successive presidents since George H.W. Bush have attempted to accede to the treaty but have been prevented by a small minority of Republican senators. The American constitutional system requires all international treaties to be passed by a two-thirds Senate majority. Since the early 1990s this minority of Republican senators has been able to consolidate more than 33 senators who have refused to accede to UNCLOS. Their primary motivation is ideologically based opposition to the UN. However, with the recent American election, and the defeat and retirement of some of the senators in question, it is anticipated that President Obama will eventually achieve success. The United States has recognized the importance of being party to a treaty that will protect its interests in the North. In anticipation of their accession, they have begun mapping their extended continental shelf. They conducted an expedition with Canada in the Beaufort Sea in 2008, 2009, and 2010, and they plan to continue mapping their continental shelf in 2011.

After ratifying UNCLOS, Canada launched a concerted effort to map its continental shelf. The 2004 budget allocated $69 million for the mapping of the Arctic and Atlantic seabeds, with the bulk of the funds expected to be spent in the North. The 2008 budget provided an additional $20 million. This investment has enabled Canadian scientists to carry on with a robust agenda that should be completed by 2010. This will give Canada the necessary time to prepare its submission to the CLCS.

The media have focused on the disputes that have the potential to develop from overlapping claims. Until all of the states have submitted their claims, it is impossible to know whether any disputes will arise or, if they do, how serious they will be. Canada, the United States, Denmark, and Norway have already issued diplomatic *démarches* against the 2001 Russian submission. After the Russians submitted their claim in 2001, the CLCS advised them to further develop the science behind it, so it is possible that a revised Russian claim may not be challenged. This would require the Russians to reduce their claimed area, which seems unlikely.

The Russians have responded to Norway's claim to an extended continental shelf in somewhat aggressive terms. In the summer of 2008, the Russian Navy resumed surface naval patrols. Specifically, two Russian warships sailed into the region that Norway has claimed around Spitsbergen, an island in the Svalbard Archipelago.[37] The Russians and the Norwegians have a long-standing dispute about that island, one that has undoubtedly been intensified by Norway's resolve to extend its continental shelf. Under international law, the Russians have the right to sail warships into the EEZ and over the continental shelf, so by sailing into the disputed region, they have not broken international law. But it is hard to avoid the conclusion that the Russians have been sending a message to the Norwegians by sailing into the disputed area. However in 2010, the Norwegians and Russians surprised many by announcing that they had resolved this dispute.

This is not the only action that the Russians have taken to support their claim. Using a mini-submarine, they dropped a Russian flag at the North Pole in the summer of 2007. The other Arctic states dismissed this as a meaningless act. "This isn't the 15th century," stated Peter MacKay, then Canada's Minister of Foreign Affairs. "You can't go around the world and just plant flags to claim territory."[38] Yet questions remain as to why the Russians would take such potent symbolic action.

The Russians are attempting to justify their claim that the North Pole should be the point dividing their claim from those of Canada and Denmark (and possibly the United States). Their initial submission to the CLCS in 2001 shows that they intend to claim up to the North Pole. While such an approach appears logical on a map, it has no basis in international law. The Russian effort seems to be based on the sector theory. This theory was first put forward by Canadian Senator Pascal Poirier in 1907 as a means of extending Canadian Arctic claims. Poirier suggested that each of the states on the Arctic Ocean should extend its boundaries northward until they meet at the North Pole. Such a suggestion was never supported by the Canadian government or by international law. One of Canada's leading experts on international law in the Arctic, Donat Pharand, conducted the definitive examination on the issue. His conclusion: such an approach is simply not valid.[39] However, the Russians are attempting to revive it. The Soviets never repudiated the principle after considering it in the 1930s. If it was accepted, this approach would benefit the Russians.

Canada and Denmark claim that the Lomonosov Ridge connects to the North American/Greenland land mass. If it does, they can make an extended claim similar to that of Russia. This means that they too can go to the North Pole. If that is the case, then Canada, Denmark, and Russia can claim almost the entire Arctic Ocean as part of their extended continental shelf. In any other part of the globe, the normal means of dividing such an overlapping claim would be to determine the equidistant point (the halfway mark) between the competing states. This point would be determined by drawing a line between the most northern Canadian, Danish, and Russian land points and then determining where the halfway mark of this line is. It is probable that this point is somewhere on the Russian side of the North Pole. Thus the pole and its surrounding area would be either Danish or Canadian depending on the precise measuring of the ridge. The support this method gains on the Russian side will only be determined once all three states have made their submission to the CLCS.

The question is whether or not all of this matters. Little examination has been undertaken of the potential location of oil and gas at the highest latitudes. The Russians have only begun exploratory drilling in this region.[40] They are

Figure 2-4 The Russian *Yamal*, a nuclear-powered "Arctic class" icebreaker.
Source: IMAGEstock

also building nuclear-powered icebreaking drill ships, but these ships are not yet operational.[41] At this point no one really knows whether the North Pole and its surrounding regions have gas and oil resources. Even if such resources are found there, the means of transporting the resources to southern markets are only now being developed. But as discussed previously, both climate change and technological development could soon make this possible.

Canada may soon have to decide whether it will challenge Russia's claim. If it does, this will be the first time that Canada has engaged in a territorial dispute with Russia since Russia and Britain resolved the land boundary between Alaska and Yukon in 1825. At the Ilulissat meeting, the Russian government promised that all disputes arising over the Arctic continental shelf would be dealt with peacefully and in a cooperative spirit.[42] However, recent events point to an increasingly assertive (and possibly aggressive) Russia. Georgia was temporarily invaded and partly occupied by Russia over a territorial dispute. Ukraine had its gas supplies temporarily suspended as it battled with the Russians over a pricing contract. It is difficult to imagine a Canadian–Russian Arctic dispute escalating to the point of conflict, but it is easy to believe that Russia could be assertive in support of its claim.

Canadian officials need to be aware of what might be involved in facing the assertive (and possibly aggressive) Russians should Canada challenge their extended continental shelf claim. The Russians have already demonstrated what such action might look like regarding the sales of its natural gas. Both Poland and Ukraine have faced Russian actions, which have included threatened gas cut-offs. The Russian Special Arctic Representative to the President (the same individual who planted the Russian flag on the seabed at the North Pole) has said in an interview that Canada talks a lot but does not do much with regard to the Arctic. In the same interview he suggested that while Russia has agreed to resolve any differences on a diplomatic basis, it would view any Canadian effort to encroach on its claim in very negative terms. Canada, then, should expect a vigorous response from Russia if it decides to go beyond the pole and into what the Russians contend is theirs in making its claims. Canadian officials should not shy away from the challenge but should be prepared for Russia to adopt "hardball" policies.

The situation facing Canada and the United States is even more confounding. Canadian scientists have made substantial efforts to determine the extent of the continental shelf in the Beaufort Sea. This country will face two problems once it submits its coordinates. First, Canada and the United States already have a substantial boundary disagreement as to how to divide the territorial waters and the EEZ in the Beaufort Sea. This disagreement stems from the interpretation of the 1825 treaty between Russia and Britain that divided the land territory of what is now Alaska from what is now Yukon. That treaty provided for the drawing of land boundaries but made no reference to maritime ones. As a consequence, the Canadians and the Americans are now disputing how to draw the boundaries for their territorial sea and the EEZ in the Beaufort. The United States contends that the border needs to be drawn at a 90 degree angle to the coastline. The Canadian position is that the maritime boundary is an extension of the land boundary. This disagreement has created a triangle-shaped disputed zone of approximately 6,250 square nautical miles, which may contain substantial oil and gas resources.

This dispute could significantly impact the determination of the Canadian continental shelf in the western Arctic. The starting point of the continental shelf will probably be determined by the tip of the top point of the farthest extent of the EEZ. The disagreement over the boundary dividing the EEZ and territorial sea may lead to a problem in dividing the extended continental shelf.

Further complicating this situation, the United States is not a party to UNCLOS. The Americans cannot formally submit a claim for their continental shelf until they accede to the convention. As mentioned earlier, the hope is that the US Senate will pass the convention. Statements by Secretary of State Hillary Clinton suggest that this will be an important priority for the Obama administration.[43]

Canada faces substantial uncertainty and challenges in determining the limits of its extended continental shelf. This uncertainty will make it difficult for Canadian officials to prepare a diplomatic campaign if there *are* in fact overlaps with the other Arctic claimant states. Canadian efforts to determine their country's continental shelf may show that Canada's claims are limited geographically and do not extend into the American, Russian, or Danish areas. It is also possible that Canadian efforts may result in considerable overlap with those three Arctic neighbours. It is doubtful that this issue will be resolved before 2020. Furthermore, the extent to which oil and gas resources will be at the heart of discussions is unknown. It may be that oil and gas resources on the extended continental shelf are limited. On the other hand, if research bodies such as the US Geological Survey are correct, Canadian control over these resources could result in substantial economic benefit for Canada.

Ultimately, the issue is one of control. The entire purpose of Canada's effort to determine the coordinates of its Arctic continental shelf is to allow for its future control over the development and exploitation of any resources that may be found there. This control will give Canada the right to set the rules as to how those resources are to be developed. It will also give Canada the right to decide whether it even wants to develop the resources. It may be that a future Canadian government may decide that it is simply better to leave the resources in the ground, but that will be for Canadians to decide. So the issue of control of this territory is important.

The Northwest Passage

The other issue that has perplexed Canadians in the Arctic is sovereignty as it relates to the Northwest Passage. As discussed earlier, this has been a major irritant in Canada–US relations since 1969. The sovereignty issue in the context of the Northwest Passage is about control of international shipping in the Northwest Passage, nothing more and nothing less.

The Canadian position is that the passage is internal Canadian waters, which gives Canada absolute control over all activities within those waters. The American position is that the passage is a strait used for international navigation. If the Canadian position is correct, then Canada has the right to control all elements of shipping in the passage, including the right to control who enters the passage and who cannot. If the American position is correct, then Canada only has the right to control international shipping with regard to international rules and standards, and thus has a limited ability to stop shipping.[44]

A number of recent articles by Canadian scholars have suggested that it may well be possible to work out a deal with the United States on this issue. Some of these articles have suggested that it should be feasible to work out a deal similar to the St. Lawrence Seaway Agreement,[45] in which there would be joint management of the passage.[46] Others have suggested that as long as Canada can show that it is serious about asserting proper control over the region and about safeguarding its security there, the Americans should respond by not pressing their position. In other words, American agreement not to challenge Canada would be exchanged for Canadian protection of the region.

In theory, this approach makes sense. The support it received from former US Ambassador to Canada Paul Cellucci suggests that it could be possible. However, such hopes were severely damaged in the last days of the George W. Bush administration amidst reports that the United States had been working on a national Arctic Policy since 2007. It seemed unlikely that it would be released as the Bush administration came to an end. But to the surprise of most observers, that administration released its policy on 9 January 2009, less than two weeks before the inauguration of Barack Obama on 20 January. On a positive note, this National Security Presidential Directive has reaffirmed in the strongest terms the American commitment to accede to the UNCLOS to ensure that American interests in the Arctic will be protected. At the same time, unfortunately, the Americans have presented one of the most direct statements of their position on the Northwest Passage. That policy states:

> Freedom of the seas is a top national priority. The Northwest Passage is a strait used for international navigation, and the Northern Sea Route includes straits used for international navigation; the regime of transit passage applies to passage through those straits. Preserving the rights and duties relating to navigation and overflight in the Arctic region supports our ability to exercise these rights throughout the world, including through strategic straits.[47]

This enunciation of the American policy makes it difficult to see how any agreement can be reached unless the Obama administration moves to repel or replace that directive. But any such movement seems very unlikely. The policy directive does not state anything that is new; it only puts the American position in stark and direct terms.

The Canadian position is further complicated by a policy statement issued by the EU in December 2008. In that statement, the EU was equally clear on its position on the Northwest Passage: while acknowledging the particular environmental needs of the waterways of the Arctic, the EU also affirms that the principle of freedom of navigation through the passage must be maintained.[48]

From the Canadian perspective, it has always been difficult to understand the American and European positions on the passage. There have been only three times when vessels transiting the passage have specifically *not* sought the Canadian government's permission to do so: the *Manhattan* in 1969 and 1970, and the *Polar Sea* in 1985. All other transits have taken place with the explicit agreement of Canadian authorities. So when both the United States and the EU maintain that the Northwest Passage is a strait used for international navigation, they are speaking of a principle and not an existing reality.

What motivates the Americans and the Europeans to oppose the Canadians on this issue? Why do they seem so intent on denying Canada the right to control shipping in what are obviously unique waterways that have not been used for international shipping? Two reasons provide the answer as to why they persist in this position regardless of the damage it may do to their relationship with Canada: the fear of setting an international precedent, and the anticipation of a substantially larger number of transpolar shipping transits.

In their Arctic policy paper, the Americans are not necessarily referencing only the Northwest Passage in their discussion about freedom of navigation. Rather, they are focused on the Strait of Hormuz, the Strait of Gibraltar, the Malacca Strait, and many other straits used for international navigation worldwide. The Americans' primary concern is to ensure that they are not perceived as weakening their support of this principle of free passage through international straits. Thus their position has always been more about precedent and less about the Northwest Passage. The Americans' concerns regarding these other straits are both strategic and economic. They are determined to ensure that countries such as Iran do not acquire the right to limit or restrict the US Navy's travel through such waters. The second and related objective of the United States is to ensure that commercial traffic continues to have the right of unfettered passage. Again, the Americans fear that a country such as Iran may stop oil tankers from entering or exiting the Strait of Hormuz to load off the coast of Saudi Arabia and Kuwait.

The EU has a similar interest in ensuring that its naval and commercial vessels retain navigational freedoms through these waters. But the EU also seems interested in the potential of the Arctic as a major shipping route. The Commission of the European Communities stated in a 2008 document that:

> EU Member States have the world's largest merchant fleet and many of those ships use transoceanic routes. The melting of sea ice is progressively opening opportunities to navigate on routes through Arctic waters. This could considerably shorten trips from Europe to the Pacific, save energy, reduce emissions,

promote trade and diminish pressure on the main trans-continental navigation channels.

It is in the EU's interest to explore and improve conditions for gradually introducing Arctic commercial navigation, while promoting stricter safety and environmental standards as well as avoiding detrimental effects.

By the same token, Member States and the Community should defend the principle of freedom of navigation and the right of innocent passage in the newly opened routes and areas.[49]

This commercial interest is the basis for the EU's desire to protect its future Arctic shipping interests.

Where does this leave Canada? As discussed earlier, even with a melting Arctic, shipping in the region will remain extremely challenging. The Canadian side of the Arctic will likely be the last region to experience the elimination of year-round ice. First-year ice will reform in the winter months, limiting shipping to only those vessels that are ice-capable. The summer months will become increasingly ice-free, but communication will remain difficult until additional communication and global positioning satellites have been placed in orbits that accommodate the high latitudes. It is difficult to imagine that the northern straits will be similar to all other straits in terms of accessibility, navigation, and communication. The great challenges to navigation well into this century will require the development of different and more powerful regulations and controls than for any other waterway. So it is clear that Canada must retain some form of control.

It is also necessary to consider the unintended results of the American and European positions on the Northwest Passage. If the passage becomes an international strait, the security of the North American Arctic will be compromised in terms of both air and maritime security. Under international law, an international strait also accords the right of overflight to all states. This means that the Russians, who recently reinstituted their long-range Tu-95 (Bear) bomber air patrols in the Arctic, would have the right to overfly the passage if it was eventually determined to be an international strait. This overflight ability would allow them to penetrate much farther into North American airspace than ever before. Relations between Canada, Russia, and the United States have been cordial in recent times. But if those relations were to become more strained, a Russian effort to assert that right could escalate tensions.

Furthermore, if the Northwest Passage were an international strait, Canada would not have the right to stop vessels that it considered a security risk unless it was able to demonstrate that the vessel in question was breaking international rules and laws. The problem for the North is that, given how sparsely populated much of it is, a vessel that was attempting to smuggle illicit products into the country would only have to *appear* to be following international rules. Absent solid evidence against the vessel, Canada would not have the right to conduct mandatory inspections or to deny passage.

In addition, countries that are not friendly to the United States or Canada would have the right of navigation without being required to ask the Canadian government for permission to transit. What would it mean for Canadian security to have a hostile navy sailing through the passage? Of course, states such as Iran have to deal with hostile US and UK navies sailing through the Strait of Hormuz. So it is possible to argue that Canada will have to deal with a similar situation as Iran. But if that is the case, then Canada and the United States will have to ensure that in the event it happens, they can provide security for the North American Arctic. It will be simple to maintain effective North American Arctic security if Canada is understood to have control over the waterway. That will not be the case if the classification of the passage changes. So it is somewhat troublesome that the policy positions of Canada's allies would increase the threat to Canadian Arctic security.

Strategic Developments

What do the new strategic realities in the Arctic mean for Canada? It is difficult to fully delineate this issue as these new realities are only now starting to take shape. Only in the past four years have most of the Arctic states begun initiating new actions regarding their security requirements in the Arctic. No one really knows what the future will look like.

The Arctic states are beginning to rebuild their military capabilities, particularly with respect to the Arctic. The driving force behind this is the recognition that new economic development in the Arctic is going to increase activity levels in the region; no one, however, can fully anticipate what this new economic activity will look like. It is expected to be substantial. Thus, Arctic nations are beginning to prepare so that they will be able to respond to new contingencies.

That being said, the driving force for most Arctic states is a concern that the Arctic is changing and that they must be prepared for the consequences of those changes. In particular, concern is rising among some Arctic states that Russia is beginning to redeploy its military to the Arctic. This concern has yet to translate into fears of an actual Russian threat, and none of the Arctic states have suggested that threat is real. Instead, the concern is to ensure that should Russian actions become more threatening, the Arctic states will be able to respond if necessary.

Figure 2-5 A CF-18 Hornet from Cold Lake, Alberta, flies next to a Russian Tu-95 "Bear" bomber in September 2007.
Source: DND

An equally nebulous concern relates to the impact of climate change. Most Arctic states have issued statements that the increasingly accessible melting Arctic is expected to facilitate new economic activities. The full nature of those activities is not yet understood; thus, the concern is to be sufficiently prepared. This desire for preparedness focuses the attention of most decision makers—Canadian included—on surveillance and enforcement capabilities. Most officials want improved means of knowing what is happening in the Arctic, and they want to have the ability to respond if unlawful action occurs.

These concerns are accompanied by a growing recognition that the Arctic remains a very expensive region in which to operate. As the Arctic states make plans to revitalize their security capacities in the Arctic, most recognize that it remains a challenging operational environment. Given the lack of existing infrastructure, any effort to improve surveillance and enforcement capabilities remains costly. The current economic crisis has only heightened concerns over how an improved Canadian Arctic capability is to be achieved.

There was general agreement at the end of the Cold War that the strategic significance of the Arctic had ended and that the need to be concerned about traditional security threats had been eliminated. The Soviet Northern Fleet with its vast number of nuclear-powered attack and nuclear-missile-carrying submarines (SSNs and SSBNs) was immediately retired. The collapse of the Soviet Union was so total that the threat posed by these submarines changed overnight from one of nuclear war resulting in the destruction of North America (and even the world) to one of a potential Arctic environmental disaster as these vessels were left to rust in northern Russian harbours with the inherent risk of a massive radionuclear spill or accident. At the same time, almost all of the other Arctic nations reduced the northern element of their own forces. From 1989 to approximately 2002, the northern military capabilities of all the Arctic states were substantially reduced.

There were some important exceptions. One of the most important, which received little attention, was the American decision to place one of two ballistic missile interceptor ground bases at Fort Greely, Alaska, in 2002. This base is now operational, meaning that missiles designed for interception are now in the ground and ready to engage incoming missiles. The location is presumed to be well suited for a missile attack on the United States from Asia. Currently, the Americans are supplementing their two bases with additional maritime mobile systems—for example, they are placing anti-ballistic missiles on board ships and are negotiating to place other interceptor sites in other countries. But with its secured silos, Fort Greely ensures that the Arctic will remain a strategic concern for the United States well into the future.

The Canadian effort to maintain military control over its Arctic ended almost as soon as the Cold War did. Any meaningful military exercises were stopped, and even the sovereignty patrols of the maritime and air forces were either stopped or reduced to symbolic levels. The maritime forces ceased their northern deployments (NORPLOYs) in 1989. The air forces reduced their northern sovereignty overflights from a high of twenty-two in 1987 to two by 1995. The only current land force presence in Canada's Arctic is the Canadian Rangers. As discussed earlier, the Rangers are a militia unit comprised of local volunteers, who are given a minimum of training, a red sweatshirt, a rifle, and some ammunition. While the Canadian Forces have traditionally provided them with very little, the Rangers provide the forces with a wealth of information and capabilities. They are important for providing surveillance of the regions they are located near. Equally important, they have always provided the CF with a rich source of traditional knowledge. They know the land and how to survive on it. Thus they have proven to be a very important asset whenever the regular forces have wanted to operate in the North.

It was not until 1999 that the CF seriously reconsidered their role in the Arctic. This was to a certain degree the result of the initiative of individual officers, who had become concerned about what they perceived to be a changing Arctic security environment.[50] These concerns led to the creation of an interdepartmental (federal and territorial) security working group named the Arctic Security Intergovernmental Working Group (ASIWG, later ASWG) as well as an internal Department of National Defence (DND) review of its Arctic capabilities. After the terrorist attacks of 11 September 2001, the entire Canadian government began to take security issues much more seriously. In 2002, Canada resumed military training operations in the North. The small-scale

Figure 2-6 A CC-138 Twin Otter from 440 squadron in Yellowknife flies over Canadian Rangers on patrol near Eureka, Nunavut, during Operation Nunalivut, 2008.
Source: DND

exercises that were conducted in August 2002 have since become annual events and are continually evolving into more complex operations.

During the Martin administration, Canadian political leaders began to share the view that Canadian Arctic security required improvement. While too short-lived to act on this realization, the Martin government either developed or began to develop policies that highlighted the need for action. The government released a set of policy papers on Defence, Diplomacy, Development, and International Trade; the need to provide for Arctic security received substantial attention in the Defence and Diplomacy papers. The DND's *Canada's International Policy Statement* (2005), which focused on the expected rise of activity in the North, stated that "the demands of sovereignty and security for the government could become even more pressing as activity in the North Continues to rise."[51] This document went on to state that Canada would need to increase its ability to act in the North.

At the same time, the Martin government was developing a domestic policy statement that would provide a Government of Canada position on the North. This statement was an attempt to move away from the traditional approach of department-specific policy; another of its aims was to provide a Government of Canada Arctic policy. Referred to as the Northern Strategy, it was to be built on seven pillars or subsections, one of which was "Reinforcing Sovereignty, National Security, and Circumpolar Cooperation."[52] Despite the Martin government's numerous meetings surrounding this document, it was not finalized before the government's defeat in the 2006 federal election.

The Harper government has fully accepted the need to improve Canada's ability to know what is happening in the North and to be able to act. It has made a large number of promises. But it remains uncertain whether those promises will be funded. Harper's government has committed itself to constructing six to eight Arctic offshore patrol vessels; to establishing a northern military training base at Resolute Bay; and to refurbishing a retired mining site at Nanisivik as a refuelling base. After making these promises, the government made the protection of Arctic sovereignty and security a priority in its Throne Speech of 16 October 2007; it also promised to construct a world-class research station in the Canadian North.[53] From a policy position and in terms of rhetoric, the Harper government has made it clear that it views the rebuilding of Canada's defence capabilities as a high priority. As discussed earlier in this chapter, it remains to be seen whether these commitments will be fulfilled.

Regardless, as of 2011, it is clear that the need to improve Canada's ability to act is being taken more seriously. Other Arctic nations have taken note as they, too, revive their capabilities. It is Norway, Russia, and the United States that are beginning to look most seriously at the need to act. From a strategic position, nuclear-powered submarines remain the principle weapons platform. At the end of the Cold War, both the Americans and the Russians found themselves with very large fleets, which were quickly deemed to be surplus. For the Russians, this, in combination with their concurrent economic collapse, meant that their submarines were simply left to rust in harbour throughout the 1990s. The direct intervention of the G8 and Norway provided the Russians with the funds and the technology to properly dispose of these submarines. At the same time, all new submarine construction was halted.

The US Navy also disposed of its older class of submarines, including the Sturgeon class, which was considered its best submarine for under-ice operations. Furthermore, the Seawolf class submarines, which were to be the new class of American SSNs, were scaled back to three vessels. A new and cheaper submarine, the Virginia class, was selected instead even though it was not given the same degree of under-ice capability as the Seawolf.[54]

In 2004 the Russians and then the Americans took action to rebuild their under-ice capabilities. On the basis of their improving financial situation, the Russian administrations of Putin and Medvedev began to rebuild their submarine forces.[55] They have just activated the nuclear reactor on their first new post–Cold War SSBN, the *Yury Dolgoruky*.[56] Under the Russian State Armaments Program 2007–15, the Russians have committed to building five SSBNs, two SSNs, and six diesel-powered submarines.[57] While it is understandable that the experience of losing much of their submarine capability in the decade and a half after the collapse of the Soviet Union may encourage them to rebuild their submarine force, the geographic reality of Russia means that most of this reconstruction will be carried out in and around their Murmansk bases. This means that the North will regain some of its strategic significance, particularly for Russia.

The Russians have also begun to consider rebuilding their surface fleet capability. Recently their naval commander-in-chief announced a plan to build up their forces to six carrier battle groups.[58] If built, most would be based on the Kola Peninsula, generating a substantial increase in naval traffic in northern waters as these vessels move in and out of harbour. This announcement has been accompanied by an increase in operations in the region. The Russians suspended their Arctic sovereignty flights in 1992, but resumed them in the summer of 2007.[59] Using its long range TU-95 (Bear) patrol and bomber aircraft, the Russians are now sending out patrols over the Arctic and as far as the Sea of Japan and Cuba. There have been no reports that the Russians have violated any other state's airspace.[60] The Russians are reported to be upgrading the TU-95 and the shorter-range TU-165 and TU-22 bombers.[61] Clearly, those bombers will be around for a long time to come.

The Russians resumed Arctic patrols by their surface naval vessels in 2008.[62] As with the long-range bombers, their naval patrols had ceased at the end of the Cold War. As a Russian naval official has stated, "the Russian Navy has restored the presence of combat ships of the Northern Fleet in the Arctic region, including in the region of Spitsbergen."[63] Two vessels, the destroyer *Severomorsk* and the cruiser *Marshal Ustinov*, made a point of sailing through several regions that at that time were the subject of ongoing diplomatic disputes between Russia and Norway.

Before considering what this means for Canada, it is necessary to examine the actions of Norway and the United States, both of which are also rebuilding their Arctic capabilities. Both are increasingly concerned about possible security threats in the Arctic as resource development increases activity.

Norway has refocused its entire defence policy on the North. In a series of recent statements, the Norwegian Defence Minister Anne-Grete Strøm-Erichsen has made it clear that Norway recognizes that resources and climate change are bringing new actors to the North. In this regard, the most recent Norwegian Defence Policy Review makes it clear that the northern regions are Norway's prime area for strategic investment. Norway's position as a significant energy exporter and as a country responsible for the administration of important natural resources extending over large sea areas, has an important bearing on security policy. We must be able to uphold our sovereignty and our sovereign rights, and to exercise authority in a proper way in areas under Norwegian jurisdiction. Even though the day-to-day challenges we face in the north are linked with economic factors, the administration of natural resources and regard for the Norwegian Security and Defence Policy environment, the Armed Forces play an important role by virtue of their operational capabilities with the emphasis on maintaining a presence and upholding national sovereignty in the North.[64]

As a result, Norway has been rebuilding its ability to operate in its Arctic region. It has a slightly easier task than the other Arctic states in that its Arctic waters seldom freeze (because the Gulf Stream warms them sufficiently). Norway is presently taking possession of five new frigates being built in Spanish yards. There is some controversy over these vessels, for they are Aegis capable and also have highly sophisticated anti-submarine capability.[65] The Aegis combat system gives these vessels the ability to search for and respond to a wide number of aerospace threats. Governments who buy this expensive system must be expecting that their ships will be operating in a dangerous environment. Clearly, these vessels have been designed to fight an advanced enemy; they are not simply for fishery and resource patrols. The Norwegians have also announced that they will be moving air assets to northern bases and increasing their defence budget. Finally, they have signed a contract to buy forty-eight F-35s, which are joint strike fighter aircraft.[66] In sum, they are building a small but modern war-fighting force.

The Americans, too, are rediscovering the Arctic. Senior officials have only recently discussed the need to reinvest in American Arctic security. These recent developments aside, the United States has always maintained vigorous Arctic capabilities. While it has decommissioned older nuclear-powered submarines, it has maintained others; indeed, it added new submarines to its navy throughout the 1990s and 2000s. The Americans have also maintained a very strong air wing in Alaska. In total, they have kept three wings of National Guard F-15s (22 aircraft per wing) as well as a number of AWACs (large aircraft that carry advanced radar and electronic systems designed to give a very detailed surveillance picture of the region around the aircraft). They have now replaced their F-15s with the newer F-22 Raptors. To support these activities, the number of serving personnel remained at about 26,000 in 2005.[67] American forces based in the North have remained substantial.

American officials are concerned mainly about the ability to operate surface vessels in ice-reduced waters. Their current icebreaking fleet officially includes three vessels, but two of those are reaching the end of their operational life, and there is some fear that neither will remain operational for long.[68] There is also some concern that one of the older icebreakers should not currently be operating. For some time now, the US Coast Guard has argued that new icebreakers need to be built.[69] But despite considerable attention being paid to this issue, little movement has been made on the decision to begin new construction.[70] The Navy has also expressed concern about its ability to operate surface vessels in an increasingly ice-free Arctic. When it first began to examine the issue in 2001, it quickly discovered that it faced substantial communication and logistical problems operating at such high latitudes.[71]

In an effort to come to terms with the changing Arctic, the Americans have been engaging in a policy development process for the past year and half. The US Executive Branch, led by the Department of State and the National Security Council,[72] has reviewed its policies for the Arctic region. That review examined the following core issues:

1) national security and homeland security;
2) international governance;
3) extended continental shelf and boundary issues;
4) international scientific cooperation;
5) shipping;
6) economic issues including energy; and
7) environmental protection and conservation of natural resources.[73]

The Bush administration released the resulting policy on 9 January 2009 as *Presidential Directive 66*.[74] That document makes it clear that national security considerations are the first priority for the United States when it comes to the Arctic. It presents five points relating to its national security and homeland security interests in the Arctic:

1. The United States has broad and fundamental national security interests in the Arctic region and is prepared to operate either independently or in conjunction with other states to safe-guard these interests. These interests include such matters as missile defense and early warning; deployment of sea and air systems for strategic sealift, strategic deterrence, maritime presence, and maritime security operations; and ensuring freedom of navigation and overflight.

2. The United States also has fundamental homeland security interests in pre-venting terrorist attacks and mitigating those criminal or hostile acts that could increase the United States vulnerability to terrorism in the Arctic region.

3. The Arctic region is primarily a maritime domain; as such, existing policies and authorities relating to maritime areas continue to apply, including those relating to law enforcement. Human activity in the Arctic region is increasing and is projected to increase further in coming years. This requires the United States to assert a more active and influential national presence to protect its Arctic interests and to project sea power throughout the region.

4. The United States exercises authority in accordance with lawful claims of United States sovereignty, sovereign rights, and jurisdiction in the Arctic region, including sovereignty within the territorial sea, sovereign rights and jurisdiction within the United States exclusive economic zone and on the continental shelf, and appropriate control in the United States contiguous zone.

5. Freedom of the seas is a top national priority. The Northwest Passage is a strait used for international navigation, and the Northern Sea Route includes straits used for international navigation; the regime of transit passage applies to passage through those straits. Preserving the rights and duties relating to navigation and overflight in the Arctic region supports our ability to exercise these rights throughout the world, including through strategic straits.[75]

It is clear from this policy position that the United States expects the Arctic to become a strategically valuable region. In addition, the Bush administration did not perceive a special relationship with Canada in the Arctic. It made it very clear that it would be increasing its challenge to Canadian claims to control over the Northwest Passage. The document states that the United States "is prepared to operate either independently or in conjunction with other states to safe-guard these interests." Furthermore, nowhere in the document does it refer to its traditional relationship of security cooperation with Canada in the Arctic. It fails to mention even the North American Aerospace Defense Command (NORAD) as the core means for ensuring aerospace security for North America in the Arctic. Clearly, unless this document is revised by the new American government, Canada should not expect the United States to be sensitive to its Arctic interests.

Where, then, does this leave Canada in regard to protecting its security? First, it is clear that the strategic environment in the Arctic is in flux. Arctic states are moving to improve their northern military capabilities. All of the main Arctic states contend that they are doing so only to provide an ability to respond to the expected increase in activity in the Arctic. But it is interesting to note that both Norway and Russia are increasing their Arctic capabilities with weapon systems that are clearly designed for fighting (i.e., rather than acting in a Coast Guard–type capacity). Furthermore, the Americans have used somewhat aggressive language in their most recent official statement, and this suggests that they, too, will be looking to further develop the strategic nature of their forces.

Canada does not face a direct military threat in the Arctic—today. But the indicators are becoming somewhat worrisome. Why would Canada's neighbours dedicate increasingly substantial resources for the harder edge of their security forces in the region unless they were beginning to see a need? Canada will need to maintain a careful watch on events as they unfold.

Conclusion

The Arctic is changing. It is changing in so many different ways and with such complexity that it seems almost impossible to comment on how best to protect Canadian Arctic sovereignty and security. Clearly, Canadian officials are going to have to make some hard decisions sooner rather than later if Canada is to ensure that it can control its section of the Arctic for the protection of Canadian interests and values.

Ultimately, it does not matter what it is called: Arctic sovereignty, Arctic security, boundary delimitation, or polar regime formation—Canada needs to be able to control what is happening in its Arctic. Very real and very substantial developments are occurring outside of Canada's borders and beyond Canada's control that will affect the Canadian North and those Canadians who call it home. Canada needs to ensure that it can and will respond to these developments promptly and decisively. Canada must assert its control of its Arctic region.

So, how is this to be done? First, Canada needs to recognize that there is no single set solution to the problem. The transformation of the Arctic is an ongoing process, one that is both rapid and complicated. It is difficult to imagine a time in the foreseeable future when the region will stabilize. Thus the government needs to be thinking in terms of process rather than result. The challenges of the Arctic require government action that transcends any one department. Currently, it is trendy to use terms such as "whole of government" when talking about efforts to break down departmental silos. The Arctic definitely requires that such silos be broken down. But Canadian Arctic policy needs to go even beyond this. The territorial governments must also be included, as well as the various northern Aboriginal peoples and their organizations. Perhaps most important, this process must have direct access to the prime minister. Canadian Arctic policy develops when the prime minister is interested. If not, other priorities quickly refocus the bureaucracy. The creation of a Cabinet committee chaired by the prime minister would be one means to ensure that attention on the Arctic is maintained. There may be other means, but the main point is that the prime minister must be continually engaged in the process.

Once the attention of the prime minister has been institutionalized, the Canadian government must follow three main sets of actions in order to establish and maintain control. To a degree, the Martin government began this process, which the Harper government continued—the critical point will be sustainability. Historically, Canadian governments have promised a wide array of policy actions only to renege on them when other political and economic issues have arisen. The question, then, is how to develop a flexible, long-term program that will be maintained. Ultimately this program will need to provide for the ability to (1) know what is happening in the Canadian North, (2) enforce Canadian rules and laws, and (3) cooperate with Canada's circumpolar neighbours.

One of the greatest political challenges now is the artificial divide that seems to be developing between Liberal and Conservative Arctic policy. A disturbing trend is emerging whereby the Conservatives while in power focus on providing Canada with enforcement and surveillance capabilities, whereas the Liberals while in power focus on diplomatic initiatives. In keeping with their policy position, the Conservatives eliminated the position of Circumpolar Ambassador and have been contented to follow the diplomatic initiatives of the other Arctic states. Throughout the Chrétien era, no discussion was ever undertaken regarding building up Canadian Arctic capabilities. This debate is increasingly being cast in unilateral versus multilateral terms. The Conservatives are perceived as focusing on Canada's military while the Liberals are viewed as focusing on the diplomatic requirements for establishing control. The reality is that both approaches are required. Canada needs to have strong surveillance and enforcement capabilities in order to control the new activities that will increasingly be taking place in the Arctic. These capabilities will be primarily the responsibility of the DND. The DND will absolutely need to work with other departments, such as the Coast Guard and the RCMP, to name two. That said, the DND's characterization as the main ministerial department should not lead to the conclusion that the Arctic is being militarized. The simple fact is that the DND has the greatest capability to provide for both surveillance and enforcement in the vast regions of the Arctic.

At the same time, Canada cannot act in isolation in the Arctic. It needs to work with its Arctic neighbours in order to develop the international frame-

Figure 2-7 HMCS *Montreal* passes an iceberg in Strathcona Sound near Nanisivik, Nunavut, during Operation Nanook 10.
Source: DND

works that will provide the international rules necessary to protect the Arctic as well as a spirit of cooperation in the region. The new accessibility of the Arctic will bring new actors and activities to the region, so it will be necessary to develop a regional set of rules and arrangements for these new activities. These include a coordinated approach to search and rescue, as well as pollution response for environmental accidents that will inevitably occur. It would also be beneficial for the entire region if agreements were reached on future economic activities. A regional approach to the expanding Arctic fisheries would head off differences before they arise over the issue of fishing new stocks as they move north. Likewise, a regional approach to all shipping coming into the Arctic could be a means of avoiding the sovereignty challenges relating to international shipping. If the Arctic nations could agree on the standards for ship construction and operation and crew requirements in Arctic waters, Canada might achieve the control it seeks over the shipping that is expected in Canadian northern waters. This almost occurred in the 1990s when Canadian officials led an initiative—to be known as the Polar Code—to develop an agreement to do precisely this. However, it failed to achieve American acceptance. The initiative was then shifted to the IMO and is now being brought about as a voluntary set of regulations. Perhaps now is the time for Canada to revisit this code at the state level.

The greatest international challenge facing Canada may be the reality that two of its Arctic neighbours are the United States and Russia. Canadian foreign relations have always focused mainly on these two states. The United States is Canada's most important trading partner and ally. At various times in Canada's recent history, the former Soviet Union has been an important ally or a dangerous enemy. Throughout the Cold War, the importance to Canada of both the United States and Russia was amplified by their geographic location as Arctic neighbours. Now that the Arctic is warming and becoming more accessible, the dynamics of this relationship are about to become even more important.

Canada must work with both the United States and Russia in the region. The problem is that with the entire Arctic becoming more accessible, these two states have developed very definitive views as to their own national interests in the Arctic. The Russians see the Arctic as the key to their future prosperity. They understand that the undeveloped oil and gas resources in their Arctic region will provide them with the economic capability to regain their status as a great power. They are also aware that from a strategic perspective, the North is their primary access to the world's oceans. Therefore, the Arctic is of central importance to them.

During the past few years, the Russians have clearly become more assertive in their foreign policy, including their policy in the Arctic. This does not mean a return to the Cold War, but it does signify that the period of complete cooperation of the 1990s has ended. Canada can still expect to work with the Russians, but any effort to cooperate now needs to be tempered by a more realistic framework. The Russians will not cooperate simply for the benefit of cooperation. Rather, it will be increasingly necessary for Canada to show the Russians why cooperation is in their interests. At the same time, when Canadian interests do not intersect with Russian interests, the Canadian government needs to be prepared for an increasingly assertive Russian response. Such would occur if Canada decides to claim any part of the Arctic continental shelf that has been claimed by the Russians. If this happens, the Russian government's reaction will set the tone for future Canadian–Russian relations. If the reaction is tempered and diplomatic, Canada should seize the moment by trying to further engage the Russians in other means of cooperation. If the reaction is more belligerent, Canada may need to garner support from its other Arctic neighbours in order to maintain its claim.

Canada's Arctic relationship with the United States will also continue to develop. It is becoming clear that the Americans recognize the Arctic's importance. It is also evident that they are increasingly aware of the transformations taking place in the region. Canada's key challenge will be to minimize, if not resolve, the various disputes over boundaries and sovereignty in the North American Arctic. The issues of control of international shipping through the Northwest Passage and the division of the Beaufort Sea are challenging. However, the two states must find ways to prevent these issues from contaminating future cooperation. Ultimately, the two states must find ways to cooperate in the Arctic, since it is in their mutual interest to do so. Both states need to ensure that the new activities in the Arctic are controlled in such a manner that environmental protection remains a core requirement. At the same time, it is also in the interests of both states to ensure that those who call the North home benefit fully from the forthcoming activities. This can best be achieved by cooperation.

Thus Canada needs to pay special attention to its relationship with Russia and the United States. While many of the issues can be addressed in a bilateral fashion, the time has arrived for Canada to renew its efforts to strengthen the region's multilateral forums. The Arctic Council is at the centre of this. The council was a Canadian initiative. Its creation had strong bipartisan support from both the Mulroney Conservatives and the Chrétien Liberals. American reluctance to strengthen multilateral bodies during the 1990s stymied Canadian efforts to give the council greater powers. Officially, the Americans continue to hold this position, as is evident in their Arctic policy released in January 2009. However, the same policy held out the possibility that they might be willing to reconsider it. It is in Canada's interests to convince the Americans that it is in their interests to have a stronger Arctic Council.

Canada will soon resume the chairpersonship of the Arctic Council. This country can serve the interests of the region and itself by dedicating its time as chair to strengthening the council. First, Canada needs to avoid directly undermining the council. For example, the Ilulissat meeting in May 2008 of the five Arctic continental shelf claimant states should have taken place within the Arctic Council. While Iceland, Sweden, and Finland do not have claims, each state will be affected by what happens within the areas claimed by others. Similarly, the Permanent Participants have interests in these regions. Yet these members of the council were excluded from this very important meeting. At that time, Canada should have insisted that the council host the meeting. Second, Canada should lead the way in creating a more powerful support system for the council. Relying on each member state to simply volunteer support is not working. Canada should establish some form of a permanent support body. Third, Canada should take the initiative to work out a series of regional agreements to deal with issues such as standards for international shipping (as it tried in the 1990s with the Polar Code), fishing, tourism, environmental protection, and so on. Canadian interests are best served by the creation of such agreements now rather than later, when many other competing interests will seek to be included.

Ultimately, Canada needs to decide what it wants its Arctic to look like in the emerging future. The time when lip service could be paid to the North is over. Transformational forces are creating a new era during which the world will be coming to the entire Arctic region. Canada can choose to simply react to the new changes, or it can take the lead, recognizing that there are both dangers and opportunities. The dangers can be mitigated by thoughtful preparation. The opportunities can best be taken advantage of by deciding what it is that Canada wants its North to look like and the level of resources that it is willing to allocate to promoting and protecting Canadian interests and values.

This will not be an easy task. Nor will it be cheap. Furthermore, any Canadian action will include missteps and mistakes. The Canadian government will ensure its control over its Arctic region if and when it takes proactive action. This ultimately means the capacity to know what is occurring in the Arctic and then the capabilities to act. But being able to know and act in the Arctic serves as the means for the real objective, which is to ensure the protection of Canadian Arctic security and sovereignty for Canadians. The protection of Canadian interests and values for Canadians must inform all Canadian actions. The actions of recent Canadian governments suggest that they understand this. The question remains whether the Canadian government is willing to pay for it.

Notes

1 Jens Bartelson, *A Genealogy of Sovereignty* (Cambridge: Cambridge University Press, 1995).

2 James Allan, *Sovereign Statehood* (London: Allen and Unwin, 1986).

3 R.R. Churchill and A.V. Lowe, *The Law of the Sea,* 3rd ed. (Manchester: Manchester University Press, 2002).

4 For the best collections of articles that address the entire discussion on the nature of security, see John Baylis, James Wirtz, Colin Gray, and Eliot Cohen, eds., *Strategy in the Contemporary World,* 2nd ed. (Oxford: Oxford University Press, 2007); and Allan Collins, ed., *Contemporary Security Studies* (Oxford: Oxford University Press, 2007).

5 Rob McRae and Don Hubert, eds., *Human Security and the New Diplomacy: Protecting People, Promoting Peace* (Montreal and Kingston: McGill–Queen's University Press, 2001).

6 Thomas Homer-Dixon, *Environment, Security, and Violence* (Princeton: Princeton University Press, 1999).

7 David Downie and Terry Fenge, eds., *Northern Lights Against POPs: Combating Toxic Threats in the Arctic* (Montreal and Kingston: McGill–Queen's University Press, 2003).

8 Their association with the Hells Angels and drugs is only alleged; they were never proved to have engaged in such activities. CBC News, "'Wild Vikings' Land in Cambridge Bay

Jail," 30 August 2007, http://www.cbc.ca/canada/north/story/2007/08/30/cambay -vikings.html, accessed 5 June 2009.

9 Kenneth J. Bird et al., "Circum-Arctic Resource Appraisal: Estimates of Undiscovered Oil and Gas North of the Arctic Circle," *US Geological Survey Fact Sheet 2008–3049* (2008), http://pubs.usgs.gov/fs/2008/3049, accessed June 5, 2009.

10 Canadian officials had hoped to use an international treaty that would create an institution that would serve as the central multilateral body for the Arctic. However, the United States refused to join if it was created by treaty. Instead the Arctic Council was created as a voluntary body with limited powers. However, since the Americans refused to allow the creation of any other bodies or treaties, it remains the most important Arctic international organization. For a discussion on the politics of the creation of the Arctic Council, see Rob Huebert, "New Directions in Circumpolar Cooperation: Canada, the Arctic Environmental Protection Strategy, and the Arctic Council," *Canadian Foreign Policy* 5, no. 2 (Winter 1998): 37–58.

11 "Japan Seeks Role in Arctic Council," *Daily Yomiuri* (Tokyo), 20 April 2009, 3.

12 Arctic Climate Impact Assessment (ACIA), *Impacts of a Warming Arctic: Arctic Climate Impact Assessment* (Cambridge: Cambridge University Press, 2004), http://www.acia .uaf.ed, accessed 5 June 2009.

13 Rheal Seguin, "Scientists Predict Seasonal Ice-Free by 2015," *Globe and Mail,* 12 December 2008, A7.

14 ACIA, *Impacts of a Warming Arctic,* 1011.

15 Anne Casselman, "Will the Opening of the Northwest Passage Transform Global Shipping Anytime Soon?" *Scientific American,* 10 November 2008, http://www.sciam.com/ article.cfm?id=opening-of-northwest-passage, accessed 5 June 2009.

16 Bird et al., "Circum-Arctic Resource Appraisal."

17 S.D. Dallimore and T.S. Elliot, eds., *Scientific Results from the Mallik 2002 Gas Hydrate Production Research Well Program, Mackenzie Delta, Northwest Territories, Canada— Geological Survey of Canada Bulletin 585* (Ottawa: Geological Survey, 2005).

18 Jeffrey Jones, "Update 2—Imperial, Exxon, Mobil Win Beaufort Sea Acreage," *Reuters,* 19 July 2007, http://www.reuters.com/article/companyNewsAndPR/idUSN194203 8220070719, accessed 5 June 2009.

19 CBC News, "Ottawa Awards BP $1.2 Billion in Exploration Permits in Beaufort Sea," 8 July 2008, http://www.cbc.ca/canada/north/story/2008/06/09/beaufort-leases.html, accessed 5 June 2009.

20 Fox Business, "Baffinland Provides Update on Mary Rivers Project," *Yours Metals News,* 5 December 2008, http://www.yourmetalnews.com/baffinland+provides+update+on+ mary+river+project_17718.html, accessed 5 June 2009.

21 Tim Bradner, "Shell Plans Alaska Drilling Program Despite Court Ruling," *Energy Current,* 27 April 2009, http://royaldutchshellplc.com/2009/04/27/shell-plans-alaska-drilling -program-despite-court-ruling, accessed 5 June 2009.

22 It is very hard to get officials to go on the record on this. Break-even points for non-Arctic resources seem to be between $25–40 for Middle Eastern producers, so an $80 cost would not seem to be unreasonable. See Richard Shaw, "Oil Predictions and Break-Even Prices," *Seeking Alpha,* 25 December 2007, http://seekingalpha.com/article/58322 -oil-price-predictions-and-break-even-prices, accessed 5 June 2009.

23 Andrew Mayeda and Randy Boswell, "Arctic Ambitions—Canada's Stake in the North: Part 3: the Rush for Oil," *Canada.com,* 17 August 2008, http://www2.canada.com/ topics/news/features/arcticambitions/story.html?id=994c07a9-7d79-4a35-927a-f78d 485df522, accessed 5 June 2009.

24 For a more complete history of the development of Canadian policy, see Rob Huebert, "Canada and the Changing International Arctic: At the Crossroads of Cooperation and Conflict," in *Northern Exposure: Peoples, Powers, and Prospects for Canada's North,* ed. Frances Abele, Thomas J. Courchene, F. Leslie Seidle, and France St-Hilaire (Montreal: Institute for Research on Public Policy, 2008), http://www.irpp.org/books/archive/AOTS4/huebert.pdf, accessed 5 June 2009.

25 Shelagh Grant, *Sovereignty or Security: Government Policy in the Canadian North 1936–1950* (Vancouver: UBC Press, 1988).

26 Edgar Dosman, "The Northern Sovereignty Crisis, 1968–70," in *The Arctic in Question,* ed. Edgar Dosman (Toronto: Oxford University Press, 1976).

27 Donald M. McRae, "The Negotiation of Article 234," in *Politics of the Northwest Passage,* ed. Franklyn Griffiths (Kingston and Montreal: McGill–Queen's University Press, 1987).

28 Rob Huebert, "Polar Vision or Tunnel Vision: The Making of Canadian Arctic Waters Policy," *Marine Policy* 19, no. 4 (July 1995), 343–63.

29 Of note, it was the efforts of CIC Senior Research Fellow, Franklyn Griffiths, whose op-eds in the *Globe and Mail* especially galvanized public and government attention.

30 Christopher Kirkey, "Smoothing Troubled Waters: The 1988 Canada–United States Arctic Co-operation Agreement," *International Journal* 50, no. 2 (1995): 401–26.

31 Peter Haydon, "The Strategic Importance of the Arctic: Understanding the Military Issues," *Canadian Defence Quarterly* (Spring 1988), 27–34.

32 Huebert, "New Directions in Circumpolar Cooperation."

33 Ilulissat Declaration, adopted at the Arctic Ocean Conference hosted by the Government of Denmark and attended by the representatives of the five coastal states bordering on the Arctic Ocean (Canada, Denmark, Norway, the Russian Federation, and the US), Ilulissat, Greenland, 27–29 May 2008, http://www.oceanlaw.org/downloads/arctic/Ilulissat_Declaration.pdf, accessed 28 May 2009.

34 UN, Oceans and Law of the Sea, Division for Ocean Affairs and Law of the Sea, "Commission on the Limits of the Continental Shelf (CLCS): Outer Limits of the Continental Shelf Beyond 200 Nautical Miles from the Baselines: Submissions to the Commission: Submission by the Russian Federation," 18 November 2008, http://www.un.org/Depts/los/clcs_new/submissions_files/submission_rus.htm, accessed 5 June 2009.

35 UN Oceans and Law of the Sea, Division for Ocean Affairs and Law of the Sea, "Chronological Lists of Ratifications of, Accessions, and Successions to the Convention and the Related Agreements as at 31 December 2008," http://www.un.org/Depts/los/reference_files/chronological_lists_of_ratifications.htm, accessed 5 June 2009.

36 "Continental Shelf Submission of Norway in Respect of Areas in the Arctic Ocean, the Barents Sea, and the Norwegian Sea Executive Summary," 2006, http://www.un.org/depts/los/clcs_new/submissions_files/nor06/nor_exec_sum.pdf, accessed 5 June 2009; and UN, Oceans and the Law of the Sea, *Report of the Secretary General,* 62nd session, UN Doc A/62/67/Add.1, 31 August 2007, paras. 48–51.

37 "Russia Sends Naval Vessels to Spitsbergen," *Barents Observer,* 15 July 2007, http://www.barentsobserver.com/russia-sends-navy-vessels-to-spitsbergen.4497720-58932.html, accessed 5 June 2009.

38 Doug Struck, "Russia's Deep-Sea Flag-Planting at North Pole Strikes a Chill in Canada," *Washington Post,* 7 August 2007, http://www.washingtonpost.com/wp-dyn/content/article/2007/08/06/AR2007080601369.html, accessed 5 June 2009.

39 Donat Pharand, *Canada's Arctic Waters in International Law* (Cambridge: Cambridge University Press, 1988).

40 Christoph Seidler, "Politicians Censor Report on Dangers of Arctic Drilling," *Spiegal Online International,* 23 January 2008, http://www.spiegel.de/international/world/ 0,1518,530454-2,00.html, accessed 5 June 2009.

41 Charles Digges, "Russia to Drill Arctic Oil with Nuclear Icebreaker," *Russian Icebreaker Fleet,* 8 July 2008, http://www.bellona.org/articles/articles_2007/sevmorput_drilling, accessed 5 June 2009.

42 Ilulissat Declaration.

43 Associated Foreign Press, "US 'Committed' to Ratifying Law of Sea Convention: Clinton," 6 April 2009, http://www.google.com/hostednews/afp/article/ALeqM5gB1OPzPfiju 89sybtB66q9Sq4f6A, accessed 5 June 2009.

44 Donat Pharand, "The Arctic Waters and the Northwest Passage: A Final Revisit," *Ocean Development and International Law* 38, nos. 1–2 (January 2007): 3–69.

45 Officially called the "Exchange of Notes Constituting an Agreement Between the United States of America and Canada Relating to the St. Lawrence Seaway Project."

46 Brian Flemming, *Canada–US Relations in the Arctic: A Neighborly Proposal* (Calgary: Canadian Defence and Foreign Affairs Institute, December 2008); Don McRae, "Arctic Sovereignty? What Is at Stake," *Behind the Headlines* 64, no. 1 (2007), 1–23.

47 White House, *National Security Presidential Directive/NSPD 66 Homeland Security Presidential Directive/HSPD 25—Arctic Region Policy.* 9 January 2009, Washington.

48 Commission of the European Communities, *Communication from the Commission to the European Parliament and the Council: The European Union and the Arctic Region,* Brussels, COM(2008) 763.

49 Ibid., 9.

50 Rob Huebert, "Renaissance in Canadian Arctic Security?" *Canadian Military Journal* 6, no. 4 (2005-2006): 17–29.

51 Department of National Defence (DND), *Canada's International Policy Statement: A Role of Pride and Influence in the World—Defence* (Ottawa: 2005), 17.

52 Canadian Arctic Resources Committee (CARC), "Renewing the Northern Strategy," *Northern Perspective* 30, no. 1 (Winter 2006): 2, http://www.carc.org/pubs/v30no1/ CARC_Northrn_Perspctves_Winter_2006.pdf, accessed 5 June 2009.

53 Government of Canada, "Protecting Canada's Future," Speech from the Throne, 16 October 2007, http://www.sft-ddt.gc.ca/eng/media.asp?id=1364, accessed 5 June 2009.

54 "SSN-774 Virginia-class New Attack Submarine [NSSN] Centurion," Globalsecurity.org, 5 September 2008, http://www.globalsecurity.org/military/systems/ship/ssn-774.htm, accessed 5 June 2009.

55 "Russian Navy Promised New Nuclear Subs with New Strategic Missiles," *Bellona,* 6 October 2008, http://www.bellona.org/news/news_2008/new_nuke_subs, accessed 5 June 2009.

56 Novosti, "Reactor on Russia's Newest Submarine Fired Up," 21 November 2008, http://en.rian.ru/russia/20081121/118453947.html, accessed 5 June 2009.

57 Ibid.

58 Defence Update, "Russia Plans to Deploy 6 Carrier Battlegroups by 2025," 2007, http://defense-update.com/newscast/0707/news/150707_russian_Navy.htm, accessed 5 June 2009.

59 BBC News, "Russia Restarts Cold War Patrols," 17 August 2007, http://news.bbc.co.uk/ 2/hi/europe/6950986.stm, accessed 5 June 2009.

60 Theophilos Argitis, "Canada's Harper Concerned over Russian Bomber Flights," *Bloomberg.com,* 19 September 2008, http://www.bloomberg.com/apps/news?pid= 20601082&sid=aZn0SgnawmtU&refer=canada, accessed 5 June 2009.

61   Martin Sieff, "Russia Upgrades Bomber-ALCM Force for the 21st Century," *UPI.com*, 5 January 2009, http://www.upi.com/Security_Industry/2009/01/05/Russia_upgrades _bomber-ALCM_force_for_21st_century/UPI-39951231177215, accessed 5 June 2009.

62   Russian Federal Ministry of Defence, "Russian Navy Resumes Presence in Arctic Area," *News Details*, 14 July 2008, http://www.mil.ru/eng/1866/12078/details/index.shtml?id =47433, accessed 5 June 2009.

63   Associated Foreign Press, "Russian Navy Boasts Combat Presence in Arctic," *Canada.com*. 14 July 2008, http://www.canada.com/topics/news/world/story.html?id=3572ff95-9a88 -4dd8-944f-58af497c3fa6, accessed 5 June 2009.

64   Norwegian Ministry of Defence, *Norwegian Defence 2008* (Oslo: 2008), http://www .regjeringen.no/upload/FD/Dokumenter/Fakta2008_eng.pdf, accessed 5 June 2009.

65   Endre Lund, "Norway's New Nansen Class Frigates: Capabilities and Controversies," *Defence Daily Industries*. 7 June 2008, http://www.defenseindustrydaily.com/norways -new-nansen-class-frigates-capabilities-and-controversies-02329, accessed 5 June 2009.

66   Doug Mellgreen, "Norway Picks US Fighter to Replace Aging Fleet," *Foxnews.com*, 20 November 2008, http://www.foxnews.com/printer_friendly_wires/2008Nov20/0,4675, EUNorwayJointStrikeFighter,00.html, accessed 5 June 2009.

67   These numbers were provided directly to the author by a senior American military official in an open briefing in Alaska on 10 March 2005.

68   Ronald O'Rourke, *Coast Guard Icebreaker Modernization: Background, Issues, and Options for Congress—CRS Report for Congress* RL 34391 (Washington: Congressional Research Service, 11 September 2008), http://fas.org/sgp/crs/weapons/RL34391.pdf, accessed 5 June 2009.

69   Committee on the Assessment of US Coast Guard Polar Icebreaker Roles and Future Needs, National Research Council, *Polar Icebreakers in a Changing World: An Assessment in a Changing World* (Washington: National Academics Press, 2007), http://books.nap.edu/ catalog.php?record_id=11753, accessed 5 June 2009.

70   Andrew Revkin, "A Push to Increase Icebreakers in the Arctic," *New York Times*, 17 August 2008, 6.

71   Office of Naval Research, Naval Ice Center, Oceanographer of the Navy and the Arctic Research Commission, *Naval Operations in an Ice-Free Arctic Symposium Final Report*, 17–18 April 2001, http://www.natice.noaa.gov/icefree/FinalArcticReport.pdf, accessed 5 June 2009.

72   Margaret F. Hayes, Director of Office of Oceans Affairs, Department of State, "Arctic Policy—Speech to Arctic Parliamentarians on Aspects of U.S. Arctic Policy," Fairbanks, 13 August 2008.

73   Ibid.

74   White House, *National Security Presidential Directive 66*.

75   Ibid., 2–3.

3

From Polar Race to Polar Saga
An Integrated Strategy for Canada and the Circumpolar World

P. Whitney Lackenbauer

John George Diefenbaker, like Sir John A. MacDonald [*sic*], was a Prime Minister with a dream, not just seeing the great expanse of the country, but the greatness that Canada and Canadians should aspire to. But he understood that to truly fulfill our national dream, we must accept the challenges and seize the opportunities presented by our North [...]

Prime Minister Diefenbaker is no longer with us, but the geopolitical importance of the Arctic and Canada's interests in it have never been greater. This is why our government has launched an ambitious Northern Agenda based on the timeless responsibility imposed by our national anthem, to keep the True North strong and free. To this end, we will encourage responsible development of the North's abundant economic resources, we will ensure jobs and opportunity and the health and good governance of Northern communities. We will protect the unique and fragile Arctic ecosystem for the generations yet to come. And of course, we will assert and defend Canada's sovereignty and security in this region.

—*Rt. Hon. Stephen Harper, Inuvik, Northwest Territories, August 28, 2008*

Fifty years ago, Diefenbaker's bold "northern vision" anticipated that the North—the last Canadian "frontier"—would soon be abuzz with activity. His vision was never implemented, and our nation-building exercise remains incomplete. Political rhetoric has once again heated up, prompted by climate change and uncertainty about Canada's hold on the Arctic. Ominous captions below images of solitary polar bears on ice floes (an iconic and distorted staple of climate change discourse) are often accompanied by unrealistic expectations about Canada's sovereignty and control in the face of allegedly malevolent circumpolar challenges. Much of this discourse affirms just how little southern Canadians actually know about the North. The promise of cooperation and dialogue with northern Canadians and our circumpolar neighbours, which seemed to frame government plans in the 1990s, has been jettisoned in favour of a "call to arms" to "stand up for Canada." If muckraking academics and journalists are to be believed, the circumpolar agenda is now dominated by a "polar race," with a concomitant sovereignty and security crisis precipitated by climate change and competing interests in "our" Arctic.

After the last round of frenzied debate over Canadian sovereignty in the wake of the 1985 *Polar Sea* voyage, Franklyn Griffiths suggested that the Arctic states had to decide whether they wanted the region to be one of enhanced civility or of military competition. In his view, accepting "an integrated concept of security—one in which military requirements are combined with an awareness of the need to act for ecological, economic, cultural, and social security"—would allow Northerners to play a more direct role in setting agendas and fostering cooperation and dialogue.[1] In the early twenty-first century, amidst rhetoric about a "new Cold War" in the Arctic, commentators suggest that cooperative arrangements are less credible. It has been alleged that in a supposed "race for resources," the Russians, Americans, Danes, and other energy-hungry nations are threatening Canada's northern inheritance. Since coming to office in 2006, the Conservative government's initiatives have emphasized the primacy of security (albeit couched in the language of sovereignty) through its commitments to enhance Canada's northern defence capabilities. Alarmism and paranoia abound, and Inuit leaders are frustrated that their voices have been pushed to the margins.[2]

The time for Canadian action in the North has indeed come, but it need not be justified by partisan political rhetoric rooted in alarmism or paranoia. After all, a crisis mentality is more conducive to symbolic reactions and hollow commitments designed to serve positive short-term optics rather than sustained investment in Canadian capabilities and northern development. While outside forces have typically driven the northern foreign policy agenda, the twenty-first century brings different problems and possibilities that require new thinking and a more careful integration of domestic and international priorities. The reactive, crisis-based mentality that governed Canada's northern strategy through the twentieth century will no longer suffice if Canada wants to seize opportunities and take a leadership role in a rapidly evolving circumpolar world.

The 2008 federal election confirmed that Canada faces a minority government situation. The development and implementation of an integrated Arctic strategy must proceed with this political consideration in mind. While political parties will also try to make political capital out of their adversaries' platforms, this chapter seeks to articulate a feasible and practical strategy that integrates elements from all of the major parties' agendas and that might be the basis for cooperative progress. It also draws upon the recommendations and priorities of other stakeholders, particularly the territorial governments and northern Aboriginal organizations.

My central contention is that a 3-D approach to circumpolar affairs may help the government produce an integrated Northern Strategy. The federal government's defence promises, if implemented fully, will ensure that Canada has more robust monitoring and enforcement capabilities in the event that international vessels begin to transit the Northwest Passage (NWP) in greater numbers. Through collaborative and sustained diplomatic engagement (something that has not been a priority in recent years), Canada can assume a leadership role and promote cooperation, coordination, and interaction in the circumpolar world. A policy framework that practically and directly engages Northerners in development and that invests in local capacity-building initiatives will ensure that cooperation and human security are central pillars of Canada's Arctic strategy.

The central question is whether Canadians are prepared to seize the opportunities of the twenty-first century, with southerners working in close cooperation with Northerners, or whether outdated rhetoric and thinking will hijack the agenda. We will need better capabilities if we are to assert control over our lands and waters, but as a nation we need to decide what we want to actually do with our Arctic. Outside forces have typically driven the northern foreign policy agenda; twenty-first-century problems and possibilities require new, proactive thinking.

Note on Definitions

The terms "Arctic" and "Northern" have been defined and debated in various ways. For the purposes of this chapter, the Arctic refers to the region north of the treeline; or to "Inuit Nunaat," which is the homeland of Canada's Inuit, comprising the land and marine areas of the Nunatsiavut, Nunavik, Nunavut, and Inuvialuit land claims settlement areas.[3] This area includes the Arctic Archipelago, the islands and waters lying to the north of the Canadian mainland. This chapter's disproportionate emphasis on Inuit Nunaat (see Map 3-1) reflects how most of the key sovereignty and security questions debated in recent years relate to this region; it also suggests why Inuit spokespersons are quoted extensively in this report.

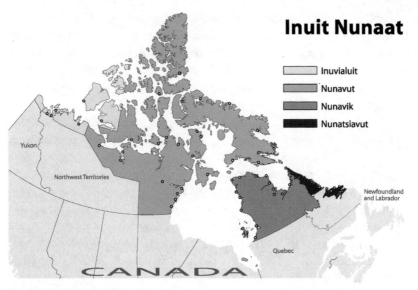

Map 3-1 Inuit Nunaat.
Source: Inuit Tapiriit Kanatami

The term "the North" is more inclusive and is used in various senses. The Territorial North refers to Yukon, the Northwest Territories (NWT), and Nunavut—also referred to as "North of 60"—with a total population of about 100,000. Only in the territory of Nunavut do Aboriginal people constitute a majority of the population. The "Canadian North" includes the territories as well as the northern regions of British Columbia, Alberta, Saskatchewan, Manitoba, Ontario, and Quebec, and also all of Labrador. For the purposes of this report, "Northerners" is meant to include the people of Yukon, NWT, Nunavut, and (where stated) Nunavik and Labrador.

Background

The current Arctic "crisis" is predicated on the idea that Canada faces a sovereignty and security crisis because previous governments have failed to protect Canadian interests. A more careful reading of the historical record suggests that the expansion and entrenchment of Canada's Arctic sovereignty through the twentieth century—albeit in an *ad hoc* and reactive manner—was a remarkable success given our parsimonious and half-hearted commitment to investing in the region.[4]

From "Crisis" to "Crisis"

Anxiety about "using or losing" our Arctic inheritance is more revealing of the Canadian psyche—particularly our chronic lack of confidence—than of objective realities. This anxiety encourages a disproportionate emphasis on national defence at the expense of a broader suite of social, economic, and diplomatic initiatives.

Crisis rhetoric conceals a history of diplomacy and successful working relationships that helps explain how and why Canada's security and sovereignty interests have been upheld over the last half century. A careful reading of historical "lessons learned" suggests that quiet diplomacy and practical, bilateral solutions have allayed most of the acute "crisis" concerns that have precipitated government reactions since the Second World War. If our goal has simply been to hang on to the North, expand our claims to include archipelagic waters, and incrementally entrench our claims in international law, twentieth-century politicians and civil servants deserve modest praise. Over the last half century, Canada's most successful unilateral actions have been backed up by negotiations with our American allies: we have long-standing precedent in "agreeing to disagree" with the United States while safeguarding our essential interests. Legal scholar Donat Pharand's latest analysis of Canada's sovereignty case is grounds for optimism, not pessimism: our internal waters case is strong.[5]

One hundred thirty years ago, Canada's sovereignty over the Arctic lands and waters was far from secure. The young Dominion inherited the islands of the High Arctic Archipelago from Britain in 1880 not because it asked for them but because Britain wanted to transfer responsibility for its nebulous rights after it received "two apparently innocent requests for concessions of Arctic territory in 1874."[6] Canada proceeded to ignore the Arctic for the next quarter century, until the Klondike Gold Rush encouraged it to look north. In the early twentieth century, the government sent official missions to the Arctic to explore and to collect customs duties and licensing fees from whalers—a modest assertion of Canadian legal authority. In the interwar years, Royal Canadian Mounted Police (RCMP) posts dotted the northern landscape, suggesting a continuous presence.[7] There was little cause for worry about lands and islands once Canadian negotiators reached agreements with Denmark and Norway to settle terrestrial sovereignty claims. American explorers complied with Canadian regulations, and geography seemed to preclude any military threat; Canada was a "fireproof house" insulated from European and Asian conflagrations by distance and isolation.

The Second World War brought the Canadian North into new strategic focus. The Americans were worried about overland and air routes to Alaska,

Figure 3-1 Canadian Ranger TooToo, an Inuk from Churchill, Manitoba, relays information to army personnel in a Penguin during Exercise Bulldog II in 1954.
Source: DND

so they entered into agreements with Canada to build airfields, a highway, and an oil pipeline in the northwest. When American personnel swept into the Canadian North to complete these tasks, Prime Minister William Lyon Mackenzie King became fearful that American developments, taken in the name of military security, would undermine Canadian sovereignty.[8] They did not. The Americans pulled out of Canada at war's end and, at Ottawa's request, the ownership of permanent facilities in the North passed into Canadian hands. Canada emerged unscathed in terms of territorial ownership, but senior officials certainly took note of the interdependency between security and sovereignty.[9]

The onset of the Cold War renewed pressures on Canada to balance sovereignty concerns with continental security imperatives. Polar projection maps revealed how Canada's strategic situation had changed now that the United States and the Soviet Union had become rivals. Arctic defences were inextricably linked to American security, and the United States pushed for access to Canada's Far North to build airfields and weather stations. Canadian officials grew apprehensive and cautious in authorizing new installations, whereas the

Americans were anxious to proceed. Journalists began to talk about a looming sovereignty crisis, and scholars cite this era as further evidence that the Americans were willing to encroach on Canadian sovereignty to achieve their ends.[10] Discussion of this encroachment has been distorted. "The Americans showed throughout a remarkable tolerance of the requirements the Canadians imposed upon them," Gordon Smith writes, "even when some of these must have seemed rather picayune, and they demonstrated a genuine willingness to observe Canadian regulations and generally accepted Canadian proprietorship." It was a "striking illustration of successful international cooperation and collaboration," with the Americans officially acknowledging Canadian ownership of the entire Arctic Archipelago.[11] Legal scholar Nigel Bankes notes that the Joint Arctic Weather Station Agreement "thus ended the last potential legal threat to Canadian sovereignty over its Arctic *lands*."[12]

As the Cold War heated up in the 1950s, however, the Americans sought extensive air defence systems extending to the northernmost reaches of the continent. This launched yet another round of "crisis" rhetoric. The Distant Early Warning (DEW) Line, built across the 70th parallel to detect Soviet bombers, was the boldest megaproject in Arctic history, dramatically altering the military, logistic, and demographic characteristics of the Canadian Arctic. The United States designed and paid for it: the Canadian military was already stretched thin by its commitments to the North Atlantic Treaty Organization (NATO) in Europe, and Canada could not afford the kind of installations that the Americans wanted. Once again, Canadian officials negotiated a very favourable agreement that protected Canada's sovereignty and that secured economic benefits for Canadian companies. Regardless, journalists and opposition politicians suggested throughout the construction and operational phases that Canada lacked practical control over its northland and that the DEW Line, in the words of *Maclean's* editor Ralph Allen, "is the charter under which a tenth of Canada may very well become the world's most northerly banana republic."[13]

Such an eventuality did not come to pass. Canada had concerns, and there were minor indiscretions, but these were managed effectively, and the United States again proved an accommodating and respectful ally. After visiting the Line in 1969, Erik Wong of the Department of National Defence's (DND) legal department noted that journalists who had taken "masochistic pleasure" in decrying American control and dwelling on potential sovereignty encroachments were misleading the public, for there was no evidence to support such concerns. It is telling that scholars have preferred to cite these sensationalizing journalists instead of considering the DEW Line a success story. The DEW Line was a major coup for Canadian sovereignty, for it reaffirmed that the Arctic islands explicitly belonged to Canada; throughout these years, the United States, as an ally, accommodated Canadian interests and sought harmony instead of relying on coercion to get its way. Wang noted in his corresponding 1969 report: "Indeed we might be tempted to congratulate ourselves ... for enjoying a 'free ride' at least in this area of our defense activities on our own soil, without any unpleasant side effects."[14] While there were no side effects in terms of sovereignty, there certainly were lasting cultural and environmental impacts.

During the Cold War, NATO and bilateral agreements with the Americans guaranteed Canadian security at relatively little expense to the federal government. "Defending against help" from our allies, historian Desmond Morton writes, meant that Canada needed only modest defence capabilities to ensure that the Americans did not take unilateral action to defend the northern approaches to North America. Canada could instead focus on being "providers" rather than "consumers" of security.[15] At various intervals, Canadian journalists and politicians panicked about Canada becoming too dependent on the United States and thus abdicating our *de facto* sovereignty. These concerns had some merit, but solid diplomacy produced sound agreements that preserved (and indeed extended) Canadian sovereignty. Conventional military threats were possible but not probable, and Canada was spared the expense of trying to defend its remote regions alone. Instead, it could afford to deploy peacekeepers abroad, contribute forces to NATO in Europe, and invest in extensive social security measures like Medicare.

The legal status of the NWP posed a more intractable dilemma than questions of terrestrial sovereignty. American and Soviet submarine activity in the Arctic raised concerns about what was going on under the sea ice in the waters of Canada's Arctic Archipelago, but Canadian politicians sent mixed messages in the late 1950s about whether it formally claimed these waters. Canadian officials discussed issuing a more decisive claim in the 1960s. In 1965 the government introduced legislation to institute an exclusive fishing zone based on straight baselines along the east and west coasts; but it did not make a similar move in the Arctic, fearing that the United States would object. Canadians hoped that the Americans might support an extension of Canada's claim to Arctic waters for reasons of defence and national security, but they did not. In the view of the US Navy, any such move could set a dangerous international precedent. Archipelagic states in Asia, such as Indonesia and the Philippines, might use such an agreement on the NWP as a pretext to unilaterally restrict freedom of the seas in strategically sensitive areas. This could affect merchant shipping and naval mobility and increase the potential for international controversy and conflict.[16] "We can't concede [Canada] the principle of territoriality [in the NWP] or we'd be setting a precedent for trouble elsewhere in the world," a Department of State official explained in 1969.[17] Ottawa retreated from its plans.[18]

The issue came to a head at the end of the decade. In 1969, American-owned Humble Oil sent an icebreaker, the *Manhattan,* through the NWP to determine whether it was a viable commercial shipping route for oil and gas from the Beaufort Sea. The Canadian media reported the voyage as a direct challenge to Canada's Arctic sovereignty. "The legal status of the waters of Canada's Arctic archipelago is not at issue in the proposed transit of the Northwest Passage by the ships involved in the Manhattan project," Prime Minister Trudeau reassured the House of Commons on 15 May 1969. His government "welcomed the *Manhattan* exercise, has concurred in it and will participate in it."[19] Humble Oil's request for Canadian cooperation seemed to imply that the passage was Canadian, even if the US State Department would not say so specifically.[20] A crisis mentality developed; according to Maxwell Cohen in 1970, the *Manhattan* voyages "made Canadians feel that they were on the edge of another American [theft] of Canadian resources and rights which had to be dealt with at once by firm governmental action."[21]

Putting aside but not renouncing any claim to sovereignty, the Liberal government announced its "functional" approach to Canadian sovereignty in 1970. It cast the Arctic as an ecologically delicate region: Canada needed to extend its jurisdiction northward to ensure that foreign vessels did not pollute Canadian waters. The Arctic Waters Pollution Prevention Act (AWPPA) allowed Canada to regulate and control future tanker traffic through the NWP by creating a pollution prevention zone one hundred nautical miles outside the archipelago as well as in the waters between the islands. The Territorial Sea and Fishing Zone Act extended Canada's territorial sea to twelve miles, subjecting the waters leading into the Passage to Canadian control. Trudeau considered this to be a show of "legal moderation," but the Americans were furious, announced that Canada's unilateral actions were unjustified in international law, and cut oil imports from Canada in retaliation.[22] While Canada increased its tempo of military activities in the North during the 1970s to "show the flag," it also set to work to consolidate its new regulations in international law. Although initially opposed to the AWPPA, in 1982 the United States supported Canadian-sponsored Article 234 of the UN Convention on the Law of the Sea (UNCLOS), which gave coastal states "the right to adopt and enforce non-discriminatory laws and regulations for the prevention, reduction and control of marine pollution from vessels in ice-covered areas within the limits of the exclusive economic zone."[23]

The August 1985 voyage of the US Coast Guard icebreaker *Polar Sea,* for reasonable operational reasons relating to the resupply of the American base at Thule, Greenland, launched another Canadian "crisis" over the NWP. The Americans refused to seek official permission from Canada, recognizing that this would prejudice their own legal position. In response, the Mulroney government announced that Canada was officially implementing straight baselines around the Arctic Archipelago effective 1 January 1986, thus claiming full sovereignty over the NWP as "historic, internal waters." Concurrently, it outlined an aggressive plan to exercise control over its waters and assert its Arctic sovereignty. This plan included a Polar 8 Class icebreaker, new maritime patrol aircraft, a new northern training centre, improved northern airfields, a dozen nuclear-powered attack submarines, and a fixed sonar detection system for the entrances to the passage. Canada also promised to negotiate with the United States—a prudent move that, owing to Mulroney's close relationship with President Ronald Reagan, yielded the 1988 Arctic Cooperation Agreement, which required American icebreakers to arrange Canadian consent for transits. By "agreeing to disagree" on the legal status of the passage, the two countries reached "a pragmatic solution based on our special bilateral relationship, our common interest in cooperating on Arctic matters, and the nature of the area"—one that did not prejudice either country's legal position or set a precedent for other areas of the world.[24]

Neither the *Manhattan* nor the *Polar Sea* voyages challenged Canadian ownership of the waters. They related to Canada's right to restrict transit passage[25] by foreign commercial or naval vessels. When the federal government perceived Canadian sovereignty to be threatened, however, it adopted unilateral legal measures to assert jurisdiction. It also demonstrated its commitment to defending Canadian sovereignty by ordering the Canadian Forces to "show the flag" and make a demonstration of Canada's presence in the North. Given that our closest military and economic ally was also our main challenger, this was a symbolic show of control. Canada could devote resources to a presence precisely because we knew that, in the end, the Americans could be relied upon to offer us security.[26] When the short-term crises faded, however, the government's willingness to deliver on its promised investments in Arctic security also melted away. Instead, Canada sought multilateral or bilateral agreements to lessen the likelihood that its claims would be challenged in the future.

With the end of the Cold War, budget pressures, promises of a "peace dividend," and few military threats on the northern horizon, the Canadian Forces' capabilities in the North were allowed to atrophy. Growing concerns about climate change, the opening of the NWP, global demands for Arctic resources, and security in the post-9/11 world have since converged to put the Arctic back on the national and international agendas. Recent laments

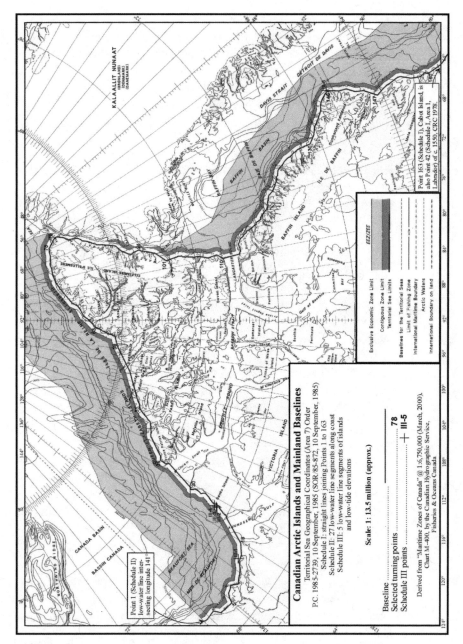

Map 3-2 Canadian Arctic islands and mainland baselines.

Source: Association of Canadian Land Surveyors

reflect a new alarmism: urgent action is again necessary because Canada's paltry capabilities are insufficient to project control over Arctic lands and waters at a time when our sovereignty is *likely* to be challenged. In a break with past practice, this latest sovereignty crisis is in anticipation of what *may* lie ahead. Nevertheless, our assessment of the past is coloured by anticipation of a future that, in the eyes of many commentators, does not look friendly.

A sober analysis of twentieth-century developments yields an unexpected set of lessons learned:

- Canadian sovereignty is not in jeopardy. This is most certain in terms of the Arctic islands and mainland. Canada has addressed potential challenges to *de facto* sovereignty over its territory through quiet diplomacy and has successfully balanced continental security priorities with its national interests. In terms of its Arctic waters, Canada has incrementally expanded its claims and, with the application of straight baselines in 1986, has established "that no right of innocent passage exists in the new internal waters of the Northwest Passage."[27]
- The Canadian–American disagreement over the legal status of the Northwest Passage is a long-standing issue that has been managed successfully on an agree-to-disagree basis. This does not support the nationalist myth that the United States has deliberately and systematically sought to undermine Canadian sovereignty. Both the Canadians and the Americans have strong reasons for their legal positions and have managed this issue sensibly without prejudice to their respective legal positions, without taking the matter to court. Indeed, to take that route would be a lose–lose proposition for Canada, for reasons I will explain later.
- Alarmism and reactionism lack staying power. They help place northern issues on the political agenda, but when anticipated threats or "crises" do not materialize as the alarmists anticipate, the political will to carry through dissipates quickly. This explains why Canadian governments have often made bold proclamations about investing in northern sovereignty and security but have largely failed to deliver on an integrated, proactive Arctic strategy.
- Canada's passive-reactive approach has succeeded insofar as it allowed Canada to expand and entrench its sovereignty in the twentieth century. This approach is not appropriate for the twenty-first century. First, it has failed to stimulate Canadian investment in northern social and economic development. Second, numerous commentators suggest that new challenges precipitated by climate change, which has heightened pressures for access to Canadian waters and Arctic resources, may lead to "loss by

dereliction."[28] An integrated Arctic strategy that incorporates defence, diplomacy, and development will allow Canada to seize the opportunities afforded by new interest in the Circumpolar North, maintain dialogue with key stakeholders, and ensure that its interests and values are promoted and protected.

Framing the Issues: Circumpolar Cooperation to "Use It or Lose It"

A decade ago, the federal government seemed poised to pursue a new course in engaging the circumpolar world. The all-party House of Commons Standing Committee on Foreign Affairs and International Trade (HCSCFAIT) approved a 1997 document that recommended that Canada's relations focus on international Arctic cooperation through multilateral governance (particularly the Arctic Council) to address pressing "human security" and environmental challenges in the region. "Nothing illustrates more dramatically the link between domestic and foreign factors than the state of the Arctic environment," committee chairman Bill Graham noted in this report. "That environment, so special and so fragile, is particularly sensitive to foreign influences." This report, *Canada and the Circumpolar World*, accepted that the concept of security had broadened beyond military issues to encompass an array of social and environmental issues. "This new agenda for security cooperation is inextricably linked to the aims of environmentally sustainable human development," it noted. "Meeting these challenges is essential to the long-term foundation for assuring circumpolar security, with priority being given to the well-being of Arctic peoples and to safeguarding northern habitants from intrusions which have impinged aggressively on them."[29]

The Liberal government under Jean Chrétien embraced this emphasis on international cooperation and reconfigured Canada's approach to Arctic sovereignty accordingly. Although the government rejected the committee's recommendation that the Arctic should become a nuclear-free zone, it did not perceive any security crisis that warranted an increased military presence beyond a modest expansion in the number of Northerners serving with the Canadian Rangers.[30] In 2000, the Department of Foreign Affairs and International Trade (DFAIT) issued *The Northern Dimension of Canada's Foreign Policy* (NDFP), which revealed how environmental and social challenges were now predominant:

> Both the tradition of transnational co-operation and the new emphasis on human security are particularly applicable to the shaping of the Northern Dimension of Canada's Foreign Policy. The circumpolar world that includes the

northern territories and peoples of Canada, Russia, the United States, the Nordic countries plus the vast (and mostly ice-covered) waters in between was long a front line in the Cold War. Now it has become a front line in a different way—facing the challenges and opportunities brought on by new trends and developments. The challenges mostly take the shape of transboundary environmental threats—persistent organic pollutants, climate change, nuclear waste—that are having dangerously increasing impacts on the health and vitality of human beings, northern lands, waters and animal life. The opportunities are driven by increasingly confident northern societies who, drawing on their traditional values, stand poised to take up the challenges presented by globalization. Whereas the politics of the Cold War dictated that the Arctic region be treated as part of a broader strategy of exclusion and confrontation, now the politics of globalization and power diffusion highlight the importance of the circumpolar world as an area for inclusion and co-operation.

Framed by principles of Canadian leadership, partnership, and ongoing dialogue with Northerners, this new northern foreign policy was rooted in four overarching objectives:

1. to enhance the security and prosperity of Canadians, especially northerners and Aboriginal peoples;
2. to assert and ensure the preservation of Canada's sovereignty in the North;
3. to establish the Circumpolar region as a vibrant geopolitical entity integrated into a rules-based international system; and
4. to promote the human security of northerners and the sustainable development of the Arctic.[31]

By the start of the new millennium, developments in Aboriginal self-government and devolution required new economic opportunities that promoted northern interests. Similarly, asserting and ensuring the preservation of Canadian sovereignty was deemed compatible with multilateral cooperation. Constructive engagement, not confrontation, would mark the twenty-first century, and the Liberal government was willing to downgrade military concerns. Accordingly, the NDFP supported activities in five key areas: strengthening the Arctic Council; establishing a University of the Arctic and a circumpolar policy research network; working with Russia to address its northern challenges; promoting sustainable economic opportunities and trade in the North; and increasing northern cooperation with the European Union (EU) and circumpolar countries.[32] Cabinet approved the NDFP in September 2000 and directed the DFAIT to allocate $10 million over five years to facilitate its implementation.

In 2005 the Inspector General at DFAIT completed an evaluation of the NDFP. Most stakeholders said that the Arctic Council was the "centre-piece" for advancing Canada's foreign policy interests in the Arctic and that it had played a "key role" in the council's working groups and in funding the Canadian-based Permanent Participants (who needed additional support). This active role had improved awareness and understanding of environmental issues, such as climate change and transboundary pollutants. In other respects, the resources and results were less satisfactory. However, the Inspector General determined that the Arctic Council needed "firmer policy direction, stronger diplomatic efforts and an enhanced role for the Ambassador of Circumpolar Affairs," as well as stronger partnerships with other federal departmental agencies, territorial governments, and land claims groups. The evaluators heard frequent complaints from northern and indigenous stakeholders that it had failed to sustain an ongoing policy dialogue.[33] Overall, the evaluation found that the NDFP warranted continuation but recommended the following: that Canada focus its energies and resources on fewer initiatives; that it strengthen DFAIT and Canadian leadership in circumpolar affairs; that it "strengthen partnerships with other federal departments and agencies, territorial governments and land claims groups in light of increasing emphasis on horizontal and whole-of-government solutions and the continuing devolution of governance in the North"; and that it strengthen initiatives to engage Canadians, particularly Northerners and indigenous groups.[34]

The focus on diplomacy and circumpolar cooperation meant that traditional preoccupations with "defending" sovereignty slipped to the back burner. The 2000 Canadian Forces' *Arctic Capabilities Study* recognized that northern security had evolved to include environmental, social, and economic aspects, but argued that the coming decades would make the North even more vulnerable to "asymmetric" security and sovereignty threats. The Canadian Forces (CF) had to be prepared to respond to challenges related to environmental protection, increased shipping as Arctic sea lanes opened due to climate change, heightened commercial airline activity, and "trans-national criminal activity" that would accompany resource development such as diamond mining. To meet its obligations in the North, improved capabilities to monitor and respond to emergencies were needed.[35] The DND decided that, given its limited budget, the equipment and programs proposed to address anything more than surveillance issues would be extremely expensive. Scarce military resources would, instead, be devoted to more pressing priorities.[36]

In 2005 the Liberals' *International Policy Statement* (IPS) identified that the Arctic was now a priority area in light of "increased security threats, a changed distribution of global power, challenges to existing international institutions, and transformation of the global economy." It was anticipated that the next two decades would bring major challenges requiring creative diplomacy as well as investments in new defence capabilities. "In addition to growing economic activity in the Arctic region, the effects of climate change are expected to open up our Arctic waters to commercial traffic by as early as 2015," the IPS noted. "These developments reinforce the need for Canada to monitor and control events in its sovereign territory, through new funding and new tools."[37] The IPS focused on surveillance, such as infrared sensors for patrol aircraft, unmanned aerial vehicles, and satellites. Prime Minister Paul Martin's government fell before it could deliver on its 2005 budget promises.

In December 2004, the Liberals announced a Northern Strategy, backed by the three territorial premiers (none of whom was a Liberal) and led at the federal level by the Department of Indian and Northern Affairs (INAC). It was framed by the following headings and goals:

- Strengthening Governance, Partnerships and Institutions
  – Proposed Goal: To strengthen governments and institutions, and support evolving relationships among them, in order to provide northerners with effective governance and greater control over decisions central to their future.
- Establishing Strong Foundations for Economic Development
  – Proposed Goal: To build strong, sustainable, diversified economies where northerners share in the benefits of northern development.
- Protecting the Environment
  – Proposed Goal: To engage all partners in the North in the protection and stewardship of the environment.
- Building Healthy and Safe Communities
  – Proposed Goal: To ensure healthy, safe and sustainable northern communities that serve and support the needs of northern residents and promote self-reliance.
- Reinforcing Sovereignty, National Security and Circumpolar Cooperation
  – Proposed Goal: To ensure that Canada plays a leading role and promotes concerted international action on circumpolar issues, and that northern concerns are taken into consideration in national efforts to reinforce sovereignty, security and circumpolar cooperation.
- Preserving, Revitalizing and Promoting Culture and Identity
  – Proposed Goal: To ensure that the importance of language, traditional knowledge and way-of-life is recognized and encouraged.
- Developing Northern Science and Research

– Proposed Goal: To ensure that Canada is a leader in northern science and technology, and to develop expertise in areas of particular importance and relevance to the North.[38]

Although the Martin government conducted public consultations on the strategy in 2005, the results were not released before the federal election at the end of that year.

Since coming to office in early 2006, Prime Minister Stephen Harper's "use it or lose it" refrain has become the dominant political message. Because it taps into primordial national anxieties about sovereignty, this threatening phrase resonates with southern Canadians who otherwise have taken little interest in their Arctic and have been led to believe that military capabilities will shield Canada from "the perfect storm" brewing in the Circumpolar North.[39] The logic of "defending sovereignty" from foreign challenges has also meant a shift away from past governments that favoured *recognition*—persuading others to accept our claims without demonstrating a capacity to enforce them—toward a Harper government that favours *enactment*.[40] Its instrument of choice is the Canadian Forces, which fits within the "Canada First" vision that pledges to defend "our vast territory and three ocean areas" through increased defence spending and more Regular and Reserve Forces.[41]

While most of Prime Minister Harper's speeches have announced a "shopping list" of military initiatives rather than a coherent vision for northern policy,[42] his government acknowledges the need for a broader strategy. His 16 October 2007 Speech from the Throne asserted that

the North needs new attention. New opportunities are emerging across the Arctic, and new challenges from other shores. Our Government will bring forward an integrated northern strategy focusing on strengthening Canada's sovereignty, protecting our environmental heritage, promoting economic and social development, and improving and devolving governance, so that northerners have greater control over their destinies.[43]

This agenda moves beyond a narrow military focus but provides few concrete details about what this integrated strategy will actually include. The 2008 federal budget reiterated the above four pillars, this time suggesting that they *were* the government's strategy. The only additional clarification came in the form of principles drawn from the territorial premiers' 2004 *Northern Vision*, discussed later:

• Self-reliant individuals live in healthy, vital communities, manage their own affairs and shape their own destinies.

- The northern tradition of respect for the land and the environment is paramount—where principles of responsible and sustainable development anchor all decision making and action.
- Strong, responsible, accountable governments work together for a vibrant, prosperous future for all—where people and governments are significant contributing partners to a dynamic, secure Canadian federation.[44]

Thus, the Conservative government claims to have an integrated northern strategy but has not made it public beyond reiterating four general pillars. This observation reflects what commentators have called Prime Minister Harper's "announcement" approach to governance: making a series of individual procurement or spending promises rather than laying out a coherent vision or agenda. Stated another way, his speeches *are* the government's strategy. A fact sheet on the government's Northern Strategy, posted to the INAC website in May 2008, corroborates this assessment. Instead of elaborating on an overarching vision—which could, of course, be criticized on a conceptual level for what it prioritizes or leaves out—it provides a series of bullets identifying discrete promises that it had made since coming into office. Although this suggests government action on some important files, it does not constitute a national strategy.[45]

Northern and Academic Stakeholders' Suggestions

Stakeholders outside the federal government have recommended various principles and elements that should be considered in an integrated northern strategy. Reviewing their policy proposals helps identify the priorities and expectations of Northerners, clarifying which additional elements should be accommodated in a proactive and comprehensive national vision.

In October 2006 the Walter and Duncan Gordon Foundation convened a two-day workshop, "The Arctic and Canada's Foreign Policy," with twenty-four participants, including northern indigenous representatives, territorial government officials, policy practitioners, academics, and industry. This report recommended that Canada complete its northern strategy, update and expand the *Northern Dimension to Canada's Foreign Policy*, re-create the position of Circumpolar Ambassador, create a domestic equivalent to the Arctic Council to ensure engagement of Northerners on Arctic issues, and take "a more visible and assertive leadership role in the Arctic Council's sustainable development activities." This report also recommended that the territorial governments and the three Canadian-based Permanent Participants to the Arctic Council (the Arctic Athabaskan Council, the Gwich'in Council International, and the Inuit Circumpolar Council) explore ways to develop and implement the NDFP.[46]

The premiers of Yukon, NWT, and Nunavut have worked to articulate a pan-territorial action plan to frame their dialogue with Canada on a northern vision.[47] In their view, Canada's sovereignty is based on Northerners' use and occupancy of lands and waters through the centuries and is enhanced by "strong and healthy communities." The theme of partnership—between the territories and the rest of Canada, as well as with Canada's circumpolar neighbours—is treated as "critical to Canada's sovereignty and security interests." In 2007 the three premiers released *A Northern Vision: A Stronger North and a Better Canada*, which clarified specific priorities. First and foremost, their report holds that sovereignty comes through sustainable communities that have robust infrastructures, educated and capable populations, and lower costs of living. In terms of security, they call for shipping regulations that balance commerce with environmental protection. Their report also encourages the federal government to collaborate with them "to enhance monitoring and enforcement capabilities in the Arctic" through modern Coast Guard icebreakers, a permanent military base in the Arctic, a deep-water port, and "strong support for the Canadian Rangers." For them, adapting to climate change means maximizing the benefits and minimizing the negative impacts through research, information sharing, cleaner energy sources, and modifications to infrastructure so that it can withstand environmental and socioeconomic changes. In circumpolar forums, the premiers have emphasized that "Northern issues must be addressed by Northern voices," and they have promised "to support increased efforts by Canada to strengthen bilateral relations with our Arctic neighbours to help ensure that our circumpolar interests remain a priority area for multilateral cooperation."[48]

Northern Aboriginal organizations have highlighted similar themes and priorities. "The rapid decline in recent years of multi-year sea ice in the Arctic Ocean has attracted considerable attention worldwide," the Arctic Athabaskan Council (AAC) observes.[49] It anticipates that

> the Arctic Ocean is destined soon to become like North America's Great Lakes— frozen over in winter and completely thawed in summer—further "opening" the region to oil, gas and mineral development and intercontinental shipping. The impacts of such development will not be confined to the coast, but will reach deep into Eurasia and North America, including areas used and occupied by Athabaskan peoples.[50]

The AAC's suggestions to the EU on policy priorities are equally relevant to Canada. These include encouraging Arctic states and Permanent Participants to strengthen the Arctic Council. Furthermore, it advocates using the Arctic as a "bridge" to engage China on environmental protection, research, and sustainable development issues. The AAC has also lobbied for the removal of barriers on Arctic wildlife products "as long as harvests accord with principles of conservation and sustainability"; for Arctic climate change issues to be addressed through the UN Framework Convention on Climate Change; and for indigenous peoples to be granted a seat on the UN Environment Program's Governing Council.[51]

The Inuit also emphasize the need for constructive engagement in the circumpolar world, particularly given that Inuit live in four Arctic countries and share a common culture, heritage, environment, language, diet, and resources. Inuit Tapiriit Kanatami (ITK) and the Inuit Circumpolar Council (Canada) (ICC), in "Building Inuit Nunaat—The Inuit Action Plan," promote a shared "vision of international agreements and activities that enhance the health, well-being, culture, and economy of the Inuit of Canada, and protect the natural environment upon which Inuit so closely and fundamentally depend."[52] This plan calls for improved communication so that Inuit stakeholders are engaged in developing Canada's positions through annual meetings with Cabinet ministers; a stronger role for Canada's Circumpolar Ambassador (a position abolished in 2006); and more funding to strengthen the capacity of the Inuit to engage government actors domestically and internationally. Priority areas for the Inuit relate to the sustainable utilization of Arctic living resources, biodiversity, environmental contamination, science and research, health, shipping, sovereignty, cooperation with the Russian Federation and its Arctic peoples, and climate change.

In January 2008, ITK released its proposal for "An Integrated Arctic Strategy" based on seven central themes. First, it suggests that the term "Arctic" be used to encompass Canada's provincial and territorial northern areas. Second, it emphasizes the need to encourage "a peaceful and stable international Arctic" that will contribute to international cooperation and security. Despite the presence of unresolved sovereignty issues in the Arctic, "the world needs positive regional examples of how peaceful and stable international relations can be constructed and pursued."[53] ITK expresses the priorities to reach this objective as follows:

- delivery on the package of multi-year Arctic oriented military initiatives set out in the October 2007 Speech from the Throne
- an early examination of the viability of a new marine authority to govern the use of Canada's internal Arctic waters for transportation purposes; close attention should be paid to the unfulfilled commitments in relation

- the creation of a Nunavut Marine Council set out in the 1993 Nunavut Land Claims Agreement
- Canadian leadership in the exploration of a more permanent footing to the Arctic Council and a more rigorous mandate for the Council
- Canadian leadership in expanded discussions among circumpolar States as to the feasibility of a regional Arctic climate change/adaptation strategy
- Canadian receptiveness to a discussion among circumpolar States as to the feasibility of an Arctic oriented approach for the sorting out of disputes regarding issues of jurisdiction over marine areas
- a review of the mandate and role of the Canadian Polar Commission as it relates to their capacity to establish research priorities[54]

The ITK's third theme stresses that efforts to reinforce sovereignty and security should also strengthen northern society; the fourth, that the peoples of the Canadian Arctic should be empowered to manage their own economic and political affairs. Fifth, the distinctive culture of Aboriginal peoples should be supported; sixth, "successful development of non-renewable resources should be combined with thoughtful use of renewable resources for reasons of economic diversification and cultural continuity and related land/marine monitoring purposes."[55] Seventh, the ITK emphasizes the need for policy making and priority setting based upon rigorous research. The strategy proposal recommends a trilateral approach to implementation that includes the federal government, provincial/territorial governments, and Aboriginal organizations.

Scenario-Based Thinking

A forward-thinking Arctic strategy is inherently predicated on future scenarios—that is, on plausible stories about future environments in which current decisions play out. Even when these are not explicit, they underpin the rationale for a particular course of action.

The academic debate between Rob Huebert and Franklyn Griffiths is a good illustration of how anticipated scenarios influence the ways in which commentators frame the issues and help set priorities. Huebert sees the Arctic as a potential battleground. Since the late 1990s, he has been forecasting a "perfect storm" over climate change, newly accessible Arctic resources, shortened transportation routes, and competing national claims to Arctic waters, seabeds, and islands. Canada is at a "crossroads" and must choose between "scal[ing] back or abandon[ing] some of their unilateral objectives and develop[ing] a multilateral framework for new governance."[56] His writings assert that the "soft law" in the region and the Americans' unwillingness to ratify UNCLOS have made the legal regime a tenuous basis for solving problems, while global competition for resources and incompatible national interests have brought circumpolar countries and other stakeholders into growing conflict. By extension, in this hostile world where only the strong will survive, Canada must take unilateral action to assert control and defend its sovereignty or its claims will be overwhelmed by those of rival powers.[57]

By contrast, Griffiths has emphasized that Canadian sovereignty is well in hand and that the government should focus on *stewardship*—"the enactment of sovereignty"—in light of uncertainties related to climate and geopolitical change.[58] Downplaying the immediacy or probability of the northern military and commercial threats emphasized by Huebert, Griffiths emphasizes the need for ongoing dialogue between southern stakeholders and northern residents with regard to setting agendas and priorities.[59] Concurrently, if Canada sees the United States as an ally rather than a polar adversary, this will offer the prospect of a working bilateral compromise on the NWP, which is the issue "that continues to tower above all other of our Arctic sovereignty concerns."[60] In short, by asserting the improbability of an existential threat to Canada's possession of its Arctic waters, Griffiths provides the conceptual space to envision schemes for constructive international engagement and cooperative management.

"The Future of Arctic Marine Navigation in Mid-Century," a series of scenario narratives produced by the Global Business Network for the Arctic Council's Protection of the Arctic Marine Environment (PAME) Working Group in May 2008, provides a framework for devising and analyzing plausible futures for Arctic marine navigation. Their matrix treats two variables as the most important and uncertain: (1) governance and resources and (2) trade. In Figure 3-2, the horizontal axis describes the degree of relative governance stability within and beyond the Arctic region:

> ← **Less stability** implies shortfalls in legal structure and transparency, as well as a propensity for actors and stakeholders to work on a more unilateral basis rather than by collaborating in a cooperative, international fashion.
>
> → **More stability** implies not only efficiently operating legal and regulatory structures, but also an international atmosphere more conducive to collaborative and cooperative development.

The figure's vertical axis describes the level of demand for Arctic resources and trade, including potential global market developments:

↑ **More demand** implies higher demand from more players and markets around the world for resources in the Arctic, including open water for trans-shipment trade.

↓ **Less demand** implies fewer players interested in fewer Arctic resources.[61]

This framework yields four scenarios. Neither "Polar Lows" nor "Polar Preserve" would bring the economic development that the Canadian government and northern stakeholders desire. The recent downturn in the global economy, coupled with falling energy and mineral prices, may foretell a future of low demand and a shift of attention away from Arctic resources. This, however, is likely a short-term trend; issues of energy security and diversity of supply still make the region attractive on a strategic level for future development. The federal government and northern stakeholders recognize that

Figure 3-2 Future scenarios: The Global Business Network (GBN) Future Arctic Marine Navigation Matrix (2008).
Source: Arctic Council

resource extraction offers the best prospects for sustained economic growth in the North; thus they encourage development. By extension, Canada obviously should not frame its foreign policy around either a "Polar Low" or a "Polar Preserve" scenario.

Much of the alarmist rhetoric swirling in the media suggests a looming "Arctic Race": more demand for resources and trade and less stable governance. The no-holds-barred race for resources in the Arctic frontier presupposes intense competition and a corresponding willingness to violate rules, growing military activity, unilateral action, and political friction over states' willingness to allow trans-Arctic passage. National interests are paramount, shared interests are few and unreliable, and rapid climate change will fuel a feeding frenzy in an anarchic region allegedly devoid of "overarching political or legal structures that can provide for the orderly development ... or mediate political disagreements over Arctic resources or sea-lanes."[62] For reasons that will be discussed, Canada cannot thrive in this anarchic scenario—and particularly not through unilateral action—given its low military, political, and economic strength relative to the Russians, the Americans, and the EU.

Is any other scenario naive, given the challenges that Canada faces from its circumpolar neighbours? Self-professed "realists" might assert this, but even the Russians seem to think that an "Arctic Race" scenario is misguided. Russian Ambassador at Large Anton Vasilyev, who is also a high-ranking participant on the Arctic Council, told reporters on 22 October 2008 that "media assessments of possible aggression in the Arctic, even a third world war, are seen as extremely alarmist and provocative. In my opinion, there are no grounds for such alarmism ... We are following the situation in the region, this also includes the military activity of other countries, but we hope cooperation will be the main feature."[63] The Russians are working to define their extended continental shelf, as are their circumpolar neighbours, including Canada, and President Dmitry Medvedev told a Russian Security Council session on 17 September 2008 that the shelf was "a guarantee of Russia's energy security and that the Arctic should become the resource base for Russia this century."[64]

If one inserted the word "Canada" in place of "Russia," this could be mistaken for one of Prime Minister Harper's speeches. Yet in September 2008, when the Russian government announced a new frontier law to define its southern Arctic claim, Harper responded that Canada was stepping up its military measures in the region because of the Russians' willingness to flout international law. "We would like to hope that this is, at best, the result of inattentive reading of the materials published by the Russian Security Council," the Russian Foreign Ministry replied, explaining that the new federal law had nothing to do with its continental shelf claim.[65] Indeed, Russian press releases have emphasized the socio-economic benefits of development, noted that the interests of indigenous peoples and environmental regulations will be taken into account, and reaffirmed that Russia will submit scientific evidence to the UN to support its shelf claim in 2009. The Russians, ironically, are accusing the Canadians and Americans of belligerence for trying to stimulate an "Arctic Race." This is disconcerting, particularly when scenario-based decision making serves as the basis for developing an integrated foreign and domestic strategy on the Arctic.

What Canada can anticipate and should seek is an "Arctic Saga"—that is, greater demand for resources and trade coupled with more stable governance. This scenario envisions "a healthy rate of development that includes concern for the preservation of Arctic ecosystems and cultures," based on a world view "driven by business pragmatism that balances global collaboration and compromise with successful development of the resources of the Arctic."[66] Shared economic and political interests, global economic prosperity, and systematic resource development will permit a range and variety of maritime activities, with navigational infrastructure and improved technology making marine transport safer, more efficient, and more economically viable. Although hypothetical and optimistic, this should encapsulate Canada's desired outcome. It incorporates what northern stakeholders have identified as key priority areas: sustainable development, constructive circumpolar engagement, and environmental protection—without sacrificing either Canadian sovereignty or security.

A basic 3-D approach—one that integrates defence, diplomacy, and development—can frame a robust and sustainable northern strategy that fits within this desired outcome. It need not succumb to alarmism, and it can prioritize Northerners' voices and interests in agenda setting and decision making. Responsible circumpolar leadership will begin with convincing Canadians that our Arctic sovereignty is not in jeopardy. Canada should frame a new discourse as a confident, sovereign northern nation willing to invest and participate in sustainable development. "If we focus only on losing, then lose we will," Sheila Watt-Cloutier highlighted in *Nunatsiaq News* on 17 January 2007. Canada is in it to win, and Northern residents will tolerate nothing less.

Defence

You don't defend national sovereignty with flags, cheap election rhetoric or advertising campaigns. You need forces on the ground, ships in the sea, and proper surveillance.

—*Prime Minister Stephen Harper, Winnipeg, 22 December 2005*

> Sovereignty is not a magic word which automatically requires or justifies a certain military set-piece. It is rather the political and territorial framework within which a state exists and functions. It is not made up of, or protected by symbols, tokens or gestures.
>
> —*External Affairs, Legal Division, August 1970*

The federal government has often turned to the Canadian Forces when faced with northern sovereignty "crises," from the *Manhattan* voyages of 1969 and 1970, to the *Polar Sea* voyage of 1985, to the latest round of concerns over Hans Island, the continental shelf, and the melting of the NWP. Over the past three years, Prime Minister Harper has announced a spate of new military measures—from a high-Arctic base to ice-strengthened frigates to more Canadian Rangers—to respond to the anticipated sovereignty challenges. These commitments to invest in new or improved capabilities should be welcomed, but they must also be rationalized, and coordinated in a more holistic, whole-of-government context than existing government announcements suggest.

A "Canada First" strategy is politically sound, but the government is unrealistic if it is setting up "Canada only" expectations for the Arctic region. Canada cannot afford the suite of necessary capabilities to defend our Arctic from any *possible* aggressor. More important, there is no need for us to try to achieve total security by ourselves. Despite the hyperbolic media rhetoric about a new Cold War brewing, there is no conventional military threat to our Far North, nor will Canada solve its boundary disputes through force of arms. We need to invest in military capabilities so that the CF can operate in all parts of the country and play a supporting role to civil authorities, particularly the Canadian Coast Guard (CCG) and the RCMP. The rationale for a more robust military presence is not so that Canada can stand up to the United States and our circumpolar neighbours with modern naval ships, intimidating them into submission. To be perceived as an antagonist would go against our national interests and values. The other argument—that military capabilities will earn us a seat at the table—is also a moot point. Canada has a seat by virtue of geography and its undisputed legal ownership of vast Arctic lands and waters. Instead, the Government of Canada must improve its defence capabilities because "a responsible government provides proper policing, surveillance, search and rescue [(SAR)] and other services throughout its territory."[67] This lacks the political glamour of saving the country from foreign challenges to its territorial and maritime integrity, but it is a sounder rationale on which to base a national sovereignty and security strategy.

Figure 3-3 After being granted Freedom of the City and marching through Iqaluit, Nunavut, members the Canadian Forces are addressed by Prime Minister Stephen Harper during the opening ceremony for Operation Lancaster, August 2006.
Source: DND

Every Arctic country has national interests at stake in the region; that is self-evident. This recognition should be neither grounds for Canada to adopt a narrow, unilateralist approach to circumpolar affairs, nor a basis for apathy borne of faith that Canada's neighbours will look after the region for us. Simply relying on our allies to protect our interests limits our range of action. Being a good neighbour means having the ability to control your territory and waters so that you do not have to rely entirely on your friends to do so. In Canada's case, having to depend too heavily on our allies, particularly the Americans, for security in the Arctic makes us jittery because it raises concerns about our *de facto* (practical) sovereignty. Even if our *de jure* (legal) sovereignty is solid, primordial Canadian concerns about American intentions tend to launch us into yet further rounds in the game of sovereignty "crisis reaction" (as was laid out earlier). Canada must be prepared, at the very least, to defend against needing too much help from its major ally, given that our interests do not always coincide.

Since coming into office in 2006, Stephen Harper's Conservatives have made the CF the centrepiece of their "use it or lose it" approach to Canadian sovereignty. The government has made frequent reference to the "critical role" that the CF play in "asserting Canadian sovereignty." These claims seem to be rooted in the notion that, if a country does not demonstrate its occupation and effective control over its territory, it can lose its sovereignty "by dereliction."[68] What does increasing Canada's military presence actually contribute to our Arctic sovereignty?

The Role of Defence in Sovereignty Assertion

The role of the Canadian Forces in asserting sovereignty is often tied to the maxim that possession is nine-tenths of the law. Surveillance and "boots on the ground" are commonly bound up with Canada's credibility in "defending" its sovereignty. By implication, a more robust CF presence is essential to "using or losing" our Arctic. Yet there has been little to no evidence given to substantiate this accepted wisdom. Recent legal opinions are obviously classified and cannot be analyzed, but history will help illuminate the issue. Discussions from the early Trudeau era on the role of the CF in protecting and maintaining sovereignty—the military's first priority, according to the then prime minister, just as it is according to the current one—reveal that improved military capabilities do not translate into stronger sovereignty claims.

In the early 1970s, defence planners emphasized the need for a persistent presence in the North, arguing that surveillance was integral to affirming Canada's legal claims over the area. A few commentators took a different view. In April 1969, international lawyer Erik Wang, who was then at Canadian Forces Headquarters before moving to the Defence Relations Division at External Affairs,[69] commented that "it is difficult to see what expanded role the Canadian Armed Forces could usefully play in support of Canada's claim to sovereignty over water between the Arctic islands." He described the problem of sovereignty in the Arctic as based in legal, economic, and political considerations. "It is *not* a military problem," Wang concluded. "It cannot be solved by any amount of surveillance or patrol activity in the channels by Canadian forces." There had to be a firm military rationale for CF involvement in the North, not "presence for the sake of presence." To develop a role merely to satisfy the "optical demands" of political sovereignty "would be to build on shifting sands ... It would not be long before somebody noticed that one visit of the Governor General, accompanied by an enthusiastic press corps, can provide a sovereign presence to a remote area much more effectively and much more cheaply than 100 [Canadian Armed Forces] surveillance overflights."[70]

In the ensuing years, the Legal Division at External Affairs took issue with DND reports and policy statements that confused "the problematic enforcement of Canada's jurisdictional claims in the Arctic waters with the problem of the legal basis for those claims." In short, a military presence did nothing to establish the "legal validity of Canada's claims" in the Arctic. Surveillance "may well be a necessary function of sovereignty, but could not be considered a basis for or sine que non of sovereignty." It was necessary for control, enforcement, and protection, but there was no legal basis for the idea that "he who is best informed has the best case."[71] Legal opinions confidently asserted that Canadian claims were strong and that "there was no need for increased presence of military forces in the North merely for the sake of presence in order to bolster our legal claim to the real estate."[72]

The military's role in support of sovereignty, External Affairs argued, was *functional*. "To the extent that Canadian legislation has asserted specific types of jurisdiction in the Arctic waters (i.e[.], pollution control) Canada must be in the position to enforce that jurisdiction," Legal Division officials argued in 1970, although it added the qualifier that enforcement was not necessarily through military agencies. As a result, it emphasized that "increased surveillance activities must be developed in response to specific *needs and interests* and not on the basis of some pious hope that aimless overflights somehow contribute to 'sovereignty.'"[73] It was senseless to boost military strength in the Arctic without a clearer sense of purpose, noted the Office of Politico-Military Affairs. Was the preoccupation with a heavier military presence supposed to allow Canadians to "somehow sleep better, or is it intended to serve as a signal to Washington of our national resolve?" The focus needed to switch to finding "roles for the military in specific areas where a useful job can be performed in support of other government agencies with operational responsibilities in the North."[74] The DND's reference to "presence" in its defence objectives seemed to imply that the government's concept of sovereignty was static and symbolic, not functional. Wang insisted that the Canadian government should identify and define specific national interests, such as anti-pollution measures and safety of navigation, and shape policy to protect them. The military's fixation on presence and surveillance was inconsistent with this approach.

In the eyes of lawyer Len Legault, the fixation on defence as a panacea for Canada's sovereignty issues was "confused and deficient." The draft White Paper *Defence in the 70s* "sometimes seems to view 'surveillance' as a sort of mystic rite rather than a functional requirement to meet well defined needs," he observed. The very suggestion that comprehensive surveillance or an increased presence was needed to perfect Canada's title "may give a misleading impression that Canada is concerned to shore up a weak legal claim to sovereign jurisdiction in the North." Continuous calls for more effective occupation and comprehensive surveillance were actually "prejudicial to the very objective of protecting sovereignty, for if Canada persistently calls into doubt its sovereignty in the Arctic then others may too begin to entertain such doubts."[75] "Functional needs should be the touchstone" for any proposed CF role in the Arctic, an External Affairs official noted in February 1972:

> Surveillance is a functional activity directed variously to the detection of military threats ([e.g.,] submarine operations and intelligence activities by potentially hostile ships and aircraft), territorial violations not strictly military in nature ([e.g.,] unauthorized overflights) and infringement of Canadian jurisdiction or legislation ... Any suggestion that surveillance might be quasi-symbolic activity required to meet certain legal formalities of sovereignty would by inaccurate and should be avoided.[76]

This irony—that harping about the need for a stronger CF presence could actually undermine Canada's sovereignty—must be remembered today. Claims that any investment in CF capabilities in the North or any increase in military activity strengthens our sovereignty are tenuous at best. From a political perspective, such claims are intended to evoke an image of government action and resolve, something best demonstrated through a whole-of-government, functional approach.

Recent Commitments

As long as its logic is grounded in functional reasons, and not in the flawed notion that military "boots on the ground" strengthens or perfects our legal sovereignty,[77] the Harper government should be commended for its promises to invest in robust defence capabilities. The Liberals modestly increased the tempo of military operations in the Arctic in the early twenty-first century and promised to augment capabilities in their 2005 Defence Policy Statement; then, in 2006, Stephen Harper's Conservatives swept into office with a much stronger resolve to make the Arctic a top priority. "We believe that Canadians are excited about the government asserting Canada's control and sovereignty in the Arctic," Harper told a *Toronto Sun* reporter on 23 February 2007:

> We believe that's one of the big reasons why Canadians are excited and support our plan to rebuild the Canadian Forces. I think it's practically and symbolically hugely important, much more important than the dollars spent. And I'm hoping that years from now, Canada's Arctic sovereignty, military and otherwise, will be, frankly, a major legacy of this government.[78]

The Harper government's main military announcements, all cast as sovereignty initiatives, include expanding the Canadian Rangers; ordering new

Arctic offshore patrol vessels to monitor and respond; building a deep-water Arctic docking and refuelling facility in Nanisivik; launching Radarsat-2 to provide enhanced surveillance and data-gathering capabilities; holding military exercises; building a Canadian Forces Arctic Training Centre in Resolute; and establishing a new CF Reserve unit in Yellowknife.

Given that each initiative was announced separately and with minimal justification—which generated criticism from opposition parties and media commentators—these commitments must be evaluated for the functional contributions they make to broader government strategy. Furthermore, the recent economic downturn and talk of a deficit budget in Ottawa will be putting pressure on the federal government to cut projects and activities. For reasons discussed below, the government should deliver on its promises and integrate them into an interdepartmental defence, security, and safety strategy.

The Canadian Rangers

Kenneth Eyre astutely noted that the Canadian military has influenced the North more than the North has influenced the military. While the historical record yields examples of the military as an environmental and social "treadmill of destruction,"[79] there have also been success stories, most notably the Canadian Rangers. For sixty years the Rangers have served as the "eyes and ears" of the armed forces in remote areas, providing a military presence in isolated northern and coastal regions of the country that cannot be covered practically or economically by other elements of the CF. Their unique military footprint in coastal and northern Canada draws on the indigenous knowledge of community members rather than on "militarizing" and conditioning them through typical military training regimes. The Rangers are a flexible, inexpensive, and culturally inclusive means of "showing the flag" and asserting Canadian sovereignty in remote regions.[80] They also provide tangible support to CF operations and training across the Canadian North—not just in the Arctic, as implied by repeated government references to the "Arctic Rangers."

The danger, in an era of "crisis response," is that even successful initiatives like the Canadian Rangers can be overextended as a result of heightened but unrealistic expectations. The Rangers have survived cycles of waxing and waning interest in northern defence mainly because of their tiny cost, minor material demands, and grounding in local communities. Recent proposals to expand their numbers from 4,200 to 5,000, under the auspices of the government's commitment to Arctic sovereignty, may be misleading—and unsustainable if government priorities shift. For example, every community along the Arctic coast that can sustain a Ranger patrol already has one. New patrols can only be created south of the treeline, where there is no perceived sovereignty threat.

FIGURE 3-4 Two Canadian Rangers from the Pangnirtung patrol listen to a range safety briefing prior to zeroing their .303 Lee-Enfield rifles during Exercise Narwhal in the Cumberland Peninsula area of Baffin Island, August 2004. Source: DND

Although the average strength of patrols in 1st Canadian Ranger Patrol Group (responsible for the Territorial North) is 27 members and the authorized limit per community is 30, the government has committed to increasing the number of Rangers by more than 900 (to a strength of 5,000 nationally). Given that 1.44 percent of the territorial population already serve as Canadian Rangers (compared to 0.27 percent of Canadians serving in the Regular Forces or Primary

Reserves), and that in some communities most able-bodied adults are already members,[81] it may not be realistic or desirable to increase enrolments to reach targets set in Ottawa.

Northern Aboriginal groups continue to see the Rangers as a key component of any integrated Arctic strategy, and the requests those groups are making have the potential to take what has been a mutually beneficial military–community partnership in new directions. ITK has called for "a reconceptualization and expansion of the Arctic Rangers program" so that its official tasks would include environmental monitoring, supplying country food to communities, "work for those unqualified or unable to work in wage employment, particularly in small communities," and sustaining land-based skills, cultures, and languages.[82] These capacities are already some of the ancillary benefits to having a patrol in a community; formalizing them, however, would transform the Rangers into a federal "program" directed at Aboriginal communities. This transformation would detract from their credibility as reserve elements in the larger CF team.

The Rangers are important in that they serve not only as a military "footprint" in northern communities but also as a bridge between the military and civilian realms. These volunteers should be provided with better uniforms, more money for wear and tear on their personal equipment during training and operations, and exciting training opportunities. They are proof that small-scale, grassroots measures can assert a national presence over Arctic lands and waters. Because Ranger activities allow Northerners to exercise jurisdiction and control, they also bolster the idea that traditional indigenous activities continue unbroken to the present and are supported by Ottawa. The Rangers, as a community-based story, must not be set up to fail. Five thousand Rangers will not provide more security or more Arctic sovereignty than 4,200 Rangers, but increasing the cap may accommodate sustainable growth if it is undertaken in a realistic and careful manner. Heightened expectations that do not take into account the demographic, social, and cultural realities of the North could undermine positive relationships that have been forged between the Rangers and other CF elements over the past half century.

Arctic/Offshore Patrol Vessels

In January 2006, Prime Minister Harper promised to build three armed heavy icebreakers for the Canadian Navy, capable of operating anywhere in the North at any time of the year. In May 2007, Cabinet announced that instead of icebreakers, it would order between six and eight Arctic offshore patrol ships (AOPSs). These Class 5 vessels will be able to operate in Arctic waters during the navigable season in up to one metre of first-year ice. They will also be able to operate in Canada's East and West coast exclusive economic zones (EEZs) the year round.

The construction of corvette-sized, ice-strengthened patrol ships lacks the dramatic and symbolic flair that the construction of major icebreakers for the Navy would have had, but it is a reasonable response to the challenges and opportunities facing the country. First and foremost, the navy did not want to develop a full icebreaking capacity, which it has not had since 1957. This capability more properly resides with the Coast Guard. At the same time, the government can still justify the procurement of AOPSs as part of its "Canada First" sovereignty posture. The proposed vessels are versatile and flexible; moreover, they reflect the government's willingness to follow CF recommendations. They also fill an existing capability gap that is not confined to the Arctic. "The Navy's current fleet of Maritime Coastal Defence Vessels (MCDVs) has limited capability to conduct operations in the EEZ," notes the AOPSs' 2008 *Statement of Operational Requirement.* "Specifically, they have reduced sea keeping capabilities, modest ability to operate outside of coastal waters, reduced capability to support open ocean boarding operations, limited speed and lack the ability to operate a helicopter."[83] In short, though they have been criticized as inadequate "slush-breakers" by former New Democratic Party leader Jack Layton, the AOPSs are a sensible platform that will allow the Navy to support other government departments in areas such as fisheries regulation, disaster response, search and rescue, immigration enforcement, and environmental protection. They will make sense, however, only if the Coast Guard fleet is also recapitalized to provide Canada with icebreaking capabilities[84] and if ice-strengthened replenishment ships are procured.[85]

Recruiting, training, and retaining personnel to serve on these ships must be a high priority. The crewing and training requirements for the AOPSs have not been firmly identified, but estimates are that each ship will require a core crew of thirty-five to forty-five personnel.[86] The Navy, however, is already facing a "crisis" when it comes to filling technical trades more generally, Captain (Navy) James Cotter has explained in a recent study. How will it "develop the necessary competencies for Arctic ship handling and navigation"? It would be logical to place selected personnel in Coast Guard ships, where Canada's icebreaking expertise resides. But there are salient differences between the two services. Cotter asks: "The coast guard operates with a month-on, month-off rotation. Would the Navy ... follow suit?" The Navy already faces a "perennial problem" with "retention and staffing into hard sea trades," making it difficult for it to maintain its *existing* competencies.[87] Given that the CCG already has the resident expertise in ice navigation, and given also that "capturing this knowledge requires years of exposure during all phases of training and operations on a fleet-wide basis, not just with a few chosen individuals," it might be more realistic to consider seconding Coast Guard officers to the Navy.[88] This raises its own set of problems, given acute personnel and training pressures in the CCG. Whatever the solution, the situation would be far worse had the government forced icebreakers onto the Navy.

Nanisivik Docking and Refuelling Facility

In August 2007, the federal government announced that it would build a deep-water Arctic docking and refuelling facility at Nanisivik on Baffin Island. Although some commentators expressed frustration at this choice, asserting that this was hardly the sort of deep-water port promised in the Conservative election platform and that a port in Iqaluit would have more civilian application,[89] the Nanisivik site has several operational advantages. First, it is near Lancaster Sound, an advantageous location to support Navy and other government department vessels operating in eastern Arctic waters and the NWP: a ship fuelling at Nanisivik is just a few hours away from the entrance to the passage, while Iqaluit is more than 1000 km to the south. Second, there is an existing port at Nanisivik "owned" by the federal government with basic ship-berthing infrastructure and fuel storage, which can be refurbished relatively quickly and cost-effectively. As a staging area for naval vessels, the Nanisivik site will allow the Navy to resupply, refuel, embark equipment and supplies, and transfer personnel throughout the navigation season.[90]

While the main purpose of the Nanisivik Naval Facility (NNF) will be military, it will also have important civilian applications, particularly for the Coast Guard. Questions remain regarding what infrastructure will be required to support future Canadian activities in the region. Should Nanisivik be treated as a limited docking/berthing and refuelling site, or should air force facilities be located nearby so that it can support Globemaster operations?[91] What about co-locating the government's promised Arctic research facility at Nanisivik? The federal government must provide more clarity on its logistic needs across the board before the DND completes its plans for the NNF in 2010.

Military Exercises and the Construction of a Canadian Forces Arctic Training Centre in Resolute

Although CF "boots on the ground" do not perfect Canada's sovereignty claim, land forces are important assets in the event of emergencies. Floods, ice storms, and blackouts in southern Canada have borne out their relevance. Without experience operating in Arctic environments, their ability to support this part of the country is weak.

The Canadian Forces' *Arctic Capabilities Study* noted that by the mid-1970s, the land forces "had developed a capability to operate in the Arctic that was second to no other first world nation." Unfortunately, Canada's land force capabilities in the North were allowed to atrophy during the 1990s, and the CF would have been "hard pressed to conduct operations in the Arctic" by the dawn of the new millennium.[92] Military exercises initiated under the Liberals and expanded under the Conservatives have allowed land force personnel to regain some experience in the Far North, and the commitment to build an Arctic training centre at Resolute is an appropriate step toward restoring operational effectiveness for probable future missions, which include surveillance and reconnaissance, patrolling, search and rescue, aid to the civil power, and emergency response.[93] The ability to house one hundred personnel in the Arctic the year round makes much more sense than building a large Arctic base or stationing a battalion full-time at Goose Bay. Regular Force personnel can deliver a more comprehensive training program for the Canadian Rangers and southern-based units, and this multi-purpose training and staging facility for operations will help support other government departments that have lead responsibilities for enforcement.

Enhanced Surveillance and Data-Gathering Capabilities

Monitoring foreign and domestic activities in northern waters is not just about observation: it involves locating, tracking, and inspecting vessels to confirm that they comply with Canadian laws and regulations. To this end, Canada should continue to develop an integrated military air/subsurface/surface intelligence, surveillance, and reconnaissance (ISR) network.[94] Project Polar Epsilon will be fully implemented in 2011, using Radarsat-2 satellite data to facilitate the tracking of large surface vessels.[95] The November 2008 announcement that McDonald Dettweiler and Associates have secured a sixteen-month contract to complete the preliminary design of the Radarsat Constellation Mission—a fleet of three satellites (successors to Radarsat-2) to be launched between 2014 and 2016—is a sign of the government's long-term commitment to maritime surveillance, disaster management, and ecosystem monitoring.[96] Defence Research and Development Canada (DRDC) has initiated the Northern Watch technology program, a series of trials to develop and integrate surface and underwater sensors that could collect surveillance data at navigation choke points.[97] Although unmanned aerial vehicles (UAVs) are currently limited to Low Arctic regions, the CF's director of space is exploring the possibilities for a comprehensive Arctic UAV surveillance system, and the 2004 Arctic Littoral Intelligence, Surveillance, and Reconnaissance Experiment demonstrated a command, control, communications, computers, intelligence,

FIGURE 3-5 CC-177 Globemaster at Alert, Nunavut, on Operation Nunalivut, 2010.
Source: DND

surveillance, and reconnaissance (C4ISR) capability in a domestic emergency scenario on southern Baffin Island.[98]

These new technologies must be coordinated with naval and air force assets. Although several countries have incorporated air-independent propulsion (AIP) technology into their submarines to allow under-ice operations, the CF has decided not to retrofit Canada's fleet with this technology. For the long term, the CF should consider incorporating AIP technology in whatever replaces the Victoria Class submarines. In the meantime, Canada might seek a formal Canada–US operations agreement to allow Canadian liaison and exchange personnel to augment US Navy submarine patrols in the Arctic.[99] If Canada does not already have an Arctic maritime information-sharing agreement in place with the United States—which would be top secret so as not to prejudice either country's legal position on the status of the NWP—it should seek one. This is consistent with the "agree to disagree" strategy discussed later. Furthermore, the new facility at Nanisivik is important to sustain naval and coast guard operations in Arctic waters, but it is not sufficient in itself. Although the Harper government has "postponed" the acquisition of new replenishment vessels (joint support ships) for the Navy because the bids were too high, it must procure these replacements soon. These ships should be double-hulled so that they can operate in Arctic waters and modestly extend the range of the forthcoming Arctic patrol vessels.[100]

Canada's air force also plays an essential role in confirming suspicious activities in the North. The fleet of eighteen Aurora (CP-140) maritime patrol aircraft, originally designed for anti-submarine warfare, are capable of self-sufficient northern deployment.[101] LCol Paul Dittmann provides a useful overview of medium-term requirements and options for long-range patrol and transport aircraft. He holds that the Aurora modernization program will carry ten airframes to 2020 and that "the introduction to service of five Globemaster transports and 17 modern Hercules transports will greatly improve strategic airlift into the Arctic and response to both national and regional emergencies." Accordingly, he recommends that the CF consider lengthening the runways at its four Arctic forward operating locations and at the Nanisivik facility to support Globemaster operations. The Cyclone helicopter, the replacement for the Sea King, is planned to enter service in 2012, and its medium-icing capability will allow it to operate in harsher conditions than its predecessor. Planners should incorporate this capability into designs for the AOPSs and new Coast Guard icebreakers.[102] New fixed-wing SAR aircraft must also be a high priority. Although the CF might explore the option of permanently basing SAR aircraft north of 60°, the probable number of incidents in the region based on past trends and anticipated traffic indicates that, for the foreseeable future, assets can be based in the south for reasons of economy.[103]

An Integrated, Whole-of-Government Approach

Overall, the government's commitments to invest in more military capabilities for the North are reasonable and proportionate to probable short- and medium-term threats. Canadians will be well served if the government delivers on the Arctic-oriented promises that it has already made. But investing additional resources in defence capabilities will not achieve greater security unless those resources are embedded in a "whole of government" strategy that situates the Canadian Forces' responsibilities in the appropriate context. Despite political and media intimations, the CF is not the lead agency in most domestic incidents and does not have a standing mandate to enforce Canadian laws. It is mandated to play a supporting role to other departments and agencies, even in scenarios such as terrorist incidents, where the RCMP or Public Safety and Emergency Preparedness Canada are the lead; escorting nuclear-powered vessels, where the RCMP has the lead; and conducting fisheries patrols and boardings, where the Department of Fisheries and Oceans (DFO) has the lead.[104]

Several federal departments and agencies have functional responsibilities for security and emergency preparedness in the Arctic, so it is important to fuse intelligence into a common governmental operating picture to ensure coordinated, timely, and effective responses. Transport Canada oversees the marine pollution prevention, preparedness, and response regime. Its Marine Security Branch administers the Marine Transportation Security Regulations, which require that all ships in Canadian waters meet a variety of reporting requirements and develop shipboard security plans.[105] When a marine pollution incident occurs north of 60°, the Canadian Coast Guard is the lead federal agency. Furthermore, although the Minister of National Defence is responsible for Canada's National SAR Program, the Coast Guard is responsible for the marine component and manages Joint Rescue Coordination Centres with DND to respond to SAR incidents.[106] The CF may be called upon to support activities such as protecting our environment and fisheries, and countering organized crime, illegal immigration, and drug trafficking, but its role is secondary.

Operation Nanook, held at Iqaluit in August 2008, tested what capabilities various federal, territorial, and municipal government stakeholders could bring to three emergency scenarios: an outbreak of a communicable disease on a cruise ship, including a quarantine and a hostage situation; a fuel spill; and a Russian vessel with a fire on board and a number of casualties. The "Team North" approach reflected in the exercises highlights the need to further develop and synchronize situational awareness. The government should continue to undertake annual Operation Nanook–type operations and eventually expand them to the winter season as well as create more complex scenarios. While press releases emphasize that these operations are important assertions of "sovereignty," they are more important as opportunities for government departments and agencies to critically analyze their policies and procedures and to refine their relationships so that they can better respond to emergencies. Exercising scenarios at the operational and strategic levels to clarify mandates and improve coordination will bolster Canadian preparedness and confidence.

Expectation management will be key. The Standing Senate Committee on National Security and Defence observes that current levels of interjurisdictional collaboration and cooperation in strategic emergency planning and management are inadequate across the country.[107] Canadians demand that the government do everything possible to keep the Arctic pristine, but the vulnerability of ecosystems, coupled with the low population and infrastructure density, makes emergency response management particularly difficult in this region.[108] Canada must establish an effective "Arctic Action Plan" with an emergency response framework and a disaster mitigation strategy covering contingencies such as a major air disaster in the High Arctic, a massive oil spill in Canada's internal waters, or an infectious disease outbreak. Government

Figure 3-6   Prime Minister Stephen Harper, Minister of National Defence Peter Mackay, and Commander Alex Grant, Commanding Officer of HMCS *Toronto*, view HMCS *Corner Brook* and CCGS *Pierre Radisson* as three CF-18 Hornets fly overhead during Operation Nanook 09 in Frobisher Bay, Baffin Island.
Source: DND

messages must resist creating a sense of alarmism (the possibility of a major oil spill, for example, is remote at present) and be realistic about what is feasible to achieve so that federal departments and agencies are not set up to fail.

To better coordinate efforts between security stakeholders and partners, security information must be analyzed and shared—as far as is legally permissible—among mandated federal, territorial/provincial, and municipal departments and agencies. This sharing also pertains to the maritime domain:

> There is no single agency that keeps up-to-date with vessel movements in Canada's Arctic waters, or is necessarily aware of all of the planned entries into those waters. This frustrates effective border clearance and on-going monitoring. It also injects a degree of uncertainty into the every-day-business of the involved officials and is an obstacle to effective risk assessment. In addition, geography, multiple entry points and the prevailing water depths leads to a somewhat unstructured approach to inward clearance, with formal ports of entry giving way to an as-needed approach with multi-functional border teams travelling as necessary to conduct inspections.[109]

Figure 3-7 Brigadier-General David Millar, the commander of Joint Task Force (North), and Kellie Mitchell, the Arctic regional officer with Public Safety Canada, co-chair a meeting of the Arctic Security Working Group in Yellowknife, 2009.
Source: DND

Although threats of terrorist and organized criminal activity in (or emanating from) the Arctic are easily overblown as national security priorities, Canada must have a modest capacity in place to prevent illegal immigration and trafficking in persons, with due consideration to distance and resource constraints. Stronger relationships for maintaining security and emergency preparedness are being built through the Arctic Security Working Group (ASWIG) and the Assistant Deputy Ministers' Committee on the Arctic, which presumably is working to sort out strategic internal relationships. Cooperation is particularly important in emergency prevention, preparedness, and disaster response—the most *probable* threat scenarios facing the Arctic.

An Arctic Marine Security Operation Centre

Marine domain awareness is integral to Canadian control over its internal waters. The 2004 National Security Policy promised funding to "better track vessels operating in Canadian waters, increase surveillance, protect marine infrastructure, and improve domestic and international coordination."[110] It also funded the creation of Marine Security Operation Centres (MSOCs), which have been tasked with collecting, analyzing, and exchanging information related to maritime security more effectively than has been done in the past. These centres have six core partners—DND, RCMP, CCG, DFO, the Canada Border Services Agency, and Transport Canada—and are expected to eventually integrate provincial and regional law enforcement agencies as well. Permanent coastal MSOCs headed by CF Maritime Command are located at Halifax and Esquimalt, with an interim centre headed by the RCMP in Niagara Region.[111]

The MSOCs still lack an essential continuous information source feed from Canada's Arctic.[112] At present, the two coastal MSOCs simply divide responsibilities at 95° west. The government should explore the possibility of creating an MSOC–Arctic using a phased-in approach. Using the interim Marine and Ports Branch Great Lakes and St. Lawrence Seaway Interim MSOC as a model, an initial team could consist of RCMP, DND, and CCG employees. That team could be based in Halifax and co-located with the East Coast MSOC. This centre could eventually grow to include more stakeholder departments and agencies, as well as a facility established at Iqaluit (co-located with the Marine Communication and Traffic Services Centre) or at Tuktoyaktuk. In the development phases, the interim MSOC–Arctic team would develop a better awareness of the Arctic region, including maritime economic and recreational trends, and increase its capability to discern which anomalies are potential security threats or warrant criminal investigation. The MSOC–Arctic would then advise the appropriate department, agency, or first responder of these activities.

Although MSOCs are national assets, Canada should consult with the United States and Denmark/Greenland to seek collaborative participation in the MSOC–Arctic. There will be limits to what information can be legally shared with our circumpolar neighbours; that said, an information sharing agreement would benefit all stakeholders and reinforce that all of the Arctic littoral states have vested interests in the security and cargo of ships.

The Canadian Coast Guard

The civilian Coast Guard, a special operating agency within the DFO, is Canada's icebreaking service and is the most visible federal marine presence in the Arctic. Although it does not have an enforcement mandate, its vessels conduct security surveillance and carry customs, immigration, RCMP, fisheries, and transport officers on possible interdiction missions.[113] Michael Turner, former Deputy Commissioner of the CCG, explained in a 2007 article:

> Sovereignty is based on the 80/20 rule. While the military's ability to deter an aggressor nation from claiming your territory or waters seems to be what this

government has focused on, that's only 20 per cent of the 'sovereignty solution.' The other 80 per cent is the ability to demonstrate the effective management and administration of your territories and the waters over which we claim jurisdiction.

Most international law experts agree that this is best done by a civilian agency or police force, rather than by a nation's military, because the use of the military option to enforce domestic law or policy is seen as heavy handed, and leaves little room for escalation of response should the "offender" decline to comply.[114]

Turner outlined convincing reasons for investing in the CCG's icebreaking capabilities rather than those of the Navy. First, it would cost two to three times as much to build, operate, and maintain an armed icebreaking warship compared to a Coast Guard vessel of similar operational capability. It would be wasteful if that vessel was used to manage and administer civilian programs such as a controlling tourist ships, enforcing laws, and surveying the seabed. Second, it takes years of practical experience to become a dependable ice navigator or icebreaker commander. The Navy rotates officers every two to three years, which results in inevitable skill fade and retraining over time; by contrast, Coast Guard officers and crews can devote their careers to developing these particular skills. In short, the government was wise not to impose

Figure 3-8 CCGS *Henry Larsen* in Strathcona Sound during Operation Nanook 10.
Source: DND

an icebreaking mission on the Navy, and instead to leave it with the Coast Guard.[115]

Human resources pose serious problems for the Coast Guard. More than 70 percent of CCG employees are between forty and fifty-nine years old, with an average age of forty-five; more than one-quarter of CCG personnel are scheduled to retire in the next five to seven years. More resources are needed for recruitment (applications to the Coast Guard college have been declining sharply in recent years, and there is domestic and worldwide competition for well-trained mariners), as well as for training and promotion.[116] The Standing Senate Committee on Fisheries and Oceans (SSCFO) also recommends that the Coast Guard recruit Inuit wherever possible, given their unique knowledge of the Arctic region.[117] Due to the Government of Nunavut's recruiting problems, as well as continuing education gaps between Inuit and southern Canadians, expectations for attracting and training Inuit for full-time careers must be modest. Concurrently, the role of the Coast Guard Auxiliary—a volunteer organization that provides year-round SAR service in remote areas—should be expanded in northern communities. Through an expanded auxiliary program, Inuit might be trained in oil spill containment and decontamination.[118] The CCG might also consider creating a Junior Coast Guard program, based on the model of the successful Junior Canadian Rangers, in partnership with community leaders. This program would help generate interest in the organization and in maritime affairs more generally, and provide useful training and activities for youth.

To remain effective, the Coast Guard desperately needs a feasible recapitalization plan. The government's 2008 budget pledge of $720 million to procure a heavy icebreaker to replace the aging CCG *Louis St. Laurent*, built in 1968, by 2017 is a step in the right direction. But it is not enough. The rest of the fleet is also aging, as well as costly to maintain and operate, and the "current replacement schedule is already becoming outdated and unrealistic," the Auditor General reported in 2007.[119] "For example, the estimated useful life of an icebreaker is 30 years, but, as currently scheduled, they will be between 40 and 48 years when they are replaced." As a result, the Coast Guard has had to scale back or cancel services and activities because of equipment failures, unplanned maintenance, and other problems exacerbated by an unrealistic "can do" philosophy.[120] According to Dr. Louis Fortier, the scientific director of ArcticNet, all of the CCG icebreakers are in the last quarter of their expected lifespan, and Canada has "virtually no capacity for rapid, efficient intervention in case of an accident or extreme ice conditions." The government should act on his recommendation that immediate plans be made for two Polar Class icebreakers and four medium icebreakers.[121] Concurrently, for the necessary expansion to take place, the Coast Guard needs to develop better mechanisms for prioritizing its needs, predicting its costs, and devising an updated and realistic fleet renewal plan.[122]

The new icebreakers must be designed as multi-mission, "all of government" support platforms.[123] The Coast Guard provides at-sea support to other government departments and agencies (including logistical and platform support to the RCMP and the CF), breaks ice for commercial vessels, delivers supplies to remote settlements and defence establishments, and provides considerable support for scientific research.[124] Accordingly, the new ships should be designed in consultation with other government departments and agencies. For example, given that the CF will not have heavy icebreaking capabilities, future Coast Guard icebreakers should be designed to accommodate the CF Cyclone helicopter.[125] They should also be designed to transport the RCMP's smaller interceptor boats.[126] Note that maintenance and refuelling facilities at Nanisivik will be suitable to better support these deployed vessels.

As the Coast Guard fleet's role in supporting maritime security evolves, questions will continue to arise about the CCG's mandate and its status as an agency of DFO. If the federal government decides to expand the mandate of the Coast Guard to include coastal security, the Privy Council Office should consider making it either a stand-alone agency or a separate operating agency within Public Safety and Emergency Preparedness Canada.[127] The SSCFO reasoned in 2004 that, since the CCG is responsible for detecting illegal incidents at sea, it should have the mandate to intervene on behalf of other agencies, including (where appropriate) the DFO, Environment Canada, the Department of Justice, Transport Canada, the Canada Border Services Agency, the Canada Revenue Agency, and Citizenship and Immigration Canada. It also suggested that the Coast Guard should arm its officers with light arms and possibly its vessels with weapons, as an example citing Iceland (where a civilian agency reports to the country's Minister of Justice, with three cutters each armed with a 40 mm cannon).[128] The Coast Guard offers maritime security training for joint work with the RCMP in the Great Lakes / St. Lawrence Seaway, such as Marine Security Enforcement Team training, which includes enhanced police defensive tactics and law enforcement familiarization.[129] This should be extended to the Arctic region.

Making NORDREG Mandatory

Canada maintains that the NWP is open to navigation by international and domestic shipping as long as conditions relating to security, the environment, and Inuit interests are satisfied. Shipping is essential to socio-economic development in this region, where resource extraction and community resupply depend overwhelmingly on maritime access. The threats that increased shipping pose to sovereignty, security, safety, and the environment must be balanced with the ideals of sustainable development: "development that substantially meets the aggregate needs and goals of federal Canada, the involved provinces and territories, northern communities and their constituent population groups."[130]

In August 2008 the Harper government announced its intention to make the Arctic marine traffic system (NORDREG) mandatory and to extend its reporting zone from 100 to 200 nautical miles (nm) (the revised extent of the Arctic Waters Pollution Prevention Act, Canada's primary regulatory vehicle in this context). Although the original 100 nm limit encompasses nearly all Arctic shipping, this proactive and benign expansion to 200 nm conforms with Article 234 of UNCLOS. Making NORDREG compulsory is a much bolder and more provocative move. Through to 2009, NORDREG remained a voluntary system—mariners were encouraged to report their location, planned route, and compliance with the Arctic Waters Pollution Prevention Act in exchange for Canadian services such as ice information, ice routing, icebreaker assistance, and SAR.[131] The Marine Communication Traffic Services Centre in Iqaluit claims that approximately 99 percent of vessels in Arctic waters already report to NORDREG. Yet under the voluntary regime, Canada does not have the right to deny entry to single-hulled vessels until 2015, at which time, according to the IMO, double-hulled tankers will be mandatory in ice-covered waters.[132] Two cases of non-reporting in 2007 and 2008 likely account for the perceived need for urgent action and the near unanimous support for making NORDREG mandatory.[133]

Despite the almost certain protests this action will generate from countries that dispute Canada's internal waters claim to the passage, few commentators seem to be weighing the consequences for Canada's legal claim of making NORDREG mandatory. If this unilateral action draws formal letters of protest from countries that contest Canada's internal waters claim (which it has not yet done, given that Canada has only expressed its *intent* to make NORDREG mandatory), then it may actually have a deleterious effect on Canada's position. The fewer letters of protest on file, the more strongly Canada can assert foreign acquiescence to its claims. The other option is to convince other countries that this action is in their best interests and encourage them to implement similar systems. This is unlikely to work, however. The SSCFO recommends encouraging the United States to implement its own mandatory notification system so that it will not be in "a position to object if NORDREG were made mandatory";[134] however, there is no challenge to US sovereignty over waters off Alaska. This devalues this option as a bargaining chip in bilateral negotiations.

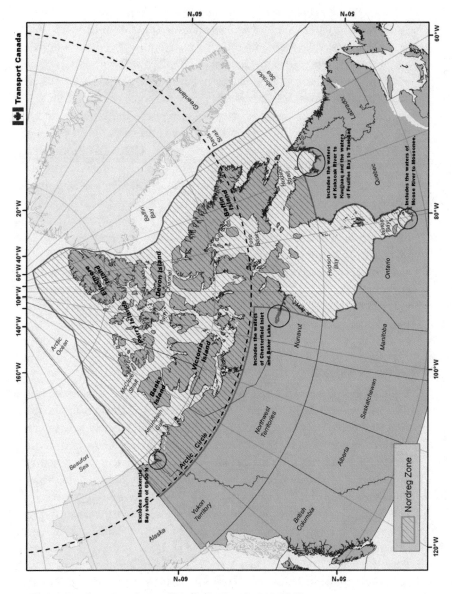

Map 3-3 Northern Canada Vessel Traffic Services (NORDREG) zone.
Source: Transport Canada

Canada could continue to upgrade its surveillance capabilities without declaring NORDREG mandatory. For example, ships are already required to be fitted with the automatic identification system (AIS), an IMO initiative. Joseph Spears, Principal of the Horseshoe Bay Marine Group, suggests linking the AIS to Radarsat-2 as a way "to go beyond NORDREG."[135] If this were done, Canada could still identify vessels that opted not to report and could "pay them a visit," as it has done in the past.[136] Furthermore, the SSCNSD notes that the Pre-Arrival Information Report (PAIR) requires a "96-hour pre-arrival vessel report that is screened by TC security experts." The PAIR is more than "just notice": Transport Canada can deny entry for non-compliance.[137] Finally, Transport Canada already has the authority under the Canada Shipping Act to ban a vessel if intelligence suggests that it does not comply with international conventions.[138] In short, Canada could choose to work with international organizations (such as the IMO) to toughen international conventions rather than take provocative actions that seem to undermine the "agree to disagree" arrangement we have in place with the Americans. (The announcement by Gail Shea, the Minister of Fisheries and Oceans, that NORDREG is mandatory effective 1 July 2010—meaning that all foreign and domestic vessels of a certain size have to report to the Canadian Coast Guard if travelling through Canada's Arctic waters—has rendered these considerations moot.)[139]

Follow-through

If the federal government breaks with the trend of previous governments by delivering on its existing military commitments and integrating them in a coherent whole-of-government strategy, then Canada should have the capabilities necessary to deal with the most probable threats to northern security. Strategic investments in Arctic-capable naval replenishment ships, fixed-wing aircraft, and Canadian Coast Guard vessels will round out an inventory of functional assets capable of asserting control and responding to emergencies. Although a stronger federal government presence in the Arctic will not strengthen our legal sovereignty case, it may reduce Canadians' insecurity about the country's lack of northern preparedness. Removing this psychological barrier will allow us to continue to work with our circumpolar neighbours in a cooperative manner. Emergency preparedness is the most pressing security issue in the circumpolar world. Canada must prioritize and clarify its domestic situation before we can develop and invest in niche capabilities that will allow us to better position ourselves within a collaborative international framework.

Since 1957, Canada and the United States have jointly monitored northern North American airspace through the North American Aerospace Defence

Figure 3-9 HMCS *Montreal*, USS *Porter*, and HDMS *Vaedderen* sail in formation on the Labrador Sea during Operation Nanook, 2010.
Source: DND

Command (NORAD). In May 2006, this agreement was expanded to incorporate a maritime warning mission, reflecting the heightened American emphasis on maritime security and on continental security more generally.[140] Through constructive diplomacy, Canada should explore creating a "Combined Arctic Command" to coordinate Canada's Joint Task Force North with US Northern Command surveillance and response efforts in the Arctic. This initiative could include a Canadian–US joint operational planning group, which would include representatives of the Canadian and US navies and coast guards located at Colorado Springs, with access to NORAD planning staff.[141] A more efficient command and control structure would allow us to work with our allies to deal with emergencies in the Arctic in a more timely and effective manner than Canada could hope to accomplish alone.[142] This would also be compatible with the "agree to disagree" framework that I lay out in the following section. Instead of emphasizing the perceived "sovereignty loss" inherent in coordinating efforts, Canadians should acknowledge that our politicians, civil servants, and senior officers have historically succeeded in finding bilateral and multilateral solutions to sovereignty and security dilemmas that protect and project Canada's national interests.

Diplomacy

> The world needs positive regional examples of how peaceful and stable international relations can be constructed and pursued.
>
> —*Inuit Tapiriit Kanatami,* Integrated Arctic Strategy *(January 2008)*

Canada's sovereignty over the Arctic lands and waters is more secure than the recent alarmist discourse would suggest. Canadian scholars and media commentators have, for years, been building the legal case for foreign countries or multinational corporations that might want to challenge our control over the NWP. They have done so with admirable intentions, trying to kick-start Canada into action, but the implications are unfortunate.

Canadians have become convinced that our sovereignty is on "thinning ice." This provides senior decision makers, based in southern Canada and possessing a distinctly southern world view, with a convenient pretext to devise "stand up for Canada" strategies that play to a southern audience. Diplomacy and dialogue are marginalized, and a positive short-term *outcome*—defined as strong political optics with the aura of decisive action—becomes more important than *process.* This has unfortunate implications for Northerners who once again face the prospect of having their voices needlessly and unconscionably relegated to the sidelines.

The circumpolar diplomacy angle has been marginalized in recent years. While this differentiates the Conservative government from its Liberal predecessors, it also goes against popular opinion: the results of a Leger Marketing poll published by the *Toronto Sun* on 23 February 2007 revealed that Canadians want the North protected, with more than half favouring diplomatic and legal tactics but fewer than 20 percent supporting a military buildup.[143] Reports produced by the territorial governments and Aboriginal groups also emphasize the need for constructive engagement through the Arctic Council. If the Canadian government is going to take a leadership role in promoting regional stability and cooperation, it needs to broaden its "Canada First" strategy to emphasize the benefits of bilateral and multilateral partnerships. It is too easy for journalists, trying to generate the next catchy headline, to miss the quiet, constructive, sustained engagement that has benefited Canada and the rest of the circumpolar world. As well, it is easy for politicians, seeking to distance themselves from previous governments, to ignore past successes and healthy relationships so that they can trumpet their own distinct contributions. A solid national northern strategy need not generate sensational headlines, nor need it downplay Canada's positive relationships. Canada has done constructive work in the circumpolar world. It is time for us to do more by reinforcing our strengths, picking the right battles, and cooperating with circumpolar stakeholders.

Rein in the Rhetoric and Alarmism

Sweeping proclamations that "the Arctic" belongs to Canada set the country up to fail. Canada is one Arctic nation among many and needs to accept this reality. Other nations have sovereignty claims that, in some cases, conflict with Canada's.[144] Rather than setting this up as a "polar race" destined to end in a resource feeding frenzy that will ignore international laws and norms, the federal government should make more effort to clarify Canada's actual claims. While sweeping "stand up for Canada" language can be beneficial politically, it sets up unrealistic expectations. All Arctic states, Russia included, are engaged in a legally established process to delimit their extended continental shelves, identifying the seabed areas outside their 200-nautical-mile EEZs where they have the exclusive right to exploit resources.

The alarmist fanfare over Hans Island is the clearest case of how a modest, manageable dispute can become a *cause célèbre*. Denmark and Canada quietly disagreed over ownership of the tiny uninhabited island for more than three decades before political theatre and hyperbolic rhetoric created a "crisis" that some commentators portrayed as the opening salvo in a coming boundary war. Both the Liberals and the Conservatives played a role in converting a relatively minor disagreement into a litmus test of Canadian sovereignty over the North. Danish and Canadian negotiators had prudently "agreed to disagree" over the status of the island in 1974 by discontinuing the continental shelf delimitation line within less than 300 metres to its north and south, as well as agreeing not to issue licences for mineral exploitation near this line without mutual agreement. The Danes, whose claim to the island seems to be based solely on the island's closer proximity to Greenland than to Ellesmere Island, sent naval vessels to the island in 2002 and 2003. Canada responded in 2005 with an inukshuk-raising and flag-planting visit by a small group of Canadian Rangers and other land force personnel, followed by a highly publicized visit by then Minister of National Defence Bill Graham. The media frenzy soon spiralled out of hand, complete with allusions to Canada's 1995 "Turbot War" with the Spanish and even to a domino-theory effect suggesting that if Canada lost Hans Island, its other Arctic islands might meet to a similar fate. Thankfully, cooler heads prevailed; the Canadian and Danish Foreign Ministers met in New York City on 19 September 2005 and agreed to a process for resolving the dispute. Despite Minister of Foreign Affairs Pierre Pettigrew's insistence that the two countries would work "to put this issue behind us,"[145] Hans Island remains a touchstone for the outstanding

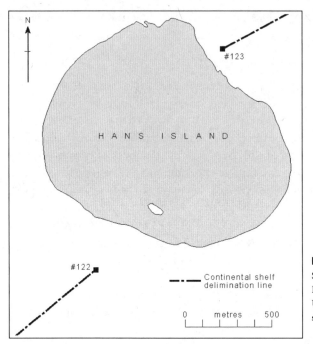

Map 3-4 Hans Island. Source: International Boundaries Research Unit, Durham University, UK

sovereignty issues that Canada faces in the North. Rob Huebert, for instance, continues to draw comparisons between it and the China–Japan dispute over the Senkaku Islands in the East China Sea.[146]

The fixation on the Hans Island dispute conceals the very positive diplomatic relations that we enjoy with Denmark, illustrating the skewed perceptions of Canada's relations with its circumpolar neighbours. Seldom do commentators highlight the working agreement quietly reached by Canadian and Danish diplomats to "agree to disagree" on ownership of the island while both countries prepare their legal claims. Since 2006, Canada has cooperated with Denmark on mapping the continental shelf north of Ellesmere Island and Greenland, as well as parts of the Labrador Sea.[147] Journalists and scholars who have downplayed the positive relationship in lieu of more sensationalist and sinister readings of Danish intentions are irresponsibly charting a collision course that does not—and need not—exist.

In a recent study, Suzanne Lalonde carefully parses the difference between claims related to Arctic waters and those related to marine seabed issues. The two are often conflated in alarmist media and political statements.[148] An editorial in the *Winnipeg Free Press* is a case in point:

At the moment, the Northwest Passage is not good for much except history lessons and romantic fancies. But if global warming is a long-term reality that leads to even partial melting of the Arctic ice, it will become a hot spot as other nations deny not just this country's claim to the passage, but to the islands around it as well.

This is already happening, to a degree. The Danish claim to Hans Island may seem frivolous, but it possibly forebodes other American and European claims to many other larger and more important islands.

If those claims were pressed, Canada might find itself hard-pressed to refute them. This country's claim to sovereignty over the archipelago is considered by rivals to be only tenuously based—some of the islands were actually discovered by Americans, Danes and Norwegians; others were ceded to Canada by Britain before they had been discovered.[149]

The threat of loss, it would seem, is palpable. The scope of this study precludes a detailed examination of the particulars of each case, but it is clear that the current alarmism is misplaced. Grouping together a series of individual—and manageable—challenges makes the alleged "storm" brewing on the horizon seem scarier than it is. There is still room, and still time, for bilateral and multilateral cooperation that will better serve Canada's national and international interests.

Extended Continental Shelf Claims

"Nobody disputes Canada's control over land in the Arctic, where Inuit have lived for countless generations, or over our 200 mile EEZ," Senator Bill Rompkey explained in a 17 July 2008 article in the *Ottawa Citizen*. "As for the seabed beyond the EEZ, claims go through an international process."[150] This is a sound assessment. UNCLOS defines the rights and responsibilities of states in using the oceans and lays out a process for determining maritime boundaries. Littoral countries are therefore mapping the Arctic to determine the extent of their claims. Canada ratified UNCLOS in November 2003 and has until 2013 to submit evidence for its extended continental shelf outside the existing 200 nautical mile EEZ. The 2004 federal budget announced $69 million for seabed surveying and mapping to establish the outer limits of Canada's continental shelves in the Arctic and Atlantic Oceans. In 2007, the government allocated another $20 million to complete the mapping of its shelf to meet the deadline, and DFAIT officials are confident that it will submit its claims on schedule.[151]

But is this scientific research merely a sideshow to the real contest that is emerging? Pessimists point to the Russian submarine expedition that planted a titanium flag on the seabed at the North Pole in August 2007, and to that country's renewed military overflights and its decision to send warships into Arctic waters in July 2008 for the first time in decades, as evidence that it has nefarious intentions.[152] That two Russian military aircraft flew close to Canadian airspace on the eve of President Barack Obama's visit to Canada in February 2009 is a recent example of these overflights. National Defence Minister Peter MacKay stated that two CF-18 fighter jets were scrambled to intercept the Russian aircraft. "I have expressed at various times the deep concern our government has with increasingly aggressive Russian actions around the globe and Russian intrusion into our airspace," Prime Minister Harper stated. "We will defend our airspace." To Russian spokespersons, this tough talk seemed misplaced. Russian news agencies reported that "the statements from Canada's defence ministry are perplexing to say the least and cannot be called anything other than a farce."[153] Following this overflight, Dmitry Trofimov, the head of the Russian Embassy's political section in Ottawa, insisted that there had been no intrusion on Canadian national airspace or sovereignty—"from the point of international law, nothing happened, absolutely nothing." He added that this had been a "minor episode"—a scheduled air patrol flight that, like Canadian military exercises, had been planned months in advance. Supportive of this argument was the notable absence of any American reaction to flights that adhered to international law—and that did not differ from similar NATO practices just beyond Russian airspace.[154] Does this, however, indicate a trend toward Russian militarization designed to bully Canada out of its sovereign rights in the Arctic?

Canada is involved in "muscle flexing," Lloyd Axworthy asserts, "even though this is a contest we cannot win."[155] Fortunately, rights to explore for resources and to control areas "beyond the 200-mile Exclusive Economic Zone are thoroughly scripted," explains David Jones, a former US diplomat. "They will be handled by duelling mapping agencies, seismic studies, and probably, ultimately by jurisprudence, but not by duelling gun boats."[156] In this light, Ron McNab, a former member of the Canadian Polar Commission, notes that "an increased investment in science may be the cheapest, and most effective, immediate means of establishing a sovereign base for our northern lands and seas."[157]

While extended continental shelf claims are usually cast as conflictual, observers are wise to remember that until the science is in, talk of "losing part of Canada"[158] is presumptive, given that we have not even identified our claims, never mind submitted them. Alan Kessel, the legal adviser at DFAIT, emphasizes that the process is unfolding according to the rules and should not be a cause for panic:

This is not a race. Therefore, there is not a beginning and an end—except that when you sign on, you have 10 years to make your submission. Those who signed on earlier make their submission earlier. Since you cannot get more than you are entitled to, whether you do it now or then does not really matter ... I will reiterate; this is not a race. We will all go to the finish line at different paces, but there is no gun starting it and there is no flag ending it.[159]

Accordingly, Canada should anticipate that all five Arctic Ocean littoral states that have the potential for extended continental shelf claims will adhere to the science-based UNCLOS process when determining the geographical extent of their national rights. That adherence was the message these states asserted in the Ilulissat Declaration of May 2008.[160]

The UN Commission on the Limits of the Continental Shelf can only review and issue recommendations based on data submitted by states; negotiations or arbitration relating to overlapping claims will occur outside the UN. Instead of lamenting this reality or setting up the expectation that we must never concede an inch—which sets up our diplomats and politicians for failure—Canada must engage in concerted diplomacy to seek support for our case rather than try to stand alone. This is best done by sharing expertise and data and by looking to areas of mutual interest to "minimize the possibility of disputes and complications" where possible.[161] This cooperation may not play to the unilateralist impulses of some strident nationalists, but it offers the most realistic and constructive means to secure our national interests.

Collaborative data collection by Canada and its closest circumpolar neighbours (countries with whom Canada supposedly has intractable disputes) is beneficial on several levels: it mitigates risks associated with data collection, reduces costs and environmental impacts, diversifies the sources of data, and encourages the joint interpretation of data, which in turn augments the credibility of Canada's case. For example, Canada and Denmark/Greenland both stand to benefit if scientists can prove that the Lomonosov Ridge (a submarine ridge north of Ellesmere Island) is a natural prolongation of the continent. Since 2006, researchers from the two countries have been cooperating in collecting seismic and bathymetric data.[162] In August 2008, these scientists presented findings linking the ridge geologically to North America.[163] That fall, in the Western Arctic, Canadian and American scientists and Coast Guard personnel on the CCG icebreaker *Louis St. Laurent* and the US Coast Guard cutter *Healy* collaborated to map the seabed in the Canada Basin, north of the Beaufort Sea.[164] They conducted another joint mapping project in the area in 2009, providing both countries with valuable scientific data. "You have to, at the very least, lay a factual foundation before we can even begin to contemplate

Figure 3-10 Icebreakers USCG *Healy* and CCGS *Louis S. St. Laurent* work together to conduct research during the five-week-long polar continental-shelf survey expedition in the Canada Basin of the Arctic Ocean in 2010.
Source: UNH-NOAA

how we would go into resolving these overlaps that would occur beyond 200 nautical miles," noted Allison Saunders, Deputy Director of the Continental Shelf Division at Foreign Affairs. Scientists anticipated another two years of joint efforts to complete mapping the seabed[165] and insisted that partnerships were integral to ensure that "Canada has the complete and high quality information needed for a comprehensive and credible submission by the end of 2013."[166]

Boundary Disputes

Canada faces several unresolved bilateral boundary disputes. These disputes must be placed in context so that they are not blown out of proportion, as has all too often been the case.

There is no great urgency to settle the issue of Hans Island, or the one over Greenland's drawing of straight baselines, which has resulted in two tiny disputed zones (31 nm² and 34 nm²) in the Lincoln Sea.[167] Canada is well advised to manage these disputes by avoiding provocation—an avoidance it displayed, for example, in the summer of 2008, when the Danes allegedly visited the island. Canada decided not to send an Aurora aircraft to fly over them; instead, it diplomatically disputed Danish actions that could prejudice Canada's claim

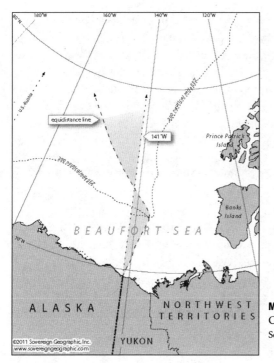

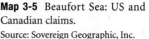

Map 3-5 Beaufort Sea: US and Canadian claims.

Source: Sovereign Geographic, Inc.

and went about quietly preparing its legal case in the event that Denmark pressed for a resolution.

The Beaufort Sea question with the United States, which involves off-shore hydrocarbon reserves, is more significant. Although the land boundary between Alaska and Yukon is fixed by the 141°W meridian, the maritime boundary is disputed. Canada claims an extension of the land boundary into the sea based on its interpretation of the 1825 Convention between Great Britain and Russia, which sold Alaska to the United States in 1867, while the Americans base their claim on a lateral boundary line equidistant from the low-water line of each country's coast. Because the coast trends in a southeasterly direction, this creates a 6250 nm² disputed zone.[168]

Once again, Canada should anticipate a negotiated solution based upon established rules of international law. Although Canada has little reason to force this issue at present, the United States might decide to push for clarity. Energy security is an American priority, and the Obama–Biden "New Energy for America" strategy is proposing a "use it or lose it" approach, which would require companies to "diligently develop" existing oil and gas leases or turn them over to another company for development.[169] Although statements made during the American election campaign indicate that Canada is considered part of a secure "domestic" supply, it is unlikely that development in the Beaufort will be kept in perpetual abeyance. Liberal MP Larry Bagnell's warning that "the present government's inaction could lose ... the Beaufort Sea" is unfounded; that said, Canada is well advised to prepare its legal case if it has not already done so. Rather than seeking a confrontation, however, it eventually should seek a negotiated, bilateral solution with its western Arctic neighbour, long-standing ally, and largest trading partner.[170] If Canada and the United States work toward a comprehensive bilateral energy plan, pursuant to the "Clean Energy Dialogue" announced during President Obama's visit to Ottawa in February 2008, the resources of the Beaufort Sea might be included.[171]

American political scientist Scott Borgerson recommends that Canada lay all Arctic issues on the table, including the NWP and Beaufort boundary, to achieve a "grand compromise" with the United States.[172] This may not be in Canada's interests, however, unless this "grand compromise" is a comprehensive bilateral package that includes non-Arctic variables such as the tar sands. Otherwise, it may be in Canada's continued interests to manage its bilateral Arctic disputes on a case-by-case basis. Regarding the Beaufort boundary, this may mean exploring alternative approaches to managing the resources and the larger ecosystem in partnership with the Americans. Although Canada's position in this boundary dispute is complicated by the Inuvialuit Final Agreement, which also uses the 141st meridian as its western maritime boundary, Canada has to accept that an "all or nothing" approach to maritime boundary delimitation negotiations is unrealistic. Trying to settle the boundary will likely involve concessions on the Canadian side, unless our position is leveraged by external issues. Instead, the government should explore the potential of treating the disputed area as a joint development zone, without prejudice to its claim; this would allow exploration and exploitation to occur and generate a deeper knowledge of the area.[173] This "agree to disagree" approach would be consistent with Canada's other strategic interests in the Arctic.

The Northwest Passage: Managing the Relationship with Our Closest Ally

The notion that countries do not have friends, only interests, sets up a false dichotomy. You can be friends and have different interests without discarding the friendship over relatively minor points of disagreement. This is the case with Canada and the United States.

In the days immediately following Stephen Harper's election as prime minister in January 2006, the spirit of goodwill and sense of common ground seemed nowhere to be found. After the US Ambassador David

Wilkins reiterated America's long-standing rejection of Canada's position that the NWP as internal waters (in response to a student question at the University of Western Ontario), Harper threw down the gauntlet: "The United States defends its sovereignty. The Canadian government will defend our sovereignty ... It is the Canadian people we get our mandate from, not the ambassador of the United States." This made for good political theatre, allowing him at once to show his nationalist resolve and to distance his government from the unpopular Bush administration. As Wilkins told reporters, however, the American position was "old news" and there was "no reason to create a problem that doesn't exist."[174]

Notwithstanding the apparent distance between the American and Canadian positions on the Arctic, the two countries' Arctic agendas have converged more than diverged. Since 2006, Canada has migrated from a broader set of circumpolar priorities toward the more "narrow and hierarchical view" held by the United States, with paramount emphasis on homeland security and defence, followed by the resource potential of the region.[175] Although the two countries have different perspectives on specific boundary and transit rights questions, they also have much in common.

No one disputes that the NWP, which runs from the Davis Strait to the western Beaufort, is "Canadian" insofar as no foreign country claims that it has stronger rights to the airspace, waters, or seabed than Canada. The sovereignty issue in this case is not about rival "ownership" in the sense of possession. Rather, the issue relates to how much power Canada has over these waters and the air corridor overhead—in short, the debate is over just how "Canadian" they are and what this means in practice. A simplistic analogy might be drawn to a public pathway crossing through a person's backyard. Does ownership of the ground imply that the owner has the right to prevent people from passing through for any reason, even if she has stated repeatedly that she encourages other people to use the route? Or does everyone have a right to pass through her property directly, continuously, and expeditiously, without wandering off the path onto the adjacent property, as long as they adhere to commonly agreed upon conditions and controls?

Canada's position is that the NWP is part of Canada's internal waters; thus, we enjoy full sovereignty and the right to regulate and control foreign navigation. In short, foreign ships have no right of transit passage. Although Canada welcomes domestic and foreign shipping in its waters, it retains the legal right to control entry to, and the activities conducted in, its internal waters as if these were land territory. The United States holds the view that an international strait runs through these Canadian waters and, therefore, commercial and naval vessels have the right of transit passage. Accordingly, the

Americans feel that Canada does not have the right to pass and enforce its own laws and regulations and that it is limited to the enforcement of international safety and maritime standards. The Americans insist that if they acquiesced to Canada's position that the NWP constitutes internal waters, then archipelagic states could use this as a precedent to restrict US naval mobility in other parts of the world.[176]

Captain Thomas Pullen, the retired Royal Canadian Navy officer who had sailed on the *Manhattan*, offered a sober reflection on the situation in September 1987:

> If push comes to shove, which is more important—Canadian Arctic sovereignty or U.S. security? When one shares a continent with a superpower, these are the facts of life; the issues of sovereignty and security are inseparable. To be squeezed between two superpowers is a costly and frustrating business. Canada should negotiate with its southern neighbour to find a mutually palatable solution to the issues of Arctic sovereignty and North American security. Surely it should be possible for the United States and Canada—friends, neighbors, and allies—to come to some agreement.[177]

In 1988, a non-prejudicial, practical arrangement on icebreaker transits—necessary to overcome a long-standing legal impasse—proved that diplomacy could trump the politics of embarrassment of the sort that so often play out in the Canadian press.[178] "The 1988 agreement represents a pause rather than an end to the Northwest Passage dispute as military, economic, and environmental pressures increase in the entire region," American political scientist Philip Briggs concluded in his study of the *Polar Sea* affair. "Continued creative diplomacy and joint efforts will be necessary to avoid future problems … However, diplomacy based upon mutual respect for each state's national interests and the growing interdependence between the two countries may yet yield a more complete solution to the Northwest Passage dispute."[179]

A more complete solution will have to acknowledge that the Americans have strategic interests in the region, and that so do we. "It's our view that the Northwest Passage is for international access and unfettered access needs to be maintained," James Steel, a US Embassy counsellor in Ottawa, said at a Montreal conference on Arctic shipping in late October 2008.[180] Any solution must recognize that, insofar as Canadians are desirous of having the United States recognize Canada's internal waters claim to the NWP, they are not going to do so. "As long as there is a United States Navy," former American diplomat David Jones insisted, "U.S. government policy will insist on maintaining international waterways as international."[181] Some Canadian commentators suggest that if Canada can demonstrate it has the rules, regulations, and capabilities to better control activities and thus increase continental security in the passage, then the United States will not contest Canada's claims and may even support them.[182] But former US Ambassador to Canada Paul Cellucci's personal opinion that the United States should recognize Canada's full sovereignty over the NWP as Canadian internal waters[183] should not be mistaken for official US policy. Simply put, the Americans will act pragmatically to ensure that their international interests are maintained, and they see global maritime mobility as integral to their economic and national security. Canada might be an accommodating ally in the Arctic, but there is no guarantee that Iran would not use the NWP case as a pretext for asserting unilateral control over the Straits of Hormuz, or Indonesia over the Malacca Strait.[184] For Canada, the NWP—as a part of Canada itself—is a special case that warrants unique attention. The United States sees the NWP in global terms and believes that it must defend its position accordingly.

Canada has various options. The status quo, "agreeing to disagree" with the Americans on the status of the NWP, with limited Canadian capabilities to respond to a challenge or an emergency, may be reasonable for the short-term, given the very modest tempo of foreign activity in the region.[185] This position, however, will put Canada at a disadvantage if the passage opens to commercial shipping and Canada cannot assert adequate control. Steps must be taken to defend against contingencies, but these should be geared toward probable threats, not all *possible* threats. It is not worth picking a fight with the United States that involves fundamental legal principles when the threat scenarios are based solely upon potentialities. Canada is wise not to provoke a crisis and jeopardize its legal claims when, as Franklyn Griffiths argues, "we are secure in the benefits of de facto control of the Northwest Passage."[186]

Canada can confidently assert that the waters of the Arctic Archipelago constitute internal waters on the basis of straight baselines, historic and continuous use by the Inuit, and vital interests related to the marine environment, the Inuit, and national security.[187] Pushing for international clarity on the legal status of the NWP, however, may place Canada in a "lose–lose" situation. First, taking the issue to court runs the risk of an unfavourable judgment. Legal scholar Donald McRae concludes that if it was determined either that the passage was not internal waters or that it constituted an international strait, this would be perceived as a major sovereignty loss (although neither scenario would seriously undermine Canada's legal authority to regulate commercial shipping).[188] On the other hand, if Canada secures international recognition that these are internal waters, this could set a precedent in other parts of the world. Our strategic mobility, and that of our allies, could be constrained as a result, with negative impacts on commerce as well as on our ability to project naval power abroad. In short, pushing too hard for American acquiescence on the NWP issue could actually work *against* Canada's grand strategic interests. If the United States is not anxious to push the point,[189] we should not provoke a battle in which we are likely to lose—either locally or globally.

Rob Huebert, who previously argued that the dispute over the NWP was essentially a sovereignty issue, has recently clarified that the heart of the matter is about control. "Canada can afford to lose the right to refer to the Northwest Passage as internal waters," he notes in his latest study, "but it cannot afford to lose control over the regulation of the ships that sail on it."[190] In this vein, Canada has practical reasons for linking with the United States on matters of regulation and control. If we fail to negotiate and work with the Americans, this may lead other countries' naval and air forces to use the route with impunity, which—as Griffiths has ably laid out[191]—is in neither country's strategic interests. Griffiths makes a convincing case that "agreeing to disagree" with the Americans on the legal status of the passage remains a viable strategy. "The Northwest Passage will see an increase in commercial shipping," he predicts, "but it will move in and out of sites in Arctic North America and not between the Atlantic and Pacific in volume any time soon." In his view, we can and should cooperate with the United States to constrain hostile states' access to Canadian Arctic waters, maintaining our legal position that they are internal waters while choosing "to govern the Northwest Passage *as though* it were an international strait."[192] This is eminently sensible, and best serves the interests of both countries.

John Noble, a Canadian diplomat assigned to the US Relations Branch, concluded that "rather than trying to make a big issue out of this matter, [Canada and the United States] should be proclaiming that the Arctic is an area where we do co-operate and have come to a pragmatic solution to a difficult legal problem."[193] We have a long history of working with the Americans in defending the North, and Canadians should not lose sight of this just because nationalists on both sides of the political spectrum do not want to see Canada conceding anything. This is counterproductive. By recasting our mindset from "use it or lose it" to an emphasis on *how* we want to use the North, rooted in the confidence that our sovereignty is secure, we can manage our internal waters with our allies and free up financial resources to invest in sustainable northern development. Canada should also be mindful that cultivating the United States as a practical ally on the NWP issue (without prejudice to legal positions) is good insurance against a critical mass of foreign countries allying against us and pushing the legal issue. The European Commission's recent statement on the EU and the Arctic shows that the United States is not the only country or group of countries that may challenge Canada's view.

Engaging the Europeans

Canada's bilateral cooperation—and disputes—with Denmark/Greenland have already been mentioned. We also engage European Arctic littoral states through the Arctic Council and other multilateral bodies. The EU's growing attentiveness to Arctic issues suggests the need for constructive engagement with this supranational body. In 2006, the EU established a Northern Dimension Policy with Iceland, Norway, and Russia to promote dialogue and sustainable development in northern Europe. This signals a salient shift from its traditional focus on central and southern Europe, one that reflects "the high visibility of the Arctic's role in the context of climate change."[194] Concurrently, the EU sees itself as uniquely positioned "to respond to the impacts of climate change on international security, given its leading role in development, global climate policy and the wide array of tools and instruments at its disposal."[195] The EC's report on the EU and the Arctic region, released on 20 November 2008, recommends that Europe play a leadership role in protecting the Arctic environment, promoting sustainable resource development, and supporting indigenous populations.[196] Canada emphasizes all of these priorities in its own Northern Strategy.

In light of the 2004 EU–Canada partnership agenda pledging cooperation in northern development and indigenous issues, Canada should welcome the EU's commitment to develop a more systematic approach to the region and should continue to identify areas for cooperation.[197] For example, Canada could partner with the EU to improve environmental and emergency response management; to protect whales within the framework of the International Whaling Commission (with accommodations for sustainable indigenous subsistence whaling); to frame a regional regime for regulating new fisheries; to secure international standards for oil and gas extraction; to propose new, multi-sector frameworks for integrated ecosystem management (such as navigational measures and rules for ensuring the sustainable exploitation of minerals); to pursue international negotiations on marine protected areas on the high seas; and to establish closer links with Arctic education networks, such as the University of the Arctic.[198] In light of the socio-economic interests of the Inuit, Canada should oppose EU proposals to ban seal products through bilateral and multilateral channels.[199]

While most Canadian public attention on the disputed status of the NWP is directed toward the United States, the EU also views it as an international strait. The member states of the EU have the world's largest merchant fleet and would benefit from transoceanic routes through Arctic waters. "This could considerably shorten trips from Europe to the Pacific, save energy, reduce emissions, promote trade and diminish pressure on the main trans-continental navigation channels," a recent report notes.[200] "But serious obstacles remain including drift ice, lack of infrastructure, environmental risks and uncertainties about future trade patterns," which means that commercial navigation in the region "will require time and effort." In the meantime, the EU is urged to improve conditions for this possibility. Canada should be a partner in promoting stricter safety and environmental standards; in this vein, it will be alarmed by the comment that EU "Member States and the Community should defend the principle of freedom of navigation and the right of innocent passage in the newly opened routes and areas."[201] This is an obvious reference to the NWP, one of the "new trade routes" that the EU sees as important "to effectively secure its trade and resource interests in the region and may put pressure on its relations with key partners."[202] Canada should not concede its position on internal waters, but—as with the Americans—this does not preclude a working relationship with the Europeans on other issues.

Engaging the Russians

In 1997, the House of Commons Standing Committee on Foreign Affairs and International Trade described Russia as a "giant jigsaw puzzle of paradoxes, contradictions, ambiguities, and uncertainties."[203] Ten years later, Russia seemed poised to flex its military and economic muscle, buoyed by a wealth of northern resources. Oil and gas revenues have allowed it to begin rebuilding its armed forces, resume northern air and naval operations, and invest heavily in the offshore sector.[204] The Russian invasion of Georgia coupled with "Russia's increasingly apparent diplomatic opposition to Western interests" has led to talk of a new Cold War.[205] Discussions of how Canada could tap into Russian markets, which were central to perceived bilateral opportunities in the 1990s, have been replaced by sabre-rattling rhetoric, much of it generated by alarmist readings of Russia's increased military activities in the polar region and its alleged intentions to unilaterally demarcate and defend its borders.[206]

Russia faces unique challenges as the only non-NATO member among the five Arctic littoral states. Sven Holtsmark neatly summarizes Russia's unique geopolitical position:

> First, there is geography. From the Bering Strait in the east to the border with Norway in the west, the Russian Arctic Ocean shore line covers nearly half of the latitudinal circle. Second are the economic factors. Because of the presence of enormous petroleum resources and other natural riches in the Russian

European High North and in Northern Siberia, as much as 20 per cent of the Russian [gross domestic product] is generated north of the Arctic Circle. At 22 per cent, the Arctic's share in Russian exports is even higher. Only a profound and long-term diversification of the Russian economy away from today's heavy reliance on energy extraction may fundamentally alter this situation. At present, there are few signs that such structural change is under way. Moreover, in decades to come, the Arctic's share in Russian petroleum extraction is expected to grow rather than diminish. Thus, there is a very real economic basis for the last years' strong focus on Arctic issues among Russian policy makers and in the Russian media. The uncertainty about Russia's will and ability to make full use of already identified and potential new offshore Arctic petroleum finds does not change this general picture.[207]

The Arctic is central to Russia's economic future, yet it finds itself surrounded by countries bound together in a military pact to which it does not belong. "The NATO countries' community of interests over a wide spectrum of issues, including security challenges, will easily outweigh even substantial bilateral or multilateral disputes," Holtsmark predicts. By extension, Western–Russian cooperation more generally is the real key to Arctic stability.[208]

Figure 3-11   Minister of Foreign Affairs Lawrence Cannon meets with his Russian counterpart, His Excellency Sergey Viktorovich Lavrov, on the margins of the Arctic Ocean Foreign Ministers' Meeting, Chelsea, Quebec, in March 2010.
Source: DFAIT

Holtsmark acknowledges that "certain aspects of Russian rhetoric and action give legitimate reasons for concern," as do unpalatable domestic practices of the Russian regime. Nevertheless, Russian foreign policy statements that emphasize the primacy of international law and multilateralism in international relations "should not be routinely dismissed." Russian policy makers may indeed "realise that adherence to international law and collective solutions are in fact in Russia's own vital interest." Of particular note, the Russian Arctic strategy approved in September 2008 supposedly emphasizes maintaining the Arctic "as an area of peace and cooperation" as one of its four main policy aims.[209] Geographical and economic realities mean that Russia has the most to gain if orderly, lawful development occurs. By extension, Holtsmark soberly concludes that:

> All decisions must be guided by a firm intent to avoid a return to the chess-board reasoning of the cold war, which presupposed that only one winner would be left on the field. This will involve multiple balancing acts between demonstrations of Allied solidarity and preparedness and the danger that they may provoke destabilizing Russian counter-measures. The approach should be analytical rather than emotional. All steps should be calculated in terms of their long-term effect on High North security and stability, and they should be predictable and legitimate in terms of the Western countries' declared policy aims. Military measures have the negative aim of avoiding the worst. Positive ambitions can only be achieved through dialogue, cooperation and compromise solutions to matters under dispute.[210]

Working with Russia to address its northern challenges was a key component of the Liberal government's *Northern Dimension of Canada's Foreign Policy*. This is echoed in Conservative government actions, such as the 2007 Joint Statement on Canada–Russia Economic Cooperation and the Memorandum of Understanding between the Ministry of Regional Development of the Russian Federation and the Department of Indian Affairs and Northern Development concerning cooperation on Aboriginal and northern development.[211] Canada and Russia should continue to reaffirm their bilateral agreements on cooperation in the Arctic and the North,[212] based on their continuing desire for partnership to serve the interests of Northerners. Priority areas should remain economic development, Arctic contaminants, Aboriginal issues, resource development, geology, tourism, and health. The governments should facilitate continued contacts among government representatives, Aboriginal organizations, other NGOs, scientists, and business associations and firms. INAC's Circumpolar Liaison Directorate should remain the lead federal

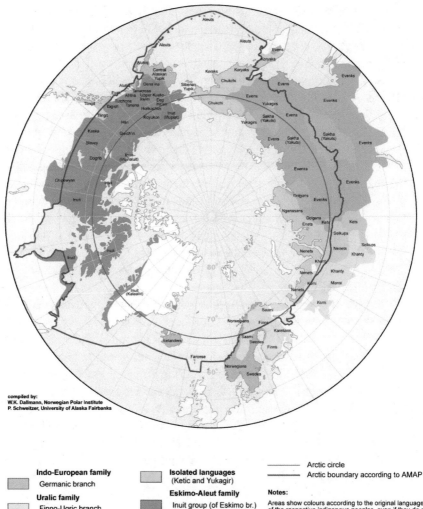

Indo-European family
Germanic branch

Uralic family
Finno-Ugric branch
Samoyedic branch

Altaic family
Turkic branch
Tungusic branch

Chukotko-Kamchatkan fam.

Isolated languages
(Ketic and Yukagir)

Eskimo-Aleut family
Inuit group (of Eskimo br.)
Yupik group (of Eskimo br.)
Aleut branch

Na-Dene family
Athabaskan branch
Eyak branch
Tlingit branch

——— Arctic circle
━━━ Arctic boundary according to AMAP

Notes:

Areas show colours according to the original languages of the respective indigenous peoples, even if they do not speak their languages today.

Overlapping populations are not shown. The map does not claim to show exact boundaries between the individual language groups.

Typical colonial populations, which are not traditional Arctic populations, are not shown (Danes in Greenland, Russians in the Russian Federation, non-native Americans in North America).

Map 3-6 Arctic peoples subdivided according to language families.
Source: Arctic Council

coordinator for implementing this agreement. Canadian Inuit groups have been strong proponents of the Russian Association of Indigenous Peoples of the North (RAIPON), encouraging Canada to help Aboriginal peoples tackle environmental and development challenges and supporting Aboriginal representation at the national and international levels.[213] Although modest technical assistance initiatives designed to share best practices (such as the Institutional Building for Northern Aboriginal Peoples in Russia program, which is continuing under a modest northern development stream, and the Canada–Russia Northern Development Partnership Program funded by the Canadian International Development Agency) may not enjoy a strong political or media profile, the Russians perceive them as constructive initiatives, and they are contributing to regional and local Aboriginal entrepreneurship as well as to improved regional governance systems. Despite all the high-level political and media talk of conflict, there is ongoing bilateral cooperation and goodwill.[214] Canada must avoid being punitive with Russia so that northern bilateral cooperation, geared largely toward indigenous capacity building, is not held hostage to global developments.

Canada also stands to learn from Russia through its experiences in managing the Northern Sea Route (NSR, or Northeast Passage) on the basis of Article 234 of UNCLOS. The NSR will have less ice and a longer navigating season than the NWP, and most careful commentators note that in the short-term at least, it will be a more attractive option for commercial vessels interested in Arctic transit. As a result, Canada is in an advantageous position to closely study scientific research and implementation issues related to the NSR, including navigational requirements, pollution standards, emergency facilities, and fees for using the route.[215] These "lessons learned" will help Canada devise its own management regime when its archipelagic waters become attractive and economically viable for commercial transit traffic.

Circumpolar Cooperation and the Arctic Council

The overall picture of transnational cooperation in the Arctic is complex; it features a mosaic of issue-specific arrangements rather than a single comprehensive and integrated regime covering an array of issues that constitute the region's policy agenda ... The continued success of region building in the Far North is by no means assured. The emerging mosaic of cooperative arrangements remains fragile ... What is more, the tides of global environmental change and globalization have triggered cascades of events that threaten to overwhelm efforts to carve out coherent agendas at the regional level and to pursue them without undue concern for the linkages between regional activities and planetary processes. Nowhere is this more apparent than in the Arctic, where externally driven environmental forces (for example, the impacts of climate change) together with the impacts of globalization (for example, the consequences for Arctic communities of political pressures relating to marine mammals) threaten to swamp cooperative initiatives at the regional level.

—Oran Young (2005)[216]

The Arctic Council was first proposed by the Mulroney government in 1989 and was eventually created in 1998 "to provide a means for promoting cooperation, coordination and interaction among the Arctic states."[217] The Arctic Council should not be dismissed as another Liberal "soft power" activity of the Axworthy era. Instead, Conservatives should see it as Liberal carry-through of a Conservative idea, and a successful one at that. The eight-nation Council is the key intergovernmental forum for regional cooperation in addressing environmental and sustainable development challenges in the Circumpolar North and plays a vital role in conveying Arctic perspectives to other international and global organizations. Although a high-level "discussional and catalytic" venue rather than a political decision-making body,[218] the council "does excellent technical work and informs and enables states to adopt progressive and

Figure 3-12   Duane Smith, president of Inuit Circumpolar Conference (Canada), speaks at the Social Development Working Group of the Arctic Council.
Source: Arctic Council

environmentally and socially responsible policies."[219] The formal status of "Permanent Participants" has been given to six indigenous peoples' organizations (IPOs) on the council. This innovative development in intergovernmental relations has enabled the region's permanent residents to contribute traditional knowledge as well as policy and political perspectives to circumpolar debate.[220] This serves broader national and international strategies related to northern capacity building and cross-cultural dialogue.

The Arctic Council continues to play an important generative role in framing and highlighting issues on the Arctic agenda.[221] Canada played a major role in pushing for a human dimension to the council and in creating the Sustainable Development Working Group, acting on Northerners' wishes to have the council's mandate extend beyond a narrow science focus. Canada continues to make valuable contributions in the various working groups,[222] and this should be highlighted in subsequent government statements. As the Arctic Athabaskan Council notes, Arctic Council activities and reports have influenced negotiations leading to international protocols on persistent organic pollutants (POPs), and this has "significantly influenced the climate change mitigation and adaptation positions of some non-Arctic as well as Arctic states," besides encouraging Arctic interests and the Small Island Developing States to cooperate on climate change adaptation and resilience-building measures.[223] Given that sound policies must be based on assessments of the best available knowledge of environmental processes affecting the Arctic, the Arctic Council's research programs and reports and assessments have been instrumental to sustainable human and economic development.

"The Arctic Council has been successful in preparing assessments, developing a regional identity and setting the Arctic agenda," the EC notes.[224] Yet Rob Huebert asserts that the Arctic Council "has been unable to formulate a regionally acceptable set of policy actions to respond to [environmental] problems" facing the region,[225] and Canada should consider a regional treaty to manage climate change and resource development issues.[226] Timo Koivurova and David Vanderzwaag note that before the "soft sleddings" of the past decade can be replaced by regional, legally binding agreements, a series of "hard questions" must be addressed: Is a legally binding agreement necessary? If so, what type of treaty and what details should be included? The various pros and cons, recapped in Koivurova and Vanderzwaag's article, need not be reiterated here. If Canada chooses to "champion" a "hard law" approach, this would be a long-term process with no assurance that all Arctic states would agree to a new treaty. It would also contradict the Ilulissat declaration, which stated clearly that the five Arctic Rim states do not believe there is a need to create a new Arctic "treaty."[227] Given the efforts required to secure an American signature on the

Arctic Council as it currently stands, the prospects of success on a formal treaty seem slim.[228] Instead, Canada should focus on strengthening the council's existing structure by supporting the creation of a permanent secretariat, and should try to expand its mandate by promoting an "International Cooperation Working Group" or a coordinating committee for external relations.[229]

The absence of an Antarctic-style treaty for the Arctic should not be seen as a failure. It is hard to envision how Arctic Aboriginal groups would have gained such an influential position if a treaty had been signed, given American desires to treat the Permanent Participants as observers.[230] Furthermore, the existing "web of soft-law declarations, informal arrangements, and growing institutional cooperation in the Arctic show that these measures often prove to be quite efficient in addressing existing challenges."[231] Canada is well advised to continue to embrace informal practices. Despite concerns that the May 2008 Illulissat declaration by the Arctic-5 has relegated the Arctic Council to a marginal role, Canada must remember that this specific meeting was focused on extended shelf claims. The participants declared that they would follow international rules, using UNCLOS to sort out competing national claims to continental shelf rights.[232] This does not relegate the Arctic Council to the sidelines of circumpolar affairs. The council remains an essential forum for "conveying Arctic perspectives, concerns and interests on climate change, contaminants, biodiversity conservation and other issues to international and global bodies."[233] Indeed, with the EU, China, India, South Korea, and others expressing interest in becoming observers to the council, one of the key challenges will be managing membership so that the permanent participants' voices are not diluted.[234]

International Standards

All Arctic stakeholders have a vested interest in when and where shipping in the Arctic will occur and under what conditions. "Governance in shipping is characterized by efforts to promote harmonization and uniformity in international maritime law," a team of Canadian international lawyers explain in a report produced for the Marine and Environmental Law Institute of Dalhousie Law School. "The reason for the global approach to shipping governance is that by definition and function, shipping is essentially an international tool in the service of global trade."[235] To this end, Canada should join with its circumpolar neighbours to promote the full implementation of existing obligations concerning navigation rules, maritime safety, routes system, and environmental standards in the Arctic.[236]

The IMO, a specialized UN agency, is responsible for creating harmonized shipping regulations and operating practices. These regulations and practices encompass safety, environmental concerns, legal matters, technical cooperation, maritime security, and the efficiency of shipping. Transport Canada led discussions on the Polar Code, which was later developed into IMO's non-mandatory *Guidelines for Ships Operating in Ice-Covered Waters*. Transport Canada is also active in the International Association of Classification Societies, where work on class harmonization and the enforcement of detailed ship construction rules for ice-strengthened ships complements the IMO's activities. Canada should continue to use its influence in these organizations to strengthen the design, construction and safety standards for ships that will operate in Arctic and Antarctic waters.[237]

Canada should strongly support further efforts to enhance IMO environmental and safety standards for shipping in Arctic waters; develop cooperative SAR procedures and assets; and support designating some Arctic navigation routes as particularly sensitive sea areas under IMO rules.[238] The need for well-designed and well-built polar vessels is not uniquely Canadian. Nations in close proximity to both poles have similar needs, and Canada is well suited to take a leadership role in promoting international standards for constructing and operating ships in ice-covered waters. Canada should work collaboratively with the United States to translate the existing guidelines into a mandatory Polar Code for International Shipping.[239]

Northerners, Diplomacies, and Foreign Policy

Canadian foreign policy must also be framed, wherever possible, in concert with Northerners' priorities. Through comprehensive land claim agreements and sovereignty assertions based upon northern indigenous use and occupancy, northern Aboriginal peoples are partners in Canada's Arctic governance and stewardship. Inuit Tapiriit Kanatami places a high policy priority on "recognition that an effective Arctic strategy requires a high and sustained level of inter-governmental and government–aboriginal cooperation."[240]

This emphasis on the foreign policy-making *process* conflicts with the prevailing tendency toward immediate, *outcome*-oriented, "crisis" decision making. The *International Dimension to the Inuit Action Plan* observes that "to address international issues, which are increasingly interdisciplinary and multifaceted, the Government of Canada establishes ad hoc and sometimes permanent interdepartmental committees and/or working groups. Canadian Inuit are sometimes invited to participate in these bodies but often after positions have been developed by Canada."[241] A November 2008 meeting of the Inuit Circumpolar Council in Kuujjuaq reaffirmed that the Inuit want to be included "as equal partners in any future talks regarding sovereignty" and that they are displeased with the lack of meaningful and direct inclusion in decision making.[242] It is telling that while federal officials insist they regularly engage Northern leaders on circumpolar issues, Northerners stridently assert that they are not embraced as active partners. Allegedly, this violates national and international obligations.

To improve cooperation and coordination, the federal government should consider establishing a domestic Arctic Council as recommended by a workshop of prominent Northerners and scholars.[243] This "Arctic Canada Council" would include representatives from key federal departments (such as INAC, DFAIT, Environment Canada, DFO, RCMP, and DND), the territorial governments, Aboriginal regional governments (including representatives from Nunavik and Nunatsiavut), ICC (Canada), ITK, AAC, and the Gwich'in Council International. The Arctic Canada Council could meet biannually and could generate a series of working groups involving leading Canadian researchers. While the agenda would invariably transcend the domestic and international spheres, and while meetings would be expensive to host given the distances involved in bringing participants together, this would be a strong mechanism to ensure that Northerners were truly engaged as ongoing partners in devising and implementing a truly integrated northern strategy for Canada.[244]

The federal government should also reinstate the position of Ambassador for Circumpolar Affairs. This position, originally created in 1994 to support the creation of the Arctic Council and to serve as Canada's senior representative at council meetings, was eliminated by the Harper government in 2006 as a cost-saving measure. Although DFAIT has the capacity to manage the Arctic file through its Aboriginal and Circumpolar Division, it is important for Canada to have a dedicated ambassador to act as our face to the world on circumpolar issues. Appointing a Northerner to this position would send a strong signal that Canada's policies reflect its northern peoples' priorities, that we intend to invest in multilateral relationships, and that we take our northern diplomatic responsibilities seriously.

Climate Change and Pollution

> Climate change is the defining issue of our time that will ultimately impact on us all. The Inuit are giving the world the gift of an early warning.
>
> —*Sheila Watt-Cloutier*[245]

The Governing Council of the United Nations Environment Programme (UNEP) has characterized the Arctic as the world's barometer of environmental change. Its February 2008 resolution, "Sustainable Development of the

Arctic Region," urges better cooperation among and between states and non-governmental stakeholders to ensure sustainable development,[246] given that the root causes of climate change are intrinsically global. The impacts are also regional and local. The effects of climate change on the Arctic ecosystem have been widely documented; they include rising temperatures, melting ice caps and glaciers, and changes in flora and fauna.[247] Potential security and sovereignty threats must be considered alongside issues of food security, cultural survival, physical health, threats to settlements on the coast or built on permafrost, and the vulnerability of critical infrastructure. Adapting and adjusting to climate change is an abiding concern for Aboriginal groups. These groups recognize that global action is needed to reduce greenhouse gases and slow the pace of change so that northern residents have time to adapt to changing conditions.[248]

"Climate change is best viewed as a threat multiplier which exacerbates existing trends, tensions and instability," the EU notes. "The core challenge is that climate change threatens to overburden states and regions which are already fragile and conflict prone."[249] While the Arctic is fragile, it is not "conflict prone." The fragility is linked to humanitarian and ecological issues, not to an anarchic arena likely to explode into military conflict. Thomas Homer-Dixon asserts that

> the most common "state-centric" concerns about the effect of climate change on the Arctic ... are exaggerated. These concerns are grounded in a set of assumptions that may have been appropriate for 19th and 20th century world affairs but are entirely inappropriate as a basis for addressing the 21st century's challenges. Indeed, these state-centric concerns divert policy attention away from far more critical issues, including the larger climate consequences of Arctic ice loss, such as more rapid melting of the Greenland icecap, invigoration of carbon-cycle positive feedbacks, and potentially dramatic changes in precipitation patterns much farther south affecting global food production ... Access to the Northwest Passage and to reserves of oil and natural gas in the Arctic basin will seem trivial in a world whipsawed by climate change shifts resulting from loss of Arctic sea ice. Policymakers need to focus on what is really important, not what fits their 20th century worldview.[250]

Unfortunately, Canada is not in a position to take a leadership role in climate change adaptation and mitigation strategies. It does, however, have an opportunity to stand beside the new "leader," Barack Obama. The US president has promised an aggressive "New Energy for America" strategy that includes re-engaging with the UN Framework Convention on Climate Change (UNFCC) and creating a Global Energy Forum of the world's largest emitters to focus exclusively on global energy and environmental issues.[251] Similarly, Adele Airoldi calls on the EU to take a leading role in climate change mitigation efforts, given the reticence or opposition of other circumpolar countries to commit to action, so that the EU can "become the main interpreter of Arctic concerns."[252]

Canada's weak record on climate change is a serious blow to our self-image as good international citizens. We need to develop an Arctic Climate Strategy that is global in its aspirations for mitigation while sensitive to the needs for local adaptation. It must contain an on-the-ground capacity (scientific and local) to monitor the physical, social, cultural, and economic impacts of global warming in Canada, as well as support similar studies abroad. In response to the 2007 Natural Resources Canada report *From Impacts to Adaptation: Canada in a Changing Climate*, Mary Simon made three key recommendations for federal action vis-à-vis the Arctic. Canada should:

1. Convene a blue ribbon panel of civil society and industry leaders to advise the Federal Government on fully understanding how climate change is affecting the Canadian Arctic and how to assist Northerners to adapt to the changes already underway. This panel would be innovative, non-partisan and empowered to consult with ordinary Canadians.
2. Then develop a comprehensive national climate change strategy for the Arctic with targets and timelines, connected to international processes, funding commitments, and tax incentives.
3. Select a model Inuit Community to evaluate strategies that will allow northern residents to cope with rapid Climate Change. We are suggesting Tuktoyaktuk. For example examining building and engineering challenges in an environment where the ground is now subject to much warmer temperatures for longer periods of time.[253]

This is an appropriate and feasible plan, one that encapsulates the multiple levels of engagement that are required. On the ground, observations and scientific reports have revealed that global warming threatens Arctic infrastructure; therefore, mitigation efforts cannot be regional. Given that pipelines, buildings, and houses built on permafrost are threatened by warming temperatures that erode the ground's bearing capacity and lead to structural damage, local adaptation will be needed long before any global action can take effect. This reality can be applied to most of the environmental challenges facing Arctic peoples.

Canada's climate change prevention and mitigation strategy must be developed in tandem with continued investment in identifying global and transboundary processes that contaminate the Arctic ecosystem. Working in

Figure 3-13   Mary Simon, representing the Inuit Tapiriit Kanatami, responds to the official apology for residential schools in the House of Commons, June 2008.
Source: Prime Minister's Office

close collaboration with northern Aboriginal peoples, the Canadian government has become a circumpolar leader in contaminants-related science, and it must continue to screen and monitor new contaminants entering the Arctic "sink." Canada should pursue opportunities to reduce pollution by persistent organic pollutants, heavy metals, and other contaminants through existing international forums, including the Arctic Council's Arctic Monitoring and Assessment Program (AMAP) and the UN's Economic Commission for Europe's Long Range Transport of Airborne Pollutants process. It should also seek agreements to reduce the risk of radionuclide contamination in the Arctic.[254]

This must be coupled with research in northern communities to assess the impacts of locally based contaminants on food supply and health. "With the environment changing so quickly, it's difficult to tell from year to year whether that food will be there or not," said Vuntut Gwich'in Chief Joe Linklater from Old Crow, Yukon, who also chairs Gwich'in Council International. Linklater also stated that the changing Arctic environment causes great uncertainty and stress for elders and youth in the region and that he hopes northern communities will be involved in developing strategies to deal with these challenges.[255] This engagement must not be an afterthought: it must be central to the process of devising a national climate change strategy.

A key risk associated with climate change is the potential for strong resentment among Northerners if southern policy makers fail to include them in discussions that impact their lives, or if they fail to take action to deal with changes that are of paramount importance to them. These tensions may be expressed domestically—as is already happening—or internationally. The recent Circumpolar Inuit Declaration on Arctic Sovereignty is telling.[256] Canada has been very fortunate to enjoy strong support from its Inuit and other northern peoples. The ringing Inuit phrase "Canadians first, first Canadians," which I have heard frequently in my northern travels, should be the envy of the world. We cannot let the spirit of cooperation and partnership wane because "crisis" thinking demands urgent action. Aboriginal issues have been the Achilles heel of Canada's good international citizenship,[257] which has been further eroded by the federal government's decision to vote against the UN Declaration on the Rights of Indigenous Peoples. We cannot take for granted our partnership with the Inuit and other northern peoples. A serious rift between northern and southern Canadians over the setting of our Arctic priorities, besides hurting us domestically, will erode our credibility globally.

Toward a Renewed Emphasis on Diplomacy

Circumpolar cooperation and diplomacy must be reinstated as an explicit and central pillar of Canada's Northern Strategy. This is essential if Canada wants to promote a "Polar Saga" scenario and assume a leading role in circumpolar affairs. The absence of diplomacy and circumpolar cooperation as main components of an integrated federal strategy has set up a false separation between sovereignty/security concerns and a stable circumpolar world predicated on the rule of law wherein Canada is a strong ally and responsible neighbour. If the original phraseology in the Northern Vision devised under the Liberals, "Reinforcing Sovereignty, National Security and Circumpolar Cooperation," is politically unpalatable for partisan reasons, the federal government should consider something along these lines: "Increase Diplomatic, Military and Scientific Cooperation with Other Circumpolar Nations."

If DFAIT has been "missing in action" on the Arctic file in recent years[258]—though perhaps it is more appropriate to say it has been frozen out of the military-centred approach since 2006—it is time for the government to swing back the pendulum and re-engage its diplomats as central players. As David Runnalls neatly summarizes:

> Action is needed around specific topics and coalitions which naturally bind the Arctic nations: a shared Arctic environment; a declared commitment to abide by UNCLOS; the Ilulissat Declaration and the Arctic Council; threatened indigenous and northern populations; and the fact that a lot is at stake, environmentally, socially and economically. A common thread for these connectors is the need to promote sustainable development in the region. The central focus for Canada should be to demonstrate through its actions that it intends to be a world leader in northern sustainable development stewardship no matter how difficult the challenges of transition created by climate change.[259]

To paraphrase an old adage, the Arctic issues are too broad to be left to the generals and the oil and gas company executives.

Development

> What happens in the North ... will be of great importance to the future of our country; it will tell us what kind of a country Canada is; it will tell us what kind of a people we are ... We think of ourselves as a northern people. We may at last have begun to realize that we have something to learn from the people who for centuries have lived in the North ... Should the future of the North be determined by the South? ... The goals, aspirations and preferences of the northern peoples should be fully explored before any decision is taken. The choice we make will decide whether the North is to be primarily a frontier for industry or a homeland for its peoples.
> —*Thomas Berger,* Northern Frontier, Northern Homeland *(1977)*

The resource potential of the Arctic is huge. The US Geological Survey estimated in July 2008 that 90 billion barrels of oil, 1,669 trillion cubic feet of natural gas, and 44 billion barrels of natural gas liquids may remain undiscovered in the Arctic, with 84 percent laying in offshore areas. Potentially exploitable minerals in the Canadian Arctic include iron ore, base metals, and diamonds. Interest in northern fisheries, tourism, and freshwater may expand as global warming opens up easier access to the region. As a result, the notion that this treasure-laden frontier may hold the key to Canada's future prosperity has re-entered the popular mind. Northern Canadians are excited by the opportunities offered by northern resource development. Concerns abound, however, about how Canada will facilitate development while protecting the northern ecosystem and sustaining northern communities and cultures.

Development issues are intrinsically domestic and international. Oil and gas exploration and production is driven by international energy prices and demand, as well as by issues of American energy security and diversity of supply. The demand and prices for minerals are also dictated by volatile international markets, leaving the North susceptible to "boom and bust" cycles.[260] World prices have largely determined the scale and pace of industrial development in the region, which is a very high-cost environment in which infrastructure is poor and often lacking.[261] Taken at face value, the current global economic downturn may point to a "polar low" scenario, in which "low demand and unstable governance bring a murky and underdeveloped future for the Arctic."[262] However, longer-term international demand for conventional energy and raw materials will continue to rise. "Nations around the world are taking steps to ward off recession and kick-start their economies," NWT Premier Floyd Roland recently noted. "They'll need energy and resources to fuel that economic growth ... The bottom line is that Canada's Arctic remains one of the last politically stable places on Earth that has abundant energy resources."[263]

Canada is a trading nation and should encourage an "Arctic Saga" scenario that balances global collaboration and compromise with sustainable Arctic resource development.[264] As the territorial premiers note in their Northern Vision,

> the strength of the northern economy is based on rich endowments of renewable, non-renewable and human resources. The northern labour force is young and skilled; billions of dollars are being invested by the private sector in mineral and gem exploration and development; the oil and gas sector is the focus of intense activity and great potential; hydro development holds great promise for clean energy; and offshore fisheries are developing into a competitive sector.[265]

In short, Canada is well positioned to exercise its sovereignty and develop its resources with, and for the benefit of, Northerners. This has been a central pillar of both the Liberal and Conservative northern strategies, one that transcends the domestic and international spheres.

Yet northern commentators continue to accuse Ottawa of having its strategy backwards. This critique usually promotes a vision that builds sovereignty "from the ground up." In a strongly worded commentary in *Nunatsiaq News* on 11 April 2008, Mary Simon observed that

> the Arctic has the country's worst housing, health and education indicators. This cannot be allowed to continue. Notwithstanding last October's Throne Speech promise of "an integrated northern strategy," a quick review of the recent federal budget shows where the federal government priorities rest at the moment: sizeable new funding for mineral development alongside earlier big ticket commitments to military facilities and hardware, with a "hold-the-line" approach to endemic social problems.
>
> In this backwards-looking focus, the aboriginal realities of the Arctic—our demographic majority, our aboriginal and treaty rights, our distinct languages and cultures—are effectively pushed out of sight.
>
> Public pronouncements on northern policy priorities rarely mention Inuit and other aboriginal peoples, and, when they do, the references are footnotes and afterthoughts. The views and suggestions of representative aboriginal organizations are sidelined …
>
> There is a core fallacy that threatens to take hold at the heart of the federal government's emerging northern and Arctic policies: that the top third of Canada can be managed and developed as if its aboriginal history, demography, and its aboriginal values and character, are peripheral and transitional. Policies built around such a misleading notion will be unsound in concept and unsustainable in practice.
>
> The "integrated northern strategy" promised in last year's Throne Speech is, at least notionally, still under construction. There is now an opportunity to get things right.[266]

To "get things right," Canada must commit to internal development in close partnership with northern leaders; discern a more central role for Northerners in governance, research, environmental monitoring, and enforcement; exercise its sovereignty; practise meaningful stewardship; and reduce its vulnerability to external criticism.

Although Canada has had a surprisingly successful track record in expanding and entrenching its legal sovereignty in the North, its record on development is disappointing.[267] The following section lays out options that the federal government may choose to support as part of an integrated northern strategy. This set of possibilities does not present a hierarchy of priorities or cost–benefit analyses—assessments that are invariably made by politicians and public servants. Political realities dictate that federal decision makers will evaluate these options according to how they fit with prevailing priorities, budgets, and desired political messaging. For example, recent federal government commitments to invest in infrastructure as part of its economic stimulus package may make "bricks and mortar" projects particularly attractive. Furthermore, the needs of the North must be balanced with those of southern Canada. Development proposals tend to be region-centric, and this extensive "menu" of policy options does not presume that there is sufficient political appetite for the federal government to bite off all of the options at once. The following, then, is intended as a sampling of policy suggestions that federal decision makers should evaluate when developing a comprehensive Arctic strategy.

Encouraging Sustainable Resource Development

With all the focus on the alleged threats to Canadian sovereignty and security in the North, predicated on foreign eagerness to undermine our claims and steal our resources, the popular discourse has been directed away from the benefits that Canada will accrue if development is attracted to the region. Indeed, some observers suggest that the Arctic Basin will not see the dramatic expansion of oil and gas exploitation and in-transit shipping that is driving the "polar race" scenarios rampant in the media. Homer-Dixon anticipates that "in a world of melting and shifting sea ice, more violent Arctic storms, and a surge of icebergs from disintegrating Greenland glaciers—exploring and extracting Arctic petroleum resources might be much more, not less, difficult than it is today."[268] Unpredictable ice conditions (including the possibility of more, not less, multi-year ice infesting Canada's internal waters), confusing regulatory regimes, inadequate infrastructure, and human capital deficits may make development unattractive to potential investors.[269] The federal government and northern stakeholders have emphasized that sustainable development and resource management are integral to future growth. To achieve this, Canada should strive where possible to make its North more competitive with other regions. This is a tall order, however, given its geographical remoteness, sparse population, and challenging climate.

Pierre Alvarez, the president of the Canadian Association of Petroleum Producers, explains that a sustainable oil and gas industry in northern Canada must meet the same requirements as in other parts of the world. "Companies compete for international investment dollars for projects," he observes, and they seek to maximize their return on investment. The prices of crude oil and natural gas are weighed against the relatively high exploration and development costs—and risks—of operating in the region, given the isolation, short drilling season, complex regulatory system, and lack of infrastructure.[270]

A recent AMAP assessment report notes that climate change will have both positive and negative effects on oil and gas activities in the Arctic.[271]

Accordingly, the federal government should continue to launch initiatives and incentives to encourage investment and development. Resource estimates often presented as "facts" in the media are based on surveys and must be followed up with in-depth research. Natural Resources Canada's geomapping program serves this need; so does the extension of the 15 percent mineral exploration tax credit to explore new mineral reserves in the North. The federal government should also implement its Regulatory Improvement Initiative to make a more efficient and effective regime out of "the spiderweb of federal regulatory authority which threatens economic development in the north."[272] Improved navigational infrastructure, aids to make marine transportation safer and more efficient, deep-sea capable port infrastructure to receive and send cargo and to service vessels, and increased road and rail networks to deliver resources to southern markets (and potentially to western markets through Russia) all warrant further study. Given the high costs and difficult logistics associated with northern development, public–private partnerships will likely be necessary.[273]

The premier of the NWT has called for a strategic federal investment to start the Mackenzie Gas Project, the largest industrial project ever undertaken in the Canadian North, which is intended to transport gas from the Mackenzie Delta to Alberta, where it can be distributed internationally.[274] Federal leadership may be necessary, given that the success of this $16.2 billion project has become "a litmus test for Canadian frontier development in general."[275] The regulatory process has been slow and cumbersome,[276] Aboriginal claims and land access issues continue to pose obstacles, and proponents insist on the need for a supportive "fiscal framework" to make the project economically feasible. Once a pipeline has been built, however, the economics of developing new gas fields in the region will be improved. Without it, the difficulties in delivering Arctic gas to market, coupled with export and technological constraints,[277] will likely inhibit development of these resources for the foreseeable future.

Canada's Atlantic and Pacific fisheries remain in crisis from overfishing and poor management and conservation policies, even while national and world demand for fish protein continues to rise. This situation is part of a global crisis during which attempts to exploit increasingly scarce resources may further destabilize ecosystems and undermine a major part of the global food supply. Fishing is partly regulated through the North Atlantic Fisheries Organization, but illegal and unreported fishing still takes place in Canadian waters, and there are indications that the pressure on fish stocks may continue to rise in the near future.[278] Climate change is likely to shift the spatial distribution of fish stocks, and reduced sea ice coverage in Arctic waters may

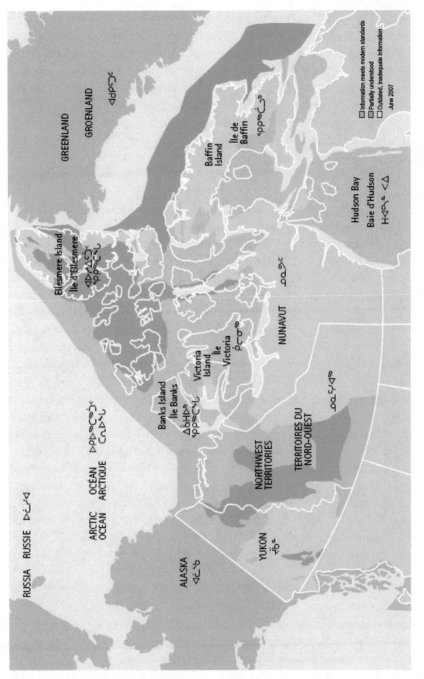

Map 3-7 Resource knowledge: oil and gas.
Source: Indian and Northern Affairs Canada

make new areas attractive to fishers trying to deal with the loss of indigenous fish stocks on their home fishing grounds. To protect against unregulated fisheries in the waters straddling Canada's EEZ and in parts of the Arctic high seas, Canada should engage the international community to enact a regulatory framework that ensures "fair and transparent management of fisheries in accordance with the Code of Conduct for Responsible Fishing."[279] Establishing one or more regional fisheries management organizations is consistent with the ecosystem-based management and "collaborative stewardship" advocated by Oran Young and Franklyn Griffiths, as well as with the UNCLOS framework for Arctic government proposed by the five Arctic coastal states.[280]

At the same time, the federal government could encourage and support a Northern Canadian commercial fishery as proposed by the government of Nunavut, and should give Nunavut companies a right of first refusal on fishing quotas in territorial waters.[281] Accordingly, fishery and small craft harbours would be an important community resource and could stimulate self-sustaining, local economic development. Currently, northern communities do not benefit commercially from offshore fish stocks because they do not have fishing vessels suitable for offshore work, nor do they have landing places for these ships, adequate charts, processing facilities, or regular air cargo services to move products to southern markets.[282] In the 2008 federal budget, the government committed $8 million over two years to build, operate, and manage a commercial harbour in Pangnirtung. This commitment is only a start, and the federal government should invest the $41.2 million over eight years that will be necessary to build harbours in six other communities identified in the DFO *Nunavut Small Craft Harbours Report* (2005). Accordingly, it should implement, with Nunavut, a comprehensive harbour development plan. This plan would entail improved Arctic marine charts, new services and infrastructure to ensure safe navigation, and aids to navigation and better port facilities.[283] At the same time, by reducing local unemployment, facilitating community resupply, and supporting subsistence hunters and fishers, investments in small craft harbours would support northern community development.

Functional harbours would enhance the potential for more tourism in the Canadian Arctic. Tourism, particularly cruise travel to the Canadian Arctic, has grown steadily since 1984 and may accelerate because of global warming. While much of the existing literature seems fixated on the threat posed by foreign tourist traffic to Canada's sovereignty claims and to the Arctic environment,[284] this overlooks the potential for foreign tourism to become part of a diverse and sustainable northern economy.

Figure 3-14 Prime Minister Stephen Harper visits Tuktoyaktuk, NWT, in August 2010.
Source: Prime Minister's Office

Marine ecotourism is a growing force in the tourism industry worldwide and can have direct material benefits at the community level. As long as environmental safeguards are in place, including restricted access to ecologically vulnerable areas, Canada should support sustainable Arctic tourism.[285] *Guidelines for Operation of Passenger Vessels in Canadian Arctic Waters*[286] encourages tour operators to consult the World Wildlife Fund codes of conduct.[287] Canada should strengthen its requirements by promoting an international agreement on instruments for managing Arctic tourism.[288] Eco-cruising at present is overwhelmingly handled by foreign-flag companies and ships, so the federal government could also explore the possibility of supporting an enhanced eco-cruise sector in the Arctic.[289]

Protecting the Arctic environment must be central to all development strategies. Canadians expect the federal government to be an effective steward of the Arctic, and they recognize that resource development could threaten northern ecosystems if these are not managed in a sustainable manner. It follows that federal support for hydrocarbon resource exploration, extraction, and transportation must be contingent on strict environmental standards. Canadians must also recognize that accidents and spills do not respect national borders and that we must work with our circumpolar neighbours to develop and implement binding international standards based upon the Arctic

Council's oil and gas guidelines, a Polar Code (through the IMO), and improved bilateral and multilateral cooperation to institute preparedness and response measures across the circumpolar region.[290] Before opening new geographical areas for resource development or constructing new infrastructure, it is also essential to consult with northern residents to ensure that their interests are taken into account, that negative effects are minimized, and that they can secure short- and long-term benefits from activities.

Sustainable Human Development

"As I've said before, 'use it or lose it' is the first principle of sovereignty in the Arctic," Prime Minister Harper declared when announcing his expanded geomapping program in August 2008. "To develop the North we must know the North. To protect the North, we must control the North. And to accomplish all our goals for the North, we must be in the North."[291] The tone and language, suggestive of an open frontier and the need for a Canadian presence, was precisely the sort of message that is offensive to many Northerners with whom I have spoken. Northern residents already provide a continuous presence. Political speeches talking about the need to prepare the Arctic for defence and resource development activities, without careful consideration of the ways in which Northerners already use the lands and waters, cause consternation. The Arctic front/frontier often characterized in southern media coverage and political speeches often bears little resemblance to the relationships that Northerners already have with and in their Arctic homeland.

As Thomas Berger's landmark 1977 report for the Mackenzie Valley Pipeline Inquiry revealed to Canadians, debates about resource development are not simply about pipelines and access to energy: they are "about the future of the North and its peoples."[292] So they remain. The Inuit assert that "sovereignty begins at home."[293] Mary Simon, president of the Inuit Tapiriit Kanatami, explains that establishing meaningful sovereignty in the North will require a strong commitment to meeting the needs of the Inuit, whose historic and ongoing use and occupation of the Arctic lands and waters is "the bedrock of Canada's status as an Arctic nation." By extension, "coherent policy-making for the Arctic must commit to two things: A credible power-sharing partnership between Inuit and the government; and a determination to overcome the obvious gaps in basic measurements of well-being that separate Inuit from all other Canadians."[294]

Sustainable human and resource development in the Arctic must go hand in hand for Canada to be a competitive and credible player in the circumpolar world. The three territorial premiers' document, *A Northern Vision: A Stronger North and a Better Canada*, asserts that northerners should be the

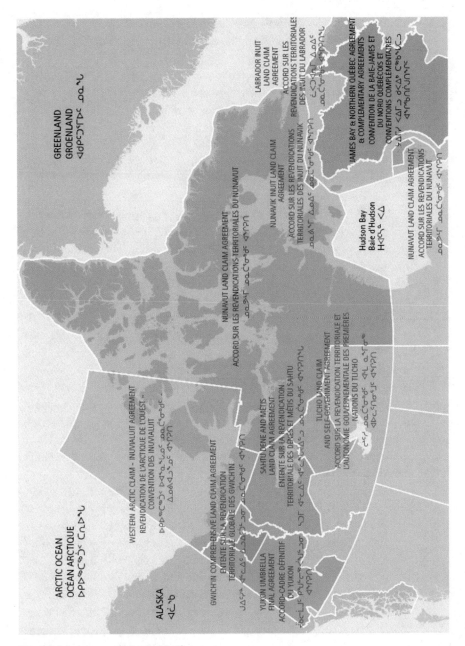

Map 3-8 Modern treaties in the North.
Source: Indian and Northern Affairs Canada

primary beneficiaries of northern resource development. In the section "Sovereignty Through Sustainability," this collaborative vision asserts that

> in order for Northerners to continue to act as stewards of Canadian sovereignty, the North needs sustainable communities. Northerners must be supported in building communities where we can live healthy lives; where opportunities for employment, education and training exist; where we can raise our families in adequate, suitable and affordable homes; where health and social services exist that are comparable to the rest of Canada; and where we can build a future for ourselves and our children.[295]

The "human dimension" of development, prioritized by northern stakeholders, relates to issues such as economic development and diversification, health care, education and training, Aboriginal issues, and northern infrastructure. Studies reveal that on Northerners' priority lists, local concerns such as housing shortages, suicide, substance abuse, violent crime, and exorbitant costs of living trump sovereignty and conventional security concerns.[296] The Harper government has committed itself to various initiatives to encourage social and economic development in the North, including affordable housing, $500 million for a socio-economic trust for communities affected by the construction of the Mackenzie Gas Project, increased deductions for northern workers, and expanded broadband connectivity in the NWT and Nunavut.[297] These investments should be welcomed by the leaders of all political parties; indeed, they must be increased to address the acute social problems that Northerners suggest represent the real crisis in the Canadian North. Proposals to build human capacity blur the lines between domestic and international policy, but they are key to Canada's future.

The model for a mutually supportive relationship is embodied in land claim agreements, but frustration is mounting over the federal government's perceived failure to fully implement them.[298] Inuit spokespersons have argued that Canada's archipelagic waters are best understood and protected as internal waters to Nunavut and the NWT, subject to local control and local use, and that control over environmental monitoring and seabed resources should be devolved to the territorial governments. Former Nunavut premier Paul Okalik described this as an in-house solution to bolster Canada's internal waters claim, and he accused the federal government of being "hypocritical," "impractical," and "colonial" in its approach to devolving governance.[299] This sort of rhetoric is harmful. The expectations of the Nunavut government in particular must be proportionate to serious management and staffing problems it faces, as well as to a host of federal considerations that should not be dismissed for the sake of a hasty agreement.[300] Nevertheless, it must be a top government priority to build regional capacity so that control over lands and resources can be transferred from Ottawa to the NWT and Nunavut governments, as has been done in Yukon.[301]

One element of the devolution process that bears directly on Canada's jurisdiction over the waters of the Arctic Archipelago is the creation of a Nunavut Marine Council (NMC), which was set out in the 1993 Nunavut Land Claims Agreement to help regulate marine development. By bringing together representatives from the Nunavut Impact Review Board, Water Board, Planning Commission, and Wildlife Management Board, an NMC would build more coherent and coordinated policies for offshore resource use, planning, and development.[302] In due course, if the NWC proves feasible and constructive, Marine Councils for the Inuvialuit, Nunavik, and Nunatsiavut governments could and should be formed. They could then be brought together as the Canadian Arctic Marine Environment Working Group under the aegis of the Arctic Canada Council proposed earlier. This would help ensure the inclusiveness of decision making related to marine governance.

Education and Arctic Research

While Canada has lagged behind in Arctic research over the past few decades, its world-leading $150 million investment in the International Polar Year (2007–9) is providing momentum for a new national commitment to excellence in Arctic research.[303] Long-term investments in physical, human, and social scientific research are needed to avoid the "feast and famine" cycle that has marked Arctic research to date. A Natural Sciences and Engineering Research Council (NSERC) and Social Sciences and Humanities Research Council (SSHRC) report has observed that Canada's northern research is in "crisis" and that if it is not better supported, Canada will be unable to fulfill its national or international science and research expectations. This report pitches Northern research activity as an "essential assertion of our sovereignty."[304]

The Canadian Arctic Research Initiative emphasizes Canada's international obligation to contribute to knowledge about the "nature, mechanisms and extent" of connections between the Arctic and the rest of the globe.[305] The federal government is carrying through on its promises to create new research infrastructure—in particular, a world-class Arctic research station[306]—and to encourage researchers to coordinate their efforts across relevant topic areas (such as resource development, transportation, health, and the environment) so that they can translate their findings into concrete policy recommendations. The international dimension of Canada's Arctic research strategy should be based on principles of transparency, information sharing, and partnership between Canada's Arctic scientists and northern peoples at all levels of planning, training, fieldwork, data analysis, and communication.[307] To become a global leader in polar science, Canada might also partner with the EU to "develop enhanced, broad international information exchange on research projects and facilitate coordination of national programmes." The establishment of the Sustained Arctic Observing Network may work in this direction.[308] Given that all circumpolar countries have a vested interest in sustainable resource development, environmental science and stewardship, climate change, and healthy and sustainable communities, Canada has a lot to teach—and to learn—through constructive engagement in circumpolar research.

Strategic research should also be targeted at priority areas that will have an impact on quality of life and that will allow Northerners to adapt to changing realities. For example, northern communities are plagued by exorbitant fuel costs to generate electricity. Canada, in concert with its circumpolar neighbours, should invest in research and development for technologies oriented toward renewable, indigenous energy sources to serve northern residents.[309] Wind power is an obvious possibility, given that the Arctic coast registers some of the highest average annual wind speeds in North America and that wind is a stable cost (in contrast to the fossil fuels that run existing generators). This could be a priority area for NSERC, which should fund a strategic partnership with researchers in Alaska and the Nordic countries to create a "wind turbine technology centre [to] undertake research design and product development for small northern communities and isolated industrial sites." Such a centre would also train northern utility workers and market the resulting technology to the circumpolar world.[310] Canada could engage the EU on this issue, given its potential interest in strengthening cooperation on "improving primary energy savings, energy efficiency and the use of renewable resources in the Arctic."[311]

There is also room for Canadian leadership in circumpolar human development. The appointment of Leona Aglukkaq (the first Inuk Cabinet minister) as Canada's new Minister of Health in November 2008 makes this an opportune time to seize the initiative. Given that "the single-most powerful reason for Canada's poor international ranking [in health indices] is the poor health and health care of our First Nation, Inuit and Métis citizens," according to the chair of the Health Council of Canada,[312] healthy northern communities must be a priority. The federal government should collaborate with the ICC to "bring Canadian Inuit health issues (best practices and challenges) to the circumpolar world and bring circumpolar issues to Canadian decision makers" through the Arctic Council's Sustainable Development

Figure 3-15 International Polar Year scientist Dr. Luke Copland sets up a monitoring beacon on the Ayles Ice Shelf on Ellesmere Island, Nunavut, April 2008.
Source: DND

Working Group, the AMAP Human Health Experts Working Group, and the International Union for Circumpolar Health.[313] Priority areas for international collaboration include mental health, alcohol and substance abuse, suicide, dietary concerns (such those related to changing lifestyles and contaminated food), tuberculosis, and delivery of health services to remote communities. The government should support the *Circumpolar Inuit Health Action Plan* proposed in the ICC's Utqiagvik Declaration (2004), as well as the Inuit Action Plan, which will identify health issues, priorities, and mechanisms to support healthy community initiatives throughout the circumpolar world. In Canada's case, investing in the health of northern residents is also essential for a northern labour force; it will reduce the current dependency on imported labour—something that makes "frontier" development very costly.

Education is also a key priority, given the young population of Canada's Arctic and the need to build human capacity so that Northerners can seize development opportunities and realize regional self-government. To support these goals, the federal and territorial governments should continue to invest resources in the University of the Arctic (UArctic), a cooperative network of universities, colleges, and Aboriginal organizations committed to higher education and research in the circumpolar world. UArctic helps build regional awareness, fosters transnational cooperation between students and researchers, and allows for innovative curriculum development. While DFAIT provided start-up funding, it should not be expected to provide ongoing financial support to UArctic operations. A long-term funding plan should be developed through INAC (with support from Human Resources and Social Development Canada) to sustain and enhance its programs.[314] The federal government also should consider special initiatives such as co-op education placements in the Aboriginal and Circumpolar Affairs directorates at DFAIT and INAC; these placements would be earmarked for university students from the North. And it should consider a national and international scholars-in-residence program at the three northern colleges (through NSERC and SSHRC), as well as visiting professorships for Canadian scholars at universities in Alaska, Europe, and Russia, in order to build educational and research networks throughout the circumpolar world.

Advisory Committee on Northern Security and Stewardship

Although regular meetings on northern issues take place in Ottawa at the deputy minister and assistant deputy minister levels, the establishment of a more formal committee would reinforce a long-term commitment to strategic planning. To orchestrate and implement its Northern Strategy, the federal government should consider re-establishing an interdepartmental Advisory Committee on Northern Development (ACND). The original ACND was created in 1948 to provide "close and continuous interdepartmental coordination" so that civil and defence developments were orchestrated within a comprehensive northern development program.[315] Although it had an uneven history and reflected the centralist tendencies of the era in which it existed, the concept remains sound provided that it is broadened to encompass the complementary pillars of defence/security and diplomacy.

The Arctic Security Working Group (ASWG), established in 1999, is a step in the direction of a "whole of government" approach, but its mandate is too narrow to encompass the full suite of issues that must be engaged at a strategic level. Regular meetings with representatives from the main stakeholder departments, as well as Aboriginal organizations and the territorial governments, would facilitate greater coordination across the 3-Ds and ensure that Canada's Arctic Strategy integrates foreign and domestic policy priorities.

Conclusion

A Mari ad Mare ad Mare: Building National Will

> Canada's Arctic is central to our national identity as a northern nation. It is part of our history. And it represents the tremendous potential of our future.
> —*Prime Minister Stephen Harper, 2007*[316]

The building of national will is difficult to cast in concrete policy terms, but it is of paramount importance if Canada is going to make a sustained investment in its North and in the circumpolar world more generally. Notwithstanding our deference to the "True North Strong and Free" line in our national anthem, very few southern Canadians really embrace the North beyond symbolism and mythology. We revere the Arctic as a touchstone of our distinctiveness—the inukshuk was, of course, the symbol for the 2010 Vancouver Olympics—but we have been unwilling to make it a national priority except at those fleeting junctures when "purveyors of polar peril"[317] tell us we might lose it. The time has come for southern Canadians to internalize their responsibilities for the North, not because it is in danger of being stolen away but because it is integral to who we are as a country. A Northern Vision has the potential to unite us all. The Arctic is a region of opportunity where we can make important contributions to constructing a more cooperative and sustainable circumpolar world.

Although many southern Canadians have lost touch with the land and the sea, it is the environment that binds us all. Our national motto, derived from Psalm 72:8 when the Fathers of Confederation dreamed of a country stretching from Atlantic to Pacific, no longer accommodates the breadth of the country we have become. "A mari usque ad mare" is an anachronism, a reminder that we have yet to embrace our northernness. Since 1880, when Canada inherited the Arctic Archipelago from the British, we have also been an Arctic nation. As a start, Canada should officially acknowledge the third ocean in our national motto by amending it to read, *A mari ad mare ad mare*—"from sea to sea to sea." In 2006, national polls showed very strong support for this proposal when it was introduced in the House of Commons. Having to change the motto on paper money, passports, federal buildings, and other places where the coat of arms appears would entail expense, but it would be a strong reaffirmation, to quote Jack Anawak, "that the North is very much a part of Canada."[318]

To build strong national will for a Northern Vision, the federal government needs to be more systematic and proactive in its Arctic strategy. The Conservative government has since 2006 been proactive in preparing for a "Polar Race." It has *not* been systematic in constructing a "Polar Saga." In a speech he gave in Whitehorse on 11 March 2009, the Minister of Foreign Affairs, Lawrence Cannon, took an important step in this direction when he adopted the language of cooperation and relationships that is essential to constructive international engagement. Implementing a comprehensive northern strategy will require an expanded vision that accommodates the broader suite of priorities articulated by the other federal political parties, northern representatives, and other stakeholders. The challenge, James Stauch of the Walter & Duncan Gordon Foundation notes, is how to balance "progress and panic" in light of the disconnection between the "real and imagined Norths" and "wildly vacillating" southern interest in the region. How can current interest be sustained and put to good effect in a manner that is responsible to Northerners' priorities and effective in promoting Canadian sovereignty, values, and interests?[319]

Before Canada can take a leadership role in the circumpolar world, it needs to have more creative leadership at home. Stephen Harper has an opportunity to build his reputation as the most northern-oriented prime minister in our history. His readiness to quote John Diefenbaker in the lead-up to the 2008 federal election, in apparent hopes of rekindling "the Chief's" energy and excitement from the 1958 Conservative campaign, indicates his desire to make northern development a key legacy of his government. Harper can improve on his predecessors by enacting an integrated Northern Vision and selling it to Canadians as a positive nation-building exercise. He can use the Arctic file as proof that he is willing to work with the opposition parties in a non-partisan manner to improve the country. Most important, he has the opportunity to invest Canadians with a sense of national purpose. Managing the economy in a time of crisis, regardless of how competently, will not earn him the title of nation builder; nor will beefing up the Canadian Forces. In looking to succeed where previous prime ministers have failed, Harper told reporters that "I'm hoping that years from now, Canada's

Arctic sovereignty, military and otherwise, will be, frankly, a major legacy of this government."[320] Building the national will to seize our northern destiny, not out of fear but out of confidence and a sense of national purpose, will contribute to a stronger, more prosperous Canada and a stable and constructive circumpolar world.

Notes

1 Franklyn Griffiths, "Civility in the Arctic," in *Arctic Alternatives: Civility or Militarism in the Circumpolar North*, ed. Franklyn Griffiths (Toronto: Science for Peace/Samuel Stevens, 1992), 279–309.

2 See, for example, Mary Simon, "Inuit Say Budget Falls Far Short of Throne Speech Promises," Inuit Tapiriit Kanatami (ITK) press release, 27 February 2008.

3 ITK and Inuit Circumpolar Council (ICC) (Canada), *Building Inuit Nunaat: The Inuit Action Plan* (2006), http://www.itk.ca/sites/default/files/Inuit-Action-Plan.pdf, accessed 28 May 2009.

4 Please note that this assessment differs from the conclusions in Ken Coates, Whitney Lackenbauer, William Morrison, and Greg Poelzer, *Arctic Front: Defending Canada's Interests in the Far North* (Toronto: Thomas Allen, 2008) but is consistent with our treatment of Canadian sovereignty from the Second World War to 1990 (the chapters for which I was primary author). Although my co-authors gave Canada a failing grade in its track record, this was largely on the basis of missed development opportunities and Canada's socio-cultural record. Rather than authoring a dissenting opinion in the co-authored book, I was encouraged to reserve it for this report.

5 Donat Pharand, "The Arctic Waters and the Northwest Passage: A Final Revisit," *Ocean Development and International Law* 38, nos. 1–2 (2007): 58–59.

6 Gordon W. Smith, "The Transfer of Arctic Territories from Great Britain to Canada in 1880, and Some Related Matters, as Seen in Official Correspondence," *Arctic* 14, no. 1 (1961): 53–73.

7 William R. Morrison, *Showing the Flag: The Mounted Police and Canadian Sovereignty in the North, 1894–1925* (Vancouver: UBC Press, 1985).

8 Shelagh Grant, *Sovereignty or Security? Government Policy in the Canadian North, 1936–1950* (Vancouver: UBC Press, 1988).

9 P. Whitney Lackenbauer, "Right and Honourable: Mackenzie King, Canadian–American Bilateral Relations, and Canadian Sovereignty in the Northwest, 1943–1948," in *Mackenzie King: Citizenship and Community*, ed. John English, Kenneth McLaughlin, and P.W. Lackenbauer (Toronto: Robin Brass Studios, 2002), 151–68.

10 For example, Grant, *Sovereignty or Security?*

11 Gordon W. Smith, "Weather Stations in the Canadian North and Sovereignty," *Journal of Military and Strategic Studies* 11, no. 3 (2009): 72–73.

12 Nigel D. Bankes, "Forty Years of Canadian Sovereignty Assertion in the Arctic, 1947–87," *Arctic* 40, no. 4 (December 1987): 285–91 at 287.

13 Ralph Allen, "Will DEWline Cost Canada Its Northland?" *Maclean's*, 26 May 1956, 16–17, 68–72.

14 E.B. Wang, "The Dew Line and Canadian Sovereignty," 26 May 1969, LAC, RG 25, file 27-10-2-2, pt. 1. See also R.J. Sutherland, "The Strategic Significance of the Canadian Arctic," in *The Arctic Frontier*, ed. R. St. J. MacDonald (Toronto: University of Toronto Press, 1966), 271.

15 Desmond Morton, "Providing and Consuming Security in Canada's Century," *Canadian Historical Review* 81, no. 1 (2000): 1–28.
16 See, for example, David L. Larson, "United States Interests in the Arctic Region," *Ocean Development and International Law* 20 (1989): 167–71 at 169.
17 Milton Viorst, "Arctic Waters Must Be Free," *Toronto Star*, 20 September 1969, 16.
18 Margaret W. Morris, "Boundary Problems Relating to the Sovereignty of the Canadian Arctic," in *Canada's Changing North*, ed. William C. Wonders (Toronto: McClelland and Stewart, 1971), 322; Gordon W. Smith, "Sovereignty in the North: The Canadian Aspect of an International Problem," in *The Arctic Frontier*, ed. R. St. J. MacDonald (Toronto: University of Toronto Press, 1966), 194–255 at 236–37; and Elizabeth B. Elliot-Meisel, *Arctic Diplomacy: Canada and the United States in the Northwest Passage* (New York: Peter Lang, 1998), 140.
19 Canada, House of Commons, *Debates*, 15 May 1969, 8720–1.
20 Elliot-Meisel, *Arctic Diplomacy*, 141.
21 Maxwell Cohen, "The Arctic and the National Interest," *International Journal* 26, no. 1 (1970–71): 72.
22 Elliot-Meisel, *Arctic Diplomacy*, 143.
23 United Nations Convention on the Law of the Sea (UNCLOS), 10 December 1982, http://www.un.org/Depts/los/convention_agreements/texts/unclos/unclos_e.pdf, accessed 28 May 2009. See Part XII: "Protection and Preservation of the Marine Environment," Section 8: "Ice-Covered Areas," Article 234: "Ice-Covered Areas." On the background to Article 234, see Donald M. McRae and D.J. Goundrey, "Environmental Jurisdiction in the Arctic Waters: The Extent of Article 234," *UBC Law Review* 16, no. 2 (1982): 197–228 at 215–22.
24 Larson, "United States Interests," 183.
25 According to UNCLOS, all ships and aircraft have the right of *transit passage* through "straits which are used for international navigation between one part of the high seas or an exclusive economic zone and another part of the high seas or an exclusive economic zone." The freedom of navigation and overflight in this context is "solely for the purpose of continuous and expeditious transit of the strait between one part of the high seas or an exclusive economic zone and another part of the high seas or an exclusive economic zone." UNCLOS, Part III: "Straits Used for International Navigation," Section 2: "Transit Passage," Articles 37–38.
26 Joseph T. Jockel, *Security to the North: Canada–U.S. Defence Relationships in the 1990s* (East Lansing: Michigan State University Press, 1991), 193.
27 Pharand, "The Arctic Waters and the Northwest Passage," 43
28 Donald M. McRae, "Arctic Sovereignty: Loss by Dereliction?" *CARC—Northern Perspectives* 22, no. 4 (1994–95): 4–9.
29 House of Commons Standing Committee on Foreign Affairs and International Trade (HCSCFAIT), *Canada and the Circumpolar World: Meeting the Challenges of Cooperation into the Twenty-First Century* (Ottawa: 1997), ix, 100.
30 DFAIT, Government Response to Standing Committee on Foreign Affairs and International Trade Report, *Canada and the Circumpolar World: Meeting the Challenges of Cooperation into the Twenty-First Century* (Ottawa: 1998).
31 DFAIT, *The Northern Dimension of Canada's Foreign Policy* (Ottawa: 2000).
32 Ibid.
33 Specifically, the department questioned whether it should continue to financially support the University of the Arctic; little progress had been made in "working with Russia to address northern challenges" or on northern cooperation with the European

Union, and activities supporting sustainable economic development and trade were "inconsistently linked to the NDFP and outcome rather than results oriented." DFAIT, *Summative Evaluation of the Northern Dimension of Canada's Foreign Policy* (May 2005), http://www.international.gc.ca/about-a_propos/oig-big/2005/evaluation/northern_program-programme_nordique.aspx?lang=eng, accessed 28 May 2009.

34 DFAIT, *Summative Evaluation.*
35 Canadian Forces Northern Area (CFNA), *Arctic Capabilities Study* (2000).
36 Rob Huebert, "Climate Change and Canadian Sovereignty in the Northwest Passage," *Isuma: Canadian Journal of Policy Research* 2, no. 4 (2001): 86–94 at 92.
37 Canada, *Canada's International Policy Statement,* Overview (Ottawa: 2005), 3.
38 Canadian Arctic Resources Committee, "Renewing the Northern Strategy," *Northern Perspectives* 30, no. 1 (2006): 1–2 at 2.
39 Rob Huebert, "Canada and the Changing International Arctic: At the Crossroads of Cooperation and Conflict," in *Northern Exposure: Peoples, Powers, and Prospects for Canada's North*, ed. Frances Abele et al. (Ottawa: Institute for Research on Public Policy, 2008), 1. http://www.irpp.org, accessed 28 May 2009.
40 Franklyn Griffiths, "Canadian Arctic Sovereignty: Time to Take Yes for an Answer on the Northwest Passage," in *Northern Exposure: Peoples, Powers, and Prospects for Canada's North*, ed. by Frances Abele et al. (Ottawa: Institute for Research on Public Policy, 2008), 3–5. http://www.irpp.org, accessed 28 May 2009.
41 Prime Minister's Office (PMO), "PM Unveils Canada First Defence Strategy," 12 May 2008. http://pm.gc.ca/eng/media.asp?id=2095, Accessed 28 May 2009.
42 David Bercuson, "Comedy of Errors: First, a Defence Strategy, Then a Shopping List," *Globe and Mail*, 21 May 2008, A17.
43 Government of Canada, "Protecting Canada's Future," Speech from the Throne, 16 October 2007. http://www.sft-ddt.gc.ca/eng/media.asp?id=1364, accessed 5 June 2009.
44 Department of Finance, "Budget 2008: Responsible Leadership," Chapter 4, "Leadership at Home," http://www.budget.gc.ca/2008/plan/chap4a-eng.asp, accessed 28 May 2009.
45 For similar comments on the government's defence strategy, see David Pugliese, "Conservatives Won't Commit Defence Strategy to Paper: 20-Year Plan for Military Be Based on 'Vision' Outlined in Harper, MacKay Speeches," *Ottawa Citizen*, 13 May 2008, A1.
46 Walter and Duncan Gordon Foundation (WDGF), "The Arctic and Canada's Foreign Policy," Report and Recommendations from a Workshop sponsored by the WDGF, 4–5 October 2006. http://www.gordonfn.org/resfiles/ForeignArcticPolicyWorkshop_Nov%202006.pdf, accessed 28 May 2009.
47 Yukon, Northwest Territories, and Nunavut Governments, *A Northern Vision: A Stronger North and a Better Canada* (Yellowknife: 2007). http://www.anorthernvision.ca, accessed 28 May 2009.
48 Ibid.
49 Arctic Athabaskan Council (AAC), "Europe and the Arctic: A View from the Arctic Athabaskan Council," presentation to Nordic Council of Ministers, Arctic Conference: Common Concern for the Arctic, Ilulissat, Greenland, 9–11 September 2008), 5.
50 Ibid., 6.
51 Ibid., 7.
52 ITK and ICC (Canada), *Building Inuit Nunaat,* 58.
53 ITK, *An Integrated Arctic Strategy* (2008), 13. http://www.itk.ca/sites/default/files/Integrated-Arctic-Stratgey.pdf, accessed 28 May 2009.
54 Ibid., 13–14.
55 Ibid., 21.

56 Huebert, "Canada and the Changing International Arctic," 2.
57 Ibid.; "The Shipping News Part II: How Canada's Arctic Sovereignty Is on Thinning Ice," *International Journal* 58, no. 3 (2003): 295–308; "Renaissance in Canadian Arctic Security?" *Canadian Military Journal* 6, no. 4 (2005–06): 17–29.
58 Franklyn Griffiths, "Our Arctic Sovereignty Is Well in Hand," *Globe and Mail*, 8 November 2006. A25.
59 Franklyn Griffiths, "The Shipping News: Canada's Arctic Sovereignty Not on Thinning Ice," *International Journal* 58, no. 2 (2003): 257–82; "Camels in the Arctic?" *The Walrus*, 4 January 2008, 46–61.
60 Griffiths, "Canadian Arctic Sovereignty," 1.
61 Global Business Network (GBN), "The Future of Arctic Marine Navigation in Mid-Century," scenario narratives produced for the Protection of the Arctic Marine Environment (PAME) Working Group, May 2008. http://www.gbn.com/articles/pdfs/GBN_Future%20of%20Arctic%20Navigation%20Mid-century.pdf, last accessed 20 June 2011.
62 Scott G. Borgerson, "Arctic Meltdown: The Economic and Security Implications of Global Warming," *Foreign Affairs* (March–April 2008): 63–77 at 71.
63 Novosti, "Russia Says Media Reports on Possible Arctic Conflict 'Alarmist,'" 22 October 2008. http://en.rian.ru/russia/20081022/117891202.html, accessed 28 May 2009.
64 Ibid.
65 Novosti, "Russia Says Arctic Marking Does Not Imply Territorial Claim," 23 September 2008. http://en.rian.ru/russia/20080923/117046775.html, accessed 28 May 2009.
66 GBN, "The Future of Arctic Marine Navigation."
67 Donald M. McRae, "Arctic Sovereignty: What Is at Stake?" *Behind the Headlines* 64, no. 1 (2007): 3.
68 McRae, "Arctic Sovereignty: Loss by Dereliction?"
69 E.B. Wang to R.P. Cameron, "Sovereignty," 20 March 1970, LAC, RG 25, vol. 10322, file 27-10-2-2, pt. 1.
70 E.B. Wang, "The Role of Canadian Armed Forces in Defending Sovereignty: A Paper by E.B. Wang, 30 April 1969," *Journal of Military and Strategic Studies* 11, no. 3 (2009): 1–23 at 22–23, ed. P. Whitney Lackenbauer.
71 Memorandum, DEXAF, Legal Division, "DND Paper on 'Canadian Defence Policy in the 1970's,'" 5 August 1970, LAC, RG 25, vol. 10322, file 27-10-2-2, pt. 1.
72 E.B. Wang, "Canadian Forces Activities in the North: Sovereignty," Memorandum to Mr. Cameron, External Affairs, 25 November 1970, LAC, RG 25, vol. 10322, file 27-10-2-2, pt. 2, acquired under Access to Information.
73 DEXAF, Memorandum, Legal Division, "DND Paper on 'Canadian Defence Policy in the 1970s,'" 5 August 1970, LAC, RG 25, vol. 10322, file 27-10-2-2, pt. 1, acquired under Access to Information,
74 DEXAF, Memorandum, Office of Politico-Military Affairs, "Role of Canadian Armed Forces in Maintenance of Sovereignty," 20 April 1970, LAC, RG 25, vol. 10322, file 27-10-2-2, pt. 1, acquired under Access to Information.
75 L.H.J. Legault, Memorandum, "Draft Paper on Defence Policy—Sovereignty Aspects," to J.A Beesley, 2 February 1971, LAC, RG 25, vol. 10322, file 27-10-2-2, pt. 2, acquired under Access to Information. See also DEXAF, Memorandum, "Draft White Paper on Defence Policy—Sovereignty Aspects," North American Defence and NATO Division to Legal Division, 28 January 1971, LAC, RG 25, vol. 10322, file 27-10-2-2, pt. 2, acquired under Access to Information.
76 DEXAF, "Comments on Draft Paper on Defence Policy," 11 February 1972, LAC, RG 25, vol. 10322, file 27-10-2-2, pt. 2, acquired under Access to Information.

77 On "undisciplined rhetoric" along these lines, see James Kraska, "The Law of the Sea Convention and the Northwest Passage," *International Journal of Marine and Coastal Law* 22, no. 2 (2007): 257–81 at 262.

78 Kathleen Harris, "Laying Claim to Canada's Internal Waters," *Toronto Sun*, 23 February 2007. http://cnews.canoe.ca/CNEWS/Canada/2007/02/22/3655342-sun.html, accessed 23 June 2011.

79 Gregory Hooks and Chad L. Smith, "The Treadmill of Destruction: National Sacrifice Areas and Native Americans," *American Sociological Review* 69 (2004): 558–75; Kevin McMahon, *Arctic Twilight: Reflections on the Destiny of Canada's Northern Land and People* (Toronto: Lorimer, 1988); P. Whitney Lackenbauer and Mathew Farish, "The Cold War on Canadian Soil: Militarizing a Northern Environment," *Environmental History* 12, no. 3 (2007): 920–50.

80 P. Whitney Lackenbauer, "The Canadian Rangers: A Postmodern Militia That Works," *Canadian Military Journal* 6, no. 4 (2005–6): 49–60.

81 Captain Conrad Schubert, letter to Commander of Joint Task Force North (JTFN), 22 October 2007, DND file 1920-1 (DCO).

82 ITK, "An Integrated Arctic Strategy," 15. http://www.itk.ca/sites/default/files/Integrated -Arctic-Stratgey.pdf, accessed 28 May 2009.

83 Chief of the Maritime Staff (CMS), *Statement of Operational Requirement: Arctic/Offshore Patrol Ship (AOPS)* (Ottawa: Department of National Defence, 2008), 6.

84 Murray Brewster, "New Arctic Patrol Vessels Approved: Plan to Build Ships Given Go-Ahead by Cabinet Committee," *Calgary Herald*, 14 May 2007, A8.

85 Larry Bagnell, "We're in Danger of Losing Part of Canada," *Embassy*, 6 November 2008.

86 CMS, *Statement of Operational Requirement*, 13.

87 Captain (Navy) Jamie Cotter, "Developing a Coherent Plan to Deal with Canada's Conundrum in the Northwest Passage," *Journal of Military and Strategic Studies* 11, no. 3 (2009): 1–51 at 16.

88 Major Paul Dittmann, "In Defence of Defence: Canadian Arctic Sovereignty and Security," *Journal of Military and Strategic Studies* 11, no. 3 (2009): 1–77 at 65.

89 CBC News, "Harper Announces Northern Deep-Sea Port, Training Site," 11 August 2007. http://www.cbc.ca/canada/story/2007/08/10/port-north.html, accessed 28 May 2009.

90 Hugues Canuel, "Nanisivik Refuelling Facility Will Enable Persistent Naval Presence," *Hill Times*, 20 August 2007, 24.

91 Dittmann, "In Defence of Defence," 61.

92 CFNA, *Arctic Capabilities Study*, 8–1, 8–3.

93 Peter Gizewski and Andrew B. Godefroy, "Force Requirements (Land)," in *Defence Requirements for Canada's Arctic*, ed. Brian MacDonald (Ottawa: Conference of Defence Associations Institute, 2007), 96–106 at 100.

94 Cotter, "Developing a Coherent Plan," 14–17; Dittmann, "In Defence of Defence," 75.

95 Dittmann, "In Defence of Defence," 72.

96 Cindy Chan, "Space Contract Awards Design Contract for Satellite Fleet," *Epoch Times*, 19 November 2008. http://en.epochtimes.com/n2/science-technology/space-agency -satellite-7444.html, accessed 28 May 2009.

97 Defence Research and Development Canada (DRDC), "Northern Watch: A Window into Canadian Arctic Surveillance," February 2008. http://www.drdc-rddc.gc.ca/news -nouvelles/spotlight-pleinfeux/index-eng.asp, accessed 3 March 2009.

98 Dittmann, "In Defence of Defence," 67–68.

99 Ibid., 75.

100 Rob Huebert, "Canadian Arctic Maritime Security: The Return to Canada's Third Ocean," *Canadian Military Journal* 8, no. 2 (2007): 9–16 at 13; "Time for Gov't to Go Beyond Arctic Promises," *Embassy*, 6 November 2008. http://www.embassymag.ca/page/view/arctic_promises-11-6-2008, accessed 28 May 2009.

101 CFNA, *Arctic Capabilities Study*, 18.

102 Dittmann, "In Defence of Defence," 61.

103 Brian MacDonald, "Force Requirements (Air)," 113.

104 LCol S.W. Moore, "Defending Canadian Arctic Sovereignty: An Examination of Prime Minister Harper's Arctic Initiatives" (Toronto: Canadian Forces College, 2007), 20–21.

105 Marine and Environmental Law Institute (MELAW), Dalhousie Law School, *Governance of Arctic Marine Shipping* (1 August 2008), 56.

106 Standing Senate Committee on Fisheries and Oceans (SSCFO), *The Coast Guard in Canada's Arctic: Interim Report* (Ottawa: June 2008), 33, 35.

107 Standing Senate Committee on National Security and Defence (SSCNSD), *Emergency Preparedness in Canada: How the Fine Arts of Bafflegab and Procrastination Hobble the People Who Will Be Trying to Save You When Things Get Really Bad ...* (Ottawa: 2008), 42.

108 Jonathan Seymour & Associates Inc. and The Mariport Group Ltd., *Canadian Arctic Shipping Assessment Scoping Study*, prepared for Transport Canada Seaway and Domestic Shipping Policy (Gibbons, BC: 2005): 2.

109 Ibid., 26.

110 Privy Council Office, *Securing an Open Society: Canada's National Security Policy* (April 2004). http://www.pco-bcp.gc.ca/docs/information/Publications/natsec-secnat/natsec-secnat-eng.pdf, accessed 28 May 2009. Specific priorities included "long-range detection technologies; enhanced screening of ships' passengers and crews; advanced reporting requirements to improve the assessment of potential risks posed by vessels, their passengers and cargo; and measures to intercept vessels of concern before they arrive on our shores."

111 *Marine Security Operations Centres Project* (MSOC), http://msoc-cosm.gc.ca/index-eng.asp, accessed 28 May 2009; RCMP, Marine and Ports Branch Great Lakes and St. Lawrence Seaway Interim Marine Security Operation Centre (GLSLS MSOC), "Frequently Asked Questions," 2008. http://www.rcmp-grc.gc.ca/fio/marine_faq_e.htm, accessed 28 May 2009; Chris Thatcher, "A Pan-Government Approach to Marine Security," *Vanguard*, 2006, http://www.vanguardcanada.com/MSOCThatcher, accessed 28 May 2009.

112 Dittmann, "In Defence of Defence," 58.

113 SSCFO, *Coast Guard in Canada's Arctic*, 28.

114 Michael Turner. "Guarding Canada's Northern Coast: It's Too Bad That the Harper Government's Preoccupation with the Military Has Caused It to Overlook a More Sensible Solution to Arctic Sovereignty," *Ottawa Citizen*, 13 July 2007, A13.

115 Ibid.

116 CBC News, "Coast Guard Faces Staffing Crunch as Arctic Demands Grow," 24 June 2008. http://www.cbc.ca/canada/story/2008/06/24/coast-guard.html, accessed 28 May 2009; SSCFO, *Coast Guard in Canada's Arctic*, 36.

117 Ibid., 39.

118 Ibid., 34.

119 Auditor General of Canada (AGC), "Managing the Coast Guard Fleet and Marine Navigational Services—Fisheries and Oceans Canada," Status Report to the House of Commons (February 2007): 2. http://www.parl.gc.ca/HousePublications/Publication.aspx?DocId=3442082&Language=E&Mode=1&Parl=39&Ses=2, accessed 10 December 2008.

120 Ibid.

121 SCCFO Proceedings, 13 May 2008. http://www.parl.gc.ca/Content/SEN/Committee/392/fish/09eva-e.htm?Language=E&Parl=39&Ses=2&comm_id=7, accessed 28 May 2009.

122 Standing Committee on Public Accounts (SCPA), *Managing the Coast Guard Fleet and Marine Navigation Services—Fisheries and Oceans* (April) (Ottawa: 2008), 7.

123 SSCFO, *Coast Guard in Canada's Arctic,* 28.

124 Ibid., 1, 3, 38.

125 Dittmann, "In Defence of Defence," 61–62.

126 Eric Lerhe, "Whither Canada's National Security Defence, the Navy, and the Coast Guard in a New Security Environment? Discussant Report," paper presented to the Future of Canada's Maritime Capabilities Conference, Centre for Foreign Policy Studies, Dalhousie University, 18–20 June 2004, 241.

127 SSCNSD, *Canadian Security Guide Book—Coasts* (March 2007), 6. http://www.ccg-gcc.gc.ca/folios/00018/docs/bp-pa-0811-eng.pdf, accessed 28 May 2009; SCPA, *Managing the Coast Guard Fleet,* 14.

128 SSCFO, *Nunavut Fisheries,* 18, 45.

129 Canadian Coast Guard, *Business Plan 2008–11,* 18; *Canadian Coast Guard 2007–2008 Year End Report,* 5. http://www.ccg-gcc.gc.ca/folios/00018/docs/2007-2008-year-end-report-eng.pdf, accessed 28 May 2009.

130 Jonathan Seymour, *Canadian Arctic Shipping Assessment,* 2.

131 SSCFO, *Coast Guard in Canada's Arctic,* 31.

132 Huebert to SSCFO, SCCFO Proceedings, 13 March 2008. http://www.parl.gc.ca/Content/SEN/Committee/392/fish/05cv-e.htm?Language=E&Parl=39&Ses=2&comm_id=7, accessed 28 May 2009.

133 For a brief discussion of the "defiance" of the cruise ships MS *Hanseatic* and MS *Bremen* as "a direct challenge to the Canadian ability to control its northern waters," see Rob Huebert, "As the Ice Melts, Control Ebbs in the Arctic," *Globe and Mail,* 18 August 2008. Both ships have ice-strengthened E4 hulls, equivalent to Type A hulls in the Arctic Waters Pollution Prevention Act, which gives them some independence in Arctic summer ice conditions. These ships also have a considerable history of circumpolar navigation and cooperation with Canadian authorities.

134 SSCFO, *Coast Guard in Canada's Arctic,* 21.

135 Spears to SSCFO, SSCFO Proceedings, 27 May 2008. http://www.parl.gc.ca/Content/SEN/Committee/392/fish/09evc-e.htm?Language=E&Parl=39&Ses=2&comm_id=7, accessed 28 May 2009.

136 Victor M. Santos-Pedro to SSCFO, SSCFO Proceedings, 15 May 2008. http://www.parl.gc.ca/Content/SEN/Committee/392/fish/09evb-e.htm?Language=E&Parl=39&Ses=2&comm_id=7, accessed 28 May 2009.

137 SSCNSD, *Canada's Coastlines: The Longest Under-Defended Borders in the World* 1 (October) (Ottawa: 2003).

138 William J. Nash to SSCFO, SSCFO Proceedings, 15 May 2008. http://www.parl.gc.ca/Content/SEN/Committee/392/fish/09evb-e.htm?Language=E&Parl=39&Ses=2&comm_id=7, accessed 28 May 2009.

139 See Transport Canada, News Release H078/10, "Government of Canada Takes Action to Protect Canadian Arctic Waters," 22 June 2010. http://www.tc.gc.ca/eng/mediaroom/releases-2010-h078e-6019.htm, accessed 23 June 2010.

140 Cotter, "Developing a Coherent Plan," 36.

141 SSCONSD, *Canada's Coastlines,* 135. This option is consistent with White House, *National Security Presidential Directive/NSPD 66, Homeland Security Presidential Directive/HSPD 25—Arctic Region Policy* (hereafter US Presidential Directive), 9 January 2009, which

notes that "the United States has broad and fundamental national security interests in the Arctic region and is prepared to operate either independently or in conjunction with other states to safeguard these interests. These interests include such matters as missile defense and early warning; deployment of sea and air systems for strategic sealift, strategic deterrence, maritime presence, and maritime security operations; and ensuring freedom of navigation and overflight."

142   Dittmann, "In Defence of Defence"; Griffiths, "Canadian Arctic Sovereignty."

143   Canadians viewed environmental issues as the greatest threat, followed by American incursions on the Arctic. Approximately 10 percent cited one of two other possible threats: foreign claims to Canadian territory, and terrorist attacks.

144   For a useful chart summarizing competing claims among the five Arctic littoral states, see David Runnalls, "Arctic Sovereignty and Security in a Climate-Changing World," in *Securing Canada's Future in a Climate-Changing World* (Ottawa: National Round Table on the Environment and the Economy, 2008), 87.

145   CBC News, "Canada, Denmark Agree to Resolve Dispute over Arctic Island," 19 September 2005. http://www.cbc.ca/world/story/2005/09/19/hans-island-20050919.html, accessed 28 May 2009.

146   "Who Owns the Arctic?" Episode of *The Agenda* with Steve Paikin, TV Ontario, broadcast on 29 September 2008. http://www.tvo.org/TVO/WebObjects/TVO.woa? video?TAWSP_Dbt_20080929_779336_0, accessed 10 October 2008.

147   Jacob Verhoef and Dick MacDougall, "Delineating Canada's Continental Shelf According to the United Nations Convention on the Law of the Sea," *Ocean Sovereignty* 3, no. 1 (2008): 1–6 at 5.

148   Suzanne Lalonde, "Arctic Waters: Cooperation or Conflict?" *Behind the Headlines* 65, no. 4 (2008): 8–14.

149   Quoted in Griffiths, "Canadian Arctic Sovereignty," 7.

150   Bill Rompkey, "Russian Flags Aren't the Real Threat to Arctic Sovereignty," *Ottawa Citizen*, 17 July 2008, A13.

151   SSCFO, *Coast Guard in Canada's Arctic,* 13.

152   See, for example, "The Arctic Contest Heats Up," *The Economist*, 9 October 2008. http://www.economist.com/world/europe/PrinterFriendly.cfm?story_id=12381767, accessed 28 May 2009.

153   Mike Blanchfield, "Harper Warns Russians after Two Bombers Intercepted," *National Post*, 28 February 2009, A10.

154   Meagan Fitzpatrick, "Russian Bombers Did Not Breach Canadian Airspace: Diplomat," *Vancouver Sun,* 23 March 2009, http://www.vancouversun.com/technology/Russian +bombers+breach+ Canadian+airspace+Diplomat/1419825/story.html, accessed 24 March 2009.

155   Lloyd Axworthy, "A New Arctic Circle," *Globe and Mail*, 22 August 2008, A15.

156   David Jones, "Don't Kid Yourselves, Canada," *Ottawa Citizen*, 15 August 2008, A15.

157   Randy Boswell, "Canada's Arctic Sovereignty Challenged: U.S. Submarines May Chart the Continental Shelf," *Vancouver Sun*, 8 March 2006, A8.

158   Bagnell, "We're in Danger of Losing Part of Canada."

159   SSCFO, *Coast Guard in Canada's Arctic,* 15.

160   Ilulissat Declaration, adopted at the Arctic Ocean Conference hosted by the Government of Denmark and attended by the representatives of the five coastal states bordering on the Arctic Ocean (Canada, Denmark, Norway, the Russian Federation, and the US), Ilulissat, Greenland, 27–29 May 2008. http://www.oceanlaw.org/downloads/arctic/ Ilulissat_Declaration.pdf, accessed 28 May 2009. The declaration stated that all states

will adhere to the existing legal framework to settle overlapping claims. Although the United States is not a signatory to the convention, there is every reason to anticipate that it will adhere to its provisions in the Arctic.

161 Michelle Collins, "Unearthing Mysteries under the Arctic Ice," *Embassy*, 6 November 2008, 20.

162 Verhoef and MacDougall, "Delineating Canada's Continental Shelf," 4–5.

163 Randy Boswell, "Research Backs Canada's Arctic Claim," *Ottawa Citizen*, 7 August 2008, A1.

164 CBC News, "Early Findings Encouraging in Canada–U.S. Mapping of Arctic Ocean Seabed," 3 November 2008. http://www.cbc.ca/canada/north/story/2008/11/03/arctic -seabed.html, accessed 28 May 2009.

165 CBC News, "Arctic Seabed Mapping Renewed," 29 July 2009. http://www.cbc.ca/news/ canada/north/story/2009/07/29/cda-us-arctic-mapping.html, accessed 29 July 2009.

166 Verhoef and MacDougall, "Delineating Canada's Continental Shelf," 5.

167 David H. Gray, "Canada's Unresolved Maritime Boundaries," IBRU *Boundary and Security Bulletin* (1997): 61–70 at 65.

168 Donat Pharand, *The Law of the Sea of the Arctic with Special Reference to Canada* (Ottawa: University of Ottawa Press, 1973), 312; Michel Frederick, "La délimitation du plateau continental entre le Canada et les Etats-Unis dans la mer de Beaufort," *Annuaire canadien de Droit international 1979* (Vancouver: UBC Press, 1979), 78, 91; Gray, "Canada's Unresolved Maritime Boundaries," 63.

169 Barak Obama, "Barak Obama and Joe Biden: New Energy for America," 2008, 5. http://www.barackobama.com/pdf/factsheet_energy_speech_080308.pdf, accessed 28 May 2009.

170 Bagnell, "We're in Danger of Losing Part of Canada."

171 Allan Woods and Tonda MacCharles, "Canada, U.S. to Open Clean Energy 'Dialogue,'" *Toronto Star*, 19 February 2009, A6.

172 Quoted in SSCFO, *Coast Guard in Canada's Arctic.*

173 Donald Rothwell, *Maritime Boundaries and Resource Development: Options for the Beaufort Sea* (Calgary: Canadian Institute of Resources Law, 1988), 45–48. This option is consistent with the 9 January 2009 US Presidential Directive, which notes that the United States should "consider the conservation and management of natural resources during the process of delimiting the extended continental shelf"; "protect United States interests with respect to hydrocarbon reservoirs that may overlap boundaries to mitigate adverse environmental and economic consequences related to their development"; "explore whether there is a need for additional fora for informing decisions on hydrocarbon leasing, exploration, development, production, and transportation, as well as shared support activities, including infrastructure projects"; and "continue to emphasize cooperative mechanisms with nations operating in the region to address shared concerns."

174 CBC News, "Wilkins Says Arctic Comment Old News," 27 January 2006. http:// www.cbc.ca/canada/story/2006/01/27/wilkins-harper060127.html, accessed 28 May 2009.

175 Douglas C. Nord, "The North in Canadian–American Relations: Searching for Cooperation in the Melting Seas," paper to the Borders and Bridges Conference, Ottawa, 18–19 October 2008, 12, 15.

176 Griffiths, "Our Arctic Sovereignty Is Well in Hand." This argument is also explicit in US Presidential Directive, 9 January 2009.

177 Thomas C. Pullen, "What Price Canadian Sovereignty?" *U.S. Naval Institute Proceedings* 113, no. 9 (1987): 66–72 at 66.

178   Christopher Kirkey, "The Arctic Waters Pollution Prevention Initiatives: Canada's Response to an American Challenge," *International Journal of Canadian Studies* 13 (1996): 41–59 at 56.

179   Philip J. Briggs, "The *Polar Sea* Voyage and the Northwest Passage Dispute," *Armed Forces and Society* 16, no. 3 (1990): 437–52 at 449.

180   Hugo Miller, "U.S. Seeks 'Unfettered' Northwest Passage," *Vancouver Province*, 21 October 2008, http://www.canada.com/theprovince/news/story.html?id=83b6126e-e345 -4317-aecb-02ff192a6212, accessed 23 June 2011.

181   Jones, "Don't Kid Yourselves, Canada."

182   Michael Byers, "Unfrozen Sea: Sailing the Northwest Passage," *Policy Options* 28, no. 5 (2007): 30–33 at 33; SSCFO, *Coast Guard in Canada's Arctic,* 24; Rompkey, "Arctic Sovereignty."

183   See, for example, Jeff Davis, "Securing the Northwest Passage Essential," *Embassy,* 6 November 2008. http://www.embassymag.ca/page/printpage/securing_northwest_ passage-11-6-2008, accessed 28 May 2009.

184   Kraska, "The Law of the Sea Convention and the Northwest Passage," 278–79; Jones, "Don't Kid Yourselves, Canada."

185   Ironically, the SSCFO's June 2008 report, *The Coast Guard in Canada's Arctic,* argues that "as long as ice conditions hazardous to international shipping remained, Canada's interests were protected. ... Until now, Canada could afford to go on 'agreeing to disagree' with the United States over its legal status" (19). This is a peculiar assertion on several levels. First, ice conditions clearly remain hazardous to international shipping, as numerous Arctic Council and marine shipping studies have amply demonstrated. The use of the past tense in the report is unwarranted. Second, no justification is offered for why "agreeing to disagree" is no longer a viable option.

186   Quoted in Paul Kaludjak, "Sovereignty and Inuit in the Canadian Arctic," Arctic Council Indigenous Peoples Secretariat, 18 November 2006, http://www.arcticpeoples.org/ index.php?option=com_k2&view=item&id=83:sovereignty-and-inuit-in-the-canadian -arctic&Itemid=2, accessed 22 June 2010.

187   Pharand, "The Arctic Waters and the Northwest Passage."

188   McRae, "Arctic Sovereignty," 18.

189   Griffiths, "Canadian Arctic Sovereignty," 15–17.

190   Huebert, "Canada and the Changing International Arctic," 17.

191   Griffiths, "The Shipping News."

192   Griffiths, "Canadian Arctic Sovereignty," 14, 22.

193   John Noble, "Arctic Solution Already in Place," *Toronto Star,* 8 February 2006, A19.

194   Adele Airoldi, *The European Union and the Arctic: Policies and Actions* (Copenhagen: Nordic Council of Ministers, 2008), 13.

195   European Union (EU), *Climate Change and International Security,* S113/08, 14 March. (Brussels: 2008), 2.

196   European Commission (EC), *The European Union and the Arctic Region,* COM(2008) 763, 20 November (Brussels: 2008).

197   Airoldi, *The European Union and the Arctic,* 26.

198   EC, *The European Union and the Arctic Region,* 12.

199   Ibid., 87–90; ITK/ICC Press Release, "Inuit of Canada: European Union Knows Proposed Seal Bay Would Be Unlawful," 27 March 2009. http://www.itk.ca/media-centre/ media-releases/itkicc-press-release-inuit-canada-european-union-knows-proposed -seal-ban, accessed 28 May 2009.

200   EC, *The European Union and the Arctic Region,* 8.

201 Ibid.

202 Ibid.

203 House of Commons Standing Committee on Foreign Affairs and International Trade (HCSCFAIT), *Canada and the Circumpolar World: Meeting the Challenges of Cooperation into the Twenty-First Century* (Ottawa: 1997), 227.

204 SSCFO, *Coast Guard in Canada's Arctic,* 8.

205 Matt Gurney, "The New Cold War: A Brief History," *National Post,* 15 August 2008, A15.

206 Natalie Mychajlyszyn, "The Arctic: Geopolitical Issues," in *The Arctic: Canadian and International Perspectives* (Ottawa: Library of Parliament InfoSeries, October 2008), 1–5 at 3; Peter O'Neil, "Russia's Militarization May Be Just Sabre-Rattling: Expert," *Canwest News Service,* 17 March 2009. Recent "tough talk" from Canadian Foreign Affairs Minister Lawrence Cannon, asserting that "Canada will not be bullied" by the Russians in light of reports that the Kremlin was planning to create a dedicated military force for the Arctic, might best be viewed as political grandstanding. After all, just five days before, Canada had announced that it was creating a "new Arctic force" over the next five years. David Pugliese, "Reserve Units to Form Core of New Arctic Force," *Ottawa Citizen,* 22 March 2009, http://www.ottawacitizen.com/news/Reserve+units+form+core+Arctic+force/ 1416657/ story.html, accessed 23 March 2009; Philip Authier, "Canada Won't Be Bullied by Russia: Cannon," *Montreal Gazette,* 27 March 2009, A12.

207 Sven G. Holtsmark, "Towards Cooperation or Confrontation? Security in the High North," research paper, Research Division—NATO Defence College Rome, no. 45, February 2009. http://www.ndc.nato.int/download/publications/rp_45en.pdf, accessed 28 May 2009.

208 Ibid., 7.

209 Ibid., 9.

210 Ibid., 7, 12.

211 DFAIT, "Joint Statement on Canada-Russia Economic Cooperation," 28–29 November 2007, http://www.international.gc.ca/commerce/zubkov/joint_state-en.asp, accessed 10 May 2009.

212 Agreement Between the Government of Canada and the Government of the Russian Federation on Cooperation in the Arctic and the North, E100317—Canada Treaty Series 1992, No. 18. http://www.treaty-accord.gc.ca/text-texte.asp?id=100317, accessed 20 May 2011.

213 ICC, *Project Description: Institutional Building for Northern Aboriginal Peoples in Russia (INRIPP-2)* (2008), http://www.inuitcircumpolar.com/index.php?ID=209&Lang=En, accessed 28 May 2009; Gary N. Wilson, "Inuit Diplomacy in the Circumpolar North," *Canadian Foreign Policy* 13, no. 3 (2007): 65–80 at 72–73.

214 See, for example,Kirill Kalinin, "Russia-Canada Cooperation in the Arctic," Embassy of the Russian Federation in Canada, Press Release, 11 March 2009. In February 2010, Chuck Strahl, Minister of Indian Affairs and Northern Development, signed a new work plan with the Honourable Viktor Fyodorovich Basargin, Minister of Regional Development of the Russian Federation, to implement concrete activities under the 2007 Memorandum of Understanding through exchanging best practices in the preservation of Aboriginal languages; building capacity for local public administration; sharing tools for Aboriginal policy research; and promoting public–private partnerships. Indian and Northern Affairs Canada, News Release 2-3317, "Canada and Russia Working Jointly for the Well-Being of the Aboriginal Peoples of the Arctic," Ottawa, 12 February 2010.

215 Mariport Group, *Canadian Arctic Shipping Assessment: Main Report,* prepared for Transport Canada (June 2007), 132, 137; MELAW, *Governance of Arctic Marine Shipping,* 66–67.

216 Oran R. Young, "Governing the Arctic: From Cold War Theatre to Mosaic of Coopera-tion," *Global Governance* 11 (2005): 10, 14.

217 Arctic Council, "About Arctic Council," 26 November 2007. http://arctic-council.org/article/about, accessed 28 May 2009.

218 Timo Koivurova and David Vanderzwaag, "The Arctic Council at 10 Years: Retrospect and Prospects," *UBC Law Review* 40, no. 1 (2007): 121–94 at 122.

219 AAC, "Europe and the Arctic," 3.

220 Ibid.

221 Young, "Governing the Arctic," 11.

222 The Council's working groups are as follows: Arctic Monitoring and Assessment Program (AMAP); Conservation of Arctic Flora and Fauna (CAFF); Emergency Prevention, Pre-paredness, and Response (EPPR); Protection of the Arctic Marine Environment (PAME); and Sustainable Development Working Group (SDWG).

223 AAC, "Europe and the Arctic," 2–3.

224 EC, *The European Union and the Arctic Region*, 10.

225 Huebert, "Canada and the Changing International Arctic," 3, 22.

226 Rob Huebert and Brooks B. Yeager, Report for the WWF, *A New Sea: The Need for a Cooperative Framework for Management and Conservation of the Arctic Marine Environ-ment*, 22 January 2008, 33–38. http://assets.panda.org/downloads/a_new_sea_jan08_final_11jan08.pdf, accessed 28 May 2009.

227 Oran Young, in rejecting the argument for a comprehensive treaty for the governance of the Arctic as a whole, notes that "the law of the sea provides a perfectly serviceable frame-work for addressing maritime issues in the far north" and that "legally binding arrange-ments typically take a long time to negotiate and bring into force, exhibit a tendency to contain provisions reflecting the lowest common denominator among the parties, and are hard to adjust or revise in a timely manner. This is a recipe for disaster in dealing with complex and dynamic systems like the Arctic." See Young, "Whither the Arctic 2009? Further developments," *Polar Record* 45 (2009): 179–81 at 180–81.

228 The US Presidential Directive, 9 January 2009, applauds the work of the Arctic Council "within its limited mandate of environmental protection and sustainable development," as well as its value as "a beneficial venue for interaction with indigenous groups." It asserts the US position that "the Arctic Council should remain a high-level forum devoted to issues within its current mandate and not be transformed into a formal international organization, particularly one with assessed contributions." The directive suggests that the United States is "open to updating the structure of the Council, including consoli-dation of, or making operational changes to, its subsidiary bodies, to the extent such changes can clearly improve the Council's work and are consistent with the general man-date of the Council."

229 Koivurova and Vanderzwaag, "The Arctic Council at 10 Years," 176–77. See also the list of recommendations in AAC, "Improving the Efficiency and Effectiveness of the Arctic Council: A Discussion Paper" (March 2007): 6–7. http://arctic-council.org/filearchive/AAC_Arctic_Council_Future_Dec_2006.pdf , accessed 10 November 2008.

230 Timo Koivurova and Leena Heinamaki, "The Participation of Indigenous Peoples in International Norm-Making in the Arctic," *Polar Record* 42, no. 221 (2006): 101–9 at 104–5.

231 Natalia Loukacheva, "Legal Challenges in the Arctic," position paper presented to the 4th NRF Open Meeting in Oulu, Finland, and Luleå, Sweden, 5–8 October 2006, 2. http://www.nrf.is/Open%20Meetings/Oulu%20Lulea%202006/Position%20Papers/Leuka cheva_4th%20NRF%20PP.pdf, accessed 28 May 2009.

232 For thoughtful reflections on the Ilulissat declaration, see Rosemary Rayfuse, "Warm Waters and Cold Shoulders: Jostling for Jurisdiction in Polar Oceans," *University of New South Wales Faculty of Law Research Series*, No. 56 (2008). http://law.bepress.com/cgi/view content.cgi?article=1131&context=unswwps, accessed 28 May 2009.

233 AAC, "Europe and the Arctic," 3.

234 Peter Kikkert notes concern among the Permanent Participants that "if more actors continue to gain access to the Council, the organization will begin to lose its specialized status and regional identity to the harm of the indigenous peoples and circumpolar states." See Kikkert, "Rising Above the Rhetoric: Northern Voices and the Strengthening of Canada's Capacity to Maintain a Stable Circumpolar World," paper delivered at Canada's Role in the Circumpolar World: A Symposium Showcasing Preeminent Graduate Students, Saskatoon, 9 March 2009, 8.

235 MELAW, *Governance of Arctic Marine Shipping*, 11.

236 See also EC, *The European Union and the Arctic Region*, 8; US Presidential Directive, 9 January 2009, 5–6.

237 Cotter, "Developing a Coherent Plan"; Jonathan Seymour, *Canadian Arctic Shipping Assessment*; MELAW, *Governance of Arctic Marine Shipping*. Rosemary Rayfuse explains that these "guidelines supplement existing flag state treaty obligations relating to ship construction, crewing and operational standards with specific reference to the unique risks posed to navigation in Arctic waters by poor weather conditions, challenging ice conditions, the relative lack of good charts, communications systems and other navigational aids, and the difficulties of rescue or clean-up. The Polar Code sets out a number of additional, specific, construction and operational standards for shipping in polar waters aimed at promoting the safety of navigation and the prevention of pollution from ship operations. For example, the Code calls for the carriage of life saving and fire-extinguishing equipment able to withstand extreme cold, the use of qualified Ice Navigators, structural arrangements adequate to resist global and local ice loads, ship design sufficient to ensure stability in ice even when damaged, installation of equipment and machinery systems designed to withstand cold and ice, carriage of appropriate survival kits and equipment, and effective and redundant navigation systems. However, the Code 'is not intended to infringe on national systems of shipping control' and it consists of voluntary guidelines only. Thus, no guarantees of national implementation and, in particular, of harmonised national implementation by all five coastal states exist." Rayfuse, "Warm Waters and Cold Shoulders," 5.

238 EC, *The European Union and the Arctic Region*, 4.

239 SSCFO, *Coast Guard in Canada's Arctic*, 21.

240 ITK, *An Integrated Arctic Strategy*, 12.

241 ITK and ICC (Canada), *Building Inuit Nunaat*, 59.

242 Jane George, "ICC Urges Stronger Inuit Voice in Sovereignty," *Nunatsiaq News*, 14 November 2008. http://www.nunatsiaqonline.ca/archives/2008/811/81114/news/nunavut/81114_1690.html, accessed 21 June 2011.

243 WDGF, "Arctic and Canada's Foreign Policy," 20.

244 Some of the networks may already be in place. The Arctic Council Core Group (ACCG), with representatives from the territorial governments, the federal departments involved in the North, and the senior Arctic official (SAO), has become a key forum for high-level discussion between the territories and the federal government. Peter Kikkert notes that "this group engages in open and frank discussions and provides all involved the opportunity to express their views and the positions they want Canada to adopt on the Arctic Council." The Arctic Council Advisory Committee (ACAC) includes the ACCG

members as well as the Canadian Permanent Participants "and is supposed to comple-ment the work of the Core Group. It too has become an important mechanism for con-sultation and dialogue." Kikkert also notes some concern may exist among territorial officials that a domestic Arctic Council would dilute their voices and become a forum for competing political agendas and priorities. Kikkert, "Rising Above the Rhetoric," 5–6.

245 Quoted in Louise Johncox, "We're in a Meltdown," *The Guardian,* 23 August 2007, 12.
246 United Nations Environment Programme (UNEP), "Revised Draft Decision on Sustain-able Development of the Arctic Region," 1 February 2008, http://www.unep.org/civil_society/GCSF9/pdfs/draft-dec-ARCTIC-1feb08.pdf, accessed 10 March 2009.
247 See, for example, Arctic Climate Impact Assessment (ACIA), *Impacts of a Warming Arc-tic: ACIA Overview Report* (Cambridge: Cambridge University Press, 2004). http://amap.no/acia, accessed 28 May 2009.
248 AAC, "Europe and the Arctic"; ITK and ICC (Canada), *Building Inuit Nunaat*; Sheila Watt-Cloutier, "Connectivity: The Arctic—The Planet," speech at Oslo Sophie Prize Cer-emony, 15 June 2005. http://www.sophieprize.org/Articles/23.html, accessed 28 May 2009.
249 EU, *Climate Change and International Security,* 2.
250 Thomas Homer-Dixon, "Climate Change, The Arctic, and Canada: Avoiding Yesterday's Analysis of Tomorrow's Crisis," in *Securing Canada's Future in a Climate-Changing World* (Ottawa: National Round Table on the Environment and the Economy, 2008), 89.
251 Obama, "Barak Obama and Joe Biden: New Energy for America," 3.
252 Airoldi, *The European Union and the Arctic,* 43; AAC, "Europe and the Arctic," 3.
253 ITK, media release, "Climate Change Report Highlights Need for Specific Measures in Arctic Regions," 2007. http://www.itk.ca/media-centre/media-releases/climate-change-report-highlights-need-specific-measures-arctic-regions, accessed 10 August 2008.
254 David L. Downie and Terry Fenge, *Northern Lights against POPs: Combatting Toxic Threats in the Arctic* (Montreal and Kingston: McGill–Queen's University Press, 2003); ITK and ICC (Canada), *Building Inuit Nunaat.*
255 CBC News, "Northern Summits Tackle Arctic Sovereignty, Environment," 6 November 2008. http://www.cbc.ca/canada/north/story/2008/11/05/arctic-summits.html, accessed 28 May 2009.
256 Patricia A.L. Cochran, ICC Chair, on behalf of Inuit in Greenland, Canada, Alaska, and Chukotka, "Circumpolar Inuit Declaration on Arctic Sovereignty," adopted by the Inuit Circumpolar Council, April 2009. http://www.itk.ca/circumpolar-inuit-declaration-arctic-sovereignty, accessed 28 May 2009.
257 P. Whitney Lackenbauer and Andrew F. Cooper, "The Achilles Heel of Canadian Good International Citizenship: Indigenous Diplomacies and State Responses in the Twenti-eth Century," *Canadian Foreign Policy* 13, no. 3 (2007): 99–119.
258 Lee Berthiaume, "DFAIT Left in the Cold on Arctic Issues," *Embassy,* 1 August 2007, 1, 10.
259 Runnalls, "Arctic Sovereignty and Security in a Climate-Changing World," 75–88 at 82.
260 Jonathan Seymour, *Canadian Arctic Shipping Assessment,* 7; Robert M. Bone, *The Geog-raphy of the Canadian North: Issues and Challenges,* 2nd ed. (Toronto: Oxford University Press, 2003), 105.
261 AAC, "Europe and the Arctic."
262 GBN, "Future of Arctic Marine Navigation," 6.
263 Floyd Roland, "Arctic Energy Resources Will Be Needed," *Embassy,* 6 November 2008, 22.
264 GBN, "Future of Arctic Marine Navigation," 6. See Appendix A.

265 Yukon et al., *A Northern Vision*, 9.
266 Mary Simon, "Does Ottawa's Northern Focus Look Backwards?" *Nunatsiaq News*, 11 April 2008, http://www.nunatsiaqonline.ca/archives/2008/804/80425/opinionEditorial/opinions.html, accessed 21 June 2011.
267 Coates et al., *Arctic Front*, 191.
268 Homer-Dixon, "Climate Change, The Arctic, and Canada," 99.
269 Griffiths, "The Shipping News"; E.J. Stewart, S.E.L. Howell, D. Draper, J. Yackel, and A. Tivy, "Sea Ice in Canada's Arctic: Implications for Cruise Tourism," *Arctic* 60, no. 4 (2007): 370–80.
270 Pierre Alvarez, "Renewing the Northern Strategy," *Northern Perspectives* 30, no. 1 (2006): 11–13 at 11.
271 Arctic Monitoring and Assessment Programme (AMAP), *Arctic Oil and Gas 2007* (Oslo: 2008). http://www.amap.no/oga, accessed 28 May 2009.
272 Peter Stoffer, New Democratic Party Member of Parliament, quoting Stephen Harper and the territorial premiers, in House of Commons *Debates*, 31 October 2006. 1015.
273 The now-closed Polaris and Nanisivik mines, for example, needed federal government seed money for facilities and transportation.
274 Roland, "Arctic Energy Resources Will Be Needed."
275 Frédéric Beauregard-Tellier, "The Arctic: Hydrocarbon Resources," Library of Parliament, Parliamentary Information and Research Service Publication PRB 08-07E, 24 October 2008, 25.
276 See, for example, Jeffrey Jones, "Ottawa Seeks Legal Advice on Arctic Pipeline Delays," *Reuters*, 16 March 2009. http://www.reuters.com/article/marketsNews/idUSN16 53185520090316, accessed 28 May 2009.
277 Dennis Bevington, "Enough Stalling on Environmental Assessment and Permitting," *Hill Times*, 20 August 2007, 28; Beauregard-Tellier, "The Arctic: Hydrocarbon Resources," 27.
278 Peter T. Haydon, "Why Does Canada Still Need a Navy?" Maritime Security Working Paper No. 1, Centre for Foreign Policy Studies, Dalhousie University, 2007, 5; Boris Worm and David Vanderzwaag, "High Seas Fisheries: Troubled Waters, Tangled Governance, and Recovery Prospects," *Behind the Headlines* 64, no. 5 (2007): 1–32.
279 EC, *The European Union and the Arctic Region*, 8; see also Huebert and Yeager, *A New Sea*, 10–12.
280 Young, "Whither the Arctic?" 180; Griffiths, "Canadian Arctic Sovereignty," 24–28.
281 Jim Bell, "Nunavut Fishing Reps Rap Feds over Docks, Quota," *Nunatsiaq News*, 21 March 2008, http://www.nunatsiaqonline.ca/archives/2008/803/80321/news/nunavut/80321 _1027.html, accessed 21 June 2011.
282 Jonathan Seymour, *Canadian Arctic Shipping Assessment*, 9.
283 SSCFO, *Coast Guard in Canada's Arctic*, 41.
284 See, for example, Huebert, "Canada and the Changing International Arctic."
285 EC, *The European Union and the Arctic Region*, 9. If the government follows through on its pledge to make NORDREG mandatory, this will ensure that foreign cruise ships entering Canadian waters comply with our marine safety, security, pollution prevention, and customs regulations.
286 Transport Canada, *Guidelines for Operation of Passenger Vessels in Canadian Arctic Waters*, TP 13670E (Winnipeg: Transport Canada, Prairie and Northern Region, Marine, 2005).
287 MELAW, *Governance of Arctic Marine Shipping*, 60.
288 Huebert, "Time for Gov't to Go Beyond Arctic Promises."
289 Jonathan Seymour, *Canadian Arctic Shipping Assessment*, 9.

290   EC, *The European Union and the Arctic Region*, 7; Huebert, "Time for Gov't to Go Beyond Arctic Promises"; AMAP, *Oil and Gas 2007*.

291   PMO, Backgrounder: "Extending the Jurisdiction of Canadian Environment and Shipping Laws in the Arctic," 27 August 2008. http://pm.gc.ca/eng/media.asp?id=2246, accessed 28 August 2008.

292   Thomas Berger, *Northern Frontier / Northern Homeland: The Report of the Mackenzie Valley Pipeline Inquiry* 1 (Ottawa: Department of Supply and Services, 1977), 1.

293   ITK, "An Integrated Arctic Strategy," 15.

294   Mary Simon, "Inuit: The Bedrock of Arctic sovereignty," *Globe and Mail*, 26 July 2007, A15.

295   Yukon et al., *A Northern Vision*, 9.

296   See, for example, Moore, "Defending Canadian Arctic Sovereignty."

297   Indian and Northern Affairs Canada (INAC), *Fact Sheet: Northern Strategy*, 28 May 2008. http://www.ainc-inac.gc.ca/ai/mr/is/n-strat-eng.asp, accessed 28 May 2009. See also Chris Windeyer, "Tories Praised for Helping Nunavut with Housing," *Nunatsiaq News*, 27 February 2009, http://www.nunatsiaqonline.ca/archives/2009/902/90227/news/nunavut/90227_1949.html, accessed 21 June 2011.

298   Terry Fenge, "Inuit and the Nunavut Land Claims Agreement: Supporting Canada's Arctic Sovereignty," *Policy Options* 29, no. 1 (2007–8): 84–88; and Michael Mifflin, "Canada's Arctic Sovereignty and Nunavut's Place in the Federation," *Policy Options* 29, no. 7 (2008): 86–90.

299   John Thompson, "Ottawa Clears Path for Devolution Talks," *Nunatsiaq News*, 14 March 2008, http://www.nunatsiaqonline.ca/archives/2008/803/80314/news/nunavut/80314_1007.html, accessed 21 June 2011.

300   Paul Mayer, *Mayer Report on Nunavut Devolution* (Ottawa: Indian and Northern Affairs Canada, June 2007).

301   Dennis Bevington, "Arctic Sovereignty Not Just a Military Concern, It's More Than That," *Hill Times*, 16 October 2006, 24.

302   Nunavut Tunngavik Inc. (NTI), *Discussion Paper: Devolution and Marine Areas*, presentation to Paul Mayer, Vancouver, 2 February 2007, 4–5. http://www.tunngavik.com/documents/publications/2007-02-02-NTI-Marine-Areas.pdf, accessed 10 July 2008.

303   Ed Struzik, "Canada Urged to Take Lead in Polar Research," *Edmonton Journal*, 25 February 2009, A3; "The True North Strong and Free but Not Cheap," *Toronto Star*, 1 December 2007, ID 01.

304   Natural Sciences and Engineering Research Council of Canada (NSERC) / Social Sciences and Humanities Research Council of Canada (SSHRC), "From Crisis to Opportunity: Rebuilding Canada's Role in Northern Research," final report to NSERC and SSHRC from the Task Force on Northern Research (Ottawa: 2000), 2, 8. http://www.nserc-crsng.gc.ca/_doc/Northern-Nordique/crisis.pdf.

305   Council of Canadian Academies, *Vision for the Canadian Arctic Research Initiative: Assessing the Opportunities* (Ottawa: Council of Canadian Academies, 2008), 4.

306   The shortlist of sites for the research facility consists of Cambridge Bay, Pond Inlet, and Resolute. Chris Windeyer, "Tories Put Three Places on Short List for Research Centre," *Nunatsiaq News*, 27 February 2009, http://www.nunatsiaqonline.ca/archives/2009/902/90227/news/nunavut/90227_1939.html, accessed 21 June 2011.

307   ITK and ICC (Canada), *Building Inuit Nunaat*.

308   EC, *The European Union and the Arctic Region*, 6.

309   Bevington, "Arctic Sovereignty Not Just a Military Concern," 24.

310   Bone, *The Geography of the Canadian North*, 224.

311 EC, *The European Union and the Arctic Region*, 4.

312 Michael Decter, "Aboriginal Health Will Be the Biggest Challenge for the New Minister," *Sault Star,* 17 November 2008 http://www.saultstar.com/ArticleDisplay.aspx?archive =true&e=1300012, accessed 23 June 2011.

313 ITK and ICC (Canada), *Building Inuit Nunaat.*

314 Charles J. Jago, "Report and Recommendations on a Government of Canada Approach Toward a Sustainable University of the Arctic (Canada)," 28 February 2008. http://ycdl4.yukoncollege.yk.ca/frontier/files/uarctic/jagouarcticcanadareportncr13.pdf, accessed 10 October 2009.

315 Memorandum, Minister of National Defence and Minister of Mines and Resources to Cabinet, "Northern Development Policy," 16 January 1948, *Documents on Canadian External Relations,* vol. 14—928, doc. 928. http://www.international.gc.ca/department/history-histoire/dcer/details-en.asp?intRefid=10616, accessed 28 May 2009.

316 Harper quoted in Max Delany, "Gas and Glory Fuel Race for the Pole," *Moscow Times,* 27 July 2007, http://www.themoscowtimes.com/news/article/gas-and-glory-fuel-race -for-the-pole/195431.html, accessed 23 June 2011.

317 Griffiths, "Canadian Arctic Sovereignty."

318 Quoted in Randy Boswell, "Bid to Put Three Seas in Canada's Motto Riding Wave," *Vancouver Province,* 11 April 2006, http://www2.canada.com/vancouversun/news/story.html ?id=278af877-e9d5-4e11-8f62-04f0e03413df&k=79100&p=1, accessed 23 June 2011.

319 James Stauch, "Sovereignty for Whom? A Closer Look at Use and Occupancy in the Canadian Arctic," presentation to the Canada in the World Conference, University of Toronto International Relations Society, 18 January 2008.

320 Quoted in Kathleen Harris, "Arctic Sovereignty Part 1: Our True North Strong and Free?" *Edmonton Sun,* 23 February 2007. http://www.torontosun.com/News/Canada/2007/02/23/3657827-sun.html, accessed 23 February 2007.

4

Towards a Canadian Arctic Strategy

Franklyn Griffiths

The Arctic is opening up at an astonishing rate. It draws more and more of us southerners to want in, but from a safe distance as though from a cruise ship. Enticed but leery, we marvel at the physical transformations that are making the region less forbidding. Climate change, the prospect of easier access, and the expectation of long-term growth in the global demand for oil and gas have evoked unprecedented interest from the world at large, and first of all from the attentive publics and decision makers of the eight nations of the region. Despite inevitable variation in the way the Arctic-8 look at things, they are now less ambiguous in their Arctic attachments, more material in their Arctic interests, and nowhere more so than in Canada. As well, we must consider the implications of the global recession that has set in. With oil and gas prices and worldwide energy demand all remaining well short of earlier highs, the level of activity in the Arctic is not what it was in 2008. Public interest persists, but resource development and—to a lesser extent—geopolitical interest in the region have been set back and will remain that way until prices recover. Over the next while, climate change and media hype about the "cold rush" for Arctic seabed rights will be the main drivers of southern attention to the northernmost part of the world. We in Canada are presented with an opportunity to plan and prepare now for cooperative stewardship, as distinct from self-help and unsustainable resource exploitation, in the cycle of renewed regional development that is sure to come upon us.

Given a very extensive saltwater frontage and, after Russia, the largest land holdings, Canada has a great deal at stake in the evolution of the Arctic as a political region—specifically, in the changing proportions of cooperation and

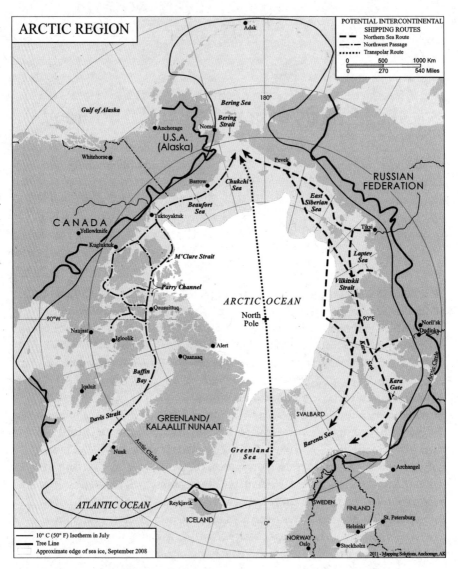

Map 4 Potential intercontinental shipping routes.
Source: Mapping Solutions

conflict among the ice states and in their dealings with non-Arctic states and
entities that may want in. Should change favour interstate conflict, not just
Canada but the entire Arctic will suffer the costs and risks of political–military rivalry, with all manner of collaboration forgone. Alternatively, should conflict be favoured only marginally when cooperation is inherently difficult to

achieve, simple neglect of the Arctic environment and its inhabitants could be the net result. Vigorous cooperation is surely Canada's preference. This chapter therefore lays out the elements of a Canadian strategy that would steer the unfolding story of the region in a direction that mutes conflict and that enables all to exercise due care in the exploitation and enjoyment of a shared natural environment. The twin watchwords of such a strategy are *stewardship* and *sovereignty*. We should have the strategy in hand and already be moving on it by the spring of 2013, when Canada assumes the chair of the Arctic Council. There is not a lot of time.

Cooperation and conflict are produced in the Arctic in particular ways that a Canadian strategy for the region will ignore at its own peril. Intimate knowledge of the regional context and of how things are accomplished locally is a precondition for the success of anything we might venture. Knowledge of this kind is the subject of the first part of the discussion that follows. It will go a long way in the structuring of an approach to the region. No less significant are the enabling actions that need to be taken if Arctic international cooperation is to unfold as it should. We distinguish here between what will first be required if we are to shape a future for the region, and what specific measures we might take for cooperative stewardship if given the capacity to act effectively. Strengthening the capacity for collective action is our second major concern and the heart of this chapter. Nor can we confine ourselves to the merits of what needs doing "out there." A strategy of stewardship will require strong leadership in this country. Such a strategy must bring us out from behind the lines of our sovereign jurisdiction and into the thick of a region that is still quite unfamiliar. This is the focus of a third set of comments. We end with recommendations.

The Arctic as an Arena

In discussions about the Arctic it is sometimes asked, "Why not follow the Antarctic pattern in regulating the affairs of the north polar region?"[1] This is a natural suggestion perhaps, but not one that can be acted upon. In thinking about the Arctic as a setting for Canadian intervention, it may therefore be useful to begin with a contrast. As polar areas, the Antarctic and the Arctic do share very similar physical conditions and present similar challenges for human understanding, occupancy, and use. Yet in a multitude of other ways, they could not be further apart. Antarctica, a continent unto itself, is governed by a treaty (1959) that has placed all territorial claims in abeyance, has demilitarized the region, bars resource development, and enjoins the parties to scientific and (more recently) environmental cooperation. The Arctic, by contrast, is a polar Mediterranean. Surrounded as it is by the territories of five coastal states—Canada, Denmark (Greenland), Norway, the Russian Federation, and the United States—and those of three other states at a remove from the Arctic Ocean—Finland, Iceland, and Sweden—international governance is minimal here. It is also difficult to compare the Arctic with the Antarctic because the former is the scene of enduring human habitation, especially in the case of indigenous peoples. It is the scene, as well, of strategic military activity, nuclear deployments included; of steadily more intensive resource exploitation and scientific research; of largely dormant but potentially sharp jurisdictional disputes; and of minimal environmental cooperation. Furthermore, while it is easy to determine where the Antarctic begins and ends, the Arctic according to certain definitions extends well beyond the ocean and the Arctic Circle to include all lands above the treeline in the eight regional countries, as well as waters down to the 10°C isotherm for the month of July. As such, it includes treeless Iceland, the Labrador Sea, the Aleutian Islands, and the entire Bering Sea. Far-flung, the Arctic amounts to some 8 percent of the Earth's surface. Relative to all of this, Antarctica is a tight little island. In no way, therefore, can we expect to follow the Antarctic precedent and come up with an omnibus treaty for the Arctic any time soon. Instead, we are faced with the difficult task of building habits and structures of cooperation as circumstance allows in the decades ahead.

Cooperation is achieved in many ways. It may come opportunistically, which is to say through joint actions on projects that are timely and achievable, reflecting whatever convergences of national interests may allow at a particular moment. In the Arctic, opportunism favours bilateral and issue-specific collaboration such as that between Norway and Russia in the Barents Sea area, or among the parties to the Polar Bear Treaty of 1973.[2] Arrangements such as these are certainly to be greeted warmly. Indeed, in the Barents subregion, international cooperation is more extensive and impressive than anywhere else in the Arctic. Nor is there anything like an equivalent practice at the regional level. If the Arctic states confined themselves to subregional opportunities, cooperation would surely proceed. But it would not be greatly cumulative, integrated, or conducive to the growth of a sense of shared purpose. Instead, the collective ability to accomplish would likely be held to "fragmented incrementalism."[3]

Alternatively—and this is something that has yet to be tried in earnest—the Arctic-8 could *also* adopt a multilateral and region-wide approach to Arctic affairs. Besides seizing opportunities as they arise, the ice states would orchestrate joint actions so as to shape the region's development according to a common strategic design. They would act not so much on what might seem currently doable—international provisions for search and rescue, oil spill response, the establishment of maritime and terrestrial protected areas, and the like—but also on what is needed to create and maintain a region that is maximally consistent with national purposes and the long view. In a collaborative approach to an awakening Arctic, the opportunistic and the incremental should not be walled off from the regional and the strategic. Quite the reverse: subregional collaboration—and even bilateral collaboration, as for example between Canada and the United States in mapping North America's Arctic continental shelf[4]—is to be valued and encouraged not only in its own right but also for the contribution it might make to the betterment of regional conditions. Still, it is the regional and strategic dimension that is underrepresented in Arctic practice and that will be emphasized here.

What we have in mind is a *via media* for the practice of Arctic cooperation—an alternative to treaty-based mandatory compliance and to the fragmented incrementalism that presently prevails. Another way would see the Arctic equipped with new capacities for voluntary coordination of, and active support for, international cooperation, be it bilateral, subregional, region-wide or extraregional. The essential requirement is an enabling central institution of governance, one that reviews and coordinates cooperation on a consensual basis while also providing financial assistance to projects in need.[5] This chapter envisages a forum that serves a diversity of processes and institutions that have been chosen or set up pragmatically to meet problems of collective action as they arise. Though at times providing the locus for collaboration among all members of the Arctic-8, such a forum would more likely greet, comment upon, observe, support, and receive the results of varied undertakings led by subsets of the eight, who more often than not would be acting in conjunction with non-Arctic actors. Short of binding regulation, it could also monitor and report on voluntary compliance with agreed guidelines—for example, as they relate to oil and gas development in the region. As well, and as a counter to the fragmentation of today, it would have the big picture in mind.

International self-regulation in the Arctic should not take the form of a series of pick-up hockey games that have no relation to one another—on fisheries management, safe and efficient navigation in ice-covered waters, abatement of land-based sources of marine pollution, conservation of marine biological diversity, and so on. On the contrary, and under the auspices of a central institution with modest means of its own, regime building would be open to overarching coordination that takes advantage of complementarities and that avoids incompatible outcomes. The net effect: cooperation that is less fragmented and less sluggishly incremental and that is more conducive to a sense of shared purpose for the Arctic as a region; but that also is respectful of sovereignty. The basis for such an institution already exists in the Arctic Council, about which we will have more to say as we go along, including on the matter of a new fund for supporting international cooperation. Yet regional practice is not common practice in the Arctic at present. This is a fact. Before considering how and why this is so and what it means for a Canadian Arctic strategy, we should make clear the chief benefit of international cooperation that is more decidedly regional.

There would be no need for regional stewardship if the Arctic-8 were individually able to achieve their Arctic environmental and social objectives on their own at acceptable cost. But no Arctic sovereign is omnipotent in its own space and its immediate surroundings. National action is insufficient when each nation depends in greater or lesser measure on the others—for example, in maintaining secure sea lanes for voyages to and from Arctic natural resource sites, or for safe and efficient intercontinental shipping. Nor is a subregional approach of great use in this kind of thing. And then there is the fact that the sovereign's holdings are subject to transboundary processes everywhere in the Arctic, be it regarding (for example) migratory fish stocks, land-based sources of environmental pollution, the long-range airborne transport of toxins, or the preservation of biological diversity. Pervasive challenges such as these do not readily yield to unilateral or subregional action.

If the sovereign is not merely to possess but also to enjoy the benefits of its jurisdiction, it will join with others in a practice of stewardship. By this we mean *locally informed governance that not only polices but also shows respect and care for the natural environment and living things in it.* Valuing the Arctic environment in its own right, including the life it supports, and not viewing it merely as a region to be exploited for human advantage, the ideal sovereign will be doubly embedded in nature and in the society of locals who are most familiar with the conditions there. Fully alert to transboundary effects, the sovereign will not rely primarily on self-help. Instead, it will collaborate. Whether or not the ideal is attained any time soon, the knowing sovereign will act as a cooperative steward in seeking to maintain not only a local milieu conducive to possession in full, but also regional and global conditions favourable to human existence in an era of rapid climate change. In short, the Arctic state needs considerably more than surety of autonomous possession. In a world of physical and human interdependence, it must also have favourable conditions of existence. The best way to achieve them is though regional practices of cooperative stewardship.

The notion of affirming Arctic sovereignty through joint stewardship on a regional basis is unconventional. Although they vary in this, the members of the Arctic-8 are not inclined to see far beyond the horizon of sovereign possession and exclusive jurisdiction. The reasons for this are complex. In surveying them, we begin to uncover the essentials of what a Canadian Arctic strategy will have to accomplish as it generates and deploys new means on behalf of cooperative stewardship at the regional level. The situation is in fact a difficult one. We need to be realistic about it while also acknowledging the potential as well as the need for change. The fundamentals can be discussed under five main headings.[6]

First of all, the Arctic areas of the ice states and, even more so, the high polar region that lies beyond national frontiers, are *peripheral* to the life of southern majorities and the agendas of their governments—less peripheral for some of the eight, but peripheral on the whole. To be specific, issues related to the boundaries and immediate surroundings of individual Arctic countries may be regarded with utmost gravity, but the region as a whole is something different. In its entirety the Arctic is populated by only some four million people, roughly half of whom are to be found in the Russian Federation. The American state of Alaska has a population of roughly 650,000, of whom perhaps one-fifth are indigenous. The Canadian Arctic—so vast that all of Europe from the Bosphorus to the English Channel could fit into Nunavut alone—has a population of some 130,000, of whom half are indigenous.[7] Overall, the demographics are such that there is not a lot of the national vote in the Arctic, nor is there a lot of knowledge of or resonance with the region down south (though nationalist identifications with the North may sell well politically in Canada and Russia). The consequence of this is a strong tendency to focus on resource development and environmental protection rather than on the human dimension of Arctic affairs.[8] All the while, it is very expensive to venture very far into the remote and difficult physical conditions of the region. Several implications follow.

As southern interest grows, attention focuses on the national domain and on resource exploitation right out to the farthest edge of jurisdiction. Assured possession—that is to say, sovereignty—becomes the natural point of departure in southerners' considerations of their national purpose in the Arctic. Just what northern residents might have in mind for their locales and for the region as a whole is thereby marginalized. At the same time, even while national pronouncements in favour of environmental protection, sustainable development, and international action for both are readily produced, the lack of strong domestic coalitions for effective (and thus costly) international Arctic cooperation makes it exceedingly difficult to coordinate and regulate national resource development in the region according to enforceable rules. As a result, Arctic policies, both national and international, acquire an official and bureaucratic character. They depend heavily on what mid-level officials can cobble together from existing mandates and already available resources. As long as the Arctic, over and above its subregions, continues to be of marginal political interest down south, even the most skilled civil servants and non-governmental organizations will continue to find that ingeniously negotiated deliverables for regional cooperation are met with little interest from senior authorities and their political masters. Not only the deliverables, but also the very appetite for them has to be created.

Second, the Arctic is *pacific* in the sense that not a lot goes on there compared to other regions of the world. This aspect of the situation is unevenly experienced. For some—in Norway and Russia, for example—the felt sense of danger may be strong enough to deny any thought of the pacific. Still, we should note that religious and ideological clashes are not to be found in the Arctic and seem unlikely to arise any time soon. The same applies to terrorists, be they home-grown or introduced from afar. While great physical violence is being done to the natural world, it is wholly absent in the way governments and peoples deal with one another within and between the region's nations unless we include human suffering from indifference and neglect as experienced violence. Nor is there any real expectation of war among the ice states as a result of conflict originating within the region. Indeed, when we look at the map and consider the full extent of settled and law-governed extensions of national jurisdiction, the Arctic is largely bereft of a physical basis for international violence as long as states refrain from trespassing upon or invading one another's established rights. By the same token, international cooperation is made difficult when most of the region is under firm national control.

When trouble arises, it is between contiguous states that may not welcome either the intervention of remote others or the application of generic regional principles. Meanwhile, even as we observe increases in tourism, low-level military preparedness, and (once again) resource exploitation, physical communication throughout the Arctic continues to be heavily oriented along north–south and not east–west lines. The exchange of people, goods, and to a lesser extent ideas across the region is stunted. For example, Canada's 2008 "Global Commerce Strategy" lists thirteen priority areas, yet the Arctic is not among them.[9] This is by no means to imply the need to create an integrated economic region in the Arctic. But it underlines the larger point that from a southern perspective, not a lot is going on in this part of the world. The thought of understanding and acting upon the region "in the round" is evidently one whose time has yet to come.

A pacific Arctic presents us all with plusses and minuses. On the negative side, the region is not merely a hinterland that is peripheral to the national purpose, but inherently something of a backwater. Compared with what might be done in Eastern Europe, the Middle East, or the Asia-Pacific region, new international engagements in the Arctic are difficult to justify. The stakes have not been there for commitments that cost money: If it ain't broke, why fix it? Where is the urgency that is required to command the attention of very busy people? At the same time—and surely this is the main point—a pacific Arctic is to be prized and built upon. How this might be accomplished is central to a regional strategy. For now we may note that thus far, the international agenda of a peaceable if peripheral Arctic has focused on the management of resources in whose exploitation all the region's states and peoples are interconnected. It is concerned with climate change, human development, long-range transport of pollutants, marine transportation, the conduct of scientific research, the maintenance of cultural and linguistic diversity, and so on. The single word for this kind of thing is, again, stewardship. Very much to be desired in its own right, an international Arctic practice of stewardship also deserves to be intensified as a means of building ever denser webs of cooperation among the Arctic-8—webs of common interest to constrain the enduring propensity of states to enter into conflict. Unfortunately, the propensity for conflict is reinforced by a third feature of the region.

When it comes to climate and weather, the Arctic is without doubt a major influence on global affairs. Even in this domain, however, the region is increasingly *dependent* on processes and events in the world outside. This is our third fundamental. Greenhouse gas emissions originating in the Arctic itself account for little of the ice and snow cover reduction of recent decades. The same applies to patterns of boom and bust in Arctic oil and gas development, to unsettling short-term variations in global energy demand and prices, and to the vagaries of the global business cycle such as we are now experiencing. Pollutants—DDT, for example—originate in and are transported to the Canadian Arctic from as far away as sub-Saharan Africa, making it impossible to address the problem effectively in Arctic forums.[10] In its priorities and practices, science performed in the Arctic is decidedly global and not regional. Much the same may be said of Arctic interstate collaboration, which itself is heavily dependent on extraregional variables. This was certainly the case during the Cold War, when the very thought of pan-Arctic cooperation was effectively banished by the demands of a military–political confrontation whose origins had nothing to do with the region as such.[11] The sequence of action and reaction between Russia and the Western countries that followed the Russian–Georgian crisis has not been forgotten. It makes for mistrust on both sides, and in the case of the North Atlantic Treaty Organization (NATO), it has prompted former Soviet members of the alliance to seek a role for the organization in the

Arctic.[12] The region does have the potential for one state to apply international sanctions against another either in direct response to enormities committed elsewhere, or simply in response to others' sanctions themselves. The Arctic therefore needs to be shielded against extraregional conflict. The alternative: a stronger likelihood that Arctic cooperation will unravel.

Arctic strategy aimed at enhanced cooperation will surely fall short of intent if it is confined to collective action by regional states on issues specific to the region. Instead, regional objectives and global strategy must be integrated. On the one hand, this means acting on the novel proposition that Arctic collaboration is capable of making a global contribution. For example, an increasingly successful practice of cooperative stewardship in the Arctic—one in which states and corporations bring one another to conform to regional standards of best practice, for example in their regional resource extraction operations—could set new global performance standards that demonstrate not only *what* to do but also *how* to get it done. As well, the more Arctic states are encultured in stewardship, the more likely they will be to contribute globally to environmental and climate protection. On the other hand, and in regard to Arctic requirements that need global action, we need consider only the example of anti-satellite weapons. Now that Canada has reaffirmed national control over Radarsat-2—in large part to ensure Arctic surveillance—Ottawa has new reason to join with others in extraregional negotiations to constrain and ultimately ban anti-satellite attack technology (ASAT) capabilities, including those based in space.[13] Global arms control and confidence-building measures may thus serve not only the national purpose writ large but also the aims of regional strategy. Done right, the Arctic and the global fuse. Done wrong, the Arctic is a place apart.

Fourth, the Arctic is physically and politically *fragmented*. To the extent that cooperation among the ice states adds up to no more than fragmented incrementalism, we have here a major part of the reason why. The actors who determine the affairs of the region differ—sometimes strongly—in their material interests and political preferences and in their rights and abilities to speak to the issues. Commonalities are of course to be found. Given similar and very demanding living conditions, Arctic residents may have more in common with their counterparts in other countries of the region than they do with fellow nationals to the south. The same applies to small communities and municipal and territorial governments, the latter gathered in the Northern Forum.[14] And down south as well, there are shared views that reach right around the region. Nobody speaks in favour of war or a remilitarization of the Arctic. All countries are prepared to address the linkages between development and the environment in the region's affairs. Yet even in such matters, biases as well as the aversions of some to the thinking and practices of others are also shared.

Geography obviously separates the Arctic-8 from non-Arctic states, as well as from intergovernmental entities such as the European Union (EU) and, increasingly, NATO, which have shown greater interest in the region. Reading between the lines, we may suggest that the eight are inclined to resist outside involvement in what they take to be their own affairs—and rightly so from our point of view, in that stewardship is a matter of locally informed governance. Among the eight, however, geography also divides the "Ocean Five" from the "Non-Littoral Three." In May 2008, the five coastal states (again, Canada, Denmark/Greenland, Norway, the Russian Federation, and the United States) met at Ilulissat, Greenland, without the three non-littorals (Finland, Iceland, and Sweden) and also without representatives of Arctic indigenous peoples. Concerned to affirm the role of the law of the sea in the resolution of competing claims to the outer continental shelf in the Arctic Ocean, they also sought to counter non-Arctic proposals to create new regional governance arrangements and otherwise to enter more directly into the determination of Arctic affairs. They produced an admirable statement of common purpose, the "Ilulissat Declaration," which, however, lent itself to interpretation as an act of exclusion.[15] Indeed, in meeting and pronouncing as they did, the five excluded the three as well as the region's indigenous peoples' organizations. In meeting separately they also opened themselves to interpretation as signalling a desire to avoid greater reliance upon the Arctic Council as an institution for regional governance. As well, the four NATO members (Canada, Denmark, Norway, and the United States) of the five could be viewed as excluding non-Arctic members of the alliance in a "regionalization" of the organization.[16] Geography thus combines with low-key power politics to produce a set of concentric circles in which more and more players now vie for position and influence.

Manoeuvring of this kind favours not so much a regional as a subregional approach to governance in which each of the Ocean Five concentrates on the national domain and adjacent areas in pursuit of natural resources without as yet a compelling concern for transboundary effects. To the extent that this is the prevailing practice, as indeed it seems to be, the Arctic is best viewed as a collection of subregions. To the Barents and Bering subregions, which have already been mentioned, we could add a North American equivalent that might one day see significant interactions among Canada, Denmark/Greenland, and the United States. And then on the Eurasian side, the Russian vastness presents not a single subregion but a set of them. Ranging all the way from the Northwest to Chukotka, Russia's Arctic areas are divided for administrative purposes into the profitable and unprofitable—those endowed with oil, natural gas, and minerals, and then those that lack economic prospects and that non-indigenous residents are urged to leave.[17] Meanwhile, seaward of the exclusive economic zones of the five, there is a high-seas sub-region that is sure to be transformed as the waters warm. Variety in the extent and intensity of human occupancy from one area to another in the region is accompanied by considerable unevenness in the readiness of Arctic states to collaborate even at the subregional level. And then we have a fundamental difference between the Russian Federation and the other members of the Arctic-8.

Russia, as noted, is not counterposed to the Western states when it comes to governance of the region. On the contrary, it is a member of the innermost circle and thus champions the rule of law in Arctic international relations. To be sure, Moscow is capable of antagonistic behaviour as it reacts to perceived attempts to neutralize its military power and to encroach upon what it takes to be its sphere of influence. It is thus able to inspire heightened threat assessments and defensive reactions from the West—for example, in response to renewed Russian strategic bomber exercises in the region.[18] But these processes are, we believe, manageable. The real problem in the relationship between Russia and the other members of the Arctic-8 owes more to culture and history than to geography and politics. It centres on the fact that relative to the region's Western nations, which are certainly not without fault, Russia is in a class by itself when it comes to Arctic environmental protection.[19] Sadly, the environmental backwardness of the Russian Federation exemplifies what a practice of cooperative stewardship would overcome.

Immensely strengthened by its oil and natural gas as long as demand and prices held, Russia continues to act on an Arctic agenda of sovereignty and security that focuses on resource exploitation. Such is the gist of Moscow's policy statement on the region, which centres on the delimitation and securing of a national "zone" that extends well out into the Arctic Ocean.[20] Averse to multilateral regulatory arrangements, Russia prefers national implementation of international legal obligations. Nor does concern for pollution figure prominently in Russia's Arctic operations, be they domestic or international. How else could it be in a country that dumped used nuclear reactors into Arctic waters not so long ago, and whose environmental awareness has yet to make much headway against the industrial imperative?[21] Lacking money and mandate, the Russian Foreign Ministry itself has had difficulty securing the participation of other government departments in Arctic Council working groups. No surprise, therefore, that Russian contributions to the work of the council have until recently been scattered, ineffectual, and in need of subsidy by other states, including for representation by officials.[22]

Russia's presence in the region is so large that effective pan-Arctic stewardship of oil and gas exploitation, marine transportation, land-based sources of oceanic pollution, and the like is impossible without it. The Russian Federation must therefore be encouraged to come forward as an environmentally responsible Arctic partner. What is needed is an end to the neglect and disarray that typically occur when the central administration is not paying close attention. The question is how to secure Moscow's attention. The size of the problem ensures that the United States will be heavily involved in the solution.

Although the Russian Federation's contribution is now becoming more substantial, Moscow very largely absented itself from the work of the Arctic Council in the decade and a half after its inception. As to the United States, it has offered powerful leadership for collaborative research but has resisted task expansion into the area of practical action.[23] Even back in the Clinton years, when the Arctic Council was being established, Washington stood out in its efforts to circumscribe the mandate and capabilities of the new regional forum. One reason is that outside of the scientific community and the State of Alaska, there has been really no coalition for national, much less international, action in the Arctic.[24] To be sure, the US Navy is perennially interested in maritime mobility, but otherwise nobody has wanted to do much beyond study and learn in the region until recently. Still, whereas Russia is deeply constrained from environmental protection, the United States has the capacity to surge forward as a regional leader on this issue. Indeed, the Obama administration's interest could surface in new Arctic initiatives. The challenge for Canada is to find a way to engage both the Russian Federation and the United States on behalf of a common design for the region.

Finally, and it follows from what has just been said, the Arctic is not well set up when it comes to international cooperation. That is to say, it is under-institutionalized. Although other regional and subregional entities exist, the Arctic Council is the central forum for pan-Arctic collaboration.[25] Established as a result of a Canadian initiative in 1996, after the end of the Cold War and before the recent rise in the geostrategic significance of the region, the council has risked being left behind in an Arctic that demands more joint action as well as self-help from each of the regional states if they, too, are not to be left behind. But cooperation is slow to come. Things have got to the point where some deride the council as an ineffective talk shop far removed from policy and the real needs of the region.[26] Though the council does well, indeed sometimes outstandingly well, at monitoring and assessment—think of the Arctic Climate Impact Assessment—the Arctic-8 need to move beyond joint observation and statements of good intentions. They need to endow the council with new resolve and new money to help coordinate not only national activities but also regional and subregional cooperation; and they need to do so on a voluntary basis until the day comes when, issue by issue, compliance with agreed principles and rules becomes mandatory. But how to begin when, even to the attentive Canadian public, the workings and limitations of the Arctic Council are all but totally unknown?

Drawing together the strands of this assessment of the Arctic as an international political region, we have to acknowledge that there is really not a lot of subregional interaction among the Arctic-8 at present. There is even less region-wide interaction. When it comes to politics, the Arctic as an arena is very largely empty. A scattering of residents, especially indigenous peoples, is to be seen in the front rows. Otherwise, there is still hardly anyone in the stands even as global warming becomes something of a draw for southerners. Out on the ice, where not long ago a few players were scrambling for a puck in the Barents subregion, Norway and the Russian Federation have succeeded in opening a new game of cooperation, this in settling on who owns what in and under a long-disputed sea area. Players are also to be seen in and around the Bering Sea. Otherwise, individuals are standing about, leaning on their sticks. There is a cluster on the Arctic Council, but they are sitting on the boards. Intent on observing the ice conditions, which they do very well, they are only now beginning to consider regional games, as in practical cooperation on search and rescue and on marine transport. The governments of the Ocean Five are still pretty well stuck to their benches—Russia alone on one side of the arena and rest spread out along the other. As to the remaining Non-Littoral Three, it is unclear, after the Ilulissat Declaration, whether they are emerging from or returning to the locker rooms. Heavily preoccupied with other things, the Five do not often look in the direction of centre ice. When they do, they tend to the piece right in front of them, to their own holdings.

In the Arctic, possession goals trump milieu goals aimed at shaping conditions beyond the limits of national jurisdiction.[27] As long as the national and at most a subregional perspective are predominant, pan-Arctic interplay will be wanting. The Arctic will remain only minimally an international political region. The opportunity to collaborate will continue to be circumscribed. The potential for conflict and for continued environmental degradation will be left to look after itself. To reduce our exposure to conflict and to ensure appropriate care for Arctic ecosystems in the next go-around of development and thereafter, we are in need of a strategy. It should tell us not so much what we as Canadians need to do on the issues, but how we might lead in the creation of new abilities to achieve shared purposes, including defence of sovereignty in conditions of interdependence. Stronger governance for cooperative stewardship will be at the heart of a Canadian endeavour to shape the future of the Arctic region.

Arctic Strategy for Canada

A new Canadian effort for stewardship in the Arctic will be governed by three main objectives. Emerging directly from the situation we face, they are inter-related and will take time to realize.

The first is to elevate the conduct of Arctic international relations to the highest political level in dealings among the regional states, and also between Arctic heads of state and those of interested non-Arctic countries. Acting accordingly, Canada would aim to energize the region's affairs by associating them with the global as well as the domestic priorities of the Arctic-8. Arctic international relations would owe less to the internal agendas of the eight and more to their global policy imperatives. As well, we would give voice to and seek greater recognition of the needs of the Arctic both globally and in the met-ropolitan centres of the Arctic countries themselves. And if we are to raise Arctic international dealings from the official to the highest political level, the prime minister will of necessity have the lead in Canada.

Our second objective will be to engage the Russian Federation on behalf of a larger collective commitment to cooperative stewardship. American involvement at the highest level is essential here. Our governing purpose in speaking to Washington and Moscow would be to achieve broader and deeper pan-Arctic collaboration by bringing international partnership support to bear on precisely those subregions most in need of assistance—namely, some in the Russian Federation. Russia's leaders would be invited to accept a new opportunity to channel the region's evolution for the common good. Specif-ically, they would be asked to act on the proposition that Arctic political devel-opment presents us all with a choice between, on the one hand, enhanced regional security and intensified international Arctic assistance, including new funds for cooperative stewardship, and, on the other, the risk of growing dis-cord, increased potential for NATO involvement, and diminished common security in the region.

Third, we would strive to invigorate the Arctic Council and its ability to coordinate and support regional and subregional stewardship projects among Arctic states, and also between them and non-Arctic states and other entities and processes such as the International Maritime Organization (IMO) and the 1992 Convention for the Protection of the Marine Environment of the North-East Atlantic (OSPAR).[28] The council would not itself do all the work of stew-ardship—for example, in the regulation of maritime tourism, in the management of new fisheries, or in the implementation of region-wide adaptive responses to climate change. It would nevertheless be strengthened as a coordinating and funding centre for stewardship operations, including those aimed at partnership with the Russian Federation. To this end, Canada would seek acceptance of Arctic Council enlargement to include direct participation by non-Arctic countries as consultative parties in an arrangement that would be without prejudice to the sovereignty of the Arctic-8 and that also would produce new funds for cooperative stewardship.

Additional objectives related to Canada's bilateral relations with the United States and non-Arctic countries are also to be considered. Still, the core of an Arctic strategy resides in the triad of *elevation, engagement,* and *invigoration*— elevation to the highest political level, engagement of the United States and the Russian Federation in the first instance, and invigoration of the Arctic Council as a forum for the coordination and support of collective action.

For starters, a Canadian effort for improved pan-Arctic governance will not go far without new intellectual and policy capital at the disposal of the Prime Minister of Canada. A bit further on we will consider northern aspects of the domestic political situation in this country and why it should fall to the prime minister to take personal responsibility in the framing and execution of a Canadian Arctic strategy. Let us say for now that no one else is up to the task, which nevertheless happens to offer potential political advantages as a new national project. Otherwise, leadership from the highest level is a precondition for success in engaging the Russian Federation in the steward's role, as surely it is for more active US regional involvement as well. In the latter case, the opportunity to make use of Arctic relationships in furthering US global interests could prove to be compelling, especially when allied with the need to offer global leadership in the face of accelerating climate change in the Arctic. Analogous opportunities for personal diplomacy could arise between the Canadian prime minister and the heads of other Arctic states, and also non-Arctic states with interests in the region—China and Germany, for example. Accordingly, we suggest that the prime minister start off with a personal effort to gain insight into Arctic affairs.

Just as the Arctic is new to most Canadians, so also is the thinking about it—thinking that is already out there in each of the region's countries. There are resources here for all who would build a community of competence in Arctic stewardship, who would find and then give voice to an Arctic identity in national policy debate and in global policy discourse bearing upon the region. With such ends in mind, the prime minister ought to convene a one- or two-day symposium of eminent Arctic persons at a location in Canada. Such an occasion would be strictly a means for personal learning on the part of the prime minister and some of his entourage. It would have no international standing. From each of the region's countries it could bring together a northern indigenous leader, an outstanding southerner in the arts or literature, and another southerner knowledgeable in matters of Arctic-related political practice. Or more simply it could draw together some of the foremost writers from around the region. Called perhaps the Arctic Identity Network, a gathering such as this ought to generate a new awareness of the values, aspirations, purposes, and practices that are common to the region. Given a rapporteur and reconvened as required, it should impart to the prime minister and some in his office (PMO) a sense of direction for the region in an era of physical transformation and renewed resource development activity. It should also alert policy makers to differences in the way Arctic countries approach similar problems.[29]

Whether or not it was called "cooperative stewardship," an equivalent conception would surely emerge as a primary concern in the network's exchanges. So also would an interest in the ethical and moral dimensions of human actions, including respect for the natural environment in its own right. Ensuing Canadian government activity in the region would more likely be grounded in an understanding of the prerequisites for cooperation—prerequisites that extend well beyond the material and financial considerations that predominate when the capacity to act is assumed. The prime minister would take the initiative personally in order to make clear from the outset the importance now attached by Canada to Arctic cooperation.

Second, in responding primarily to the phenomena of a fragmented region, Canada should seek an agreement on Basic Principles of Arctic International Relations—in other words, a Basic Principles Agreement (BPA) among the Arctic-8. Given the priority need for Russian engagement on behalf of cooperative stewardship, the question for Canada and the region's other Western states is how to gain Moscow's interest. Part of the answer is to be had in an exchange in which Russian stewardship on Arctic environmental and human issues is forthcoming in return for increased security. The assumption here is that a diminished Russia, moved physically northwards with the dissolution of the Soviet Union and identifying increasingly with the Arctic as a source of geopolitical strength, is uncertain about its future possessions and regional standing at a time when NATO countries are encroaching upon the federation from the west and the south. Some of the reassurance Moscow needs could come from an Arctic BPA and conforming behaviour equivalent in essence to what was prescribed in the Agreement on Basic Principles of Soviet–American Relations, as was proposed by the Soviet Union in 1972.[30]

An Arctic BPA would see each of the Arctic-8 undertake the following: to refrain from any effort to obtain unilateral advantage at the expense of another party; to seek measures of nuclear arms reduction and arms control in global forums; and, as the need arose, to work out regional arrangements for confidence building and the avoidance of incidents with confrontation potential. As well, the eight would commit themselves to negotiating measures of cooperative stewardship to guard the region's environment against further degradation and to ensure direct consultation with Arctic residents—above all, with indigenous peoples—who may be most directly affected by central determinations. In this way, international security and regional stewardship would be linked in an Arctic BPA. Having in its own view been hard done by at the hands of the Western countries after the fall of the Soviet Union, Russia should welcome the creation of an equitable and actionable basis for its Arctic foreign relations—in particular, for those pertaining to the United States. As to the latter, a BPA ought to provide the occasion for a new departure in Russian–American relations as well as for continuing high-level American political engagement in the region's affairs. Experience with the 1972 BPA shows, however, that this kind of instrument will be of little use if the parties do not review compliance at regular intervals.

Canada should start the ball rolling when the time is right by raising the issue of an Arctic BPA at the official level with the US State Department and the Russian Foreign Ministry. Depending on the initial results, the prime minister might propose a trilateral negotiation to prepare an agreement for consideration and adoption at a heads-of-state meeting of the Arctic Council. This agreement would allow for a review of compliance at regular intervals either by the council as presently constituted or by a council enlarged. This brings us to the institutional preconditions for effective international cooperation at the regional level.

Reluctant to countenance central regional governance institutions, the Arctic-8 have presided over an Arctic Council that broadly suits them. The question is whether and how the member countries may be brought to strengthen the council's ability to contribute to Arctic stewardship. For the eight to move in this direction, they will need prompting and assistance from down south, which is to say from their own southern majorities and/or from non-Arctic states and peoples. In coming years, we may expect climate change to move the public in some of the ice states to new levels of regional awareness, to concern for the living conditions of Arctic inhabitants, and to sharper demands for Arctic environmental protection. As well, if encouraged to do so, non-Arctic actors could prove effective in bringing new drive and resources to the council. It would be best of all if the governments of the eight responded to southern promptings and proceeded themselves to take the initiative in moving toward stronger governance by having the council encourage and coordinate specific stewardship projects, be they subregional or regional, Arctic-only or inclusive of non-Arctic participation. In our view, the prospects for cooperative stewardship are greatest when it comes to interested non-Arctic states and intergovernmental entities. To see how non-Arctic participation might enhance the outlook for cooperative stewardship, we need first to consider the council as it is.

The Arctic Council is a standing conference with two tiers of participants and a growing gallery of state, intergovernmental, and non-governmental observers who may mingle with the Arctic-8 in the corridors but have little or no right to speak formally. At the council's meeting in November 2008, there were 160 people present.[31] The proceedings are consensual. There are no votes and therefore no formal decisions. There is, however, a somewhat informal hierarchy.

In the top tier, the Arctic-8 alone have the right to state the consensus of the council, be it at ministerial meetings every two years, at periodic gatherings of senior Arctic officials (SAOs), or in the various working groups where the real work of the Arctic Council has so far been done. In tier two, we have the Permanent Participants, who represent international Arctic indigenous peoples: the Aleut International Association, the Arctic Athabaskan Council, G'wichin Council International, the Iniut Circumpolar Council, the Russian Association of Indigenous Peoples of the North (RAIPON, a national organization), and the Saami Council. Permanent Participants enter freely into the deliberations of the eight. Although they must yield to the Arctic states when unbridgeable differences arise, Permanent Participants do shape the council's consensus. And then, below tier two, we have an array of non-participants consisting of "observer states" such as France, Germany, the Netherlands, Poland, Spain, and the United Kingdom; "ad hoc observer states" such as China, the EC, Italy, and South Korea; and "observer organizations," which include the Association of World Reindeer Herders, the International Arctic Science Committee, the Nordic Council of Ministers, and the World Wildlife Federation. We are principally concerned here with state observers: regular, pending ("ad hoc"), intergovernmental, and national. Non-Arctic states and the EC are not entitled to speak at council meetings except perhaps when one of them, the Netherlands for example, summarizes the views of all in a three- or four-minute intervention at the end of a SAO meeting. When the Aleut International Association is entitled to speak freely and the non-Arctic states virtually not at all, we have to ask why the observer states are there at all. Before answering that question, we need to make a few things clear.

In the practice of indigenous non-governmental organizations dealing directly with nation-states, we encounter the single most vital attribute of the Arctic Council. The direct engagement of Permanent Participants helps ensure that the assessments and the underlying judgments of Arctic governments far removed from the scene are properly adapted to real-life situations on site, including in very small indigenous communities. As well, the ability of Permanent Participants to intervene makes it more likely that collective action in the Arctic is not merely respectful of the realities but also ethical. Effects of this kind are achieved when those who are most vulnerable to the human and environmental consequences of collective actions are directly involved in the processes whereby situations are evaluated and state actions are coordinated. No way, therefore, can we jeopardize the ability of the Permanent Participants to make their contributions. Yet something must be done to enhance the council's capacity for collective action and for cooperative stewardship in particular.

The question for Canada and the rest of the Arctic-8 is whether non-Arctic states can be brought into the governance of the region, their interests thereby channelled to the benefit of cooperative stewardship, without compromising either the sovereignty of Arctic states or the position of the Permanent Participants. We believe this is possible. We therefore propose that selected non-Arctic states and intergovernmental entities be included as *consultative parties* to the Arctic Council.[32]

Although they will certainly vary in this, non-Arctic states and intergovernmental entities are in a position to bring substantial benefits to a regional practice of cooperative stewardship. Approaching the Arctic from the outside, they are likely not only to bring a stronger regional perspective to the work of the council, but also to prompt greater awareness of the regional as distinct from the subregional and local in the approaches of the Arctic-8 themselves. Moved by what we take to be enduring interests in climate protection, energy security, resource transportation, pollution prevention, and conflict avoidance, as well as by the rule of law, non-Arctic states stand to strengthen through their participation a discourse and practice of cooperative stewardship in the council's work. Indeed, whereas the council's work takes place at present in working groups that are occupied mostly with monitoring and assessment, the presence of non-Arctic states should help shift the focus to plenary sessions, to priorities for the region as a whole, and to common practices of stewardship. Furthermore, we would expect those with consultative-party status to contribute to an Arctic Fund with amounts to be matched by the eight and applied to the costs of collective action, for which at present there is little or no money beyond that provided by the proponents of Working

Group projects. Why, though, should non-Arctic participants make a financial contribution?

The answer is the same as for why non-Arctic states sit in the council as observers today: future considerations. Shipping, for example, is one of China's three stated priorities in observing. Energy security and climate change are among the key concerns of the EC. Non-Arctic actors are building positions in an area of the world that they see as affecting them and in which they one day will want to operate safely, efficiently, and sustainably. Meanwhile, they also have responsibilities for what happens in the region. For example, the 490 million people of the present-day EU have over the generations contributed to the mounting climate change crisis in the Arctic. They have an obligation to help ameliorate it. Whether this obligation touches on existing or future advantage, the fit between non-Arctic motivations and an agenda of cooperative stewardship should be a good one.

Accordingly, we propose that the Arctic Council be enlarged to admit a third tier of capable non-Arctic states as consultative parties with speaking rights equivalent to those of the Arctic-8 and the Permanent Participants. Candidates, presumably beginning with those already present as observers, would be asked to provide a statement of interest in the region, a plan of action on behalf of cooperative stewardship, and an annual contribution to the Arctic Fund. All proceedings of the council—its subsidiary bodies included—would remain consensual in the manner they are today. This is a critical proviso.

The Arctic-8 would continue to state the consensus of council, including as it relates to funding allocations. They would, however, need to hear and take due account of the views of those outside others that are actually or potentially affected by regional cooperation (or the lack of it). Some adjustment in the understandings and preferences of the eight regarding regional political development would be expected from a discussion that placed greater emphasis on extraregional and global considerations. The regional states would no doubt come forward with stronger regional perspectives themselves. In our view, this would be all to the good. At the same time, the eight could themselves expect a reduction in the dependence of national Arctic conditions on non-Arctic processes and events.

As to Permanent Participants, they would continue to take part on a par with states large and small in an enlarged forum, one that is now open in principle to numerous countries with significant interests in this part of the world. They would also find themselves coping with a considerably more elaborate agenda, one that extends from assessment to the coordination and support of joint action through varying arrangements of Arctic and non-Arctic states and intergovernmental organizations—arrangements that would be configured according to the particular purposes of cooperation. Hard-pressed to deal effectively with the steadily more technical business of the Arctic Council as it presently exists, Permanent Participants would surely risk being sidelined in a larger and more effective forum if new support for policy development, staffing, and quite simply attendance at meetings were not forthcoming. In our view, enlargement should be seen as presenting not a threat but an opportunity to strengthen the capacity of Permanent Participants to make contributions over and above present levels. This opportunity would arise with the creation of an Arctic Fund, which must be seen as an essential element of our proposal for enlargement.

Financial assistance for Permanent Participant capacity building should be accepted as the first priority of a new fund. Furthermore, and in a return to original Canadian thinking about the ethical dimension of the council's activities, the Arctic-8 could consider granting Permanent Participants a direct say in the council's consensus (in effect, a veto and the opportunity to bargain) with regard to issues on which the Arctic states could be persuaded of an existential threat to indigenous peoples.[33] In helping the Permanent Participants play a larger role in the coordination and support of stewardship in the region, a restructured council should not only maintain but also strengthen the capacity for adapted and ethical action on the part of interested states. Still, there is a big question.

Even if we assume that non-Arctic actors and Permanent Participants could be brought to accept enlargement along the lines being discussed here, why should the Arctic-8 go along? Granted that they would retain control over the consensus, why should they not only admit but also hear from China, India, and Japan, to say nothing of Poland, Spain, and the United Kingdom? Would this not open the door to progressively wider foreign infringement in matters better left to the individual Arctic states and—if there is to be cooperation—to transactions among the eight and subsets thereof? And in a similar vein, why should the eight agree to assessed contributions when the United States, for one, has expressly opposed the idea?[34]

In admitting non-Arctic observers, the Arctic-8 have already declared in favour of a non-Arctic interest in the conduct of Arctic affairs. Having cracked open the door, they cannot close it without in effect declaring the Arctic to be governable by the eight alone. The region is, we repeat, heavily dependent on global processes that are best addressed in conjunction with non-Arctic actors engaged in the region's affairs as influentials, resource users and producers, and recipients of Arctic transboundary effects on a global level. Furthermore, within non-Arctic countries denied enhanced access to the chief forum for an increasingly accessible region, some are sure to seek other ways to make themselves heard. Playing in particular on differences between Russia and the seven others, they could make the Arctic into a more conflicted region, thereby imposing new direct and opportunity costs upon the eight. All this being understood, the Arctic states might nevertheless opt to keep the door just as it is: they could maintain the status quo of minimal regional governance and maximal freedom of national action, which is to say fragmented incrementalism. In so doing, we submit, they would pay a price.

Arctic sovereigns must engage non-Arctic others if they are to bend conditions of interdependence to the national interest. To engage others, the Arctic-8 must at a minimum grant them the right to speak, and not only on matters of direct interest to them. Not to engage is to accept avoidable deprivation when the sovereign should be optimizing conditions of the national domain. The same applies to the projection of an Arctic voice in global councils, a task whose performance will be all the stronger when there are informed allies on the outside. Most important from the standpoint of the eight, Arctic Council enlargement for cooperative stewardship would add legitimacy to an arrangement that continued to privilege them. Stewardship as we understand it insists on the primacy of the local in Arctic governance. The Arctic states have themselves yielded to the local in undertaking to hear directly in the council from indigenous peoples' organizations as representatives of those most directly concerned and informed. In our view, this gives them an authentic claim on non-Arctic actors to yield to those with the most immediate knowledge and greatest stake in collective action.

Accordingly, we believe it best for the Arctic-8 not to leave the Arctic Council as is. On the contrary, they should bring selected non-Arctic states and intergovernmental entities to the table in an arrangement that maintains their power of determination and that enhances their sovereignty in conditions of interdependence. As to a formula for contributions to an Arctic Fund, it should not be difficult to find once enlargement is agreed upon in principle.[35]

Moving from the multilateral in our search for greater capacity to make things happen in the region, we recommend that Canada also develop *new bilateral Arctic strategic relationships* with the United States, Europe, and China. Russia is not on the list because it is best dealt with in the company of others. Given the familiar Canada–US commonalities and the continuing pre-eminence of American power, Washington comes first.

Although the Obama administration could surprise us with Arctic initiatives of its own, experience suggests that other issues and other areas of the world will continue to crowd the region off the priority list for the US government. Still, if a regional practice of cooperative stewardship is to advance, the United States must be engaged. This applies above all to Arctic Council enlargement. Canada's task here is not to encourage the United States to commit to new governance arrangements or to the region itself. Rather, it is to persuade Washington that new Arctic engagements can serve US global interests effectively. We have already argued that an Arctic BPA should be promoted by the prime minister as a means for the United States to renew the collaborative dimension in US–Russian relations worldwide. To what has been said, we would add only two items, one small and one large. First, to counter predictions of sharpening Arctic conflict that could be fulfilled if left unchallenged, and also to demonstrate basic principles in action, Canada and the United States ought to lead in a joint oil spill response exercise at the North Pole by icebreakers of the Arctic-8 and interested non-Arctic countries. More important, the Canadian prime minister needs, at the appropriate moment, to open a conversation with the American president on Arctic opportunities—especially in the matter of Arctic Council enlargement—in order to break free of the past in matters of climate change.

In the near-term future, issues of climate change will be secondary to those of economic recovery; but they will also be primary when it comes to elaborating new approaches to the environment that focus on alternative energy sources. On both accounts, economic and environmental, Canada is all but certain to follow in the wake of American thinking and decisions. There is, however, an opportunity as well as a need for Canada to lead. It seems certain that science will show that climate change in the Arctic is accelerating. Climate change may in addition present us with non-linear developments for which we have no adequate understanding. Taken up by a more receptive US government, new Arctic change reports are likely to authorize proposals for collective action that have thus far been excluded from mainstream discourse. Even before his inauguration, Barack Obama made clear the need to "reinvigorate international institutions to deal with transnational threats, like climate change, that we can't solve on our own."[36] Arctic Council enlargement for stronger cooperative stewardship would seem to be in line with this kind of thinking.

Addressing the challenge of climate change, the prime minister should, when the time is right, invite President Obama to join in the creation of a binational Canada–US panel to chart a way for cooperative stewardship in the Arctic and to make that panel's work exemplary for the planet as a whole. Although its focus should be made tight, the panel's ambit could in principle range from environmental ethics, to the provision of adaptive support for isolated small communities, to the eradication of black carbon (sooty smokestack emissions from ships, which make for an easily reduced share of global warming owing to their melting effects on Arctic ice and snow), and an out to the need for geophysical and chemical engineering to save the climate in which we have thrived.[37] And there is still more to be done with the United States.

Together with stewardship, security should also be sought in a unified North American approach to the evolution of the Arctic as an international political region. For Canada, this means first of all overcoming insecurities of our own that have kept us at arm's length from the United States when it comes to the Arctic. The issue here is the Northwest Passage. Canada is now in a position to take the initiative in strengthening the Canada–US agreement to disagree over the international legal status of the waters of the Arctic Archipelago. As elaborated elsewhere, this agreement has steadily become stronger—largely by dint of our own efforts.[38] We should now surround it with a bodyguard of bilateral Arctic cooperation. This means cooperative stewardship that is mutually beneficial, that runs counter to the Canadian inclination to think of the Arctic in terms of "use it or lose it," and that opens a way to joint leadership in shaping the future of the Arctic as a region.

The range of potential bilateral stewardship activities for Canada and the United States is formidable. It runs from the development of ecosystem-based joint management of the Beaufort Sea, where our two countries have a boundary delimitation dispute;[39] to Coast Guard cooperation in search and rescue operations; to improvement of oil spill clean-up capabilities; to joint environmental monitoring; to planning for small-community adaptation to climate change; to precautionary fisheries management; to new arrangements to protect the Porcupine caribou herd; to harmonization of vessel identification and notification systems; to control of cruise ship navigation in icy waters; and so on out to strategic planning for intercontinental shipping in the Arctic waters of North America. On this last point, do our two countries want an increase in the volume of commercial navigation sufficiently to encourage it? Is it in our shared economic as well as geopolitical interests to underwrite international use of the Northwest Passage, and if so, for which cargoes, between which destinations, against which alternative routes, and with the provision of how much icebreaker and other support for convoys as opposed to independent navigation by ice-capable merchantmen? In all of this it should be possible for us in Canada to achieve a position of confidence and strength as distinct from the needless vulnerability that prevails today; of cooperative stewardship as distinct from imperilled sovereignty; and of attention to milieu as distinct from possession goals.

Besides developing cooperative stewardship arrangements to contribute to a steadily more secure Canada–US relationship in the Arctic, we need more coordinated action for the physical security of Arctic North America. Arctic maritime domain awareness and control need to be enhanced as priorities of the North American Aerospace Defence Command (NORAD). More important, the Obama administration seems likely to provide new international security openings, which Canada could take up as they relate to Russia's capacity for cooperative stewardship. The issues here are missile defence and the weaponization of space. On both of these, the administration's preference to scale down is sure to be opposed within the United States. On both of these, Russia has been not only adamantly opposed but also committed to countermeasures, which include the acquisition of new strategic nuclear missiles.[40] Should US commitments to missile defence and space weaponization persist, we ought to expect not only Russian military involvement but also regional and political countermeasures, including in the Arctic. Cooperative stewardship is likely to be among the victims.

To avert sequences such as these, Canada needs now to take public diplomacy as well as formal negotiating positions in global forums that offer the US government strong support, and even outdo it, not only on the militarization of space and on missile defence but also on an ASAT ban. No way should we be interpreted here to be urging an Arctic "wag the dog" when it comes to Canada's global security stance. All we are saying is that if we are to treat the evolution of the Arctic as a strategic priority, then we must view global security processes in the light of our ambitions for the future of the region that is now emerging from the cold before our very eyes. Greenland remains one last area of joint concern for Canada and the United States.

A unified North American approach to the Arctic requires that Canada and the United States pay considerably greater attention to Greenland. Inhabiting what is now a self-governing area of the Danish realm, the 55,000 Greenlanders, all but a small minority of them Inuit, seem certain to declare independence without delay in the event that they strike oil or natural gas in sufficient quantities.[41] The Arctic-8 would become the Arctic-9 or, more likely, Denmark would withdraw to the rank of observer. Permanent participants on the Arctic Council would to some extent gain in their ability to shape the consensus. Alert to new opportunity, non–North American and non-Arctic countries could soon be showing greater interest in Greenlandic affairs. So also should Canada and the United States, whether or not independence is in the offing. Danish rule has worked strongly for a European orientation among Greenlanders, even as they view the EU with an aversion that stems from past experience with the sealskin ban and European overfishing in Greenlandic waters. North America does not really figure in Greenland's view of its future. Although US–Greenland relations have generally been good with the exception of the forced relocation of a high northern community to make way for the base at Thule, ties with Canada have been minimal. Both Ottawa and Washington need to change things. To begin, they ought to include Greenland in any planning for harmonized management of the Arctic waters of North America, including on the question of whether or not in the first place intercontinental commercial shipping is to be encouraged when the global economy allows. As well, Ottawa needs to promote and finance broader and deeper relations between Nunavut and Greenland with Denmark's support. In due course, Canada, Greenland, and the United States should bring an integrated North American perspective to bear in pan-Arctic discussions of the region's future.

As for Europe, Canada has much to consider in terms of generating greater capacity for stewardship in the Arctic. Dialogue on the present situation, on the region's future, and on the potential for joint action is needed to build this capacity. Specifically, we think it would be useful to discuss access to Canadian High Arctic reserves of natural gas, Arctic Council enlargement, and possible implications for the Arctic of Russian proposals for a renewed Conference on Security and Cooperation in Europe (CSCE). Aside from the EC, Canada should be talking principally to the German government owing *inter alia* to German fascination with things northern and Arctic. Where Arctic gas is concerned, Canada has great reserves in Nunavut's Sverdrup Basin. We are advised that these are unlikely to go to American markets until Western Canadian shale gas has been used up or becomes too expensive. Instead, when conditions are right, High Arctic Canadian natural gas will be liquefied and shipped year-round by icebreaking liquefied natural gas (LNG) tankers to European or Asian markets.

We think that the EU (including Germany) should have first preference in view of its desire to reduce dependence on Russian supplies and its potential to contribute to pan-Arctic stewardship once it is directly involved in the region's affairs.[42] At the same time, the EU would need to adapt to Canadian views and those of the Inuit Circumpolar Council on the issue of seal hunting if it were to pursue the option of consultative-party status in a restructured Arctic Council.[43] Whatever the outcome of bilateral dialogue on energy, marine transportation, indigenous peoples', and Arctic governance issues, the Canadian interest in cooperative stewardship warrants an ambitious effort to create common ground with the EU. Meanwhile, matters of common security should also be discussed with Berlin and Brussels as they relate to the Arctic.

Moscow is seeking to convene a renewed CSCE as a means of restructuring the security architecture of Europe.[44] As with an Arctic BPA, the question for a Canadian–European dialogue is whether the CSCE project might also be used to bring Russia to provide stewardship in exchange for security in the Arctic. It is still early days, but we believe the project should be explored. A new CSCE would be a vast and unwieldy affair including everyone from Kazakhstan to Ireland plus Canada and the United States represented at the head-of-government level in a sequence of consensual gatherings set up by preparatory conferences. Whereas the original CSCE was dominated by issues of human rights and military confidence building, a contemporary version would presumably focus on energy, climate change, and the economy. It would also consider a rearrangement of the European security system that would include the Russian Federation as a central player. Inimical to NATO as it stands, the Russian proposal is problematic. At the same time, partly at the prompting of Norway, which feels itself inordinately exposed to Russian pressure, and partly in response to the 2008 events in South Ossetia, there is a tendency in NATO to inch toward a role in the Arctic in the event that this part of the world becomes more conflictual so that alliance interests need a stronger defence.

In our view, with five of the Arctic-8 being NATO members, there is no present need for new alliance commitments in the region. There may, however, be the elements of a deal in a renewed CSCE. In a new Arctic "basket"—to use the 1970s term—commitments to build good relations in the Arctic could be elaborated in conjunction with extensive new stewardship activities for climate and environmental protection. Initiatives such as these might go some of the way toward reducing the need for a new NATO role, while also fostering a greater Russian commitment to cooperative stewardship. Meanwhile, there would be no reason for either the eight or the Permanent Participants on the Arctic Council to be concerned about extraregional infringement on the council's mandate: the eight would be present—and, necessarily, Permanent Participants as well—in a renewed CSCE process in which all commitments would be consensual, as would collective reviews of implementation.

China comes last in this discussion of bilateral relations that Canada might foster in strengthening the capacity for collective action at the regional level. A major force in world politics today and assuredly a pre-eminent power in the future, China is already present in the Arctic. It conducts scientific research at a station in Norway's Svalbard Archipelago, periodically operates an icebreaker as a science platform in Arctic waters, and is present as a would-be observer at the Arctic Council. China is also and foremost a great trading nation. We fully expect one day to see not only Chinese commercial vessels but also the Chinese Navy in the Arctic. As for Canada, it has a strong interest in trade expansion with China and should now be preparing the way for Chinese as well as EU participation in the exploitation of High Arctic natural gas.

Given present interests and future prospects in Canadian–Chinese Arctic relations, an active effort should now be made to bring the Chinese directly into the Arctic region as a steward and as a new member of the community, rather than have them come in later as intruders and in a manner that is likely to cause conflict. Just as Canada led the way in recognizing the Communist government of China, so let us now be among the first to open wide the Arctic door to Beijing. Trade, joint industrial production, and investment—call it commerce for short—should be the focus.

As has been noted, in the Arctic the east–west flow of goods, people, and (in lesser measure) ideas is impoverished. Cross-border transactions between Norway and Northwestern Russia are an exception.[45] Overall, the effect is Arctic solidarity forgone—the solidarity that comes with the experience of shared effort and mutual benefit and that could be needed in times of stress among the Arctic-8. Another result of the lack of commerce in particular: an entire domain of normal human activity has been left very largely indolent, and, with it, habits of cooperation. The repercussions of this could well spill over into the political domain. We say this in the belief that commercial activity is a source of stability. Because it prompts a desire to maintain good relations and to avoid giving offence, commercial interaction makes for civility, which is to say respect and consideration for the other that is not unlike the care that is characteristic of stewardship. That being so, Canada should endeavour to provide regional leadership in the development of Arctic commercial relations in cooperation with China. Here we could well benefit from a trilateral relationship with Norway.

In a seeming replay of CSCE agenda items, Norway has shown great imagination in promoting the free flow of people and goods across its northernmost border with the Russian Federation. As well, StatoilHydro plans to work closely with its Russian counterpart Gazprom in the exploitation of hydrocarbon reserves under the Barents Sea, until recently an area of contested jurisdiction between the two countries. One predictable effect of Norwegian–Russian collaboration such as this is to enculture the Russian oil and gas industry in best global commercial practices, including on matters of environmental protection—practices to which it would otherwise not be exposed. To the extent that a leading Russian industry with global reach is made more environmentally aware in the course of joint industrial operations in the Barents Sea, the Arctic serves not only as the recipient of extraregional influences but also as a contributor to global well-being. There is a precedent here that might be followed more broadly: in both regional and global affairs, stewardship should engage commerce and industry as well as governments and those communities most exposed to the consequences of centralized decision making.

Although Canada and Norway on their own could elaborate and present to the Arctic Council a commercial strategy for regional solidarity and cooperation, we suggest that if agreeable to Norway, China be invited to join an exploration of the potential for new Arctic trade and joint industrial ventures. On the last, for example, why not barge-mounted nuclear-powered or LNG electricity generation for small Arctic communities? Regarding trade and intercontinental marine transportation, China has already indicated an interest and doubtless has something to offer. In short, if China is to become a consultative party to the Arctic Council, let us consult with the Chinese. Then let us seek wider support for a regional commercial strategy that is not only fully justifiable on the merits, but also able to foster pan-Arctic solidarity.

In wrapping up this proposal for a Canadian strategy, we might go on to identify and prioritize the chief governance requirements, starting with the marine environment.[46] Alternatively, we could delve into one or two particular issues—for instance, those relating to adaptation to climate change or to the management of Arctic marine transportation—in order to illustrate the benefits of an international practice of stewardship. Or we could begin thinking about how to rank competing projects for support from an Arctic Fund once capacity building for permanent participants had been tended to. All well and good enough, we choose not to enter a discussion of desired outcomes at this time. In place of outcomes, we insist on the primacy of preconditions. As long as the preconditions are lacking, talk of Arctic cooperation is unlikely to be followed by effective joint action. Working with the available materials, we need first to heighten the interest of Arctic and non-Arctic states in the region's affairs. We need to find ways of moving Arctic stewardship from the domain of situation reports and useful guidelines toward that of active coordination of and support for voluntary cooperative arrangements. These are arrangements that will arise not from the mind of a governing institution, but from the perceived needs of Arctic and non-Arctic states as brought together in a central coordinating forum.

We have suggested that the key objectives of a Canadian Arctic strategy come down to elevation, engagement, and invigoration. We have sought to show how these varied objectives may be pursued in an interrelated fashion. Still, if there is one proposal in this chapter that is absolutely essential in achieving a stronger regional capacity for cooperative stewardship, it is Arctic Council enlargement. We believe it to be negotiable, not quickly but over time, provided that a sustained effort is made. There are three main reasons for optimism. First, future considerations will continue to make non-Arctic players want in. Serious discussion of enlargement within the council will make the Arctic-8 more amenable, which is our impression after talking to senior officials. Second, accelerating climate change, as well as the prospect and arrival of unheard-of energy prices, will make the state of the Arctic ever more a global concern. Lastly, it is becoming easier and easier to envisage the rise of a global awareness that the fate of what we've been pleased to call civilization depends on nothing less than our ability to keep the Arctic cold. Amidst sharpening controversy, issue-based sectoral and regional cooperative stewardship could give way to strategic global intervention in Arctic affairs, climate geo-engineering included. If so, cooperative stewardship will have served well in preparing us for the next steps. If not, it will have served us well on its own.

Domestic Sources of Stewardship

Having dwelt at length on the need for Canada to show leadership in building new capacity for stewardship in the Arctic, it would be irresponsible not to consider how Canada might itself summon the will to lead. In our view the stakes are such that Canada has no choice but to join with others in a common effort to intensify and channel Arctic political interaction to the benefit of cooperative stewardship. But that is our view. Regrettably—and it is necessary to be realistic about this as well—we Canadians share the reluctance of other Arctic nations to come out of the shell of concern over our possessions and to take milieu goals to heart. Vigorous leadership will be required if we are to leave our Arctic disabilities behind. Ways must be found for far removed southern Canadians to take heed from Northerners, especially our Arctic indigenous peoples, who together constitute a kind of distant early warning line for climate change.[47] But little of enduring value will happen, avoidable losses will be inflicted upon us, and excellent opportunities squandered, unless, as we have already stated, the prime minister leads personally. But why should we and, especially, the prime pinister venture into the Arctic when it is so challenging to lead not only out there but also in here? What *is* at stake?

Since we Canadians tend to focus more easily on losses than on gains, let us first deal with the downside of failure to rise to the occasion in the Arctic. The more inattentive we are to a part of the world that is close to us and should be home to us, the more likely we are to yield to the values, interests, and decisions of others. The primary casualty of a failure to take decisive action in the Arctic will be self-marginalization and, in due course, loss of self-respect. Then there are the transboundary processes and resources that we will have left to themselves in passing on improved pan-Arctic governance for cooperative stewardship: new and old migratory fish species, oil spill disasters from vessels or drilling platforms at sea, the plentiful non-CO_2 sources of global warming in cruise ship smokestack emissions, Arctic and global land-based sources of ecosystem degradation that ignore Canadian lines of jurisdiction, and so on. In these matters it is sovereignty, in the sense of the ability to fully possess and enjoy what's ours by right, that would suffer.

If all this were not enough, there is the potential for major direct and opportunity costs in the event that negligence—on the part of Canada and the rest of the Arctic-8—saw regional and extraregionally generated conflict outstrip the growth of governance in the Arctic. We would be hard-pressed alone to defend the entirety of our Arctic Archipelago in a heavily conflicted and militarized region; furthermore, the absolute costs and the opportunities forgone as a result of defence spending and other missions in the world—to say nothing of social programs and tax reductions—could well be insupportable. Although developments such as these may seem improbable today, it would be foolhardy for us to exempt ourselves now from a vigorous effort to accentuate the pacific in the Arctic's political development. No less important and perhaps more germane, given a renewed play for Arctic resources and geopolitical position before too long, it would be self-defeating to leave ourselves open to a full-on regional replay of the unsustainable resource exploitation that has brought the planet's climate to its present state.

As to the gains that may come from a strategy of stewardship, they arise from an extraordinary act of anthropogenic fate. The Arctic is not the region that has always been there. Rather, Canada is being given a third ocean, beckoning as a shared international space. Of all the regions of the world, the sea and land area of the Arctic is surely the one in which Canada can most readily make a difference for the better. The opening Arctic presents Canada with a unique opportunity for a fresh start. We should seize it. We should offer leadership in the design of an agreed future for the region, in the creation of improved means of governance, in the avoidance of unsustainable development, and in the construction of a new political space in which all will begin to show greater respect in their relations with the world of nature and one another.

Lest all this seem overly lyrical, we should also be aware of the direct benefits that are to be had from new linkages between the Arctic and our global interests. Rather than remain a place apart, under a strategy of stewardship the Arctic would bring us new advantages in our trade, political, and military relations with major powers of the world. Plenty is to be gained here that has not even been tentatively considered by Canadians in their approach to the region thus far. And all along, there are the unexploited contributions to Canadian sovereignty that could come from a strategy of cooperative stewardship. When national holdings are very largely assured—as we believe they are in this part of the world—the sovereign is in a position to do more than see to possession. The sovereign should use the opportunity to improve the quality of life in his or her domain by not only reducing unfavourable transboundary effects but also containing national occupancy costs, which could rise if the potential for regional conflict were left unattended.

No way, we submit, can Canada walk away from the opportunities and let losses come as they may in the Arctic. Canadians have no alternative but to engage in the region's affairs, and to engage vigorously. *How* we engage will be determined, though, not only by the situation in the Arctic at large, but also by obstacles to engagement as they exist in this country. They are to be found, we believe, in public opinion and in the inclinations of federal government officials, which broadly reflect those of the general public. As well, some resistance may be encountered from the territorial governments and Canadian Arctic indigenous peoples' organizations faced with the possibility of being sidelined in an invigorated Arctic Council.

Though perhaps less focused as a result of the recession, public interest in the Arctic and in climate change is still substantial in Canada. Especially where the archetypal issue of the Northwest Passage is evoked, sovereignty is the chief concern and point of departure. Indeed, climate change first entered the Canadian imagination not so much as a problem in its own right but as a threat to sovereignty in that reduced ice cover was thought to make for easier intrusion into our waters by unauthorized foreign vessels. Today, the prototypical possession goal, sovereignty, still has precedence over the quintessential milieu goal, climate protection, in the way we tend to frame the issues in the Arctic. "Use it or lose it" thinking has inhibited us from looking very far beyond what is ours. Instead, we have surrendered to possession anxiety.

Promoted by academic purveyors of polar peril and amplified by the media, an unwarranted sense of Arctic vulnerability has come upon us. Prone to exaggerated threat assessment and overly insistent on the need for hardware to assert control, Canadians in the grip of possession anxiety are given to self-doubt when actually the outlook is good. Certainly this is true for the Northwest Passage.[48] The same may be said of our share of the Arctic outer continental shelf, whose delineation is governed by the law of the sea and backed by a correlation of forces that is heavily in favour of Canada if ever we must call upon it.[49] Yet Canadians worry, and journalists and editorialists feed on this worry. Sensationalism becomes the order of the day in commentary on a part of the world that very few know much about. Politicians, especially in a minority government situation, are readily spooked by news of impending Arctic danger and the need to defend. They join a misguided discourse and reinforce it by committing to still more resolute defences of sovereignty. Or they turn the Arctic sovereignty issue to use in "identity politics" so as to bolster appearances of attachment to the True North and to put political distance between themselves and the United States.[50] Net effect: a Canadian public that would have us move knowingly and confidently into the Arctic is not here today. It will have to be created if a Canadian Arctic strategy of cooperative stewardship is to become domestically viable. And then there is the federal government apparatus.

Bureaucracy does two things well—crisis and routine—and not a lot in between. A new Arctic strategy falls naturally into the in-between. In our experience, Canada is gifted with a truly admirable federal civil service. Given the right political leadership, it does great things. But given the peripheral standing of the region in the scheme of things as seen from the south, officials are loath to take on new Arctic commitments. Instead, interviews conducted in federal departments with an interest in the Arctic made clear the existence of a consensus that Canada is already well engaged in the region under the "Northern Strategy," which has been a work in progress of governments Liberal as well as Conservative for much of the present decade.[51] Actually, the Northern Strategy is all but fully concerned with the development and well-being of Canada's domestic North. Thus far the pan-Arctic dimension is slight. This is not surprising, given that Indian and Northern Affairs Canada (INAC) has the lead in the strategy, and as the Department of Foreign Affairs and International Trade (DFAIT) is but one of many other government departments involved.

Nor in the circumstances is it surprising to read in a 2006–8 DFAIT position paper on Canadian priorities for the Arctic Council that the council is to be used to further the government's northern priorities, which include the well-being of northern people and protection of the northern environment.[52] There can be no objection to this, as far as it goes. But Canada's foreign relations are not front and centre in such a view. Instead, the Arctic is approached as an extension of our North. Under this approach we are playing with only half the deck in a region that is effectively severed from our wider involvement in the world. This DFAIT position paper also strikes a restrictive note in affirming that the current structure of the Arctic Council reflects and responds well to the priorities of the Arctic-8, Canada thereby included. Say goodbye, therefore, to Arctic Council enlargement for as long as the old political guidance persists. Not long ago in an interview, we also heard from a senior official in the department that sustained interest in the Arctic is hard to find above the director-general or middle-management level. Say goodbye also to a lead role for DFAIT in a Canadian strategy for a region for as long as the initiative is left to the bureaucracy. Given the right instruction from the government, indeed from a majority federal government, much could change, and rapidly so.

Meanwhile, territorial governments, which do not enjoy the advantages of Permanent Participants in the Arctic Council, may not be all that well disposed to what we are proposing. They may instead prefer the status quo under the Northern Strategy and its domestic priorities. The same may be true of the Inuit Tapiriit Kanatami and possibly the Canadian office of the Inuit Circumpolar Council, to the extent these organizations could be sidelined in Canada and internationally in an increasingly global Arctic hurly-burly. At the same time, Inuit not only may feel confident but also, surely, will excel in global operations as well as in an invigorated Canadian debate, especially if assured of new support for capacity building. In our view, Canadian Arctic indigenous peoples and the natural environment on which they depend are more likely to fare better in an energized Arctic than if they were to hold principally to a domestically oriented Northern Strategy.

Put all this together—public predispositions, official reluctance to act, and potential resistance on the part of Canadian Arctic indigenous peoples and their organizations—and it is clear that the construction and implementation of a Canadian Arctic strategy present a leadership problem. But there are opportunities as well.

The prime minister is in a position to summon into being a new coalition and a new appeal by himself acting to fuse (a) the widespread interest in Arctic sovereignty with (b) the more deeply held and mobilized Canadian concern over climate change into (c) a new national commitment to cooperative stewardship in the Arctic. There is no need here to rehearse the arguments for stewardship as the best defence of sovereignty in conditions of interdependence. Nor should we at this moment endeavour ourselves to develop the case in full for an Arctic focus in Canada's climate protection effort. Suffice it to say that as climate change mounts as a public concern, as the fate of the world boils down as it were to the fate of the Arctic, a pan-Arctic focus may be made compelling to Canadians. The Arctic is also an area of the world in which Canada has a singular opportunity—to say nothing of a duty—to be effective. We made things happen here with the creation of the Arctic Council. We can do so again and, as contrasted with other aspects of our climate effort, stewardship activity in the Arctic could yield a fresh and encouraging sense of responsibility well met. Taking the regional lead in Arctic stewardship, Canadians might unexpectedly find nothing less than a twenty-first-century equivalent of international peacekeeping. Viewed in such a light, an innovative approach to sovereignty and stewardship could become a new national project, this time in our own front yard. There is enough in all of this, we submit, for the prime minister to take a close look at the option of leading for cooperative stewardship in the Arctic.

If the prime minister is indeed prepared to consider bringing Canada out of the Passage, so to speak, and into the opening Ocean, emissaries might well be sent on a tour of the Arctic countries to report on the prospects for and possible first steps in an Arctic strategy. Given enough promise on their return, a senior figure in the PMO could be assigned responsibility for policy development, sequencing of initiatives, and coordination of federal departments. Sooner or later a new Secretary of State for the Arctic would be appointed. Housed in DFAIT as the chief executor of a prime ministerial priority, this secretary of state would have responsibility for international and domestic Canadian representation and networking, together with stakeholder consultations in Canada. Consultation with Canadian Arctic indigenous peoples should figure prominently in his or her agenda.

In developing an Arctic strategy, we to the south have much to learn from Inuit and other Arctic indigenous peoples. Unlike ours, their cultures and practices are embedded in nature. They do not aspire to dominion. Yet they find themselves on the cutting edge of climate change brought on by southern desires for mastery. If stewardship is to mean respect for, and civility to, the Other in nature and humanity, Inuit in particular must be directly involved in creating and following through on an integrated, ethical, and enduring Canadian approach to the region. And when stewardship resides in locally informed governance, not merely the involvement but the opportunity for Arctic indigenous peoples themselves to show leadership will be an essential part of it. If we are to preach stewardship abroad, we should practise it at home.

New forums are therefore needed for North–south consensual policy dialogue in Canada. Patterned on the Marine Council that is promised in the 1993 Nunavut Land Claim Agreement, a new forum would not reinvent the wheel that already exists in Ottawa-based northern policy consultation.[53] Drawing together federal departments and Arctic stakeholders, it would serve as a locus for monitoring and priority setting in our own high Arctic and the region beyond. Equipped with a small secretariat and co-located with Canada's new High Arctic science facility, it would physically mark the new northward transfer of the Canadian imagination and political purpose. The determination and details of Canadian action in the Arctic would still, however, be done in Ottawa. To help bring North and south together down south, a new Standing Committee on the Arctic should be established in the House of Commons.

In closing these remarks on the challenge of leadership, we should note that in Lawrence Cannon, the former Minister of Foreign Affairs, we had for the first time in a decade a within-government champion of Arctic international cooperation. Speaking in Whitehorse on 11 March 2009, he made a series of undertakings that promised to move the federal government forward into the region.[54] Attaching "utmost priority" to the development of bilateral relations with Arctic countries and first of all the United States, the minister promised to "re-energize" the Arctic Council and provide it with new "resources" as a "high level" forum for the coordination and making of regional policies; to work with the United States on a common agenda for the council as of 2013, when Canada gains possession of the chair of the council until 2015 (followed directly by the United States until 2017); and to foster an international environment that will assist in the implementation of the Northern Strategy. Cannon also announced that he would soon be making a tour of the Arctic countries to start things moving. Not exactly the "elevation," "engagement," and "invigoration" we have been talking about in this paper, but getting close to it and all of a sudden.

The prime minister being the leader he is, any new forwardness in Canada's Arctic diplomacy will owe a great deal to him personally. Still, DFAIT is now mobilized to a degree that seemed hardly possible a short while ago. Let us hope that the new minister, John Baird, will be able to enlarge upon the opportunity that has been revealed for Canada to exercise Arctic international leadership.

The Arctic foreign policy of today continues primarily to generate support for the Northern Strategy from the international setting. As mentioned, the priorities of the strategy—environmental protection, economic and social development, sovereignty and devolution and governance—are essentially domestic in nature. And as we have said, it is entirely appropriate for the sovereign to pursue milieu goals that look to the well-being of her or his domain and its inhabitants. Still, what Canada needs for the Arctic is an international strategy. This is one that speaks to the interests of Canadians in general and to Northerners in particular. It is one that recognizes not only that cooperation is hard to come by in the Arctic, but also that it is harder than it needs to be when most of what we want to talk about to others stems directly from our internal agenda. A strategy that is regional and global in scope is required. Other Arctic actors have come forward with strategy statements of their own. The prime minister should order a Canadian equivalent without delay. But who is to be directly responsible for its development and implementation?

Over the past nine years, by our count, Canada has had nine foreign ministers. The position is in danger of losing its former gravitas. Meanwhile, the start-up, public consultations, and operation of an Arctic strategy will call for more time and imagination than a foreign minister should be expected to give. Furthermore, for an Arctic strategy to succeed, it must be handled in a manner that elevates the issues to the highest political level and that in so doing raises public interest. Active and visible leadership from the prime minister is essential. We therefore propose that, rather than the foreign minister, a secretary of state should be appointed to preside, as the prime minister's chief agent, over the implementation of a strategy whose design and operations are centred in the PMO.

To end, the Arctic is of critical importance to Canada. We have yet to realize fully what is happening in it and to us. Nevertheless, as a foreign policy domain in a changing world, the region is starting to close in on Canada–US relations in terms of its significance for this country. The success or failure of our performance in the Arctic is inseparable from the conduct of our relationship with the United States, which is the preserve of the prime minister. Primary responsibility for Arctic stewardship should now be seen as an essential feature of the prime minister's job description.

Recommendations

To end, we reduce our reflections on a Canadian Arctic strategy to a set of recommendations. They come in two parts, principal and following.

Principal recommendations

1) Prime Minister (PM) to take the lead.
2) PM to initiate development of a domestic political strategy to transmute Canadian public interest in climate protection and Arctic sovereignty into support for pan-Arctic stewardship.
3) PM to dispatch Foreign Minister and/or other emissaries on a tour of Arctic and certain non-Arctic capitals to report on the outlook for and likely first steps in a strategy of cooperative stewardship. Priority here to talks with the United States.
4) PM to demonstrate personal commitment, create opportunity for personal learning, and acquire an appreciation of the region and regional visions for the future, all by convening an international Arctic Identity Network or brains trust from the Arctic-8.
5) PM to assign a senior official in the PMO (PMO-A) and requisite staff with primary responsibility for policy planning and the machinery-of-government dimensions of a Canadian Arctic strategy, including generation of an initial strategy statement.

6) PM to appoint a Secretary of State for the Arctic (SS-A) in DFAIT responsible for international networking and representation together with domestic stakeholder consultations, all with an eye to formal development of an Arctic strategy for Canadian chairmanship of the Arctic Council between 2013 and 2015.

7) PM to strengthen public awareness of need and opportunity to enhance Arctic cooperation with the United States as a means of stabilizing the agreement to disagree on the Northwest Passage and generating an effective North American lead for cooperative stewardship throughout the region to 2017 and beyond.

8) PM, when appropriate in the larger context of Canada–US relations, to seek to interest the US president in Arctic Council enlargement and an Agreement on Basic Principles of Arctic International Relations as a means to improved relations with the Russian Federation together with effective Arctic governance.

9) PMO-A, coordinating with INAC and the evolution of the Northern Strategy, to take the lead in Canada's pan-Arctic strategy planning, sequencing of initiatives, and instructions to SS-A including on stakeholder consultations.

10) PMO-A to be responsible for design of and federal interdepartmental participation in a new north–south Canadian consultative forum on pan-Arctic affairs patterned on the provision for a Marine Council in the Nunavut Land Claim Agreement.

11) PMO-A to join with appropriate others in discussion and ensuing action to constitute a Standing Committee on the Arctic in the House of Commons.

12) PMO-A to guide SS-A in launching Canada's effort for Arctic Council enlargement in conversations with the Arctic-8 and non-Arctic observers, including on the creation of an Arctic Fund.

Following recommendations

1) SS-A to represent Canada in the Arctic Council.

2) SS-A to explore potential for the establishment of a binational Canada–US panel on opportunities for cooperative stewardship in the Arctic.

3) SS-A to pursue, initially with US counterparts, the development of an integrated subregional approach to the management of the Arctic waters of North America.

4) SS-A to deliver maximal Canadian support for US global negotiating positions on missile defence, weaponization of space, and ASAT prohibition as they relate to the Arctic.

5) SS-A to seek US agreement to lead a joint search and rescue exercise at the North Pole with icebreakers from the Arctic and interested non-Arctic states.

6) SS-A, in dialogue with counterparts, to lay the basis for Arctic-derived trade, security, climate change, and other initiatives by the PM in encounters with other heads of state, notably American, Chinese, and German.

7) SS-A to explore the potential of a renewed Conference on Security and Cooperation in Europe evoke a greater commitment to cooperative stewardship from the Russian Federation.

8) SS-A to consult with counterparts in Berlin and Brussels on access to High Arctic natural gas, Arctic Council enlargement, climate change, and European security.

9) SS-A to consult with Chinese counterparts on High Arctic LNG, Arctic Council enlargement, Arctic marine transportation, and Canada–China trade relations.

10) SS-A to consult with Norwegian counterpart on a trilateral Canadian–Chinese–Norwegian working group to prepare recommendations on regional trade expansion and industrial cooperation for presentation to the Arctic Council.

11) SS-A to ensure Arctic Fund support for Arctic Council Permanent Participant capacity building, and to seek a direct say for Permanent Participants in the council's consensus on matters of existential significance to indigenous peoples.

12) SS-A to lead public hearings for an Arctic strategy, and for the establishment of a Marine Council or equivalent.

13) SS-A to obtain Government of Nunavut and Energy, Mines, and Resources Canada commitment to the development of Sverdrup Basin natural gas for LNG export to European and Asian markets.

14) SS-A, in conjunction with the Government of Nunavut, to widen and deepen Canada's relations with Greenland with Danish support.

15) SS-A to consult with Swedish counterpart on transition and pre-negotiation of Canadian items prior to Canadian assumption of the Arctic Council chair.

Notes

1 This paper is based on personal experience as an observer of Arctic international relations, interviews with officials and others in Ottawa and abroad, and principally on thought about the policy problems encountered. Excellent introductions to Arctic affairs are to be found in the *Arctic Human Development Report* and the *Arctic Climate Impact Assessment*. See *Arctic Human Development Report* (Akureyri: Steffanson Arctic Institute,

2004), http://www.svs.is/AHDR/AHDR%20chapters/English%20version/AHDR_ first%2012pages.pdf, accessed 28 February 2009; and Arctic Climate Impact Assessment, *Impacts of a Warming Arctic: ACIA Overview Report* (Cambridge: Cambridge University Press, 2004), http://amap.no/acia, accessed 28 May 2009. Our present observations of Canadian policy and Arctic international relations stem from Franklyn Griffiths, "A Northern Foreign Policy," *Wellesley Papers* 7 (Toronto: Canadian Institute of International Affairs, 1979); and "Introduction: The Arctic as an International Political Region," in *The Arctic Challenge: Nordic and Canadian Approaches to Security and Cooperation in an Emerging Interntional Region*, ed. Kari Möttölä (Boulder: Westview Press, 1988), 1–14. We benefited greatly from conversations with private analysts as well as officials in Ottawa (23–25 June, 21–23 July, 22–23 October, and 10 November 2008), New York (2–3 June 2008), Washington (7–11 July 2008), and Oslo (6–10 October 2008). As well, over the last year or so we were fortunate to attend a series of international conferences on Arctic affairs, especially in Iceland (30 January 2009) and Berlin (11–13 March 2009). The latter, a gathering on "New Chances and New Responsibilities in the Arctic Region" was on the invitation of the German Federal Foreign Office and provided an opportunity to test certain proposals.

2 In parallel with the growth of Norwegian–Russian cooperation in the area, collaboration in the Barents region has expanded with the creation of the Barents Euro-Arctic Region, or BEAR (1993), and, subsequently, its inclusion of high northern Swedish and Finnish counties together with Russian republics (Karelia and Komi) and the Nenets region to the east in Archangel province. Furthermore, the Northern Dimension of the EU has brought European interests into the interplay. BEAR is one of the key institutions examined in Olav Schram Stokke and Geir Hønneland, eds., *International Cooperation and Arctic Governance: Regime effectiveness and northern region building* (London: Routledge, 2007). See also Stokke, "Sub-Regional Cooperation and Protection of the Arctic Marine Environment in the Barents Sea," in *Protecting the Polar Marine Environment: Law and Policy for Pollution Prevention*, ed. Davor Vidas (Cambridge: Cambridge University Press, 2000), Chapter 6. On the Polar Bear treaty, see Anne Fikkan et al., "Polar Bears: The Importance of Simplicity," in *Polar Politics: Creating International Regimes*, ed. Oran R.Young and Gail Osherenko (Ithaca: Cornell University Press, 1993), 96–151.

3 The phrase is from David VanderZwaag, "Land-Based Marine Pollution and the Arctic: Polarities Between Principles and Practice," in *Protecting the Polar Marine Environment: Law and Policy for Pollution Prevention*, ed. Davor Vidas (Cambridge: Cambridge University Press, 2000), 197.

4 Norval Scott, "U.S., Canada Chart Path for Arctic Future," *Globe and Mail*, 2 July 2008, A7.

5 Our thinking is not far removed from that of Professor Oran Young of the University of California at Santa Barbara and Ambassador Hans Corell, former Legal Counsel to the United Nations. See Oran R. Young, "Arctic Governance: The Next Phase," paper commissioned by the Standing Committee of Parliamentarians of the Arctic Region (June 2002), http://www.arcticparl.org/_res/site/File/static/conf5_scpar2002.pdf, accessed 26 February 2009; Hans Corell, "Reflections on the Possibilities and Limitations of a Binding Legal Regime for the Arctic," address to the Seventh Conference of Parliamentarians of the Arctic Region, 3 August 2006, http://www.havc.se, accessed 28 February 2009; Oran Young, "Whither the Arctic? Conflict or Cooperation in the Circumpolar North," *Polar Record* 45, no. 1 (2009): 73–82; and Hans Corell. "Mounting Tensions and Melting Ice: Exploring the Legal and Political Future of the Arctic," address at a symposium of the *Vanderbilt Journal of Transnational Law*, 6 February 2009, http://www.havc.se, accessed 28 February 2009.

6   Here we enlarge upon "The Long-Term Need for an Arctic Council," an Annex we provided for the Arctic Council Panel in its report, *To Establish an International Arctic Council: A Framework Report* (Ottawa: Canadian Arctic Resources Committee, 1991).

7   Population numbers are from Oran R. Young and Neils Einarsson, "Introduction: Human Development in the Arctic," in *Arctic Human Development Report*, 17–19.

8   For Russian identifications, see Franklyn Griffiths. "The Arctic in the Russian Identity," in *The Soviet Maritime Arctic,* ed. Lawson W. Brigham (London: Belhaven Press, 1991), 83–107. As to the Canadian identity, see Franklyn Griffiths. "The Shipping News: Canada's Arctic Sovereignty Not on Thinning Ice," *International Journal* 58, no. 2 (2003): 257–82, esp. 273–75.

9   Government of Canada. *Seizing Global Advantage: A Global Commerce Strategy for Securing Canada's Growth & Prosperity.* (Ottawa: Public Works Canada, 2008).

10   David L. Downie and Terry Fenge, *Northern Lights against POPS: Combating Toxic Threats in the Arctic* (Montreal and Kingston: McGill–Queen's University Press, 2003).

11   The story is well told by Willy Østreng in "National Security and the Evolving Issues of Arctic Environment and Cooperation," in *National Security and International Environmental Cooperation in the Arctic—The Case of the Northern Sea Route,* ed. Willy Østreng (Dordrecht: Kluwer Academic Publishers, 1999), ch. 1.

12   Observations to this effect were heard in Reykjavik on 30 January 2009 at an international conference that we attended following a seminar organized by NATO and the Government of Iceland on Security Prospects in the High North.

13   On Radarsat, see Paul Taylor, "A Hawkeyed Addition to Canada's Arctic Arsenal," *Globe and Mail,* 10 December 2007, A7. On Chinese and Russian antipathy to space weaponization, see Pavel Podvig and Hui Zhang, *Russian and Chinese Responses to U.S. Military Plans in Space* (Cambridge, MA: American Academy of Arts and Sciences, 2008).

14   Established in 1991, the Northern Forum brings together subnational and regional governments from eight northern countries. Website is http://www.northernforum.org.

15   Ilulissat Declaration. Adopted at the Arctic Ocean Conference hosted by the Government of Denmark and attended by the representatives of the five coastal states bordering on the Arctic Ocean (Canada, Denmark, Norway, the Russian Federation, and the US), Ilulissat, Greenland, 27–29 May 2008. http://www.oceanlaw.org/downloads/arctic/Ilulissat_Declaration.pdf, accessed 28 May 2009. As to exclusion, the European Commission felt it necessary by November 2008 to say that "the EU should promote broad dialogue and negotiated solutions and not support arrangements which exclude any Arctic EU Member States or Arctic EEA EFTA countries." See Commission of the European Communities, *Communication from the Commission to the European Parliament and the Council: The European Union and the Arctic Region* (Brussels: COM(2008) 763), Section 4. http://ec.europa.eu/external_relations/arctic_region/docs/com_08_763_en.pdf, accessed 28 February 2009.

16   Seminar on Security Prospects in the High North, sponsored by NATO and the Government of Iceland, "Chairman's Conclusions," 29 January 2009. The concluding statement has not so far as we know been published. For the seminar, visit www.nato.int/docu/update/2009/01-january/e0128a.html, accessed 27 February 2009.

17   Helge Blakkisrud. "What's to Be Done with the North?" in *Tackling Space: Federal Politics and the Russian North,* ed. Helge Blakissrud and Geir Hønneland (Lanham: University Press of America, 2006), 37–40.

18   See, for example, Rowan Scarborough, "Russian Flights Smack of Cold War," *Washington Post,* 26 June 2008, A1; and Steven Chase, "Ottawa Rebukes Russia for Military Flights in the Arctic," *Globe and Mail,* 28 February 2009, A4. In the latter piece, the NORAD

Commander is quoted as saying, "The Russians have conducted themselves professionally; they have maintained compliance with international rules of airspace sovereignty
and have not entered the internal airspace of either of the countries."

19 Geir Hønneland and Jørgen Holten Jørgensen, "The Ups and Downs of Environmental
Governance," in *Tackling Space: Federal Politics and the Russian North*, ed. Helge Blakkisrud
and Geir Hønneland Blakissrud and Hønneland (Lanham: University Press of America,
2006), Chapter 7. See also Jonathan D. Oldfield, *Russian Nature: Exploring the Environmental Consequences of Societal Change* (Burlington: Ashgate, 2005).

20 Russian Federation, Security Council, "Press-reliz po Osnovam gosudarstvennoi politiki
Rossiskoi Federatsii v Arktike na period do 2020 goda i dalneishuyu perspektivy" [Press
Release on the Foundations of the State Policy of the Russian Federation in the Arctic
for the Period to 2020 and Beyond], *Novosti*, 27 March 2009, http://www.scrf.gov.ru/
news/421.html, accessed 30 March 2009. An unofficial translation of the full statement
is available at "Google Translations."

21 On nuclear dumping, see Olav Schram Stokke, "Radioactive Waste in the Barents and Kara
Seas: Russian Implementation of the Global Dumping Regime," in *Protecting the Polar
Marine Environment: Law and Policy for Pollution Prevention*, ed. Davor Vidas (Cam-
bridge: Cambridge University Press, 2000), 200–20.

22 Private communications including from Senior Arctic Officials. See also the insightful
discussion in Elana Wilson Rowe, "Russian Multilateralism: The Case of the Arctic Council," in *The Multilateral Dimension in Russian Foreign Policy*, edited by Rowe and Stina
Torjesen (London: Routledge, 2009), chapter 9.

23 According to the US Arctic policy directive of 9 January 2009, the Arctic Council "should
remain a high-level forum devoted to issues within its current mandate and not be transformed into a formal international organization, particularly one with assessed contributions. The United States is nevertheless open to updating the structure of the Council."
See White House, Office of the Press Secretary, "National Security Presidential Directive
NSPD 66: Arctic Region Policy" (9 January 2009). http://www.fas.org/irp/offdocs/
nspd/nspd-66.htm, accessed 27 February 2009.

24 Franklyn Griffiths, "Environment in the U.S. Discourse on Security: The Case of the
Missing Arctic Waters," in *National Security and International Environmental Cooperation in the Arctic*, ed. Willy Østreng (Dordrecht: Kluwer Academic Publishers, 1999),
Chapter 5. In fairness, as the member of the Arctic Five that is least aware of itself as an
Arctic country and least troubled by threats to Arctic sovereignty, the United States has
the greatest potential to take the regional view in acting for cooperative stewardship as
well as assured sovereign possession.

25 For detail on the Council, see http://www.arctic-council.org, accessed 28 February 2009.
There is also a growing literature on the Arctic Council. The best is Timo Koivurova and
David L. VanderZwaag, "The Arctic Council at 10 Years: Retrospect and Prospects," *UBC
Law Review* 40, no. 1 (2007): 121–94. Also, in regard to regime- and region-building,
see Stokke and Hønneland, *International Cooperation and Arctic Governance;* and E.C.H.
Keskitalo, *Negotiating the Arctic: Construction of an International Region* (London: Rout-
ledge, 2004).

26 Young, "Whither the Arctic? Conflict or Cooperation."

27 The distinction between possession and milieu goals is introduced in Arnold Wolfers,
Discord and Collaboration: Essays on International Politics (Baltimore: Johns Hopkins
University Press, 1962), chapter 5.

28 The OSPAR Convention of 1992 gathers fifteen European states and the European Commission in a common effort to protect the marine environment of the Northeast Atlantic,

whose northern region is taken to include Arctic waters reaching to the North Pole. See http://www.ospar.org, accessed 28 February 2009.

29 On this last point, see Elana Wilson Rowe, "Arctic Unity, Arctic Difference: Mapping the Reach of Northern Discourses," *Polar Record* 43, no. 2 (2007): 125–33.

30 The agreement was signed on 29 May 1972. It can be found at "Agreement on Basic Principles of Relations between the United States of America and the Union of Soviet Socialist Republics," *International Legal Materials* 11 (29 May 1972): 756–60.

31 DFAIT communication to the author, also providing an update on Arctic Council participation, 23 December 2008. The Arctic Council's website is http://www.arctic-council.org.

32 A proposal to grant non-Arctic states and intergovernmental organizations "a recognized status in the governance system of the Arctic" has already been made by Professor Oran Young. See Young, "Whither the Arctic? Conflict or Cooperation," 80.

33 Arctic Council Panel, "To Establish an International Arctic Council," 32.

34 See note 24 above.

35 Quite apart from whatever President Obama and his people might prefer, the Bush administration's opposition to assessed contributions was expressed in a context of resistance to change in the council's mandate and status as a "forum." What we are proposing here—enlargement for cooperative stewardship—requires no change of mandate. Nor do we seek to change the council into a formal international organization. Still, in calling for matching contributions we are proposing to endow the Council with new capability. Best, in our view, would be for the Eight to begin by setting non-Arctic membership dues as function of what, to begin with, needs doing and what the Eight are themselves prepared to pay and how: according to GNP, which of course would require very heavy reliance on the United States; in equal contributions, which presumably would allow Iceland to set the rate owing to ability to pay; or by another formula arising from talks with today's observers.

36 John Ibbitson, "Ambitious Agenda Awaits New Cabinet," *Globe and Mail,* 18 December 2008, A21.

37 On black carbon, see Martin Mittelstaedt, "The High Cost of Blowing Smoke on the High Seas," *Globe and Mail,* 1 April 2009, A11, which reports a joint Canada–US proposal to the International Maritime Organization to establish emission control zones off the east and west coasts but not in Arctic North America. As to climate engineering, see David G. Victor et al., "The Geoengineering Option," *Foreign Affairs* 88, no. 2 (March–April 2009): 64–76.

38 Franklyn Griffiths. "Canadian Arctic Sovereignty: Time to Take Yes for an Answer on the Northwest Passage," in *Northern Exposure: People, Powers, and Prospects for Canada's North,* ed. Frances Abele, Thomas J. Courchene, F. Leslie Seidle, and France St-Hilaire (Montreal: Institute for Research on Public Policy, 2009). http://www.irpp.org/books/archive/AOTS4/griffiths.pdf, accessed 28 May 2009.

39 Norway is the regional leader in ecosystem-based joint management. Royal Norwegian Ministry of the Environment, *Report No. 8 to the Storting (2005–2006): Integrated Management of the Marine Environment of the Barents Sea and the Sea Areas off the Lofoten Islands* (Oslo: Government Publications, 2006).

40 Podvig and Zhang, *Russian and Chinese Responses to U.S. Military Plans in Space.*

41 "The dominating political current in Greenland these years is aiming at more political independence from Denmark." Remark made by Juliane Henningsen, MP Denmark/Greenland, at a gathering of the Conference of Parliamentarians of the Arctic Region, New York, 4 June 2008, www.arcticparl.org/reports.aspx?id=2966, accessed 27 February 2009. For now, the trend is being expressed in movement toward "self-rule."

42 The EU's recent Arctic policy statement speaks of "facilitating the sustainable and environmentally friendly exploration, extraction and transportation of Arctic hydrocarbon resources" in the context of "enhancing the EU's security of supply." Commission of the European Communities, *Communication,* Section 3.1.

43 Currently the EU is moving in the opposite direction. See Keith Doucette, "EU Closer to Total Ban on Canadian Seal Products," *Globe and Mail,* 3 March 2009, A8.

44 Organization for Security and Cooperation in Europe (OSCE), press release, "Russian Deputy Foreign Minister Discusses European Proposal with OSCE states," 18 February 2009, http://www.osce.org/itm/36321.html, accessed 26 February 2009.

45 See Norwegian Ministry of Foreign Affairs, *The Norwegian Government's High North Strategy* (Oslo, December 2006), Part 4.

46 Timo Koivurova and Erik J. Molenaar, "International Governance and Regulation of the Marine Arctic: A Report Prepared for the WWF International Arctic Programme," 20 January (Oslo: WWF Arctic Programme, 2009), http://assets.panda.org/downloads/gap_analysis_marine_resources_130109.pdf, accessed 28 February 2009. The WWF is to be commended for this report, which amounts to a very lengthy shopping list for Arctic international cooperation on marine-related matters. The authors do not, however, establish criteria of relative importance, consider interdependencies between issues, or prioritize international action on the "regulatory gaps" they identify.

47 A discussion of the issues is available in Franklyn Griffiths, "Camels in the Arctic?" *The Walrus,* November 2007, 46–61.

48 Griffiths, "Canadian Arctic Sovereignty."

49 Nevertheless, in response to a bit of Russian bluster about the creation of an Arctic special forces unit, we have little hesitation in saying we will not be "bullied." Steven Chase, "Russia Won't Bully Canada in Arctic, Cannon Vows," *Globe and Mail,* 28 March 2009, A4. Bullied, when Russia's conventional military power has crashed since the fall of the Soviet Union? When four of the five Arctic littoral states are NATO members? When any coercion of Canada in the Arctic will inevitably be treated as an act of coercion against the United States?

50 Tom Flanagan, *Harper's Team: Behind the Scenes in the Conservative Rise to Power* (Montreal and Kingston: McGill–Queen's University Press, 2007), 245–46.

51 We have seen PowerPoint versions of the strategy, but the most that is generally available is in Prime Minister's Office (PMO), Backgrounder: "Northern Strategy, 10 March 2008, http://pm.gc.ca/eng/media.asp?id=2016, accessed 28 February 2009.

52 Department of Foreign Affairs and International Trade (DFAIT), "Arctic Council Priorities 2006–2008: Canadian Position Paper," 8 February 2007 version.

53 *Agreement Between the Inuit of the Nunavut Settlement Area and Her Majesty the Queen in Right of Canada* (Ottawa: Tungavik and Minister of Indian Affairs and Northern Development, 1993), Article 15.4.1. Still to be acted upon.

54 Hon. Lawrence Cannon, "Notes for an Address by the Honourable Lawrence Cannon, Minister of Foreign Affairs, on Canada's Arctic Foreign Policy," 11 March 2009, Whitehorse, http://www.international.gc.ca/media/aff/speeches-discours/2009/386933 .aspx?lang=en, accessed 19 March 2009. Mr. Cannon was appointed Foreign Minister following the federal election of November 2008.

Sovereignty, Security, and Stewardship
An Update

P. Whitney Lackenbauer

T he Arctic agenda has continued to gain momentum since the authors submitted their final reports to the CIC in the spring of 2009. Climate change,
resource issues, undefined continental shelf boundaries, potential maritime
transportation routes, and security issues continue to factor into the domestic and foreign policy agendas of the Arctic states. The region has also attracted
the attention of non-Arctic states and organizations, some of which assert the
need to protect the Arctic "global commons" from excessive national claims
and are alleged to covet Arctic resources. Commentators continue to debate
the implications of these geopolitical dynamics and what they mean for Canadian foreign, defence, and Arctic policy. These conclusions summarize what
has transpired over the past two years and highlight how developments relate
to some of the major debates raised in the preceding chapters about Canada's
strategic direction in the changing circumpolar world. These include the ones
over Canada's Northern Strategy; the emerging security environment; Canada's
relations with Russia, the United States, and Denmark; and international governance in the Arctic.

Canada's Northern Strategy

The Canadian government unveiled its long-awaited Northern Strategy on
26 July 2009. This was nearly a month after Griffiths asserted in the *Globe
and Mail* that Canada still had no strategy for the region in its entirety[1] and
a day after the CIC published the reports by Lackenbauer and Huebert. The
Northern Strategy reinforces a message of partnership: between the federal

government and northern Canadians, and between Canada and its circumpolar neighbours. Critics suggested that the strategy simply reiterated previous government commitments, while supporters suggested that the official document outlined a more coherent framework that shifts emphasis away from narrow security concerns and sovereignty loss. Although it trumpets the government's commitment to "putting more boots on the Arctic tundra, more ships in the icy water and a better eye-in-the-sky," it also emphasizes that Canada's disagreements with its neighbours are "well-managed and pose no sovereignty or defence challenges for Canada." This is a rather abrupt change of tone from previous political messaging.[2]

The "use it or lose it" message that had been frequently mobilized to justify the government's agenda was absent from *Canada's Northern Strategy*. Instead, the government echoed those commentators who see space for cooperation in the circumpolar world. The document casts the United States as an "exceptionally valuable partner in the Arctic" with which Canada has managed its differences responsibly since the Second World War. It also emphasizes opportunities for cooperation with Russia and "common interests" with European Arctic states, as well as a shared commitment to international law. Implicitly, this confirms that bilateral and multilateral engagement is key to stability and security in the region. "We're not going down a road toward confrontation," Foreign Affairs Minister Lawrence Cannon emphasized. "Indeed, we're going down a road toward co-operation and collaboration. That is the Canadian way. And that's the way my other colleagues around the table have chosen to go as well." Cannon insisted that his government saw the Arctic as an "absolute priority" and that the needs of Northerners would be at the heart of Arctic policy.[3]

Balancing an Arctic security agenda with domestic imperatives to improve the quality of life of Northerners, while grappling with the challenges and opportunities accompanying climate change, remains difficult. "Policy is only as good as the action it inspires," Cannon noted at the unveiling ceremony. As the chapters in this book indicate, the litmus test of government resolve would be follow-through. "Laying out a broad, integrated, and positive strategy is a step in the right direction," Lackenbauer concurred in the *Toronto Star*. "Converting the strategy to deliverables that produce a more constructive and secure circumpolar world will be the real challenge."[4]

The Emerging Arctic Security Regime?

While the Department of Foreign Affairs and International Trade has put forward its vision for improving Canada's partnership with its Arctic neighbours,

Figure 5-1 Left to right: Brigadier-General David Millar, Nunavut Premier Eva
Aariak, and Danish Rear Admiral Henrik Kudsk at the conclusion of Operation
Nunalivut at Alert, Nunavut, April 2010.
Source: P. Whitney Lackenbauer

the Department of National Defence (DND) / Canadian Forces (CF) pro-
ceeds with its plans to enhance Canada's military presence and capabilities in
the Arctic. The *Canada First Defence Strategy* directs the forces to demonstrate a visible presence in the region, to have the capacity to defend our Arctic territory, and to assist other departments when called upon. The tenor is
one of defensive rather than offensive capabilities, but it is clearly intended to
enhance the sovereignty pillar of the government's broader Northern Strategy. At the same time, the Standing Committee on Fisheries and Oceans has

recommended that the Canadian Coast Guard arms its vessels to increase Canada's enforcement capability.[5]

While decision makers are moving to improve the capabilities of the Canadian Forces and other agencies to better protect and enforce Canadian laws and regulations in the Arctic, recent speeches by senior officers in the Canadian Forces have tended to amplify the theme of international cooperation. In late April 2010, Canada's Chief of the Maritime Staff, Vice Admiral Dean McFadden, emphasized that economic interests should not lead to the militarization of the North. "While our Russian counterparts regularly conduct military exercises in the region," he noted, "this is rather more a demonstration of their intention to protect their national interests, and not the foreshadowing of a new armed standoff over resources." The real challenges relate to safety and security—environmental spills, search and rescue, and climate change causing distress to communities—rather than to conventional military threats. Accordingly, the CF role was to support other government departments, not to lead Canada's charge in a military showdown. "All countries involved in the Arctic need to move forward in a spirit of cooperation," he encouraged.[6] This optimistic message suggests space for constructive engagement.

Given that most Arctic disputes relate to maritime jurisdiction, the Navy factors heavily into Canada's promised investments. The Arctic offshore patrol ships (AOPSs) and the deepwater berthing and refuelling facility at Nanisivik are both in the project definition phase. The first ship is planned to be delivered in 2014, with full operational capability by 2020, but these dates now appear unrealistic. Physical infrastructure requirements for Nansivik are still being considered, and plans see the facility opening in 2015.[7] Meanwhile, Defence Research and Development Canada continues its Northern Watch Technology Demonstration project on the southwest corner of Devon Island, Nunavut, at Gascoyne Inlet and Cape Liddon on Barrow Strait.[8]

The Chief of the Air Staff's February 2010 planning directive promises that "the Air Force will become a more relevant, responsive, and effective Arctic capable aerospace power." Planners are still identifying which airframes, infrastructure, and training this Arctic mission will entail. The debate about the procurement of F-35 aircraft has been tied directly to Arctic sovereignty and security, particularly in response to Russian bomber flights toward Canadian airspace. Furthermore, some commentators call for the stationing of dedicated search and rescue assets in the Arctic, while others suggest that southern-based assets are more appropriate, given the relatively low rate of incidents in this vast region. New platforms also indicate that the CF has significantly improved its capabilities to move personnel and equipment quickly to respond to emergencies into remote regions. A CC-177 Globemaster III aircraft landed on a gravel-impregnated ice and snow runway for the first time ever during Operation Nunalivut in April 2010, and these aircraft were used again for Operation Nanook that August. The proven ability of the CC-177 to land on Arctic runways in both summer and winter conditions also demonstrates enhanced SAR capabilities in the region. Similarly, the arrival of CH-47F (Chinook) heavy-lift helicopters will allow the CF to move Rangers and other soldiers around the North much more rapidly than before. There are plans for an expanded hub-and-spoke system in the North, so that long-haul heavy aircraft can put down large numbers of troops and equipment on prepared airstrips and smaller, lighter aircraft can deploy out to austere locations on the ice or tundra.[9] If these plans are realized, the air force will enhance its ability to respond to routine, contingency, and crisis operations in the Arctic.

The army has also expanded its presence and tempo of activity in the North. It conducts Advanced Winter Warfare Training courses at the new CF Arctic Training Centre in Resolute, which is expanding with the Polar Continental Shelf facility run by Natural Resources Canada. Furthermore, the four Land Force Areas have established Arctic Response Company Groups (comprised of three infantry platoons, a company HQ, and an administrative/medical platoon), which conduct Northern exercises. During Operation Nanook 10,

Figure 5-2 Canadian Ranger Pauloosie (Paul) Atagoota instructs soldiers from the Arctic Response Company Group near Resolute, Nunavut, during Operation Nanook, 2010.
Source: DND

for example, soldiers from 32 Brigade Group (Ontario) deployed to Nunavut as an ARCG. The army is still determining mobility and equipment requirements related to northern operations, but senior officers anticipate that land forces will have an even greater Arctic focus once Canada's mission in Afghanistan winds down at the end of 2011.[10] The army's northern footprint expanded when a subunit to the Loyal Edmonton Regiment was stood up in Yellowknife in August 2009, marking the return of the Primary Reserves north of 60.

Finally, plans to expand the Canadian Rangers are on target, and Rangers have begun to receive additional equipment. There is no consensus on whether the Rangers should be "enhanced" to have a more combat-oriented role akin to the Primary Reserves—a suggestion that prompted some Rangers to indicate that they would quit rather than fight. "I didn't become a Canadian Ranger to go fight in combat," Master Cpl. Warren Esau of the Sachs Harbor patrol explained. "I'd have a big problem if they decided to do something like this … I'd rather be out shooting caribou and geese, not humans. It's not what I want to be doing as a Ranger."[11]

While the Northern Strategy appeared to represent a softening of the government's "use it or lose it" approach to sovereignty and security, "hard security" trends have led Rob Huebert to warn that confrontation remains a real possibility. He insists that there is an "Arctic arms race,"[12] an idea frequently echoed by national and international reporters, who raise the spectre of a new Cold War in the region.[13] Huebert concedes that there is little likelihood of conflict in the Arctic at present, but he points to three emerging trends to suggest that optimism may be short-lived. First, all the Arctic states have recently developed Arctic foreign and defence policy statements. These tend to begin with a commitment to cooperate, but warn that the country will take unilateral action to defend its Arctic interests when threatened. Within these documents, most of the Arctic states have also begun to re-emphasize a central role for their military forces. Second, almost all the Arctic states have begun to conduct larger and more complex military exercises in the Arctic. Third, and most important, several of the Arctic states—the United States, Canada, Norway, Denmark, and Russia—have begun to substantially strengthen their militaries' abilities to operate in the High North.[14] Taken as a whole, Huebert observes, Arctic states are dedicating considerable effort and resources to bolster their combat capabilities in the Arctic—clear evidence that they feel it is necessary to rearm themselves and suggesting that they perceive a possible military challenge in the region.

Other commentators insist that these activities do not portend military conflict. Lawson W. Brigham replied to Huebert in November 2010:

There has indeed been some modest military buildup by the Arctic states. But that buildup hardly signals aggressive designs. Rather, it seems little more than a prosaic response to continued resource development—national and commercial investment demand some sort of protection—and to the greater transport and increased communication lines that will accompany the opening of the Arctic seascape ... It's not a surprise ... that Arctic states are revising their security postures in light of new economic opportunities and political priorities in the region. Those states increasing their military presence are acting to deter aggressive challenges from Arctic and non-Arctic states alike, thereby increasing stability ... The Arctic situation has shifted from a Cold War posture to an emphasis on cooperative resource use, law enforcement, and environmental security. Thankfully, direct military conflict among the Arctic states is an increasingly distant possibility.[15]

Commentators like Brigham suggest that nationalist political rhetoric and scenarios about prospects for conflict deflect attention from the stability and cooperation prevailing in the region.

Brigham has also cautioned that public discussions about the possibility of conflict may become self-fulfilling prophesies. We may be witnessing in the Arctic a classic security dilemma—states misperceive one another's intentions and, in striving to be defensively secure, others perceive their actions as threatening. Or is this a case of political theatre in the High Arctic, staged by politicians to convince their domestic constituencies that they are protecting vital national interests—a convenient pretext to justify major investments in defence? As Arctic states reveal their plans to invest in military capabilities, questions linger about how to read their intentions. Are these plans a signal that Arctic countries believe military conflict is possible, if not probable? Are intentions offensive or defensive? Is "tough talk" about protecting Arctic interests merely political rhetoric designed to appeal to domestic audiences, or is it primarily messaging intended for other states with Arctic interests? Or are the leaders of the Arctic state becoming increasingly concerned that conflict may occur despite their positive rhetoric?

Regardless of the answers, Canada faces stern international critics who accuse it of unilateralism and provocation. US Navy Captain James Kraska, the Howard S. Levie Chair of Operational Law at the US Navy War College, chastises Canada for ignoring international law in pursuit of its aggressive, expansionist agenda in the Arctic:

Canada is under the unilateralist spell of oceans sovereignty, going it alone in the Arctic Ocean in a vain attempt to grasp a future of stability and security amidst a rapidly changing geophysical Arctic climate and unsettling and dynamic Arctic politics. Canada has resurrected "sovereignty" patrols, loudly trumpeted plans to construct ice-strengthened patrol vessels to enforce unilateral rules in the Northwest Passage, and retreated behind the mythos of Canadian Arctic sovereignty. The storyline is recycled by the government–media–academic complex to obtain the approval—or at least the acquiescence—of the international community, especially the United States.[16]

Likewise, some international newspaper commentators cast Canada as a destabilizing force in the circumpolar world. Timothy Bancroft-Hinchey's article in *Pravda* on 25 March 2010 is an extreme example. "What does Prime Minister Stephen Harper have in common with the Canadian Minister of Defence? He shares a sinister, hypocritical and belligerent discourse bordering on the lunatic fringe of the international community," Bancroft-Hinchey proclaims. "From Canada, Russia has become used to seeing and hearing positions of sheer arrogance, unadulterated insolence and provocative intrusion." Behind the hyperbolic language is a serious message: other countries perceive Canada's messaging as belligerent and threatening. On the other hand, other Arctic states have already moved to build up their military capabilities while most of Canada's commitments remain in the planning process.

Russia

If Americans are traditionally cast in the role of the primary threat to Canadian sovereignty, the Russians have been recast in the familiar Cold War role of the primary security threat.[17] Huebert insists that Moscow's political strategy is "an iron fist in a velvet glove."[18] He points to Russia's "escalatory" military activities in the North and around the world: the war in Chechnya, strategic bomber flights in the Arctic, missile test firings near the North Pole, nuclear submarine cruises in the region, and commitments to expand land force activities.

Tough rhetoric persists. Canadian politicians reacted sharply when Russia stated its intention to drop paratroopers at the North Pole in the spring of 2010. While a Russian embassy spokesman insisted that the mission was a "solely symbolic" event aimed at celebrating the sixtieth anniversary of a Cold War achievement by two Soviet scientists, Minister Peter MacKay was emphatic that Canada was going to "protect our sovereign territory. We're always going to meet any challenge to that territorial sovereignty, and I can assure you any country that is approaching Canadian airspace, approaching Canadian territory, will be met by Canadians."

Similar rhetoric about "standing up for Canada" followed the CF-18 interception of Russian Tu-95 bombers off the east coast of Canada in July 2010, once again outside of Canadian airspace. Journalists and military analysts immediately tied the issue to Arctic sovereignty and security, casting the Russians in the familiar role of provocateurs attempting to violate Canada's jurisdiction.[19] Even Cannon's speeches, which emphasize and promote circumpolar cooperation, also point to the need to defend against outside challenges—specifically, Russian activities that purportedly "push the envelope" and "challenge" Canadian sovereignty and security in the North. These alleged threats are mobilized to affirm that the Canadian Forces have a "real role" to play in defending our Northern sovereignty.[20] Like much of the government's rhetoric, however, the precise nature of this role, and the nature of the Russian threat, remains ambiguous.

Despite these high stakes, some commentators suggest that Russia is less bellicose than popular media perceptions convey. Lackenbauer and Katarzyna Zysk, for example, contend that listening only to the "hard security" discourse leads to an inflated assessment of the probability for Arctic conflict. The key audience for confrontational rhetoric is domestic. In its official policy and statements on the High North, they argue, Russia follows a pragmatic line and pursues its territorial claims in compliance with international law. The Russian Arctic strategy prioritizes maintaining the Arctic "as an area of peace and cooperation." Russian leaders dismiss foreign criticisms that they are flexing their muscles to extend their claims beyond their legal entitlement.[21] The prevailing *international message* that Russia seeks to project is that it will abide by international law—but that it will not be pushed around by neighbours who might encroach on its Arctic jurisdiction.

The United States and Denmark

Raising the Russian security threat also raises issues related to alliances. Canada is a member of NATO and a partner in NORAD. Former Danish Prime Minister Anders Fogh Rasmussen, Secretary General of NATO, has emphasized the "potentially huge security implications" of Arctic climate change. "I think it is within the natural scope of work for NATO to be the forum for consultation and discussion on [selected Arctic] issues," he noted in October 2009. Russia, however, has indicated that it will not cooperate with NATO on Arctic matters.[22] Accordingly, the question remains about how to leverage relationships with allies to address common security and safety concerns without destabilizing the region or undermining Canada's sovereignty position.

While nationalist concerns over sovereignty—originally directed toward the United States over the Northwest Passage and the Beaufort Sea, and the

Figure 5-3 Canadian Chief of the Defence Staff General Walt Natynczyk and his Danish counterpart, General Knud Bartels, sign a Memorandum of Understanding on Arctic Defence, Security, and Operational Cooperation, May 2010.
Source: DND

Danes over Hans Island—triggered intense political interest in the Arctic, Canada's relations with its closest Arctic neighbours have been painted in a more positive light over the past year. The most public indication of warmer relations arose during military exercises, when the CF invited the Arctic neighbours with whom it has boundary disputes to participate in High Arctic operations. During Operation Nunalivut 10, for example, the Canadian Rangers were joined by the Danish (Greenland) Sirius Dog Patrol on a joint mission on the sea ice off northern Ellesmere Island and Greenland.

Lackenbauer and Ron Wallace, a fellow with the Canadian Defence and Foreign Affairs Institute, suggested that these joint operations marked something more significant than the de-escalation of past territorial disputes between Canada and Denmark over Hans Island. "Rather, the CF have initiated, and demonstrated, an operational level of cooperation and understanding between NATO allies that may prove to be a fundamental model for accelerated and expanded political cooperation." Significantly, the work begun by Operation Nunalivut 10 culminated in Ottawa in mid-May 2010, when both nations' Chiefs of Defence Staffs, Canadian General Walt Natynczyk and Danish General Knud Bartels, signed a Memorandum of Understanding on Arctic Defence, Security, and Operational Cooperation.[23] Similarly, the US

Navy, the US Coast Guard, and the Royal Danish Navy participated in Operation Nanook 10, held in Nunavut in August 2010.

Governance: Boundaries

Some of the most exciting developments since early 2009 relate to governance. This includes peaceful efforts to resolve boundary disputes, the emergence of new actors interested in the region, and initiatives to improve the Arctic Council.

In his Whitehorse speech on 11 March 2009, Foreign Affairs Minister Cannon acknowledged that geological research and international law—not military clout—would resolve boundary disputes. His statement emphasized collaboration and cooperation. "The depth and complexity of the challenges facing the Arctic are significant, and we recognize the importance of addressing many of these issues by working with our neighbours—through the Arctic Council, other multilateral institutions, and our bilateral partnerships," Cannon expressed. "Strong Canadian leadership in the Arctic will continue to facilitate good international governance in the region."[24] The Northern Strategy reaffirmed that the process for determining Canada's continental shelf, "while lengthy, is not adversarial and is not a race."[25]

Various Arctic states continue to collect data to support their claims to the continental shelf beyond 200 nautical miles. DFAIT is responsible for preparing and presenting Canada's submission, backed up by scientific and technical work by Natural Resources Canada (Geological Survey of Canada) and the Department of Fisheries and Oceans (Canadian Hydrographic Service). While Canada conducts some mapping missions on its own, it also continues to conduct joint surveys with the United States and Denmark. Betsy Baker, a professor at Vermont Law School, suggests that the model for cooperative seabed mapping has applicability in the Beaufort Sea, where the countries have shared interests but disagree about maritime boundaries. Gathering regional data together can serve as a "foundation for joint ecosystem-based, integrated management of the triangle—a principle that is already central to each country's approach to oceans management." In her assessment, collaborative research can strengthen both countries' sovereignty over their respective maritime zones while confirming international law and filling gaps in Arctic governance and regulation.[26] Such perspectives emphasize the importance of scientific cooperation in supporting regional stability and determining sovereign rights in the Arctic basin.

The issue that Canada will face in 2013 when it submits its claims is the response of its neighbours. If the Canadian submission does not overlap with that of Russia, Denmark, and the United States, there will be no problem. If there is an overlap with some or all of its neighbours' claims, it remains to be seen how committed the Arctic states will be to an orderly resolution of the issue.

The prospects that outstanding boundary disputes will be solved through diplomatic channels received a boost in April 2010, when Russia and Norway resolved a forty-year disagreement over the division of the Barents Sea.[27] To optimists, this agreement signalled the appropriateness of efforts to promote a secure, stable region characterized by international cooperation and responsible resource exploration. Cajoling Canada to take note of this landmark resolution, Sergey Lavrov and Jonas Gahr Støre (the Russian and Norweigan foreign ministers, respectively) noted that "the Law of the Sea provided a framework that allowed us to overcome the zero-sum logic of competition and replace it with a process focused on finding a win–win solution. We hope that the agreement will inspire other countries in their attempts to resolve their maritime disputes, in the High North and elsewhere, in a way that avoids conflict and strengthens international co-operation."[28] Canada and the United States have recently initiated bilateral discussions about the Beaufort Sea boundary at the technical level, and Canadian and Danish negotiators have indicated that they expect to resolve their dispute over Hans Island before Canada submits its extended continental shelf claim to the United Nations in 2013.[29]

The lingering question of transit rights through the Northwest Passage remains the primary source of Canadian sovereignty concerns, despite official insistence from the Department of Foreign Affairs that Canadian ownership of the waters is not in doubt.[30] Although the *Arctic Marine Shipping Assessment 2009 Report* predicted that the Northwest Passage would not be an attractive commercial route for the foreseeable future,[31] the tempo of yacht and cruise ship activity in Canadian waters continues to rise.[32] Projections of increased maritime activity continued to generate warnings about possible environmental incidents and the need for tools to protect the environment and the livelihood of northern communities. Accordingly, Canada extended its jurisdictional limit under the Arctic Waters Pollution Prevention Act from 100 to 200 nautical miles in August 2009. In addition, Canada brought into force regulations requiring vessels of 300 tons or more to report when entering and operating within Canadian Arctic waters (NORDREG) effective 1 July 2010.[33] Canada noted that these rules were consistent with UNCLOS; internationally, however, they did not resolve the ongoing debate about the status of the Northwest Passage.[34]

Some commentators suggest that the NWP issue can be resolved, in Canada's favour, through bilateral negotiations. International lawyers Michael Byers and Suzanne Lalonde, for example, continue to promote Canadian investments in policing capabilities to allay American concerns about Canada's inability to control these waters. In their view, improved enforcement will convince the Americans to accept Canada's internal waters position in the interests of continental security.[35] Dissenters suggest that this line of thinking fails to appreciate broader international realities. Would this set a legal precedent for other countries to reach their own bilateral treaties to control traffic through strategic straits? Furthermore, the Northwest Passage is not simply a Canada–US issue. "Any bilateral agreement between the two countries would not affect the rights of other states such as Korea, China, or Germany," James Kraska notes. In his view, the International Maritime Organization (IMO) already represents "an effective multilateral forum for increasing coordination and cooperation throughout the Arctic generally and the Northwest Passage specifically."[36] There is no easy solution to the disagreement over the NWP that addresses both Canadian and American concerns, but commentators note that there is room for cooperation without settling the longstanding dispute.[37] Griffiths, for one, has proposed that Canada, without in any way stepping back from its internal waters claim and corresponding practice with regard to private vessels, should unilaterally declare that it will govern the Northwest Passage *as though* it were an international strait for the sovereign ships of other countries.[38]

Governance: New Actors

To the surprise of many Canadians, the Arctic has elicited growing attention from non-Arctic actors. Non-Arctic European and Asian states are requesting entry to both the region and its governance systems. This has prompted discussions about their interests in the region. In a joint media appearance with Minister Cannon in June 2009, US Secretary of State Hillary Clinton stated:

> Obviously, there are questions of sovereignty and jurisdiction that have to be acknowledged and respected, but what we don't want is for the Arctic to become a free-for-all. If there is going to be greater maritime passageways through the Arctic, if there is going to be more exploration for natural resources, if there are going to be more security issues, I think it's in the Canadian and the United States' interests to try to get ahead of those, and try to make sure we know what we're going to do to resolve them before countries that are not bordering the arctic are making claims, are behaving in ways that will cause us difficulties.[39]

The shift away from bilateral disputes toward an emphasis on Arctic states working together to protect common interests has revealed acute concerns about outside claimants encroaching on their sovereign rights. As of late 2010, however, no one has improved on Griffiths's proposal that the Arctic Council be enlarged to accommodate non-Arctic participation without diluting the roles of either the Arctic-8 or the Permanent Participants.

Particular attention has turned to China, given its growing appetite for natural resources and its increasing power and profile in global affairs. *China Prepares for an Ice-Free Arctic*, a report released by the Stockholm International Peace Research Institute in March 2010, generated global media debate about China's polar research capabilities, its commercial interests in transpolar voyages, and its general aspirations in the Arctic region. Notwithstanding China's "wait-and-see approach to Arctic developments," author Linda Jakobson quoted top Chinese experts who stated that "circumpolar nations have to understand that Arctic affairs are not only regional issues but also international ones." They were keen on resolving the interests of littoral and non-Arctic states through diplomacy, and they had applied for Permanent Observer status on the Arctic Council.[40] Other reports have noted Chinese concerns about perceived security issues emerging in the region. "The current scramble for the sovereignty of the Arctic among some nations has encroached on many other countries' interests," a Chinese admiral stated in March 2010. Accordingly, China has had to "make short and long term ocean strategic development plans to exploit the Arctic because it will become a future mission for the navy."[41] How do Arctic resources fit into China's strategic plans?

The EU has also adopted an increasingly vigorous position on Arctic issues. Over the past few years, it has been developing policy positions that call for its inclusion in the emerging Arctic governance regime. These efforts have been viewed with suspicion by the various northern indigenous organizations. They recall the EU's decision to ban the trade in marine mammals and seal products, imposed in August 2010, and have opposed the EU's application for Permanent Observer status at the Arctic Council, where their place at the table could continue to hurt Aboriginal interests.

Russia has also accused the Europeans of sowing seeds of regional discord. "Regrettably, we have seen attempts to limit Russia's access to the exploration and development of the Arctic mineral resources," President Dmitry Medvedev suggested in March 2010 after European suggestions that the EU needed to "keep the Kremlin in check." Medvedev argued that this was "absolutely inadmissible from the legal viewpoint and unfair given [Russia's] geographical location and history."[42] Instead, Russian officials insisted that the Arctic littoral states—the Arctic-5—would divide up the Arctic resources, and they welcomed restricted meetings where the coastal states could discuss technical issues related to their claims and sovereign rights. According to this logic, it was not in their national interests "to allow any other outside players to be part of this system."[43]

The Arctic-5 and the Arctic Council

The debate over the Arctic-5 took on heightened profile when the Canadian Foreign Affairs Minister invited his counterparts from Russia, the United States, Norway, and Denmark to discuss "new thinking on economic development and environmental protection" in Chelsea, Quebec, on 29 March 2010. Canadian critics accused the government of marginalizing the Arctic Council and the Permanent Participants representing northern Aboriginal peoples. Duane Smith, the president of Inuit Circumpolar Conference (Canada), argued that Inuit needed direct representation as "a coastal people, because this summit is about the Arctic Ocean coast, and because Mr. Cannon underlined the importance of our involvement in multilateral meetings outside the Arctic Council."[44] Liberal Senator Bill Rompkey contended that excluding Inuit and First Nations from future discussions on cooperation in the Arctic demonstrated a colonialist mentality. "This is really saying that land claims mean nothing; that self-government means nothing; that historical occupancy of the Arctic for thousands of years means nothing," Rompkey

Figure 5-4   Representatives at the Arctic Ocean Foreign Ministers' Meeting in Chelsea, Quebec, 29 March 2010. From left to right: Jonas Gahr Støre, Minister of Foreign Affairs, Kingdom of Norway; Sergey Viktorovich Lavrov, Minister of Foreign Affairs, Russian Federation; Lawrence Cannon, Minister of Foreign Affairs, Canada; Hillary Rodham Clinton, Secretary of State, United States of America; Lars Barfoed, Minister of Justice, Kingdom of Denmark.
Source: DFAIT

alleged. "It reveals that the government meant all along to pay only lip service to aboriginal rights in the Arctic." Why invite foreign nations to formulate Arctic plans and exclude the Aboriginal representatives whose lands and
waters were being discussed?[45]

The international reception was mixed. Iceland—a member of the Arctic
Council that, like Arctic non-littoral states Sweden and Finland, was left out of
the Arctic-5 talks—expressed public frustration that it had not been invited.
The EU also opposed what it saw as the narrowing of the Arctic agenda, and
the United States indicated that it did not support these littoral state meetings.
"Significant international discussions on Arctic issues should include those
who have legitimate interests in the region," Secretary of State Hillary Clinton
told reporters. Vermont Law School professor Betsy Baker, however, saw this
as less a repudiation than a "friendly reminder of the need to support the Arctic Council."[46] Given Russia's predisposition to deal with boundary and continental shelf resource issues among the littoral states, Russian media coverage
of the Chelsea meeting was positive. When the Arctic-5 dealt with continental
shelf and other issues governed by state-based international law, how were
these meetings incompatible with the Arctic Council and other multilateral
forums? Were northern indigenous groups not involved in domestic policy-
making processes through advisory committees? The debate over the role of Arctic Council versus the responsibilities of the Arctic coastal states continues.

More broadly, commentators differ on the broader issues of Arctic governance. In light of the tremendous transformation taking place in the region,
is the Arctic Council in danger of being supplanted by other forms of governance? Can, and should, it remain the main forum for studying and debating
Arctic issues?[47] Journalist Ed Struzik breaks the debate into two main camps:
the "hard-liners" and "soft-liners." Idealists like Timo Koivurova and Rob Huebert suggest that the soft law approach currently in place will prove ineffective in managing challenges related to climate change, resource development,
and increased shipping in the region. They advocate strong regional institutions with legal powers or an ambitious new Arctic treaty architecture mod-
elled on the Antarctic Treaty.[48] Given that the Arctic Council evolved from
the Arctic Environmental Protection Strategy, is a treaty-based body the next
logical step toward more ambitious governance? The Arctic states do not think
so, and in international statements beginning with the Ilulissat Declaration in
2008, they have argued against an overarching treaty.

Realists like Oran Young, Lawson Brigham, and Franklyn Griffiths point
out that Antarctica is a continent whereas the Arctic Ocean is maritime and
thus covered by the UN Convention on the Law of the Sea. Rather than pushing for a treaty (which the Arctic-8 would not accept), they seek to harness

Figure 5-5 Members of the Canadian delegation on the margins Arctic Council Ministerial Meeting on April 29, 2009, in Tromsø, Norway. From left to right: Chair of the Gwich'in Council International, Chief Joe Linklater; President of the Inuit Circumpolar Council (Canada), Duane Smith; Chair of the Arctic Athabaskan Council, Chief Bill Erasmus; Minister of Foreign Affairs Lawrence Cannon; Canada's Senior Arctic Official, Adèle Dion; and Liard McMillan, Chief of the Liard First Nation in Watson Lake, Yukon.
Source: DFAIT

regional cooperation within existing regimes. Young envisions a "somewhat messy patchwork made up of disparate pieces"—a soft law approach for a region experiencing dramatic changes. "Unlike treaties that are rigid and take tremendous time and effort, informal agreements can be made more quickly," he notes. "They can have more substance and they can provide for greater adaptability."[49] The Arctic Council may play a stronger role in administering these soft laws, which raises questions of whether—and how—it can move "beyond the existing paradigm of producing non binding technical guidance or fairly abstract policy recommendations," sponsoring scientific assessments, and serving "as a platform for environmental protection and sustainable development discussions between the established Arctic actors."[50]

The Arctic Council has enjoyed recent successes in developing guidelines for offshore oil and gas activity (2009) and best practices in ecosystem-based oceans management (2009), as well as in creating a task force that has produced the council's first legally binding multilateral instrument—a regional search and rescue agreement endorsed at the ministerial meeting in Nuuk, Greenland, in May 2011.[51] Ongoing discussions about strengthening the Arctic Council, however, raise key questions about its structure and its future. Should the council adopt more normative/prescriptive decisions in the future? Is there a need for the Arctic Council to move from *ad hoc* funding to permanent financial contributions from the member states and other participants? If a permanent secretariat is needed, where should it be located? Should non-Arctic states and organizations like the EU get better representation on the Arctic Council? If so, what responsibilities should this entail? Will the addition of more Permanent Observers dilute the status or influence of the Permanent Participants?

Northern Aboriginal peoples, represented by the Permanent Participants on the Arctic Council, continue to express concerns about their involvement in national and international decision making. For example, the Inuit Circumpolar Council adopted *A Circumpolar Inuit Declaration on Sovereignty in the Arctic* in 2009 which emphasized that "the inextricable linkages between issues of sovereignty and sovereign rights in the Arctic and Inuit self-determination and other rights require states to accept the presence and role of Inuit as partners in the conduct of international relations in the Arctic." The declaration envisions the Inuit playing an active role in all deliberations on environmental security, sustainable development, militarization, commercial fishing, shipping, health, and socio-economic development.[52]

Inuit insist that they have rights rooted in international law, land claims, and self-government processes,[53] and have opposed state actions that they feel violate their interests. In August 2010, for example, the Qikiqtani Inuit Association secured an injunction to halt seismic testing in Lancaster Sound on the grounds that this activity could affect whales, polar bears, and other marine life and change migration patterns. Does this signal that northern indigenous groups increasingly will use the legal rights recognized in land claims to enforce Canadian sovereignty over the NWP by unilaterally restricting foreign shipping?[54] They have also expressed acute concerns about "militarization" of the region. ITK president Mary Simon explains:

> Remembering that the respectful sharing of resources, culture, and life itself with others is a fundamental principle of being Inuit, and is the fabric that holds us together as one people across four countries, it is incumbent upon all Arctic states to work cooperatively with each other, and with Inuit, to settle disputes that may arise with regard to territorial claims and/or natural resources. While we recognise the right of every country to defend its borders we must

remain mindful that the military solution … is both unproductive and could potentially be a destructive solution as far as Inuit are concerned. Inuit are not interested to returning to the position of being *the people in the middle of another cold war*.[55]

Canada's Arctic Foreign Policy (2010)

The Department of DFAIT released its *Statement on Canada's Arctic Foreign Policy* in August 2010. This document, reproduced in this volume as an appendix, emphasizes the importance of the Arctic in Canada's national identity and its role as an "Arctic power." The overall message mirrors the Northern Strategy, outlining a vision for the Arctic as "a stable, rules-based region with clearly defined boundaries, dynamic economic growth and trade, vibrant Northern communities, and healthy and productive ecosystems." These themes—which bear striking resemblance to the *The Northern Dimension of Canada's Foreign Policy*, released in 2000—reinforce that the strategic messaging from Ottawa reflects an approach to circumpolar issues that began under the Liberals and has been pushed more forcefully by the Conservatives. Implementing a vision that supports sovereignty, security, and stewardship will entail ongoing discussions about how to balance the interests of the Arctic states, northern peoples, non-Arctic states and organizations, development and transportation companies, and other groups with interests in the region. Implementing a vision will also require moving beyond messaging and into action.

Predictably, the first and foremost pillar of Canada's foreign policy was "the exercise of our sovereignty over the Far North." The "hard security" message that had figured prominently in some statements was muted, and the tone of cooperation with circumpolar neighbours and Northerners rang loudest. Accordingly, the statement committed Canada to "seek to resolve boundary issues in the Arctic region, in accordance with international law" and to secure its rights to the extended continental shelf. Ottawa upped the political ante by suggesting an urgent need to deal with outstanding boundary issues—particularly in the wake of the Russia–Norway agreement over the Barents Sea. "Everyone else is sorting out their differences, we really are the laggards," Arctic pundit Michael Byers noted. "The parallels to the Canada–U.S. dispute [in the Beaufort Sea] are quite close."[56] While these well-managed disputes posed no acute sovereignty or security concerns to Canada, most commentators saw them as a political liability. In terms of safety and security issues, the statement emphasized that Canada would work with international partners bilaterally and through multilateral bodies like the Arctic Council. The document reiterated, however, that if cooperation fails, Canada will defend its rights and interests.

Other dimensions of the *Statement on Canada's Arctic Foreign Policy* reflected the interaction between domestic and international agendas in Canada's Arctic strategy. Trade and investment in resource development—one of the primary catalysts for the surge in Arctic interest over the previous decade—was held up as a main priority. This obviously requires a framework of international cooperation in the region—it is unlikely that Canada can "create appropriate international conditions for sustainable development" in a region beset with intense competition and conflict. Nevertheless, the development of northern resources will continue to be buffered by local and international events. The catastrophic Deepwater Horizon oil spill in the Gulf of Mexico in April 2010 and debates over oil drilling off the west coast of Greenland have generated public concerns about the potential environmental consequences of oil and gas development in the region. In anticipation of future drilling activities in the Beaufort, the National Energy Board launched a review of safety regulations and environmental impacts related to offshore drilling in Canada's Arctic.[57]

Although there are currently no drilling applications before the NEB, hydrocarbon and other resource development plans continue to serve as the basis for the future northern economy. The creation of the Canadian Northern Economic Development Agency (CanNor) in August 2009, which also hosts the Northern Project Management Office (NPMO) responsible for streamlining regulatory processes and coordinating federal involvement in northern resource development projects, is a prime example of federal efforts to stimulate economic growth.[58] The creation of the Inuit-owned Nunavut Resources Corporation in April 2010 demonstrates how Northerners are seizing opportunities to become more fully involved in the North's resource development activities and are seeking to ensure that they derive primary benefits from Arctic resources. On the other hand, opposition to seismic testing in Lancaster Sound that August revealed that Inuit remained concerned about the long-term impact of exploration and drilling.[59] "On the controversial issue of hydrocarbon development, we are realistic," Mary Simon explained. "We need non-renewable resource development if we are to achieve economic self-sufficiency. But the terms of such development must ensure the protection of our environment and the continuation of our way of life. On that, there can be no compromise."[60]

The August 2010 statement is filled with references to the central place of Northerners in decision making related to the Arctic. In it, the government commits to engaging Northerners on foreign policy, supporting Indigenous

Permanent Participant organizations, and providing Canadian youth with opportunities to participate in the circumpolar dialogue. More generally, it promises to "encourage a greater understanding of the human dimension of the Arctic to improve the lives of Northerners." What this means in practical terms remains to be seen. Northern representatives continue to express concern about the Harper government's centralized approach to decision making and its focus on military investments rather than on acute social issues such as a lack of housing and other basic infrastructure, as well as gaps in education, employment rates, and health. On the other hand, Canada's endorsement of the UN Declaration on the Rights of Indigenous Peoples in November 2010 might be held up as a reiteration of the government's "commitment to continue working in partnership with Aboriginal peoples in creating a better Canada."[61]

Northern Aboriginal spokespersons emphasize the foremost imperative to protect the Arctic environment that sustains their communities. In this sense, Udloriak Hanson told the Canadian Council for International Law in October 2010 that "international and domestic politics and policy making in the Arctic cannot be divorced ... They are two sides of the same coin."[62] Initiatives to better integrate science, law, and policy to regulate shipping, protect marine environments, and sustain human and ecological health continue. Efforts through the Arctic Council, the UN Environment Programme (such as work to prepare a global, legally binding instrument on mercury), the UN Framework Convention on Climate Change, and the International Maritime Organization to develop a mandatory Polar Shipping Code by 2012 have highlighted progress on key issues on the international level. Ongoing discussions on how Northerners can benefit from commercial fishing opportunities in the Arctic,[63] and on the need to fill governance gaps by strengthening the Arctic Council or by establishing a new Arctic Ocean regional fisheries management organization to protect fish stocks as climate change alters Arctic ecosystems, point to the interrelations among local, regional, and global interests.[64] Internally, Canada continues to develop collaborative processes for marine spatial and conservation planning, including the establishment of marine protected areas.[65] In December 2010, for example, the federal government announced that it would establish a new marine protected area in Lancaster Sound. Environment Minister John Baird declared that this would signal to the world Canada's sincerity about protecting the Arctic—but that it would not prevent commercial shipping.[66] The *Arctic Marine Shipping Assessment* of 2009, which set out set out various strategic directions for shipping governance at the national, regional, and global levels, confirmed that challenges transcend jurisdictions and remain highly speculative given the multifaceted impacts of climate change in the region.

Climate change remains the overarching issue that has dominated Canadian and international interest and concerns in the region. Infrastructure degradation, concerns about food security, and the rapid disappearance of multi-year ice—to name but a few direct impacts of climate change—continue to generate uncertainty about what the future will hold. The *Statement on Canada's Arctic Foreign Policy* promises to contribute to and support "international efforts to address climate change in the Arctic," but these efforts cannot be relegated to the region. Promised investments to make Canada a global leader in Arctic science (including the expansion of the Polar Continental Shelf facility in Resolute and the creation of the Canadian High Arctic Research Station in Cambridge Bay) will support ongoing research, but substantive action to mitigate climate change requires global political action. The disappointing results of the Climate Change Conference in Copenhagen (COP 15) in December 2009 have left gaping questions about what an effective post-2012 climate regime will look like—with obvious implications for efforts to protect the Arctic.

Official policy statements set expectations and point to desired outcomes. In the end, their credibility is measured by the actions they inspire. Does the combination of the Northern Strategy and the *Statement on Canada's Arctic Foreign Policy* represent a new era in Canada's engagement with the circumpolar world, moving beyond the *ad hoc*, reactive approach that has marked previous governments' records? What are we to make of the prime minister when he says, "I want to be absolutely clear about this: while we are giving more detail in the paper than we have in the past and we will continue to make announcements in a wide range of areas, all of these things serve our No. 1 and, quite frankly, non-negotiable priority in northern sovereignty, and that is the protection and the promotion of Canada's sovereignty over what is our North"?[67] Will promised Arctic investments survive the government's recent emphasis on eliminating deficit spending? If a sense of urgent sovereignty or security "crisis" abates, will the government be able to sustain popular support for its northern strategy? Will the Harper government or a successor display the political will to carry through on an Arctic vision? Will cooperative stewardship emerge as a primary means of securing a safe and stable Arctic region? Future developments will challenge or confirm current assumptions, requiring ongoing analysis of possible, probable, and *desirable* futures.

Notes

1 Franklyn Griffiths, "On This Day, Grab a Cold One and Think Pan-Arctic Thoughts," *Globe and Mail*, 30 June 2009, A11.

2 *Canada's Northern Strategy: Our North, Our Heritage, Our Future* (Ottawa: Indian and Northern Affairs Canada, 2009).

3 CBC News, "Canada Unveils Arctic Strategy," 26 July 2009. http://www.cbc.ca/canada/north/story/2009/07/26/arctic-sovereignty.html, accessed July 26, 2009.

4 P.W. Lackenbauer, "New Northern Strategy Trades Sabre-Rattling for Partnership," *Toronto Star*, 29 July 2009, A19.

5 Standing Senate Committee on Fisheries and Oceans, *Controlling Canada's Arctic Waters: Role of the Canadian Coast Guard*, 15 April 2010.

6 VAdm Dean McFadden, speaking notes, "The Evolution of Arctic Security and Defense Policies: Cooperative or Confrontational," Center for Strategic and International Studies Conference, Washington, 28 April 2010. See also audio version at http://csis.org/multimedia/audio-us-strategic-interests-arctic-panel-3.

7 Lawson Brigham, "The Fast-Changing Maritime Arctic," US Naval Institute *Proceedings* (May 2010), 57–58.

8 There is still no information on the future of the joint supply ship—the replacements for the Navy's existing replenishment vessels. The original intention was to give these vessels limited ice capability to operate in the Canadian North. With the rejection of the submitted bids, it is unknown whether the Navy will get new ships, what type they will be, and whether they will be Arctic capable.

9 BGen David Millar, "Northern Presence," *Airforce* 34, no. 1 (Spring 2010): 29–30.

10 Defence minister Peter McKay's announcement in November 2010 that 950 CF personnel would train Afghan military forces through 2014 does not change this emphasis.

11 Andrew Livingstone, "Make Rangers Reservists: Senate Report," *Northern News Services*, 20 May 2009. For a more positive view, see Darrell Greer, "Not as Slow as Some May Think," *Kivalliq News*, 20 May 2009.

12 See, for example, Rob Huebert, *The Newly Emerging Arctic Security Environment* (Calgary: Canadian Defence and Foreign Affairs Institute, 2010), http://www.cdfai.org/PDF/The%20Newly%20Emerging%20Arctic%20Security%20Environment.pdf, accessed 20 June 2011; Scott Borgerson, "Arctic Meltdown: The Economic and Security Implications of Global Warming," *Foreign Affairs* (March–April 2008), 63–77.

13 Some of these developments are summarized in Bruce Campion-Smith, "Geopolitics of the Far North," *Toronto Star*, 9 August 2009, A8; and Centre for Military and Strategic Studies, "Arctic Timeline—Developments in Foreign Policy," http://cmss.ucalgary.ca/foreignpolicy, accessed 21 June 2011.

14 For succinct summaries of the various countries' security positions, see Rob Huebert, *The United States Arctic Policy: The Reluctant Arctic Power*, School of Public Policy Briefing Papers: Focus on the United States 2, no. 2 (May 2009): 1–26; Huebert, *The Newly Emerging Arctic Security*; Katarzyna Zysk, "Russia's Arctic Strategy: Ambitions and Constraints," *Joint Force Quarterly* 57, no. 2 (2010): 103–10; and David Rudd, "Northern Europe's Arctic Defence Agenda," *Journal of Military and Strategic Studies* 12, no. 3 (2010), http://www.jmss.org/jmss/index.php/jmss/article/view/311/332, accessed 18 November 2010.

15 Letters, "True North," *Foreign Policy* (November 2010), available online at http://www.foreignpolicy.com/articles/2010/10/11/true_north, accessed 16 November 2010.

16 James Kraska, "International Security and International Law in the Northwest Passage," *Vanderbilt Journal of Transnational Law* 42 (2009): 1109–32 at 1121.

17 Rob Huebert, "Welcome to a New Era of Arctic Security," *Globe and Mail*, 24 August 2010, A15.

18 Quoted in Randy Boswell, "Polar Posturing: Canada, Russia Tensions in Arctic Part Politics, Experts Say," *CanWest News Service*, 19 October 2009, http://byers.typepad.com/arctic/2009/08/polar-posturing-canada-russia-tensions-in-arctic-part-politics-experts-say.html, accessed 21 June 2011.

19 Brian Lilley, "The Russians Are Coming," *Brantford Expositor*, 30 July 2010, http://brantfordexpositor.ca/ArticleDisplay.aspx?e=2691522&auth=BRIAN%20LILLEY,%20PARLIAMENTARY%20BUREAU&archive=true, accessed 23 June 2011.

20 Address by Minister Cannon to the Economic Club of Canada, "The Global Economy and Canada's Response," No. 2009/58, Toronto, 23 November 2009.

21 Katarzyna Zysk, "Russia and the High North: Security and Defence Perspectives," in *Security Prospects in the High North: Geostrategic Thaw or Freeze?* (Rome: NATO College, 2009), 106; and P. Whitney Lackenbauer, "Mirror Images? Canada, Russia, and the Circumpolar World," *International Journal* 65, no. 4 (Autumn 2010): 879–97.

22 Ronald O'Rourke, "Changes in the Arctic: Background and Issues for Congress," Congressional Research Service report 7-5700, October 8, 2010, 35.

23 Ron Wallace and P. Whitney Lackenbauer, "Unstoppable Momentum: The Real Meaning and Value Behind *Operation Nunalivut 10*," Canadian Defence and Foreign Affairs Institute Policy Update Paper, May 2010. General Natynczyk noted at the Ottawa signing: "This arrangement will help promote solid defence and security co-operation between our two countries in the Arctic region. Working together to enhance our ability to respond to emergencies through cooperative exercises in the Arctic is key to safety and to strengthening interoperability in the Arctic."

24 Notes for an Address by the Honourable Lawrence Cannon, Minister of Foreign Affairs, on Canada's Arctic Foreign Policy, Whitehorse, 11 March 2009. Cannon also insisted the same month that Canada "won't be bullied" by Russia after the Kremlin released a military strategy emphasizing the importance of the Arctic. Philip Authier, "Canada Won't Be Bullied by Russia: Cannon," *Montreal Gazette*, 27 March 2009, A12.

25 *Canada's Northern Strategy*, 12.

26 Betsy Baker, "Filling an Arctic Gap: Legal and Regulatory Possibilities for Canadian–U.S. Cooperation in the Beaufort Sea," *Vermont Law Review* 34 (2009): 58, 59.

27 Walter Gibbs, "Russia and Norway Reach Accord on Barents Sea," *New York Times*, 10 April 2010, A10.

28 Sergei Lavrov and Jonas Gahr Støre, "Canada, Take Note: Here's How to Resolve Maritime Disputes," *Globe and Mail*, 21 September 2010, A17.

29 John Ibbitson, "Dispute over Hans Island Nears Resolution: Now for the Beaufort Sea," *Globe and Mail*, 27 January 2011, A21.

30 See, for example, Alan Kessel, Legal Advisor, testimony to the Standing Senate Committee on National Security and Defence, Minutes of Proceedings, 15 March 2010, http://www.parl.gc.ca/40/3/ parlbus/commbus/senate/Com-e/defe-e/01mn-e.htm?Language=E&Parl= 40&Ses=3&comm_id=76, accessed 10 June 2010.

31 Arctic Council, *Arctic Marine Shipping Assessment 2009 Report*, 2009, http://pame.arctic portal.org/images/ stories/PDF_Files/AMSA_2009_Report_2nd_print.pdf, accessed 10 September 2010. See also Frédéric Lasserre, "High North Shipping: Myths and Realities about Arctic Shipping Routes," in *Security Prospects in the High North: Geostrategic Thaw of Freeze?*, ed. Sven G. Holtsmark and Brooke A. Smith-Windsor (Rome: NATO Research Division, 2009), 179–199; and Lasserre's edited volume *Passages et mers arctiques. Géopolitique d'une région en mutation* (Québec: Presses de l'Université du Québec, 2010).

32 In 2009, American scholar Lawson Brigham reports, thirteen vessels (eleven yachts and
    two ice-strengthened tour ships) sailed the routes of the Northwest Passage between the
    Pacific and Atlantic oceans. "Of the 135 full transits of the various routes of the Passage
    since Roald Amundsen's historic voyage in 1903–06 (60 voyages since 2000)," he observed,
    "the 13 vessels represent the highest number of full transits in a single summer season."
    Brigham, "The Fast-Changing Maritime Arctic," US Naval Institute *Proceedings* (May
    2010): 56.
33 Transport Canada, news release H078/10, "Government of Canada Takes Action to Pro-
    tect Canadian Arctic Waters," 22 June 2010. http://www.tc.gc.ca/eng/mediaroom/releases
    -2010-h078e-6019.htm, accessed 23 June 2010.
34 At least one major international shipping organization saw the changes to NORDREG as
    a "drastic" and potential threat to the right to "innocent passage" on the world's oceans.
    It also argued that Canada should have submitted its new Arctic regulatory regime to the
    IMO, which oversees global maritime traffic, before enacting it. Randy Boswell, "'Dras-
    tic' Arctic Shipping Rules Draw Fire," *Ottawa Citizen*, 10 July 2010, A3.
35 Michael Byers and Suzanne Lalonde, "Who Controls the Northwest Passage?" *Vander-
    bilt Journal of Transnational Law* 42 (2009): 1133–210.
36 Kraska, "International Security and International Law," 1127–28.
37 See, for example, Ted McDorman, "The Northwest Passage: International Law, Politics,
    and Cooperation," in *Changes in the Arctic Environment and the Law of the Sea*, ed.
    Myron H. Nordquist, Tomas H. Heidar, and John Norton Moore (Leiden: Martinus
    Nijhoff Publishers, 2010), 227–50; and Charles Doran, presentation to the Standing
    Senate Committee on National Security and Defence, 29 March 2010, http://www.parl.gc
    .ca/40/3/parlbus/commbus/senate/Com-e/defe-e/02cv-e.htm?Language=E&Parl=40&Ses
    =3&comm_id=76, accessed 10 September 2010.
38 Franklyn Griffiths, "Canadian Arctic Sovereignty: Time to Take Yes for an Answer on
    the Northwest Passage," in *Northern Exposure: Peoples, Powers and Prospects in Canada's
    North*, ed. Frances Abele, Thomas J. Courchene, F. Leslie Seidle, and France St-Hilaire
    (Montreal: Institute for Research on Public Policy, 2009), 129–30. http://www.irpp.org,
    accessed 28 May 2009.
39 Hillary Clinton, US Secretary of State, Remarks with Canadian Foreign Minister Can-
    non, 13 June 2009, http://ottawa.usembassy.gov/content/textonly.asp?section=can
    _usa&document= Sec_State_Minister_Cannon, accessed 10 September 2010.
40 Linda Jakobsen, *China Prepares for an Ice-Free Arctic*, Stockholm International Peace
    Research Institute, Insights on Peace and Security 2010/2.
41 "Admiral Urges Government to Stake Claim in the Arctic," *South China Morning Post*,
    6 March 2010, 7.
42 Randy Boswell, "Arctic Coastal States Meet as EU, Inuit Left on Sidelines," *Nunatsiaq
    News*, 29 March 2010, http://www.nunatsiaqonline.ca/stories/article/290310_arctic
    _coastal_states_meet_as_eu_inuit_left_on_sidelines/, accessed 21 June 2011.
43 Russian Embassy charge d'affaires Sergey Petrov, quoted in Alexander Panetta, "Rus-
    sians Say Canada Ally—Not Rival—in Arctic Sovereignty Fight," CNEWS, 30 June 2009,
    http://cnews.canoe.ca/CNEWS/Canada/2009/06/ 30/9987336-cp.html, accessed 10 July
    2009.
44 Quoted in Randy Boswell, "Arctic Native Leaders Say They've Been Left Out of Sum-
    mit," Canwest News Service, 15 February 2010.
45 Senator Bill Rompkey, press release, 18 February 2010, http://www.liberalsenateforum.ca/
    In-The-Senate/Publication/8731_Time-to-control-our-Arctic-waters, accessed 15 May
    2010.

46   CBC News, "Clinton's Arctic Comments Cheer Inuit," 31 March 2010. http://www.cbc.ca/news/canada/story/2010/03/31/clinton-arctic.html, accessed 1 April 2010.

47   Timo Koivurova, "Limits and Possibilities of the Arctic Council in a Rapidly Changing Scene of Arctic Governance," *Polar Record* 46 (2009): 146–56.

48   Ed Struzik, "As the Far North Melts, Calls Grow for Arctic Treaty," *Yale Environment 360*, 14 June 2010, http://e360.yale.edu/content/feature.msp?id=2281, accessed September 22, 2010; Rob Huebert, "The Need for an Arctic Treaty: Growing from the United Nations Convention on the Law of the Sea," *Ocean Yearbook* 23 (2009), 27–28; Hans H. Hertell, "Arctic Melt: The Tipping Point for an Arctic Treaty," *Georgetown International Environmental Law Review* 21 (2009): 565–91; Timo Koivurova and Erik J. Molenaar, *International Governance and Regulation of the Marine Arctic: Overview and Gap Analysis* (Oslo: World Wildlife Foundation, 2009).

49   Canada and Greenland, for example, recently signed an agreement to deal with the increasingly unsustainable hunting of polar bears in Baffin Bay. The two countries are collaborating to determine how many bears can be hunted on each side of the maritime border. It will be left to each country, not a legally binding treaty, to honour the agreement.

50   Koivurova, "Limits and Possibilities," 3.

51   Brigham, "The Fast-Changing Maritime Arctic," 57; *Agreement on Cooperation on Aeronautical and Maritime Search and Rescue in the Arctic*, 12 May 2011, http://arctic-council.org/filearchive/Arctic%20SAR%20Agreement%20EN%20FINAL%20for%20signature%2021-Apr-2011.pdf, accessed 20 May 2011.

52   ICC, *A Circumpolar Inuit Declaration on Sovereignty in the Arctic* (2009). http://inuitcircumpolar.com/files/uploads/icc-files/PR-2009-04-28-Signed-Inuit-Sovereignty-Declaration-11x17.pdf, accessed 10 January 2010.

53   Timo Koivurova, "Sovereign States and Self-Determining Peoples: Carving Out a Place for Transnational Indigenous Peoples in a World of Sovereign States," *International Community Law Review* 12 (2010): 191–212.

54   CBC, "Inuit Win Injunction on Seismic Testing," 8 August 2010, http://www.cbc.ca/canada/story/2010/08/08/nunavut-lancaster-injunction.html#ixzz15sa8WqcS, accessed 9 August 2010.

55   Mary Simon, "The Militarization of the Arctic," ITK blog, 5 October 2010, http://www.itk.ca/blog/mary-simon/oct-05-2010-militarization-arctic, accessed 8 October 2010. Italics in original.

56   Paul Koring, "Russia–Norway Pact on Arctic Zone Puts Pressure on Canada," *Globe and Mail*, 15 September 2010, A19.

57   CBC News, "Arctic Oil and Gas Joint Venture Formed," 3 August 2010, http://www.cbc.ca/news/canada/north/story/2010/08/03/beaufort-sea-oil-exploration-venture.html, accessed 4 August 2010. The National Commission on the BP Deepwater Horizon Oil Spill and Offshore Drilling's report to the President, *Deep Water: The Gulf Oil Disaster and the Future of Offshore Drilling* (January 2011) recommended that the United States take a lead in developing and adopting shared international standards for offshore oil and gas developers operating in the Arctic region.

58   Prime Minister's Office, "PM Launches New Regional Economic Development Agency for Canada's North," 18 August 2009, http://pm.gc.ca/eng/media.asp?category=1&id=2751, accessed 3 September 2009.

59   See, for example, Gabriel Zarate, "Arctic Bay Opposes Seismic Testing in Lancaster Sound," *Nunatsiaq News*, 6 June 2010, http://www.nunatsiaqonline.ca/stories/article/98789_arctic_bay_opposes_seismic_testing_in_lancaster_sound, accessed 6 June 2010; and Josh Wingrove, "Lancaster Sound: A Seismic Victory for the Inuit," *Globe and Mail*, 13 August 2010, F5.

60 Mary Simon, speech to Canada–UK Colloquium, "The Arctic and Northern Dimensions of World Issues," Iqaluit, 4 November 2010.

61 Indian and Northern Affairs Canada, "Canada's Statement of Support on the United Nations Declaration on the Rights of Indigenous Peoples," 12 November 2010, http://www.ainc-inac.gc.ca/ap/ia/dcl/stmt-eng.asp, accessed 13 November 2010.

62 Udloriak Hanson, "Geopolitics in the Arctic—Speaking Points for CCIL Conference," 29 October 2010, http://ccil-ccdi.squarespace.com/ccil-conference-papers/2010, accessed 15 March 2011.

63 Standing Senate Committee on Fisheries and Oceans, "The Management of Fisheries and Oceans in Canada's Western Arctic" (May 2010).

64 See, for example, Jennifer Jeffers, "Climate Change and the Arctic: Adapting to Changes in Fisheries Stocks and Governance Regimes," *Ecology Law Quarterly* 37 (2010): 917–77. The US Arctic Fishery Management Plan, released in 2009, prohibits the expansion of commercial fishing in Arctic federal waters until researchers have gathered enough information on fish stocks and the Arctic marine environment to implement sustainable fisheries. In May 2010, the Standing Committee on Fisheries and Oceans of the Canadian Senate recommended that the federal government institute a similar moratorium on commercial fishing in the Beaufort. See Magdalena Muir, "Illegal, Unreported, and Unregulated Fishing in the Circumpolar Arctic," *Arctic* 63, no. 3 (September 2010): 374.

65 Critics suggest that "an unorganized, piecemeal approach" to marine conservation planning contributes to a disparity in marine policy between Nunavut and the western Arctic, where a comprehensive integrated ocean management plan guides activities in the Beaufort. Ongoing negotiations about devolution of government responsibilities from the federal government to the Nunavut government, as well as pressures to formalize a Nunavut Marine Council, will shape a comprehensive marine conservation strategy in that territory. Tyson Daoust, Wolfgang Haider, and Sabine Jessen, "Institutional Arrangements Governing Marine Conservation Planning in the Canadian Arctic: The Case of Nunavut, Canada," *Environments Journal* 37, no. 3 (2010): 73–93 at 75.

66 Gloria Galloway, "Ottawa Sets Up Arctic Marine Park," *Globe and Mail,* 6 December 2010, http://www.theglobeandmail.com/news/politics/ottawa-notebook/ottawa-sets-up-arctic-marine-park/article1826548/, accessed 21 June 2011. Federal legislative tools available for marine conservation designation include the Oceans Act, under which the Minister of Fisheries and Oceans has the authority to establish Oceans Act marine-protected areas within the integrated management framework. The Canada Wildlife Act and the Migratory Birds Convention Act authorize Environment Canada to establish and manage National Wildlife Areas, Marine Wildlife Areas, and Migratory Bird Sanctuaries. Parks Canada can designate and manage National Marine Conservation Areas under the National Marine Conservation Areas Act. Other federal legislation, such as the Fisheries Act and the National Parks Act, contains conservation mechanisms, and statutes such as the Species at Risk Act can support and strengthen legislation that focuses on marine conservation. David VanderZwaag and J.A. Hutchings, "Canada's Marine Species at Risk: Science and Law at the Helm, but a Sea of Uncertainty," *Ocean Development and International Law* 36 (2005): 219–59; Daoust et al., "Institutional Arrangements Governing Marine Conservation Planning"; and Suzanne Lalonde, "A Network of Marine Protected Areas in the Arctic: Promises and Challenges," in *Changes in the Arctic Environment and the Law of the Sea,* ed. M. Nordquist, J.N. Moore, and T.H. Heidar (Leiden: Martinus Nijhoff Publishers, 2010): 131–42.

67 Mark Kennedy, "Ottawa Unveils Sovereignty Blueprint," *National Post*, 21 August 2010, A11.

Appendix
Department of Foreign Affairs and International Trade, *Statement on Canada's Arctic Foreign Policy: Exercising Sovereignty and Promoting Canada's Northern Strategy Abroad*, August 2010

In August 2010, the Department of Foreign Affairs and International Trade released its statement on Canada's Arctic foreign policy—the "international lens" of Canada's Northern Strategy.[1] The document articulates Canada's priorities for exercising sovereignty, promoting economic and social development, protecting the environment, and governing the Arctic region. It outlines how and where Canada "will show leadership and work with others to demonstrate responsible stewardship and to build a region that is responsive to Canadian interests and values."[2] We have reproduced the statement in full so that readers can compare and contrast it with the analysis and recommendations provided in the preceding chapters.

Introduction

The Arctic is fundamental to Canada's national identity. It is home to many Canadians, including indigenous peoples, across the Yukon, the Northwest Territories and Nunavut, and the northern parts of many Canadian provinces. The Arctic is embedded in Canadian history and culture, and in the Canadian soul. The Arctic also represents tremendous potential for Canada's future. Exercising sovereignty over Canada's North, as over the rest of Canada, is our number one Arctic foreign policy priority.

Our vision for the Arctic is a stable, rules-based region with clearly defined boundaries, dynamic economic growth and trade, vibrant Northern communities, and healthy and productive ecosystems. This Arctic foreign policy statement articulates how the Government of Canada will promote this vision, using leadership and stewardship. It elaborates on Canadian interests in the Arctic and how Canada is pursuing these.

New opportunities and challenges are emerging across the Arctic and North, in part as a result of climate change and the search for new resources. The geopolitical significance of the region and the implications for Canada have never been greater. As global commerce charts a path to the region, Northern resources development will grow ever more critical to Northern economies, to the peoples of the North and to our country as a whole. The potential of the North is of growing interest to Canada, to other Arctic states and, increasingly, to others far from the region itself.

While the opportunities are great, there are also important social, economic and environmental challenges. Some of these have important international dimensions. Over time, increased access to the Arctic will bring more traffic and people to the region. While mostly positive, this access may also contribute to an increase in environmental threats, search and rescue incidents, civil emergencies and potential illegal activities. How the region as a whole evolves will have major implications for Canada and our role as an Arctic power.

The Government of Canada has launched an ambitious Northern Strategy to respond to these opportunities and challenges. Our Northern Strategy lays out four areas where Canada is taking action to advance its interests both domestically and internationally and to help unlock the North's true potential: exercising sovereignty; promoting economic and social development; protecting our environmental heritage; and improving and devolving Northern governance. In pursuing each of these pillars in our Arctic foreign policy, Canada is committed to exercising the full extent of its sovereignty, sovereign rights and jurisdiction in the region.

> "The geopolitical importance of the Arctic and Canada's interests in it have never been greater. This is why our government has launched an ambitious Northern Agenda based on the timeless responsibility imposed by our national anthem, to keep the True North strong and free."
> —*Prime Minister Stephen Harper, August 28, 2008, Inuvik, Northwest Territories*

Given our extensive Arctic coastline, our Northern energy and natural resource potential, and the 40 percent of our land mass situated in the North, Canada is an Arctic power. We are taking a robust leadership role in shaping the stewardship, sustainable development and environmental protection of this strategic Arctic region, and engaging with others to advance our interests.

As we advance the four pillars of our Northern Strategy, our international efforts will focus on the following areas:

- engaging with neighbours to seek to resolve boundary issues;
- securing international recognition for the full extent of our extended continental shelf;
- addressing Arctic governance and related emerging issues, such as public safety;
- creating the appropriate international conditions for sustainable development;
- seeking trade and investment opportunities that benefit Northerners and all Canadians;
- encouraging a greater understanding of the human dimension of the Arctic;
- promoting an ecosystem-based management approach with Arctic neighbours and others;
- contributing to and supporting international efforts to address climate change in the Arctic;
- enhancing our efforts on other pressing environmental issues;
- strengthening Arctic science and the legacy of International Polar Year;
- engaging Northerners on Canada's Arctic foreign policy;
- supporting Indigenous Permanent Participant organizations; and
- providing Canadian youth with opportunities to participate in the circumpolar dialogue.

Exercising Sovereignty

In our Arctic foreign policy, the first and most important pillar towards recognizing the potential of Canada's Arctic is the exercise of our sovereignty over the Far North. Canada has a rich history in the North, and Canada's sovereignty is the foundation for realizing the full potential of Canada's North, including its human dimension. This foundation is solid: Canada's Arctic sovereignty is long-standing, well established and based on historic title, founded in part on the presence of Inuit and other indigenous peoples since time immemorial.

> "In exercising our sovereignty ... we are not only fulfilling our duty to the people who called this northern frontier home, and to the generations that will follow; we are also being faithful to all who came before us ..."
>
> —*Prime Minister Stephen Harper, August 28, 2008, Inuvik, Northwest Territories*

Canada exercises its sovereignty daily through good governance and responsible stewardship. It does so through the broad range of actions it undertakes as a government—whether related to social and economic development, Arctic science and research, environmental protection, the operations of the Canadian Forces or the activities of the Canadian Coast Guard and Royal Canadian Mounted Police. We exercise our sovereignty in the Arctic through our laws and regulations, as we do throughout Canada.

We are putting the full resources of the Government of Canada behind the exercise of our sovereignty, sovereign rights and jurisdiction in the Arctic. We are taking a whole-of-government approach. Since taking office, the Prime Minister and many federal cabinet ministers have made regular visits to Canada's North. Further evidence of the priority the Government of Canada is placing on the North was the meeting of G-7 finance ministers in Nunavut in February 2010.

Since 2007, the Government of Canada has announced a number of initiatives to enhance our capacity in the North and to exercise, responsibly, our sovereignty there. These include significant new commitments to allow Canada to better monitor, protect and patrol its Arctic land, sea and sky and to keep pace with changes in the region.

Within the next decade, Canada will launch a new polar icebreaker. This will be the largest and most powerful icebreaker ever in the Canadian Coast Guard fleet.

The *Canada First* Defence Strategy will give the Canadian Forces the tools it needs to provide an increased presence in the Arctic. Through this strategy, Canada is investing in new patrol ships that will be capable of sustained operation in first-year ice to ensure we can closely monitor our waters as they gradually open up and maritime activity increases. In order to support these and other Government of Canada vessels operating in the North, Canada is investing in a berthing and refuelling facility in Nanisivik.

Canada is also expanding the size and capabilities of the Canadian Rangers, drawn primarily from indigenous communities, that provide a military presence and Canada's "eyes and ears" in remote parts of Canada. A new Canadian Forces Arctic Training Centre is also being established in Resolute Bay.

Canada and the United States work together to better monitor and control Northern airspace through our cooperation in NORAD, the North American Aerospace Defence Command. Canadian Forces will also take advantage of new technologies to enhance surveillance capacity of our territory and its approaches.

Canadian Forces Operation Nanook, an annual sovereignty operation that takes place in Canada's Arctic, shows the government's commitment to protecting and demonstrating control over the air, land and sea within our jurisdiction. In 2010, Operation Nanook will include collaboration with the United States and Denmark in order to increase interoperability and exercise a collective response to emerging cross-border challenges.

This increased Canadian capacity demonstrates Canada's presence in the region and will also ensure that we are better prepared to respond to unforeseen events.

Moving forward, our international agenda will complement these efforts further. Three priority areas that Canada will pursue in the Arctic are: seeking to resolve boundary issues; securing international recognition for the full extent of our extended continental shelf wherein we can exercise our sovereign rights over the resources of the seabed and subsoil; and addressing Arctic governance and related emerging issues, such as public safety.

On the first priority, Canada will seek to resolve boundary issues in the Arctic region, in accordance with international law. Our sovereignty over Canadian Arctic lands, including islands, is undisputed—with the single exception of Hans Island, a 1.3-square-kilometre Canadian island which Denmark claims.

With regard to Arctic waters, Canada controls all maritime navigation in its waters. Nevertheless, disagreements exist between the United States and Canada regarding the maritime boundary in the Beaufort Sea (approximately 6,250 square nautical miles) and between Canada and Denmark over a small part of the maritime boundary in the Lincoln Sea. All disagreements are well managed, neither posing defence challenges for Canada nor diminishing Canada's ability to collaborate and cooperate with its Arctic neighbours. Canada will continue to manage these discrete boundary issues and will also, as a priority, seek to work with our neighbours to explore the possibility of resolving them in accordance with international law.

On the second priority, Canada will secure international recognition for the full extent of our extended continental shelf wherein we can exercise our sovereign rights over the resources of the seabed and subsoil. Most known Arctic natural resources lie within the exclusive economic zones of Arctic states—200 nautical miles extending from the coastal baselines. States have sovereign rights to explore and exploit living and non-living marine resources in their respective exclusive economic zones. Arctic coastal states also have existing rights to resources on their extended continental shelves beyond their exclusive economic zones.

The United Nations Convention on the Law of the Sea (UNCLOS) explicitly recognizes the rights of coastal states such as Canada over the natural resources of the seabed and subsoil beyond 200 nautical miles from their coastal baselines and sets out a process by which a state may determine the limits within which it may exercise those rights. Canada will make its submission to the United Nations Commission on the Limits of the Continental Shelf in December 2013 and is currently engaged in the scientific, technical and legal work needed to delineate the outer limits of its continental shelf. Autonomous underwater vehicles—with Canadian technology at their heart—are being used to collect some of the needed data. Canada is investing significantly to ensure that Canada secures international recognition for the full extent of its continental shelf in both the Arctic and Atlantic oceans.

The other Arctic coastal states also have extended continental shelves and are involved in a similar process. To maximize data collection in a challenging physical environment, encourage exchange of information and minimize future differences, Canada has been working closely with neighbouring Arctic Ocean coastal states. We will act on a priority basis to ensure Canada has a sound submission by the 2013 deadline. Any overlaps with the submissions of neighbouring states will be resolved through peaceful means in accordance with international law.

Beyond concrete steps on boundaries, Canada's sovereignty agenda will also address Arctic governance and related emerging issues, such as public safety. Increasingly, the world is turning its attention northward, with many players far removed from the region itself seeking a role and in some cases calling into question the governance of the Arctic. While many of these players could have a contribution to make in the development of the North, Canada does not accept the premise that the Arctic requires a fundamentally new governance structure or legal framework. Nor does Canada accept that the Arctic nation states are unable to appropriately manage the North as it undergoes fundamental change.

Canada, like other Arctic nations, stands by the extensive international legal framework that applies to the Arctic Ocean. Notably, UNCLOS, as referred to earlier, provides the legal basis for delineation of continental shelves and goes well beyond this to address the protection of the marine environment, freedom of navigation, marine scientific research, conservation and utilization of marine living resources, and other uses of the sea.

However, within this broad legal framework, new challenges are emerging. Until now, the Arctic Ocean's inaccessibility has meant that the region was largely insulated from the sort of safety and law enforcement challenges present in regions further south. However, decreasing ice cover will lead, over time, to increases in shipping, tourism and economic development in the Arctic Ocean region. While the full extent of the changes will take many decades to realize, Canada and other Arctic Ocean coastal states must begin to prepare for greater traffic into the region, with sometimes negative effects.

Regional solutions, supported by robust domestic legislation in Arctic states, will be critical. Canada will work in concert with other Arctic nations through the Arctic Council[3] (the primary forum for collaboration among the eight Arctic states), with the five Arctic Ocean coastal states on issues of particular relevance to the Arctic Ocean, and bilaterally with key Arctic partners, particularly the United States.

We will need to consider how to respond to issues such as emergency response and search and rescue capability and potential future problems related to emergencies (including environmental), organized crime, and illegal trafficking in drugs and people. One very important initiative is the current effort within the Arctic Council to negotiate a search and rescue agreement for the Arctic. Information sharing, coordination of efforts, and pooling resources are all concrete ways in which partnership may be beneficial.

The recently held Arctic Ocean Foreign Ministers meeting was an important step not only in advancing our collaboration on continental shelf delineation but also in encouraging forward thinking on the emerging issues in the region. The meeting publicly demonstrated leadership and partnership by Canada and other coastal states on responsible management of the Arctic Ocean.

Protecting national sovereignty, and the integrity of our borders, is the first and foremost responsibility of a national government. We are resolved to protect Canadian sovereignty throughout our Arctic.

Promoting Economic and Social Development

Creating a dynamic, sustainable Northern economy and improving the social well-being of Northerners is essential to unleashing the true potential of Canada's North and is an important means of exercising our sovereignty.

> "Not only is the North a land of raw and majestic beauty that has inspired generations of authors, artists and adventurers, and not only is it the home to a rich culture shaped through the millennia by the wisdom of Aboriginal people, but it also holds the potential to be a transformative economic asset for the country."
> —*Prime Minister Stephen Harper, August 18, 2009, Iqaluit, Nunavut*

The potential for wealth and job creation through resource development, both living and non-living, is great. Canada is the world's third largest diamond producer. It is estimated that one-fifth of the world's petroleum reserves lie in the Arctic. That is why the Government of Canada is investing significantly in mapping the energy and mineral potential of the North. Managed in a sustainable manner, Canada's incredible endowment, including living marine resources such as fisheries, will contribute to the prosperity of Northerners and all Canadians for generations. These resources can and will be a cornerstone of sustained economic activity in the North and a key to building prosperous indigenous and Northern communities.

In addition to investments in mapping in the North, the Government of Canada has made a wide variety of recent commitments related to promoting Northern social and economic development. These include measures to improve regulatory systems across the North, to address infrastructure needs including housing, to create the Canadian Northern Economic Development Agency, and to support improvement in indigenous skills and employment.

Ensuring sustainable development in the Arctic involves working closely with territorial governments and Northerners and through key international institutions like the Arctic Council to build self-sufficient, vibrant and healthy communities. The well-being of the people of the North—its inhabitants and communities—is fundamental.

Canada will actively promote Northern economic and social development internationally on three key fronts: take steps to create the appropriate international conditions for sustainable development, seek trade and investment opportunities that benefit Northerners and all Canadians, and encourage a greater understanding of the human dimension of the Arctic to improve the lives of Northerners.

First, Canada will take steps to create the appropriate international conditions for sustainable development in the Arctic, complementing domestic measures to support economic development. This involves understanding the opportunities and challenges of Arctic energy and resource development and developing regulations, guidelines and standards that are informed by Arctic science and research, including traditional knowledge. In no area is this more critical than in oil and gas development.

As an emerging clean energy superpower, Canada will continue to support the responsible and sustainable development of oil and gas in the North. Along with the rest of the international community, we have witnessed the terrible environmental, social and economic impacts of the oil spill in the Gulf of Mexico.

Canada recognizes and values the importance of working closely with other Arctic states and will take every step possible to prevent such an event in Canadian waters. Canada is showing leadership at home in Arctic safety and environmental requirements for offshore drilling through the review undertaken by the National Energy Board. Moreover, Canadians and our Arctic neighbours can be assured that no drilling will occur in Canada's deep Beaufort Sea until at least 2014.

Canada is a party to a number of bilateral and multilateral agreements and is actively engaged in various international forums, including the Arctic Council, on matters relating to the protection of the marine environment. In the wake of the oil spill in the Gulf of Mexico, we are furthering our collaboration at the appropriate levels, in particular with the United States and Denmark/Greenland in light of our common interests in the Arctic marine environment.

The 2007 Arctic Council Oil and Gas Assessment examined the impacts of current oil and gas activities in the Arctic and potential impacts related to possible future activities. The Oil and Gas Assessment found that while extensive oil and gas exploration activity and production have occurred in parts of the Arctic, much potential exists for future oil and gas development. Related risks need to be managed carefully. Canada made significant contributions to the Assessment.

The Arctic Council, with significant Canadian participation, updated its Arctic Offshore Oil and Gas Guidelines in 2009. These guidelines recommend standards, technical and environmental best practices, management policy and regulatory controls for Arctic offshore oil and gas operations. Canada will act on the request from the Arctic Council that all states apply these guidelines as minimum standards throughout the Arctic and will encourage others to do so as well.

Arctic shipping is another key area of focus. The 2009 Arctic Marine Shipping Assessment is the first comprehensive review of circumpolar shipping activities and provides important information about possible future shipping activities and their potential impacts. Among its findings, the Assessment noted that Arctic shipping has increased significantly, with more voyages to the Arctic and between Arctic destinations. However, the various Canadian internal waterways known as Canada's "Northwest Passage" are not predicted to become a viable, large-scale transit route in the near term, in part because mobile and unpredictable ice in the Passage poses significant navigational challenges and other routes are likely to be more commercially viable.

The Arctic Marine Shipping Assessment also provides guidance on enhancing Arctic marine safety, protecting Arctic peoples and environment, and building Arctic marine infrastructure. Based on these recommendations, the 2009 Arctic Council Ministerial supported the development of a mandatory polar code for shipping by the International Maritime Organization (IMO). As an IMO member, Canada will continue to play a leading role in the development of this code. We, along with other Arctic Council states, have also agreed to work together towards an international agreement on search and rescue operations for the Arctic by 2011.

Within the IMO context, Canada has also assumed responsibility for providing navigational warning and meteorological services to facilitate the safe management of marine traffic in two Arctic areas. These cover substantial areas of Arctic waters, including the Northwest Passage. Through this initiative, Canada will deliver services that help mitigate the risks associated with increased Arctic shipping. These services will also enhance environmental protection of the Arctic marine environment, support Northern residents in their maritime activities, and provide necessary services for coastal and marine-based resource development.

Canada is playing a key role in the creation of the Arctic Regional Hydrographic Commission to improve our understanding of the features of the Arctic Ocean and its coastal areas, essential knowledge for safe navigation. Canada has offered to host the Commission's inaugural meeting in fall 2010.

Second, Canada will continue to seek trade and investment opportunities that benefit Northerners and all Canadians.

Canada will enhance its trading ties with other Arctic states. We have recently implemented a free trade agreement with the European Free Trade Association (EFTA) member countries, which include Iceland and Norway. This agreement has the potential to enhance trade and investment between Northern regions of our respective countries. We are also seeking to build new trade ties with other Arctic states to create these same links between our respective Northern regions. These Northern commercial relationships can serve as conduits to expand trade and investment relations not only with our immediate Northern neighbours but also with other states such as those in central Asia and Eastern Europe.

Improving air and sea transportation links to create enhanced access across the polar region can help encourage Arctic trade and investment opportunities. For instance, investments have been made to upgrade the Port of Churchill, Manitoba, to facilitate increased export options and the flow of two-way trade with other Northern ports.

Third, Canada will continue to encourage a greater understanding of the human dimension of the Arctic to improve the lives of Northerners, particularly through the Arctic Council. The Arctic Council's Arctic Human Development Report was the first comprehensive assessment of human well-being to address the entire Arctic region. Canada will continue to play a leadership role in Arctic Council initiatives in this area and to host the Secretariat for the Council's Sustainable Development Working Group. For example, the

2008 Arctic Indigenous Languages Symposium, organized by the Inuit Circumpolar Council with support from the Government of Canada, underlined the importance of preserving and strengthening indigenous languages.

Addressing human health issues in Northern communities is also critically important. Canada has been supporting efforts through the Arctic Council and International Polar Year research to better understand the issues and then develop and implement appropriate health policies. The results of international collaboration are all aimed at improving the health conditions of residents in the Arctic. Canada will play a lead role in the Arctic Council on a range of new health-related projects, including the development of a circumpolar health observatory, a comparative review of circumpolar health systems, and a comparative review of circumpolar nutritional guidelines.

Canada's commitment to Northern economic and social development includes a deep respect for indigenous traditional knowledge, work and cultural activities. Going forward, Canada will promote a better understanding of the interests, concerns, culture and practices of Northerners, including with regard to seals and polar bears. In this context, Canada is committed to defend sealing on the international stage. Seals are a valuable natural resource, and the seal hunt is an economic mainstay for numerous rural communities in many parts of Canada including the North.

Protecting the Arctic Environment

The Arctic environment is being affected by events taking place far outside the region. Perhaps the most well-known example is climate change, a phenomenon which originates outside the Arctic but is having a significant impact on the region's unique and fragile environment. The resulting rapid reduction in Arctic multi-year sea ice has had, and will continue to have, profound consequences for the peoples and communities of the Arctic. What happens in the Arctic will have global repercussions on accelerating climate change elsewhere.

Strong environmental protection, an essential component of sustainable development, starts at home and is another important way in which Canada exercises its sovereignty in the North. Canada has long been at the forefront in protecting the Arctic environment. As far back as the 1970s, Canada enacted the Arctic Waters Pollution Prevention Act (AWPPA) to protect its marine environment, taking responsibility for enacting and enforcing anti-pollution and shipping safety laws applicable to a larger area of Arctic waters. In August 2009, the application of the AWPPA was extended from 100 to 200 nautical miles. In addition, regulations requiring vessels to report when entering and operating within Canadian Arctic waters have been finalized and are in force from July 1, 2010.

> "Canada takes responsibility for environmental protection and enforcement in our Arctic waters. This magnificent and unspoiled region is one for which we will demonstrate stewardship on behalf of our country, and indeed, all of humanity."
> —*Prime Minister Stephen Harper, August 27, 2008,*
> *Tuktoyaktuk, Northwest Territories*

These measures and others such as plans to establish a national marine conservation area in Lancaster Sound send a clear message to the world. Canada takes responsibility for environmental protection and enforcement in our Arctic waters. We are demonstrating stewardship in this magnificent ecological region.

Canada is committed to planning and managing Arctic Ocean and land-based activities domestically and internationally in an integrated and comprehensive manner that balances conservation, sustainable use and economic development—ensuring benefits for users and the ecosystem as a whole. We are acting domestically while cooperating internationally. Internationally, we will act in the following four ways: promote an ecosystem-based management approach with our Arctic neighbours and others; contribute to and support international efforts to address climate change in the Arctic; enhance efforts on other pressing international issues, including pursuing and strengthening international standards; and strengthen Arctic science and the legacy of International Polar Year.

First, Canada will continue to promote an ecosystem-based management approach with its Arctic neighbours and others.

In accordance with Canada's Oceans Act, Canada is working with land claim authorities, governments, industry and communities to implement an ecosystem approach in the Beaufort Sea and has identified ecologically significant marine species and places. This is part of a broader ecosystem approach in the Arctic by the Government of Canada that also includes activities related to the international co-management of species in the Arctic whose habitat crosses national borders (e.g. caribou, polar bears and Arctic birds). These activities fall under international conventions and agreements such as the United Nations Convention on Biological Diversity, the Migratory Bird Treaty, and the Agreement on the Conservation of Polar Bears. International collaborative Arctic science and research is a fundamental aspect of the Government of Canada's participation in such agreements.

Canada and its Arctic neighbours are the stewards of unique wildlife such as polar bears. The Government of Canada recognizes the importance of indigenous knowledge and the need to use it in tandem with Western science in our efforts to better understand polar bears and their habitat.

Canada has signed a Memorandum of Understanding with the United States for the conservation and management of a shared polar bear population. In addition, Canada has developed agreements with other Arctic nations to jointly manage polar bears, narwhals and belugas. This work must continue in order to manage other shared species.

As part of its mandate, the Arctic Council has been playing a lead role in identifying large marine ecosystems in the region and determining best practices in ocean management. Canada will play a leadership role in the Arctic Council's Arctic Ocean Review which aims to strengthen and ensure the sustainable development of the Arctic Ocean. In pursuing strengthened Arctic Ocean stewardship, we will work with other interested partners and users of the Arctic Ocean as well as through regional and international organizations, including the Arctic Council and the IMO.

2010 is the International Year of Biodiversity and the Arctic is the focus of considerable attention. Canada will continue to lead the Arctic Council's Circumpolar Biodiversity Monitoring Program to ensure information on population status and trends for Arctic species and ecosystems is available and supports initiatives such as the Arctic Biodiversity Assessment. The Council has recently developed the Arctic Species Trend Index, which provides decision-makers with a valuable tool for managing and predicting Arctic wildlife populations. Tracking the index over time will facilitate this prediction of trends and identify species and groups experiencing rapid change.

Canada will continue to establish terrestrial and marine protected areas in the Arctic and monitor biodiversity and ecological integrity. Canada recognizes that ecologically sensitive areas are essential for the conservation of Arctic species including polar bears, caribous, migratory birds, and marine mammals and other aquatic species. These sensitive areas play a key role in the survival and recovery of species at risk. They also provide significant ecotourism opportunities to an expanding market of Canadians and international visitors.

Canada has made significant progress in establishing protected areas in over 10 percent of our North, designating 80 protected areas covering nearly 400,000 square kilometres. These areas include 11 national parks, six national wildlife areas and 16 migratory bird sanctuaries and will protect habitat for a wide variety of species.

Canada continues to plan for additional protected areas in the North and has an ambitious program to expand the national park system, including the creation of three new national parks. The Government of Canada is moving forward in consultation with communities and industry to add nearly 70,000 square kilometres to Canada's Northern protected areas network. Canada will be finalizing a Policy Framework for Canada's National Network of Marine Protected Areas that will guide marine protected area establishment, including the five marine ecoregions found in the Arctic. The creation of the majority of existing national parks in the Arctic proceeded hand-in-hand with land claim negotiations, as are all of the new national park proposals.

Second, Canada will continue to actively contribute to and support international efforts to address climate change in the Arctic, including both mitigation and adaptation in the Arctic. Climate change is having a disproportionate impact on the Arctic, and the Arctic Council's 2004 Arctic Climate Impact Assessment heightened global awareness of the problem.

Canada recognizes that climate change is a global challenge requiring a global solution. To that end, the government is committed to contributing to the global effort by taking action to reduce Canada's greenhouse gas emissions through sustained action domestically to build a low-carbon economy, working with our North American partners and constructively engaging with our international partners to negotiate a fair, environmentally effective and comprehensive international climate change regime based on the Copenhagen Accord. Canada has been, and continues to be, very active in these international negotiations, and will seek to ensure that consideration is given to the Arctic's unique set of climate change-related challenges in every relevant forum.

New evidence suggests that certain short-term factors are having an impact on the rate of climate change. The 2009 Arctic Council Ministerial approved the formation of a task force on "short-lived climate forcers" in the Arctic. While climate agents or forcers, such as black carbon,[4] contribute significantly to climate change, they can potentially be brought under control much more quickly than long-term contributors such as carbon dioxide. The task force will identify existing and new measures to reduce emissions of these forcers and will recommend further immediate action.

Canada has been, and will continue to be, active in climate change adaptation initiatives. Canada played an important role in the Arctic Council's recent Vulnerability and Adaptation to Climate Change in the Arctic project. Underlining the importance of community involvement in planning for and responding to climate change adaptation is one of Canada's key contributions. Canada recognizes that enhanced action on adaptation will be a significant component of the post-2012 climate change negotiations under the

United Nations Framework Convention on Climate Change. Canada plays an active and constructive role in those discussions.

In support of these objectives, the Government of Canada has been working in close partnership with Northern communities and governments to assess risks, vulnerabilities and opportunities related to a changing climate. Over the last two years, over 60 projects have been funded in the Canadian Arctic that have led to the development of community and regional adaptation plans, increasing knowledge and understanding of climate-related implications and the development of strong partnerships essential to implementing adaptation action.

Third, Canada will enhance its efforts on other pressing environmental issues, including pursuing and strengthening international standards, where appropriate. Canada will continue to engage in the negotiation of an international regime on access to genetic resources and the sharing of their benefits, under the Convention on Biological Diversity. Researchers around the world are interested in genetic resources found in extreme environments like the Arctic. We recognize the importance of these issues to Northerners and Northern communities.

Persistent organic pollutants and mercury, released far from the Arctic, have had serious impacts on Arctic peoples. Canada and the Inuit Circumpolar Council[5] played an important role in the negotiation of the Stockholm Convention on Persistent Organic Pollutants. Canada will continue to address the problems arising from these contaminants, including waste management practices in the North, and will engage actively in global negotiations to reduce mercury emissions.

Canada is setting an international example with the Federal Contaminated Sites Action Plan. The government is providing $3.5 billion over 15 years to address federal contaminated sites, with the majority of resources directed to contaminated sites in the North. Canada is contributing to the global effort to address mercury emissions with a plan to implement new environmental performance standards that will reduce greenhouse gas emissions and pollutants such as mercury from coal-fired electricity generating plants. An international agreement on the reduction of mercury emissions will help reduce the impact of mercury on the health and the environment of Canadians, particularly in the North.

Fourth, Canada will contribute to strengthening Arctic science and the legacy of International Polar Year. Arctic science forms an important foundation for Canada's Northern Strategy, providing the knowledge necessary for sound policy and decision-making both on domestic and international issues. To ensure that Canada remains a global leader in Arctic science, the Government of Canada has committed to establishing a new world-class research station in the High Arctic that will serve Canada and the world, and work is proceeding on its development. The station will anchor a strong research presence in Canada's Arctic and to complement these efforts, Canada has also invested in upgrading existing research facilities in over 30 sites across the Arctic.

Canada made one of the largest single contributions of any country to International Polar Year and will be hosting its final wrap-up event in Montreal in April 2012. Canada is also taking a lead role in the Arctic Council's Sustaining Arctic Observing Networks project. Its purpose is to further international engagement in developing sustained and coordinated pan-Arctic observing and data-sharing systems, particularly related to environmental, social, economic and cultural issues.

Improving and Devolving Governance: Empowering the Peoples of the North

The Government of Canada is committed to providing Canadian Northerners with more control over their economic and political destiny. Canada is taking steps to endorse the United Nations Declaration on the Rights of Indigenous Peoples in a manner fully consistent with Canada's Constitution and laws. In recent decades, Canada's Northern governments have taken on greater responsibility for many aspects of their region's affairs. Progress is continuing in this area and represents another way in which Canada is exercising its sovereignty in the Arctic. Canada's North is also home to some of the most innovative, consultative approaches to government in Canada and the world. Through land claim and self-government agreements, indigenous communities are developing made-in-the-North policies and strategies to address their unique economic and social challenges and opportunities.

> "We're committed to helping the region and its residents realize their true potential."
>
> —*Prime Minister Stephen Harper, March 10, 2008,*
> *Yellowknife, Northwest Territories*

Canada recognizes and values the important role Northern governments, Arctic Indigenous organizations at the Arctic Council (known as Permanent Participant organizations) and other Northerners have played, and will continue to play, in shaping Canada's international actions. Canada's Arctic foreign policy bolsters our domestic efforts for strong governance in the North in the following three ways.

First, Canada will engage with Northerners on Canada's Arctic foreign policy. Through the Canadian Arctic Council Advisory Committee, Northern governments and Indigenous Permanent Participant organizations in Canada[6] will have the opportunity to actively participate in shaping Canadian policy on Arctic issues. We will continue to meet regularly in Canada's North to find common ground and work towards common objectives.

Second, the Government of Canada will continue to support Indigenous Permanent Participant organizations in Canada, including financially, to contribute to strengthening their capacity to fully participate in the activities of the Arctic Council. Furthermore, Canada will encourage other Arctic Council states to support the participation of their Permanent Participant organizations. Canada will also support the continued unique status of Permanent Participant organizations at the Arctic Council, which was created to provide for their active participation and full consultation. As interest by non-Arctic players in the work of the Council grows, Canada will work to ensure that the central role of the Permanent Participants is not diminished or diluted.

Third, Canada will provide Canadian youth with opportunities to participate in the circumpolar dialogue. The Canadian Arctic Council Advisory Committee chose three young Canadians to attend the 2009 Arctic Council Ministerial meeting. Their participation enhanced the contribution of the Canadian delegation at this meeting, and this successful initiative is one that Canada will continue to support.

The Way Forward

The rapid pace of change and growing importance of the Arctic requires that we enhance our capacity to deliver on Canada's priorities on the international scene. Facing the challenges and seizing the opportunities that we face often require finding ways to work with others: through bilateral relations with our neighbours in the Arctic, through regional mechanisms like the Arctic Council, and through other multilateral institutions.

The United States is our premier partner in the Arctic and our goal is a more strategic engagement on Arctic issues. This includes working together on issues related to the Beaufort Sea, on Arctic science, on Aboriginal and Northern issues, and on a common agenda that we might pursue when first Canada and then the United States chairs the Arctic Council starting in 2013. We are also working with Russia, Norway, Denmark, Sweden, Finland and Iceland to advance shared interests such as trade and transportation, environmental protection, natural resource development, the role of indigenous peoples, oceans management, climate change adaptation and scientific cooperation.

However, the key foundation for any collaboration will be acceptance of and respect for the perspectives and knowledge of Northerners and Arctic states' sovereignty. As well, there must be recognition that the Arctic states remain best placed to exercise leadership in the management of the region.

Canada was the first chair of the Arctic Council (1996-98) and will be chairing the Council again starting in 2013. The Arctic Council is the leading multilateral forum through which we advance our Arctic foreign policy and promote Canadian Northern interests. It is a consensus-based, high-level intergovernmental forum that promotes the environmental, social and economic aspects of sustainable development and environmental protection in the Arctic region. The unique structure of the Council brings both the eight Arctic states and the six Arctic Indigenous Permanent Participants together around a common agenda—enhancing the strength and effectiveness of this unique multilateral forum.

Canada will engage with Northern governments and Permanent Participants to ensure that the Arctic Council continues to respond to the region's challenges and opportunities, thus furthering our national interests.

From Canada's perspective, the Council needs to be strengthened to ensure that it is equipped to address tomorrow's challenges. Canada will act on several fronts.

First, we will pursue a greater policy dialogue within the Council. The Council has traditionally played a strong role in science, research, monitoring and assessments, and the development of guidelines (e.g. for oil and gas) in some select areas. Canada will play a proactive role as the Council moves forward to encourage the implementation of guidelines, the development of "best practices" and, where appropriate, the negotiation of policy instruments. The current negotiation of a regional search and rescue agreement (the first ever attempt at a binding instrument under the rubric of the Arctic Council) will serve as an important test case and will inform the scope for future policy endeavours. Canada will also work to ensure that the research activities of the Council continue to focus on key emerging issues to ensure that solid knowledge underpins the policy work of the Council.

Second, Canada will lead efforts to develop a more strategic communications role for the Arctic Council. As the profile of the Arctic increases, the image of the Council and information about the broad range of cutting-edge work that it is doing need to be bolstered. In this vein, a greater outreach role for the Council will increase both the understanding of the interests of Arctic states and people, and of the Council and its mandate.

Third, Canada will work with other member states to address the structural needs of the organization. While the current informal nature of the body has served Canada well for many years, the growing demands on the organization may require changes to make it more robust. Canada will work with other Arctic states to develop options, including with respect to the role of the Council, related "secretariat" functions, and funding issues.

Beyond the Arctic Council, Canada will work through other multilateral institutions such as the International Maritime Organization and the United Nations Framework Convention on Climate Change towards global solutions to issues like polar shipping regulations and climate change. Arctic-specific organizations such as the Standing Committee of Parliamentarians for the Arctic Region, the Northern Forum, and the University of the Arctic are important partners on a variety of issues.

The increasing accessibility of the Arctic has led to a widespread perception that the region could become a source of conflict. This has led to heightened interest in the Arctic in a number of international organizations including NATO and the Organization for Security and Co-operation in Europe. Canada does not anticipate any military challenges in the Arctic and believes that the region is well managed through existing institutions, particularly the Arctic Council. We will continue to monitor discussion of Arctic issues in other international forums and intervene when necessary to protect Canada's interests.

Canada is taking other steps to demonstrate leadership, such as the 2010 Arctic Ocean Foreign Ministers meeting. In addition, a new Arctic regional policy and program centre at Canada's Embassy in Norway has been established, strengthening our on-the-ground interaction and influence in the region. This Canadian International Centre for the Arctic Region is part of a broader concerted effort to support Canada's foreign policy goals and commercial linkages through analysis, advocacy and outreach—further enhancing Canada's presence on Arctic issues abroad.

Conclusion

Through our Arctic foreign policy, we will deliver on the international dimension of our Northern Strategy. We will show leadership in demonstrating responsible stewardship while we build a region responsive to Canadian interests and values, secure in the knowledge that the North is our home and our destiny.

Through our Arctic foreign policy, we are also sending a clear message: Canada is in control of its Arctic lands and waters and takes its stewardship role and responsibilities seriously. Canada continues to stand up for its interests in the Arctic. When positions or actions are taken by others that affect our national interests, undermine the cooperative relationships we have built, or demonstrate a lack of sensitivity to the interests or perspectives of Arctic peoples or states, we respond.

Cooperation, diplomacy and respect for international law have always been Canada's preferred approach in the Arctic. At the same time, we will never waver in our commitment to protect our North.

> "The True North is our destiny...To not embrace its promise now at the dawn of its ascendancy would be to turn our backs on what it is to be Canadian ... As Prime Minister Diefenbaker said ... in 1961, 'There is a new world emerging above the Arctic Circle.' It is this world, a new world for all the peoples of the Arctic regions that we in Canada are working to build."
>
> —*Prime Minister Stephen Harper, August 2008, Inuvik, Northwest Territories*

Notes

1 Hon. Lawrence Cannon, Address by Minister Cannon at Launch of *Statement on Canada's Arctic Foreign Policy*, Ottawa, 20 August 2010, DFAIT speech 2010/57, http://www.international.gc.ca/media/aff/speeches-discours/2010/2010-057.aspx?lang=eng, accessed 25 June 2011.

2 See DFAIT, "Statement on Canada's Arctic Foreign Policy: Exercising Sovereignty and Promoting Canada's Northern Strategy Abroad," http://www.international.gc.ca/polar-polaire/canada_arctic_foreign_policy-la_politique_etrangere_du_canada_pour_arctique.aspx?lang=eng, accessed 25 June 2011.

3 The Arctic Council brings together eight member states (Canada, Denmark, Finland, Iceland, Norway, Russia, Sweden and the United States) and six Arctic indigenous groups called Permanent Participants.

4 Black carbon (soot and methane), released by car engines and fires, can darken ice and snow, increasing their rate of melting.

5 Formerly the Inuit Circumpolar Conference.

6 There are six Arctic Council Permanent Participant organizations, of which three have significant membership in Canada. These are the Inuit Circumpolar Council, the Gwich'in Council International, and the Arctic Athabaskan Council.

Bibliography

"Admiral Urges Government to Stake Claim in the Arctic." *South China Morning Post*, 6 March 2010, 7.

"Agreement on Basic Principles of Relations between the United States of America and the Union of Soviet Socialist Republics." *International Legal Materials* 11 (29 May 1972): 756–60.

Agreement Between the Inuit of the Nunavut Settlement Area and Her Majesty the Queen in Right of Canada. Ottawa: Tungavik and Minister of Indian Affairs and Northern Development, 1993.

Agreement Between the Government of Canada and the Government of the Russian Federation on Cooperation in the Arctic and the North. E100317—Canada Treaty Series 1992. No. 18. Accessed 20 June 2011. http://www.treaty-accord.gc.ca/text-texte.asp?id=100317.

Airoldi, Adele. *The European Union and the Arctic: Policies and Actions.* ANP 2008: 729. Copenhagen: Nordic Council of Ministers, 2008.

Allan, James. *Sovereign Statehood.* London: Allen and Unwin, 1986.

Allen, Ralph. "Will DEWline Cost Canada Its Northland?" *Maclean's*, 26 May 1956, 16–17, 68–72.

Alvarez, Pierre. "Renewing the Northern Strategy." *Northern Perspectives* 30, no. 1 (2006): 11–13.

Arctic Athabaskan Council (AAC). "Europe and the Arctic: A View from the Arctic Athabaskan Council." Presentation to Nordic Council of Ministers, Arctic Conference: Common Concern for the Arctic, Ilulissat, Greenland, 9–11 September 2008. Accessed 10 November 2008. http://www.norden.org/sv/nordiska-ministerraadet/samarbetsministrarna-mr-sam/arktis/common-concern-for-the-arctic/europeiska-unionen-och-arktis/europe-and-the-arctic-a-view-from-the-arctic-athabaskan-council-aac-pdf.

———. "Improving the Efficiency and Effectiveness of the Arctic Council: A Discussion Paper." March 2007. Accessed 10 November 2008. http://arctic-council.org/filearchive/AAC_Arctic_Council_Future_Dec_2006.pdf.

Arctic Climate Impact Assessment (ACIA). *Impacts of a Warming Arctic: ACIA Overview Report*. Cambridge: Cambridge University Press, 2004. Accessed 28 May 2009. http://amap.no/acia.

"The Arctic Contest Heats Up." *The Economist*, 9 October 2008. Accessed 28 May 2009. http://www.economist.com/world/europe/PrinterFriendly.cfm?story_id=1238176.

Arctic Council. "About Arctic Council." 26 November 2007. Accessed 28 May 2009. http://arctic-council.org/article/about.

———. *Arctic Marine Shipping Assessment 2009 Report*. http://pame.arcticportal.org/images/stories/PDF_Files/AMSA_2009_Report_2nd_print.pdf.

Arctic Council Panel. *To Establish an International Arctic Council: A Framework Report*. Ottawa: Canadian Arctic Resources Committee, 1991.

Arctic Human Development Report (AHDR). Akureyri: Stefansson Arctic Institute, 2004. Accessed 28 February 2009. http://www.svs.is/AHDR/AHDR%20chapters/English%20version/AHDR_first%2012pages.pdf.

Arctic Monitoring and Assessment Programme (AMAP). *Arctic Oil and Gas 2007*. Oslo: 2008. Accessed 28 May 2009. http://www.amap.no/oga.

Argitis, Theophilos. "Canada's Harper Concerned over Russian Bomber Flights (Update1)." *Bloomberg.com*. 19 September 2008. Accessed 5 June 2009. http://www.bloomberg.com/apps/news?pid=20601082&sid=aZn0SgnawmtU&refer=canada.

Associated Foreign Press. "Russian Navy Boasts Combat Presence in Arctic." *Canada.com*, 14 July 2008. Accessed 5 June 2009. http://www.canada.com/topics/news/world/story.html? id=3572ff95-9a88-4dd8-944f-58af497c3fa6.

Auditor General of Canada (AGC). "Managing the Coast Guard Fleet and Marine Navigational Services—Fisheries and Oceans Canada." Status Report to the House of Commons. February 2007. Accessed 10 December 2008. http://www.parl.gc.ca/HousePublications/Publication.aspx?DocId=3442082 &Language=E&Mode=1&Parl=39&Ses=2.

Authier, Philip. "'Canada Will Not Be Bullied' by Russia." *Montreal Gazette*, 28 March 2009, A12.

Axworthy, Lloyd. "A New Arctic Circle." *Globe and Mail*, 22 August 2008, A15.

Bagnell, Larry. "We're in Danger of Losing Part of Canada." *Embassy*, 6 November 2008.

Baker, Betsy. "Filling an Arctic Gap: Legal and Regulatory Possibilities for Canadian–U.S. Cooperation in the Beaufort Sea." *Vermont Law Review* 34 (2009): 57–119.

Bankes, Nigel D. "Forty Years of Canadian Sovereignty Assertion in the Arctic, 1947–87." *Arctic* 40, no. 4 (1987): 285–91.

Bartelson, Jens. *A Genealogy of Sovereignty*. Cambridge: Cambridge University Press, 1995.

Baylis, John, James Wirtz, Colin Gray, and Eliot Cohen, eds. *Strategy in the Contemporary World*. 2nd ed. Oxford: Oxford University Press, 2007.

BBC News. "Russia Restarts Cold War Patrols," 17 August 2007. Accessed 5 June 2009. http://news.bbc.co.uk/2/hi/europe/6950986.stm.

Beauregard-Tellier, Frédéric. "The Arctic: Hydrocarbon Resources." Library of Parliament, Parliamentary Information and Research Service Publication PRB 08-07E. 24 October 2008.

Bell, Jim. "Nunavut Fishing Reps Rap Feds over Docks, Quota." *Nunatsiaq News*, 21 March 2008. Last accessed 21 June 2011. http://www.nunatsiaqonline.ca/archives/2008/803/80321/news/nunavut/80321_1027.html.

Bercuson, David J. "Comedy of Errors: First, a Defence Strategy, Then a Shopping List." *Globe and Mail*, 21 May 2008, A17.

———. "Continental Defense and Arctic Security, 1945–50: Solving the Canadian Dilemma." In *The Cold War and Defense*. Edited by K. Neilson and R.G. Haycock. New York: Praeger, 1990. 153–70.

Berger, Thomas. *Northern Frontier / Northern Homeland: The Report of the Mackenzie Valley Pipeline Inquiry* 1. Ottawa: Department of Supply and Services, 1977.

Berthiaume, Lee. "DFAIT Left in the Cold on Arctic Issues." *Embassy*, 1 August 2007, 1, 10.

Bevington, Dennis. "Arctic Sovereignty Not Just a Military Concern, It's More Than That." *Hill Times*, 16 October 2006, 24.

———. "Enough Stalling on Environmental Assessment and Permitting." *Hill Times*, 20 August 2007, 28.

———. "Time for Territories to Have Control over Their Non-Renewable Resources." *Hill Times*, 19 March 2008, 30.

Bird, Kenneth J., Ronald R. Charpentier, Donald L. Gautier, David W. Houseknecht, Timothy R. Klett, Janet K. Pitman, Thomas E. Moore, Christopher J. Schenk, Marilyn E. Tennyson, and Craig J. Wandrey. "Circum-Arctic Resource Appraisal: Estimates of Undiscovered Oil and Gas North of the Arctic Circle." *U.S. Geological Survey Fact Sheet 2008–3049* (2008). Accessed 5 June 2009. http://pubs.usgs.gov/fs/2008/3049.

Blakkisrud, Helge. "What's to Be Done with the North?" In *Tackling Space: Federal Politics and the Russian North*. Edited by Helge Blakkisrud and Geir Hønneland. Lanhham: University Press of America, 2006. Chapter 2.

Blanchfield, Mike. "Harper Warns Russians after Two Bombers Intercepted." *National Post*, 28 February 2009, A10.

Bone, Robert M. *The Geography of the Canadian North: Issues and Challenges*. 2nd ed. Toronto: Oxford University Press, 2003.

Borgerson, Scott G. Arctic Meltdown: The Economic and Security Implications of Global Warming." *Foreign Affairs* 87, no. 2 (March–April 2008): 63–77.

Boswell, Randy. "Arctic Coastal States Meet as EU, Inuit Left on Sidelines." *Nunatsiaq News*, 29 March 2010. Accessed 21 June 2011. http://www.nunatsiaqonline.ca/stories/article/290310_arctic_coastal_states_meet_as_eu_inuit_left_on_sidelines/.

———. "Arctic Native Leaders Say They've Been Left Out of Summit." Canwest News Service, 15 February 2010.

———. "Bid to Put Three Seas in Canada's Motto Riding Wave." *Vancouver Province*, 11 April 2006. Accessed 23 June 2011. http://www2.canada.com/vancouversun/news/story.html?id=278af877-e9d5-4e11-8f62-04f0e03413df&k=79100&p=1.

———. "Canada's Arctic Sovereignty Challenged: U.S. Submarines May Chart the Continental Shelf." *Vancouver Sun*, 8 March 2006, A8.

———. "'Drastic' Arctic Shipping Rules Draw Fire." *Ottawa Citizen*, 10 July 2010, A3.

———. "Polar Posturing: Canada, Russia Tensions in Arctic Part Politics, Experts Say." *Canwest News Service*, 16 August 2009. Accessed 21 June 2011. http://byers.typepad.com/arctic/2009/08/polar-posturing-canada-russia-tensions-in-arctic-part-politics-experts-say.html.

———. "Research Backs Canada's Arctic Claim." *Ottawa Citizen*, 7 August 2008, A1.

———. "U.S. Shifts Priorities in Arctic to Security." *Vancouver Sun*, 9 August 2008, A8.

Bradner, Tim. "Shell Plans Alaska Drilling Program Despite Court Ruling." *Energy Current*, 27 April 2009. Accessed 5 June 2009. http://royaldutchshellplc.com/2009/04/27/shell-plans-alaska-drilling-program-despite-court-ruling.

Brewster, Murray. "New Arctic Patrol Vessels Approved; Plan to Build Ships Given Go-Ahead by Cabinet Committee." *Calgary Herald*, 14 May 2007, A8.

Briggs, Philip J. "The *Polar Sea* Voyage and the Northwest Passage Dispute." *Armed Forces and Society* 16, no. 3 (1990): 437–52.

Brigham, Lawson. "The Fast-Changing Maritime Arctic." US Naval Institute *Proceedings* (May 2010): 54–59.

———. "True North." *Foreign Policy*, November 2010, online edition. Accessed 1 December 2010. http://www.foreignpolicy.com/articles/2010/10/11/true_north.

Byers, Michael. "Unfrozen Sea: Sailing the Northwest Passage." *Policy Options* 28, no. 5 (2007): 30–33.

Byers, Michael, and Suzanne Lalonde. "Who Controls the Northwest Passage?" *Vanderbilt Journal of Transnational Law* 42 (2009): 1133–210.

Campion-Smith, Bruce. "Geopolitics of the Far North." *Toronto Star*, 9 August 2009, A8.

Canada. *Arctic Waters Pollution Prevention Act*. R.S.C. 1985, c. A-12. 1970.

———. *Arctic Shipping Pollution Prevention Regulations*. C.R.C., c. 353. 1978.

———. *Arctic Waters Pollution Prevention Regulations*. C.R.C., c. 354. 1978.

———. *Canada Shipping Act, 2001*. S.C. c. 26. 2001.

———. *Canada's International Policy Statement*. Overview. Ottawa: 2005.

———. "Protecting Canada's Future." Speech from the Throne. 16 October 2007. Accessed 5 June 2009. http://www.sft-ddt.gc.ca/eng/media.asp?id=1364.

———. *Seizing Global Advantage: A Global Commerce Strategy for Securing Canada's Growth and Prosperity*. Ottawa: Public Works Canada, 2008.

Canada's Northern Strategy: Our North, Our Heritage, Our Future. Ottawa: July 2009.

Canadian Arctic Resources Committee. "Renewing the Northern Strategy." *Northern Perspectives* 30, no. 1 (2006): 1–2.

Canadian Coast Guard. *Business Plan 2008–11.* Accessed 28 May 2009. http://www .ccg-gcc.gc.ca/folios/00018/docs/bp-pa-0811-eng.pdf.

Canadian Coast Guard Agency. *2007–2008 Year End Report.* Accessed 28 May 2009. http://www.ccg-gcc.gc.ca/folios/00018/docs/2007-2008-year-end-report-eng.pdf.

Canadian Forces Northern Area (CFNA). *Arctic Capabilities Study.* 2000. Acquired through Access to Information.

Cannon, Hon. Lawrence. Address to the Economic Club of Canada: "The Global Economy and Canada's Response." Foreign Affairs and International Trade Canada, No. 2009/58. Toronto, 23 November 2009. Accessed 21 June 2011. http:// www.international.gc.ca/media/aff/speeches-discours/2009/58.aspx?lang=eng.

———. Notes for an Address by the Honourable Lawrence Cannon, Minister of Foreign Affairs, on Canada's Arctic Foreign Policy, Whitehorse, 11 March 2009. Accessed 19 March 2009. http://www.international.gc.ca/media/aff/speeches -discours/2009/386933.aspx?lang=en.

———. Address by Minister Cannon at Launch of *Statement on Canada's Arctic Foreign Policy,* Ottawa, 20 August 2010. Foreign Affairs and International Trade Canada speech no. 2010/57. Accessed 25 June 2011. http://www.international .gc.ca/media/aff/speeches-discours/2010/2010-057.aspx?lang=eng.

Canuel, Hugues. "Nanisivik Refuelling Facility Will Enable Persistent Naval Presence." *Hill Times,* 20 August 2007, 24.

Casselman, Anne. "Will the Opening of the Northwest Passage Transform Global Shipping Anytime soon?" *Scientific American,* 10 November 2008. Accessed 5 June 2009. http://www.sciam.com/article.cfm?id=opening-of-northwest-passage.

CBC News. "Arctic Oil and Gas Joint Venture Formed." 3 August 2010. Accessed 4 August 2010. http://www.cbc.ca/news/canada/north/story/2010/08/03/beaufort -sea-oil-exploration-venture.html.

———. "Arctic Seabed Mapping Renewed." 29 July 2009. Accessed 29 July 2009. http://www.cbc.ca/news/canada/north/story/2009/07/29/cda-us-arctic-mapping .html.

———. "Canada, Denmark Agree to Resolve Dispute over Arctic Island." 19 September 2005. Accessed 28 May 2009. http://www.cbc.ca/world/story/2005/09/19/ hans-island-20050919.html.

———. "Canada Unveils Arctic Strategy." 26 July 2009. Accessed 26 July 2009. http://www.cbc.ca/canada/nPaikorth/story/2009/07/26/arctic-sovereignty.html.

———. "Clinton's Arctic Comments Cheer Inuit." 31 March 2010. Accessed 1 April 2010. http://www.cbc.ca/news/canada/story/2010/03/31/clinton-arctic.html.

———. "Coast Guard Faces Staffing Crunch as Arctic Demands Grow." 24 June 2008. Accessed 28 May 2009. http://www.cbc.ca/canada/story/2008/06/24/coast-guard .html.

———. "Early Findings Encouraging in Canada–U.S. Mapping of Arctic Ocean Seabed." November 3, 2008. Accessed 28 May 2009. http://www.cbc.ca/canada/north/story/2008/11/03/arctic-seabed.html.

———. "Harper Announces Northern Deep-Sea Port, Training Site." 11 August 2007. Accessed 28 May 2009. http://www.cbc.ca/canada/story/2007/08/10/port-north.html.

———. "Inuit Leaders to Work on Arctic Rights Declaration." 10 November 2008. Accessed 28 May 2009. http://www.cbc.ca/canada/north/story/2008/11/10/inuit-summit.html?ref=rss.

———. "Inuit Win Injunction on Seismic Testing," 8 August 2010. Accessed 12 August 2010. http://www.cbc.ca/canada/story/2010/08/08/nunavut-lancaster-injunction.html#ixzz15sa8WqcS.

———. "Northerners Divided over Proposed Arctic Military Facilities." 13 August 2007. Accessed 28 May 2009. http://www.cbc.ca/canada/north/story/2007/08/13/arctic-reax.html.

———. "Northern Summits Tackle Arctic Sovereignty, Environment." 6 November 2008. Accessed 28 May 2009. http://www.cbc.ca/canada/north/story/2008/11/05/arctic-summits.html.

———. "Ottawa Awards BP $1.2 Billion in Exploration Permits in Beaufort Sea." 8 July 2008. Accessed 5 June 2009. http://www.cbc.ca/canada/north/story/2008/06/09/beaufort-leases.html.

———. "'Wild Vikings' Land in Cambridge Bay Jail." 30 August 2007. Accessed 5 June 2009. http://www.cbc.ca/canada/north/story/2007/08/30/cambay-vikings.html.

———. "Wilkins Says Arctic Comment Old News." 27 January 2006. Accessed 28 May 2009. http://www.cbc.ca/canada/story/2006/01/27/wilkins-harper060127.html.

Centre for Military and Strategic Studies. "Arctic Timeline—Developments in Foreign Policy." Accessed 21 June 2011. http://cmss.ucalgary.ca/foreignpolicy.

Chan, Cindy. "Space Contract Awards Design Contract for Satellite Fleet." *Epoch Times,* 19 November 2008. Accessed 28 May 2009. http://en.epochtimes.com/n2/science-technology/space-agency-satellite-7444.html.

Chase, Steven. "Ottawa Rebukes Russia for Military Flights in the Arctic." *Globe and Mail,* 28 February 2009, A4.

———. "Russia Won't Bully Canada in Arctic, Cannon Vows." *Globe and Mail,* 28 March 2009, A4.

Chief of the Maritime Staff (CMS). *Statement of Operational Requirement: Arctic/Offshore Patrol Ship (AOPS).* Ottawa: Department of National Defence, 2008.

Christensen, Kyle D. "The Navy in Canada's Northern Archipelago." In *Defence Requirements for Canada's Arctic.* Edited by Brian MacDonald. Ottawa: Conference of Defence Associations Institute, 2007. 79–95.

Church, Ian. "Strategies for Ecosystem Security in the Arctic." In *Securing Canada's Future in a Climate-Changing World.* Ottawa: National Round Table on the Environment and the Economy, 2008. 102–115.

Churchill, R.R., and A.V. Lowe. *The Law of the Sea,* 3rd ed. Manchester: Manchester University Press, 2002.

Clinton, Hillary. Remarks with Canadian Foreign Minister Cannon, 13 June 2009. Accessed 10 February 2011. http://ottawa.usembassy.gov/content/textonly.asp?section=can_usa&document=Sec_State_Minister_Cannon.

Coates, Ken, Whitney Lackenbauer, William Morrison, and Greg Poelzer. *Arctic Front: Defending Canada's Interests in the Far North.* Toronto: Thomas Allen, 2008.

Cochran, Patricia A.L., ICC Chair, on behalf of Inuit in Greenland, Canada, Alaska, and Chukotka. "Circumpolar Inuit Declaration on Arctic Sovereignty." Adopted by the Inuit Circumpolar Council, April 2009. Accessed 28 May 2009. http://www.itk.ca/ circumpolar-inuit-declaration-arctic-sovereignty.

Cohen, Maxwell. "The Arctic and the National Interest." *International Journal* 26, no. 1 (1970–71): 52–81.

Collins, Allan, ed. *Contemporary Security Studies.* Oxford: Oxford University Press, 2007.

Collins, Michelle. "Unearthing Mysteries under the Arctic Ice." *Embassy,* 6 November 2008, 20.

Commission of the European Communities. *Communication from the Commission to the European Parliament and the Council. The European Union and the Arctic Region.* Brussels: COM(2008) 763.

Committee on the Assessment of U.S. Coast Guard Polar Icebreaker Roles and Future Needs. National Research Council, *Polar Icebreakers in a Changing World: An Assessment in a Changing World.* Washington: National Academics Press, 2007. Accessed 5 June 2009. http://books.nap.edu/catalog.php?record_id=11753.

"Continental Shelf Submission of Norway in Respect of Areas in the Arctic Ocean, the Barents Sea, and the Norwegian Sea Executive Summary." 2006. Accessed 5 June 2009. http://www.un.org/depts/los/clcs_new/submissions_files/nor06/nor_exec_sum.pdf.

Corell, Hans. "Mounting Tensions and Melting Ice: Exploring the Legal and Political Future of the Arctic." Address at a symposium of the *Vanderbilt Journal of Transnational Law,* 6 February 2009. Accessed 28 February 2009. http://www.havc.se.

———. "Reflections on the Possibilities and Limitations of a Binding Legal Regime for the Arctic." Address to the Seventh Conference of Parliamentarians of the Arctic Region, 3 August 2006. Accessed 28 February 2009. http://www.havc.se.

Cotter, Captain (Navy) Jamie. "Developing a Coherent Plan to Deal with Canada's Conundrum in the Northwest Passage." *Journal of Military and Strategic Studies* 11, no. 3 (Spring 2009): 1–51. Accessed 28 May 2009. http://www.jmss.org.

Council of Canadian Academies. *Vision for the Canadian Arctic Research Initiative: Assessing the Opportunities.* Ottawa: Council of Canadian Academies, 2008.

Daoust, Tyson, Wolfgang Haider, and Sabine Jessen. "Institutional Arrangements Governing Marine Conservation Planning in the Canadian Arctic: The Case of Nunavut, Canada," *Environments Journal* 37, no. 3 (2010): 73–93.

Dallimore, S.D., and T.S. Elliot, eds. *Scientific Results from the Mallik 2002 Gas Hydrate Production Research Well Program, MacKenzie Delta, Northwest Territories, Canada—Geological Survey of Canada Bulletin 585*. Ottawa: Geological Survey, 2005.

Davis, Jeff. "Securing the Northwest Passage Essential." *Embassy*, 6 November 2008. Accessed 28 May 2009. http://www.embassymag.ca/page/printpage/securing _northwest_passage-11-6-2008.

Decter, Michael. "Aboriginal Health Will Be the Biggest Challenge for the New Minister." *Sault Star*, 17 November 2008. Accessed 23 June 2011. http://www.saultstar .com/ArticleDisplay.aspx?archive=true&e=1300012.

Defence Research and Development Canada (DRDC). "Northern Watch: A Window into Canadian Arctic Surveillance." February 2008. Accessed 3 March 2009. http://www.drdc-rddc.gc.ca/news-nouvelles/spotlight-pleinfeux/index-eng.asp.

Defence Update. "Russia Plans to Deploy 6 Carrier Battlegroups by 2025." 2007. Accessed 5 June 2009. http://defense-update.com/newscast/0707/news/150707_russian _Navy.htm.

Delany, Max. "Gas and Glory Fuel Race for the Pole." *Moscow Times*, 27 July 2007. Accessed 23 June 2011, http://www.themoscowtimes.com/news/article/gas-and -glory-fuel-race-for-the-pole/195431.html.

Department of External Affairs (DEXAF). "Comments on Draft Paper on Defence Policy." 11 February 1972. LAC, RG 25, vol. 10322, file 27-10-2-2, pt. 2. Acquired under Access to Information.

———. Office of Politico-Military Affairs. Memorandum: "Role of Canadian Armed Forces in Maintenance of Sovereignty." 20 April 1970. LAC, RG 25, vol. 10322, file 27-10-2-2, pt. 1. Acquired under Access to Information.

———. Memorandum. "Draft White Paper on Defence Policy—Sovereignty Aspects." North American Defence and NATO Division to Legal Division. 28 January 1971. LAC, RG 25, vol. 10322, file 27-10-2-2, pt. 2. Acquired under Access to Information.

———. Memorandum, Legal Division. "DND Paper on 'Canadian Defence Policy in the 1970s." 5 August 1970. LAC, RG 25, vol. 10322, file 27-10-2-2 pt. 1. Acquired under Access to Information.

Department of Finance. "Budget 2008: Responsible Leadership." Chapter 4, "Leadership at Home." Accessed 28 May 2009. http://www.budget.gc.ca/2008/plan/ chap4a-eng.asp.

Department of Fisheries and Oceans (DFO) and Government of Nunavut. *Small Craft Harbours Report*. Ottawa: November 2005.

Department of Foreign Affairs and International Trade (DFAIT). "Arctic Council Priorities 2006–2008: Canadian Position Paper." 8 February. Ottawa: 2007.

———. *Government Response to Standing Committee on Foreign Affairs and International Trade Report "Canada and the Circumpolar World: Meeting the Challenges of Cooperation into the Twenty-First Century*. Ottawa: 1998.

————. "Joint Statement on Canada-Russia Economic Cooperation." 28–29 November 2007. Accessed 10 May 2009. http://www.international.gc.ca/commerce/zubkov/joint_state-en.asp.

————. *The Northern Dimension of Canada's Foreign Policy*. Ottawa: 2000.

————. *Statement on Canada's Arctic Foreign Policy: Exercising Sovereignty and Promoting Canada's Northern Strategy Abroad*. 20 August 2010. Accessed 25 June 2011. http://www.international.gc.ca/polar-polaire/canada_arctic_foreign_policy-la_politique_etrangere_du_canada_pour_arctique.aspx?lang=eng.

————. *Summative Evaluation of the Northern Dimension of Canada's Foreign Policy*. May 2005. Accessed 28 May 2009. http://www.international.gc.ca/about-a_propos/oig-big/2005/evaluation/northern_program-programme_nordique.aspx?lang=eng.

Department of National Defence (DND). *Canada's International Policy Statement: A Role of Pride and Influence in the World—Defence*. Ottawa: 2005.

Digges, Charles. "Russia to Drill Arctic Oil with Nuclear Icebreaker." *Russian Icebreaker Fleet*. 8 July 2008. Accessed 5 June 2009. http://www.bellona.org/articles/articles_2007/sevmorput_drilling.

Dittmann, Major Paul. "In Defence of Defence: Canadian Arctic Sovereignty and Security." *Journal of Military and Strategic Studies* 11, no. 3 (Spring 2009): 1–77. Accessed 28 May 2009. http://www.jmss.org.

Doran, Charles. Presentation to the Standing Senate Committee on National Security and Defence. 29 March 2010. http://www.parl.gc.ca/40/3/parlbus/commbus/senate/Com-e/defe-e/02cv-e.htm?Language=E&Parl=40&Ses=3&comm_id=76.

Dosman, Edgar. "The Northern Sovereignty Crisis, 1968–70." In *The Arctic in Question*. Edited by Edgar Dosman. Toronto: Oxford University Press, 1976.

Doucette, Keith. "EU Closer to Total Ban on Canadian Seal Products." *Globe and Mail*, 3 March 2009, A8.

Downie, David L., and Terry Fenge. *Northern Lights Against POPs: Combatting Toxic Threats in the Arctic*. Montreal and Kingston: McGill–Queen's University Press, 2003.

Elliot-Meisel, Elizabeth B. *Arctic Diplomacy: Canada and the United States in the Northwest Passage*. New York: Peter Lang, 1998.

————. "Still Unresolved after Fifty Years: The Northwest Passage in Canadian-American Relations, 1946–1998." *American Review of Canadian Studies* 29, no. 3 (1999): 407–30.

European Commission (EC). *The European Union and the Arctic Region*. COM(2008) 763. 20 November. Brussels: 2008.

European Union (EU). *Climate Change and International Security*. S113/08. 14 March. Brussels: 2008.

Eyre, Kenneth C. "Forty Years of Military Activity in the Canadian North, 1947–87." *Arctic* 40, no. 4 (1987): 292–99.

Fenge, Terry. "Inuit and the Nunavut Land Claims Agreement: Supporting Canada's Arctic Sovereignty." *Policy Options* 29, no. 1 (2007–8): 84–88.

Fikkan, Anne, Gail Osherenko, and Alexander Arikainen. "Polar Bears: The Importance of Simplicity." In *Polar Politics: Creating International Regimes*. Edited by Oran R. Young and Gail Osherenko. Ithaca: Cornell University Press, 1993. 96–151.

Fitzpatrick, Meagan. "Russian Bombers Did Not Breach Canadian Airspace: Diplomat." *Vancouver Sun*, 23 March 2009. Accessed 24 March 2009. http://www.vancouversun.com/technology/Russian+bombers+breach+ Canadian+airspace +Diplomat/1419825/story.html.

Flanagan, Tom. *Harper's Team: Behind the Scenes in the Conservative Rise to Power*. Montreal and Kingston: McGill–Queen's University Press, 2007.

Flemming, Brian. *Canada–US Relations in the Arctic: A Neighborly Proposal*. Calgary: Canadian Defence and Foreign Affairs Institute, December 2008.

Fox Business. "Baffinland Provides Update on Mary Rivers Project." *Your Metals News*. 5 December 2008. Accessed 5 June 2009. http://www.yourmetalnews.com/ baffinland+provides+update+on+mary+river+project_17718.html.

Frederick, Michel. "La délimitation du plateau continental entre le Canada et les Etats-Unis dans la mer de Beaufort." In *Annuaire canadien de Droit international 1979*. Vancouver: UBC Press, 1979. 30–98.

Galloway, Gloria. "Ottawa Sets Up Arctic Marine Park." *Globe and Mail (Breaking News)*, 6 December 2010Accessed 21 June 2011. http://www.theglobeandmail.com/ news/politics/ottawa-notebook/ottawa-sets-up-arctic-marine-park/article1826548/.

George, Jane. "ICC Urges Stronger Inuit Voice in Sovereignty." *Nunatsiaq News*, 14 November 2008. Accessed 21 June 2011. http://www.nunatsiaqonline.ca/ archives/2008/811/81114/news/nunavut/81114_1690.html.

Gibbs, Walter. "Russia and Norway Reach Accord on Barents Sea." *New York Times*, 10 April 2010, A10.

Gizewski, Peter, and Andrew B. Godefroy. "Force Requirements (Land)." In *Defence Requirements for Canada's Arctic*. Edited by Brian MacDonald. Ottawa: Conference of Defence Associations Institute, 2007. 96–106.

Global Business Network (GBN). "The Future of Arctic Marine Navigation in Mid-Century." Scenario narratives produced for the Protection of the Arctic Marine Environment (PAME) Working Group. May 2008. Accessed 20 June 2011. http:// www.gbn.com/articles/pdfs/GBN_Future%20of%20Arctic%20Navigation%20 Mid-century.pdf.

Grant, Shelagh. *Sovereignty or Security? Government Policy in the Canadian North, 1936–1950*. Vancouver: UBC Press, 1988.

Gray, David H. "Canada's Unresolved Maritime Boundaries." *IBRU Boundary and Security Bulletin* (1997): 61–70.

Greer, Darrell. "Not as Slow as Some May Think." *Kivalliq News*, 20 May 2009. Accessed 21 June 2011. http://www.nnsl.com/frames/newspapers/2009-05/may20_09 edit.html.

Griffiths, Franklyn. "The Arctic in the Russian Identity." In *The Soviet Maritime Arctic*. Edited by Lawson W. Brigham. London: Belhaven Press, 1991.

———. "Camels in the Arctic?" *The Walrus*, November 2007, 46–61.

———. "Canadian Arctic Sovereignty: Time to Take Yes for an Answer on the Northwest Passage." In *Northern Exposure: Peoples, Powers and Prospects for Canada's North*. Edited by Frances Abele, Thomas J. Courchene, F. Leslie Seidle, and France St-Hilaire. Ottawa: Institute for Research on Public Policy, 2009. 107–36.

———. "Civility in the Arctic." In *Arctic Alternatives: Civility or Militarism in the Circumpolar North*. Edited by F. Griffiths. Toronto: Science for Peace/Samuel Stevens, 1992. 279–309.

———. "Environment in the U.S. Discourse on Security: The Case of the Missing Arctic Waters." In *National Security and International Environmental Cooperation in the Arctic—The Case of the Northern Sea Route*. Edited by Willy Østreng. Dordrecht: Kluwer Academic Publishers, 1999.

———. "Introduction: The Arctic as an International Political Region." In *The Arctic Challenge: Nordic and Canadian Approaches to Security and Cooperation in an Emerging International Region*. Edited by Kari Möttölä. Boulder: Westview Press, 1988. Chapter 1.

———. "A Northern Foreign Policy." *Wellesley Papers* 7. Toronto: Canadian Institute of International Affairs, 1979.

———. "Our Arctic Sovereignty Is Well in Hand." *Globe and Mail*, November 8, 2006, A25.

———. "On This Day, Grab a Cold One and Think Pan-Arctic Thoughts." *Globe and Mail*, 30 June 2009, A11.

———. "The Shipping News: Canada's Arctic Sovereignty Not on Thinning Ice." *International Journal* 58, no. 2 (2003): 257–82.

Gurney, Matt. "The New Cold War: A Brief History." *National Post*, 15 August 2008, A15.

Hanson, Udloriak. "Geopolitics in the Arctic—Speaking Points for CCIL Conference." 29 October 2010. Accessed 15 March 2011. http://ccil-ccdi.squarespace.com/ccil-conference-papers/2010.

Harris, Kathleen. "Arctic Sovereignty Part 1: Our True North Strong and Free?" *Edmonton Sun*, 23 February 2007. Accessed 23 February 2007. http://www.torontosun.com/News/Canada/2007/ 02/23/3657827-sun.html.

———. "Laying Claim to Canada's Internal Waters." *Toronto Sun*, 23 February 2007. Accessed 23 June 2011. http://cnews.canoe.ca/CNEWS/Canada/2007/02/22/3655342-sun.html.

Haydon, Peter T. "The Strategic Importance of the Arctic: Understanding the Military Issues." *Canadian Defence Quarterly* (Spring 1988): 27–34.

———. "Why Does Canada Still Need a Navy?" *Maritime Security Working Paper* no. 1. Centre for Foreign Policy Studies, Dalhousie University, 2007.

Hayes, Margaret F. Director of Office of Oceans Affairs. Department of State. "Arctic Policy—Speech to Arctic Parliamentarians on Aspects of U.S. Arctic Policy." Fairbanks, 13 August 2008.

Hertell, Hans H. "Arctic Melt: The Tipping Point for an Arctic Treaty." *Georgetown International Environmental Law Review* 21 (2009): 565–91.

Holtsmark, Sven G. "Towards Cooperation or Confrontation? Security in the High North." Research Paper, Research Division—NATO Defence College Rome. No. 45. February 2009. Accessed 28 May 2009. http://www.ndc.nato.int/download/publications/rp_45en.pdf.

Homer-Dixon, Thomas. "Climate Change, The Arctic, and Canada: Avoiding Yesterday's Analysis of Tomorrow's Crisis." In *Securing Canada's Future in a Climate-Changing World*. Ottawa: National Round Table on the Environment and the Economy, 2008. 89–101.

———. *Environment, Security, and Violence*. Princeton: Princeton University Press, 1999.

Hooks, Gregory, and Chad L. Smith. "The Treadmill of Destruction: National Sacrifice Areas and Native Americans." *American Sociological Review* 69 (2004): 558–75.

Hønneland, Geir, and Jørgen Holten Jørgensen. "The Ups and Downs of Environmental Governance." In *Tackling Space: Federal Politics and the Russian North*. Edited by Helge Blakkisrud and Geir Hønneland. Lanham: University Press of America, 2006. Chapter 7.

House of Commons Standing Committee on Foreign Affairs and International Trade (HCSCFAIT). *Canada and the Circumpolar World: Meeting the Challenges of Cooperation into the Twenty-First Century*. Ottawa: 1997.

Huebert, Rob. "As the Ice Melts, Control Ebbs in the Arctic." *Globe and Mail*, 16 August 2008, A17.

———. "Canada and the Changing International Arctic: At the Crossroads of Cooperation and Conflict." In *Northern Exposure: Peoples, Powers, and Prospects for Canada's North*. Edited by Frances Abele, Thomas J. Courchene, F. Leslie Seidle, and France St-Hilaire. Ottawa: Institute for Research on Public Policy, 2009. 77–106.

———. "Canadian Arctic Maritime Security: The Return to Canada's Third Ocean." *Canadian Military Journal* 8, no. 2 (2007): 9–16.

———. "Canadian Arctic Security: Preparing for a Changing Future." *Behind the Headlines* 65, no. 4 (2008): 14–21.

———. "Climate Change and Canadian Sovereignty in the Northwest Passage." *Isuma: Canadian Journal of Policy Research* 2, no. 4 (2001): 86–94.

———. "The Need for an Arctic Treaty: Growing from the United Nations Convention on the Law of the Sea." *Ocean Yearbook* 23 (2009): 2–28.

———. "New Directions in Circumpolar Cooperation: Canada, the Arctic Environmental Protection Strategy, and the Arctic Council." *Canadian Foreign Policy* 5, no. 2 (Winter 1998): 37–58.

———. *The Newly Emerging Arctic Security Environment*. Calgary: Canadian Defence and Foreign Affairs Institute, 2010. Accessed 20 June 2011. http://www.cdfai.org/PDF/The%20Newly%20Emerging%20Arctic%20Security%20Environment.pdf.

———. "A Northern Foreign Policy: The Politics of Ad Hocery." In *Diplomatic Departures: The Conservative Era in Canadian Foreign Policy, 1984–93*. Edited by N. Michaud and K.R. Nossal. Vancouver: UBC Press, 2001. 84–112.

———. "Polar Vision or Tunnel Vision: The Making of Canadian Arctic Waters Policy." *Marine Policy* 19, no. 4 (July 1995): 343–63.

———. "Renaissance in Canadian Arctic Security?" *Canadian Military Journal* 6, no. 4 (2005–6): 17–29.

———. "The Shipping News Part II: How Canada's Arctic Sovereignty Is on Thinning Ice." *International Journal* 58, no. 3 (2003): 295–308.

———. "Time for Gov't to Go beyond Arctic Promises." *Embassy*, 6 November 2008. Accessed 28 May 2009. http://www.embassymag.ca/page/view/arctic_promises -11-6-2008.

———. *The United States Arctic Policy: The Reluctant Arctic Power*. School of Public Policy Briefing Papers 2, no. 2. Calgary: University of Calgary, May 2009. Accessed 4 July 2009. http://policyschool.ucalgary.ca/files/publicpolicy/SPP Briefing-HUEBERTonline.pdf.

———. "Welcome to a New Era of Arctic Security." *Globe and Mail*. 24 August 2010, A15.

Huebert, Rob, and Brooks B. Yeager. *A New Sea: The Need for a Cooperative Framework for Management and Conservation of the Arctic Marine Environment*. Report for WWF. 22 January 2008. Accessed 28 May 2009. http://assets.panda.org/downloads/ a_new_sea_jan08_final_11jan08.pdf.

Ibbitson, John. "Ambitious Agenda Awaits New Cabinet." *Globe and Mail*. 18 December 2008, A21.

———. "Canada and Denmark Make Headway in Dispute over Hans Island." *Globe and Mail*, 27 January 2011, A5.

Ilulissat Declaration. Adopted at the Arctic Ocean Conference hosted by the Government of Denmark and attended by the representatives of the five coastal states bordering on the Arctic Ocean (Canada, Denmark, Norway, the Russian Federation, and the US). Ilulissat, Greenland, 27–29 May 2008. Accessed 28 May 2009. http://www.oceanlaw.org/downloads/arctic/Ilulissat_Declaration.pdf.

Indian and Northern Affairs Canada (INAC). *Fact Sheet: Northern Strategy*. 28 May 2008. Accessed 28 May 2009. http://www.ainc-inac.gc.ca/ai/mr/is/n-strat-eng .asp.

———. News Release 2-3317, "Canada and Russia Working Jointly for the Well-Being of the Aboriginal Peoples of the Arctic." 12 February. Ottawa: 2010.

———. "Canada's Statement of Support on the United Nations Declaration on the Rights of Indigenous Peoples." 12 November 2010. Accessed 13 November 2010. http://www.ainc-inac.gc.ca/ap/ia/dcl/stmt-eng.asp.

International Boundaries Research Unit, Durham University. "Maritime Jurisdiction and Boundaries in the Arctic Region." Accessed 22 June 2009. http://www.dur .ac.uk/ibru/resources/arctic.

Inuit Circumpolar Conference (ICC) (Canada). The Utqiagvik Declaration. As declared by the Inuit of Alaska, Canada, Greenland, and Russia on the occasion of the 10th General Assembly. 9–13 July 2006.

ICC. *A Circumpolar Inuit Declaration on Sovereignty in the Arctic.* 2009. Accessed 10 January 2010. http://inuitcircumpolar.com/files/uploads/icc-files/PR-2009-04-28 -Signed-Inuit-Sovereignty-Declaration-11x17.pdf.

———. *Project Description: Institutional Building for Northern Aboriginal Peoples in Russia (INRIPP-2).* 2008. Accessed 28 May 2009. http://www.inuitcircumpolar.com/ index.php?ID=209&Lang=En.

Inuit Tapiriit Kanatami (ITK). Media Release. "Climate Change Report Highlights Need for Specific Measures in Arctic Regions." 2007. Accessed 10 August 2008. http://www.itk.ca/media-centre/media-releases/climate-change-report-highlights -need-specific-measures-arctic-regions.

ITK. *An Integrated Arctic Strategy.* 2008. Accessed 28 May 2009. http://www.itk.ca/ sites/default/files/Integrated-Arctic-Stratgey.pdf.

ITK and Inuit Circumpolar Council (ICC) (Canada). *Building Inuit Nunaat: The Inuit Action Plan.* 2006. Accessed 28 May 2009. http://www.itk.ca/sites/default/files/ Inuit-Action-Plan.pdf.

ITK/ICC. Press Release. "Inuit of Canada: European Union Knows Proposed Seal Ban Would Be Unlawful." 27 March 2009. Accessed 28 May 2009. http://www.itk.ca/ media-centre/media-releases/itkicc-press-release-inuit-canada-european-union -knows-proposed-seal-ban.

Jago, Charles J. "Report and Recommendations on a Government of Canada Approach Toward a Sustainable University of the Arctic (Canada)." 28 February 2008. Accessed 10 October 2009. http://ycdl4.yukoncollege.yk.ca/frontier/files/uarctic/ jagouarcticcanadareportncr13.pdf.

Jakobsen, Linda. *China Prepares for an Ice-Free Arctic.* Stockholm: Stockholm International Peace Research Institute, Insights on Peace and Security 2010/2.

"Japan Seeks Role in Arctic Council." *Daily Yomiuri* (Tokyo), 20 April 2009, 3.

Jaremko, Gordon. "Arctic Fantasies Need Reality Check." *Edmonton Journal,* 4 April 2008, D1.

Jeffers, Jennifer. "Climate Change and the Arctic: Adapting to Changes in Fisheries Stocks and Governance Regimes." *Ecology Law Quarterly* 37 (2010): 917–77.

Jockel, Joseph T. *Security to the North: Canada–U.S. Defence Relationships in the 1990s.* East Lansing: Michigan State University Press, 1991.

Johncox, Louise. "We're in Meltdown." *The Guardian.* 23 August 2007, 12.

Jonathan Seymour and Associates Inc. and The Mariport Group Ltd. *Canadian Arctic Shipping Assessment Scoping Study.* Prepared for Transport Canada Seaway and Domestic Shipping Policy. Gibbons, BC: 2005.

Jones, David. "Don't Kid Yourselves, Canada." *Ottawa Citizen,* 15 August 2008, A15.

Jones, Jeffrey. "Ottawa Seeks Legal Advice on Arctic Pipeline Delays." *Reuters,* 16 March 2009. Accessed 28 May 2009. http://www.reuters.com/article/marketsNews/ idUSN1653185520090316.

———. "Update 2—Imperial, Exxon, Mobil Win Beaufort Sea Acreage." *Reuters.* 19 July 2007. Accessed 5 June 2009.

Kalinin, Kirill. "Russia–Canada Cooperation in the Arctic." Embassy of the Russian Federation in Canada, Press Release, 11 March 2009.

Kaludjak, Paul. "The Inuit Are Here, Use Us." *Ottawa Citizen,* 18 July 2007, A15.

———. "Sovereignty and Inuit in the Canadian Arctic," *Arctic Council Indigenous Peoples Secretariat,* 18 November 2006. Accessed 22 June 2011. http://www.arctic peoples.org/index.php?option=com_k2&view=item&id=83:sovereignty-and -inuit-in-the-canadian-arctic&Itemid=2

Kennedy, Mark. "Ottawa Unveils Sovereignty Blueprint." *National Post,* 21 August 2010, A11.

Keskitalo, E.C.H. *Negotiating the Arctic: Construction of an International Region.* London: Routledge, 2004.

Kessel, Alan. Testimony to the Standing Senate Committee on National Security and Defence, Minutes of Proceedings, 15 March 2010. Accessed 10 June 2010. http://www.parl.gc.ca/40/3/ parlbus/commbus/ senate/Com-e/defe-e/01mn-e .htm?Language=E&Parl= 40&Ses=3&comm_id=76.

Kikkert, Peter. "Rising above the Rhetoric: Northern Voices and the Strengthening of Canada's Capacity to Maintain a Stable Circumpolar World." Paper delivered at Canada's Role in the Circumpolar World: A Symposium Showcasing Preeminent Graduate Students, Saskatoon, 9 March 2009.

Kirkey, Christopher. "The Arctic Waters Pollution Prevention Initiatives: Canada's Response to an American Challenge." *International Journal of Canadian Studies* 13 (1996): 41–59.

———. "Smoothing Troubled Waters: The 1988 Canada–United States Arctic Co-operation Agreement." *International Journal* 50 (1995): 401–26.

Koivurova, Timo. "Limits and Possibilities of the Arctic Council in a Rapidly Changing Scene of Arctic Governance." *Polar Record* 46 (2009): 146–56.

———. "Sovereign States and Self-Determining Peoples: Carving Out a Place for Transnational Indigenous Peoples in a World of Sovereign States." *International Community Law Review* 12 (2010): 191–212.

Koivurova, Timo, and Leena Heinamaki. "The Participation of Indigenous Peoples in International Norm-Making in the Arctic." *Polar Record* 42, no. 221 (2006): 101–9.

Koivurova, Timo, and Erik J. Molenaar. "International Governance and Regulation of the Marine Arctic: A Report Prepared for the WWF International Arctic Programme." 20 January. Oslo: WWF Arctic Programme, 2009. Accessed 28 February 2009. http://assets.panda.org/downloads/gap_analysis_marine_resources _130109.pdf.

Koivurova, Timo, and Erik J. Molenaar. *International Governance and Regulation of the Marine Arctic: Overview and Gap Analysis.* Oslo: World Wildlife Foundation, 2009.

Koivurova, Timo, and David Vanderzwaag. "The Arctic Council at 10 Years: Retrospect and Prospects." *UBC Law Review* 40, no. 1 (2007): 121–94.

Koring, Paul. "Russia–Norway Pact on Arctic Zone Puts Pressure on Canada." *Globe and Mail*, 16 September 2010, A19.

Kraska, James. "International Security and International Law in the Northwest Passage." *Vanderbilt Journal of Transnational Law* 42 (2009): 1109–32.

———. "The Law of the Sea Convention and the Northwest Passage." *International Journal of Marine and Coastal Law* 22, no. 2 (2007): 257–81.

Lackenbauer, P. Whitney. "Canada's Northern Defenders: Aboriginal Peoples in the Canadian Rangers, 1947–2005." In *Aboriginal Peoples and the Canadian Military: Historical Perspectives*. Edited by P.W. Lackenbauer and Craig Mantle. Kingston: CDA Press, 2007. 171–208.

———. "The Canadian Rangers: A Postmodern Militia That Works." *Canadian Military Journal* 6, no. 4 (2005–6): 49–60.

———. "Mirror Images? Canada, Russia, and the Circumpolar World." *International Journal* 65, no. 4 (Autumn 2010): 879–97.

———. "New Northern Strategy Trades Sabre-Rattling for Partnership." *Toronto Star*, 29 July 2009, A19.

———. "Right and Honourable: Mackenzie King, Canadian-American Bilateral Relations, and Canadian Sovereignty in the Northwest, 1943–1948." In *Mackenzie King: Citizenship and Community*. Edited by John English, Kenneth McLaughlin, and P.W. Lackenbauer. Toronto: Robin Brass Studios, 2002. 151–68.

Lackenbauer, P. Whitney, and Andrew F. Cooper. "The Achilles Heel of Canadian Good International Citizenship: Indigenous Diplomacies and State Responses in the Twentieth Century." *Canadian Foreign Policy* 13, no. 3 (2007): 99–119.

Lackenbauer, P. Whitney, and Matthew Farish. "The Cold War on Canadian Soil: Militarizing a Northern Environment." *Environmental History* 12, no. 3 (2007): 920–50.

Lalonde, Suzanne. "Arctic Waters: Cooperation or Conflict?" *Behind the Headlines* 65, no. 4 (2008): 8–14.

———. "A Network of Marine Protected Areas in the Arctic: Promises and Challenges." In *Changes in the Arctic Environment and the Law of the Sea*. Edited by M. Nordquist, J.N. Moore, and T.H. Heidar. Leiden: Martinus Nijhoff Publishers, 2010. 131–42.

Launteaume, Sylvie. "US 'Committed' to Ratifying Law of Sea Convention: Clinton." Agence France Presse, 6 April 2009. Accessed 23 June 2011. http://www.google.com/hostednews/afp/article/ALeqM5gB1OPzPfiju89sybtB66q9Sq4f6A.

Larson, David L. "United States Interests in the Arctic Region." *Ocean Development and International Law* 20 (1989): 167–91.

Lasserre, Frédéric. "High North Shipping: Myths and Realities about Arctic Shipping Routes." In *Security Prospects in the High North: Geostrategic Thaw of Freeze?* Eidted by Sven G. Holtsmark and Brooke A. Smith-Windsor. Rome: NATO Research Division, 2009. 179–99.

———, ed. *Passages et mers arctiques. Géopolitique d'une région en mutation*. Québec: Presses de l'Université du Québec, 2010.

Lavrov, Sergei, and Jonas Gahr Støre. "Canada, Take Note: Here's How to Resolve Maritime Disputes." *Globe and Mail*, 21 September 2010, A17.

Legault, L.H.J. Memorandum, "Draft Paper on Defence Policy—Sovereignty Aspects," to J.A. Beesley. 2 February 1971. LAC, RG 25, vol. 10322, file 27-10-2-2, pt. 2.

Lerhe, Eric. "Whither Canada's National Security Defence, the Navy, and the Coast Guard in a New Security Environment? Discussant Report." Paper presented to conference, "The Future of Canada's Maritime Capabilities." Centre for Foreign Policy Studies, Dalhousie University, 18–20 June 2004. Accessed 28 May 2009. http://centreforforeignpolicystudies.dal.ca/pdf/msc2004/msc2004lerhe.pdf.

Lilley, Brian. "The Russians Are Coming." *Brantford Expositor*, 30 July 2010. Accessed 23 June 2011. http://brantfordexpositor.ca/ArticleDisplay.aspx?e=2691522&auth=BRIAN%20LILLEY,%20PARLIAMENTARY%20BUREAU&archive=true.

Livingstone, Andrew. "Make Rangers Reservists: Senate Report." *Northern News Services*, 20 May 2009.

Loukacheva, Natalia. "Legal Challenges in the Arctic." Position paper presented to the 4th NRF Open Meeting in Oulu, Finland, and Luleå, Sweden, 5–8 October 2006. Accessed 28 May 2009. http://www.nrf.is/Open%20Meetings/Oulu%20Lulea%202006/Position%20Papers/Leukacheva_4th%20NRF%20PP.pdf.

Lund, Endre. "Norway's New Nansen Class Frigates: Capabilities and Controversies." *Defence Daily Industries*, 7 June 2008. Accessed 5 June 2009. http://www.defenseindustrydaily.com/norways-new-nansen-class-frigates-capabilities-and-controversies-02329.

MacDonald, Brian. "Force Requirements (Air)." In *Defence Requirements for Canada's Arctic*. Edited by Brian MacDonald. Vimy Paper. Ottawa: Conference of Defence Associations Institute, 2007. 107–16.

Marine and Environmental Law Institute (MELAW). Dalhousie Law School. *Governance of Arctic Marine Shipping*. 1 August. Halifax: 2008.

Marine Security Operations Centres Project (MSOC). Accessed 28 May 2009. http://msoc-cosm.gc.ca/index-eng.asp.

Mariport Group. *Canadian Arctic Shipping Assessment: Main Report*. For Transport Canada. June. Ottawa: 2007.

Mayeda, Andrew, and Randy Boswell. "Arctic Ambitions—Canada's Stake in the North: Part 3: The Rush for Oil." *Canada.com*. 17 August 2008. Accessed 5 June 2009. http://www2.canada.com/topics/news/features/arcticambitions/story.html?id=994c07a9-7d79-4a35-927a-f78d485df522.

Mayer, Paul. *Mayer Report on Nunavut Devolution*. Ottawa: Indian and Northern Affairs Canada, June 2007.

McDonald, Ben. "Establishing Strong Foundations for Economic Development." *Northern Perspectives* 30, no. 1 (2006): 13–15.

McDorman, Ted. "The Northwest Passage: International Law, Politics, and Cooperation." In *Changes in the Arctic Environment and the Law of the Sea*. Edited by Myron H. Nordquist, Tomas H. Heidar, and John Norton Moore. Leiden: Martinus Nijhoff Publishers, 2010. 227–50.

McFadden, VAdm Dean. Speaking notes, "The Evolution of Arctic Security and Defense Policies: Cooperative or Confrontational." Center for Strategic and International Studies Conference, Washington, 28 April 2010.

McMahon, Kevin. *Arctic Twilight: Reflections on the Destiny of Canada's Northern Land and People.* Toronto: Lorimer, 1988.

McRae, Donald M. "The Negotiation of Article 234." In *Politics of the Northwest Passage.* Edited by Franklyn Griffiths. Kingston and Montreal: McGill–Queen's University Press, 1987.

———. "Arctic Sovereignty: Loss by Dereliction?" *CARC—Northern Perspectives* 22, no. 4 (1994–5): 4–9. Accessed 28 May 2009. http://www.carc.org/pubs/v22no4/loss.htm.

———. "Arctic Sovereignty: What Is at Stake?" *Behind the Headlines* 64, no. 1 (2007): 1–23.

McRae, Donald M., and D.J. Goundrey. "Environmental Jurisdiction in the Arctic Waters: The Extent of Article 234." *UBC Law Review* 16, no. 2 (1982): 197–228.

McRae, Rob and Don Hubert, eds. *Human Security and the New Diplomacy: Protecting People, Promoting Peace.* Montreal and Kingston: McGill–Queen's University Press, 2001.

Mellgreen, Doug. "Norway Picks US Fighter to Replace Aging Fleet." *Foxnews.com.* 20 November 2008. Accessed 5 June 2009. http://www.foxnews.com/printer_friendly_wires/2008Nov20/0,4675,EUNorwayJointStrikeFighter,00.html.

Mifflin, Michael. "Canada's Arctic Sovereignty and Nunavut's Place in the Federation." *Policy Options* 29, no. 7 (2008): 86–90.

Millar, BGen David. "Northern Presence." *Airforce* 34, no. 1 (Spring 2010): 29–30.

Miller, Hugo. "U.S. Seeks 'Unfettered' Northwest Passage." *Vancouver Province*, 21 October 2008. Accessed 23 June 2011. http://www.canada.com/theprovince/news/story.html?id=83b6126e-e345-4317-aecb-02ff192a6212.

Minister of National Defence and Minister of Mines and Resources. To Cabinet, "Northern Development Policy." 16 January 1948. *Documents on Canadian External Relations.* Vol. 14–928, doc. 928. Accessed 28 May 2009. http://www.international.gc.ca/department/history-histoire/dcer/details-en.asp?intRefid=10616.

Mittlestaedt, Martin. "The High Cost of Blowing Smoke on the High Seas." *Globe and Mail,* 1 April 2009, A11.

Moore, Dene. "Housing Crisis a Greater Issue for Nunavut Than Arctic Sovereignty." *Canadian Press,* 14 August 2006.

Moore, LCol S.W. "Defending Canadian Arctic Sovereignty: An Examination of Prime Minister Harper's Arctic Initiatives." Toronto: Canadian Forces College, 2007.

Morris, Margaret W. "Boundary Problems Relating to the Sovereignty of the Canadian Arctic." In *Canada's Changing North.* Edited by William C. Wonders. Toronto: McClelland and Stewart, 1971. 310–37.

Morrison, William R. "Eagle over the Arctic: Americans in the Canadian North, 1867–1985." *Canadian Review of American Studies* (1987): 61–85.

———. *Showing the Flag: The Mounted Police and Canadian Sovereignty in the North, 1894–1925.* Vancouver: UBC Press, 1985.

Morton, Desmond. "Providing and Consuming Security in Canada's Century." *Canadian Historical Review* 81, no. 1 (2000): 1–28.

Muir, Magdalena. "Illegal, Unreported, and Unregulated Fishing in the Circumpolar Arctic." *Arctic* 63, no. 3 (September 2010): 373–78.

Mychajlyszyn, Natalie. "The Arctic: Geopolitical Issues." In *The Arctic: Canadian and International Perspectives.* Library of Parliament InfoSeries. October 2008. 1–5.

National Commission on the BP Deepwater Horizon Oil Spill and Offshore Drilling (United States). Report to the President. *Deep Water: The Gulf Oil Disaster and the Future of Offshore Drilling.* 11 January 2011. Accessed 5 March 2011. http://www.oilspillcommission.gov/final-report.

Natural Sciences and Engineering Research Council of Canada (NSERC) / Social Sciences and Humanities Research Council of Canada (SSHRC). "From Crisis to Opportunity: Rebuilding Canada's Role in Northern Research." Final report to NSERC and SSHRC from the Task Force on Northern Research. Ottawa: 2000. http://www.nserc-crsng.gc.ca/_doc/Northern-Nordique/crisis.pdf.

Noble, John. "Arctic Solution Already in Place." *Toronto Star*, 8 February 2006, A19.

Nord, Douglas C. "The North in Canadian–American Relations: Searching for Cooperation in the Melting Seas." Paper presented to the Borders and Bridges Conference, Ottawa, 18–19 October 2008.

Norwegian Ministry of Defence. *Norwegian Defence 2008.* Oslo: 2008. Accessed 5 June 2009. http://www.regjeringen.no/upload/FD/Dokumenter/Fakta2008_eng.pdf.

Norwegian Ministry of the Environment. *Report No. 8 to the Storting (2005–2006): Integrated Management of the Marine Environment of the Barents Sea and the Sea Areas Off the Lofoten Islands.* Oslo: Government Publications, 2006.

Norwegian Ministry of Foreign Affairs. *The Norwegian Government's High North Strategy,* Oslo, December 2006, Accessed 18 June 2011. http://www.regjeringen.no/upload/UD/Vedlegg/strategien.pdf.

Novosti. "Reactor on Russia's Newest Submarine Fired Up." 21 November 2008. Accessed 5 June 2009. http://en.rian.ru/russia/20081121/1 18453947.html.

———. "Russia Says Arctic Marking Does Not Imply Territorial Claim." 23 September 2008. Accessed 28 May 2009. http://en.rian.ru/russia/20080923/117046775.html.

———. "Russia Says Media Reports on Possible Arctic Conflict 'Alarmist.'" 22 October 2008. Accessed 28 May 2009. http://en.rian.ru/russia/20081022/117891202.html.

Nunavut Tunggavik Inc. (NTI). *Discussion Paper: Devolution and Marine Areas.* Presentation to Paul Mayer, Vancouver, 2 February 2007. Accessed 10 July 2008. http://www.tunngavik.com/documents/publications/2007-02-02-NTI-Marine-Areas.pdf, accessed 10 July 2008.

Obama, Barak. "Barak Obama and Joe Biden: New Energy for America." 2008. Accessed 28 May 2009. http://www.barackobama.com/pdf/factsheet_energy_speech_080308 .pdf.

Office of Naval Research, Naval Ice Center. Oceanographer of the Navy and the Arctic Research Commission. *Naval Operations in an Ice-Free Arctic Symposium Final Report.* 17–18 April 2001. Accessed 5 June 2009. http://www.natice.noaa.gov/ icefree/FinalArcticReport.pdf.

Okalik, Paul. "Arctic Priorities: A Northern Perspective." *Behind the Headlines* 65, no. 4 (2008): 3–8.

Oldfield, Jonathan D. *Russian Nature: Exploring the Environmental Consequences of Societal Change.* Burlington: Ashgate, 2005.

O'Neil, Peter. "Russia's Militarization May Be Just Sabre-Rattling: Expert." *Canwest News Service,* 17 March 2009.

O'Rourke, Ronald. "Changes in the Arctic: Background and Issues for Congress." Congressional Research Service report 7-5700. 8 October. Washington: 2010.

———. *Coast Guard Icebreaker Modernization: Background, Issues, and Options for Congress—CRS Report for Congress* RL 34391. 11 September. Washington: Congressional Research Service, 2008. Accessed 5 June 2009. http://fas.org/sgp/ crs/weapons/RL34391.pdf.

Organization for Security and Cooperation in Europe. Press release, "Russian Deputy Foreign Minister Discusses European Proposal with OSCE states." 18 February 2009. Accessed 26 February 2009. http://www.osce.org/itm/36321.html.

Østreng, Willy. "National Security and the Evolving Issues of Arctic Environment and Cooperation." In *National Security and International Environmental Cooperation in the Arctic—The Case of the Northern Sea Route."* Edited by Willy Østreng. Dordrecht: Kluwer Academic Publishers, 1999.

Panetta, Alexander. "Russians Say Canada Ally—Not Rival—in Arctic Sovereignty Fight." CNEWS, 30 June 2009. Accessed 10 July 2009. http://cnews.canoe .ca/CNEWS/Canada/2009/06/30/9987336-cp.html.

Pharand, Donat. "The Arctic Waters and the Northwest Passage: A Final Revisit." *Ocean Development and International Law* 38, nos. 1–2 (2007): 3–69.

———. *Canada's Arctic Waters in International Law.* Cambridge: Cambridge University Press, 1988.

———. *The Law of the Sea of the Arctic with Special Reference to Canada.* Ottawa: University of Ottawa Press, 1973.

Podvig, Pavel, and Hui Zhang. *Russian and Chinese Responses to U.S. Military Plans in Space.* Cambridge, MA: American Academy of Arts and Sciences, 2008.

Prime Minister's Office (PMO). Backgrounder: "Expanding Canadian Forces Operations in the Arctic." 10 August 2007. Accessed 20 August 2007. http://pm.gc.ca/ eng/media.asp?id=1785.

———. Backgrounder: "Extending the Jurisdiction of Canadian Environment and Shipping Laws in the Arctic." 27 August 2008. Accessed 28 August 2008. http://pm.gc.ca/eng/media.asp?id=2246.

————. Backgrounder: "Northern Strategy." 10 March 2008. Accessed 28 February 2009. http://pm.gc.ca/eng/media.asp?id=2016.

————. "PM Announces Plan to Identify and Defend Northern Resources." 26 August 2008. Accessed 28 May 2009. http://www.pm.gc.ca/eng/media.asp?category =1&id=2242.

————. "PM Unveils Canada First Defence Strategy." 12 May 2008. Accessed 28 May 2009. http://pm.gc.ca/eng/media.asp?id=2095.

————. "PM Launches New Regional Economic Development Agency for Canada's North," 18 August 2009. Accessed 3 September 2009. http://pm.gc.ca/eng/ media.asp?category=1&id= 2751.

Privy Council Office. *Securing an Open Society: Canada's National Security Policy.* April 2004. Accessed 28 May 2009. http://www.pco-bcp.gc.ca/docs/information/ Publications/natsec-secnat/natsec-secnat-eng.pdf.

Pugliese, David. "Conservatives Won't Commit Defence Strategy to Paper: 20-Year Plan for Military Be Based on 'Vision' Outlined in Harper, MacKay Speeches." *Ottawa Citizen,* 13 May 2008, A1.

Pugliese, David. "Reserve Units to Form Core of New Arctic Force." *Ottawa Citizen,* 22 March 2009. Accessed 23 March 2009. http://www.ottawacitizen.com/news/ Reserve+units+form+core+Arctic+force/1416657/ story.html.

Pullen, Thomas C. "What Price Canadian Sovereignty?" *U.S. Naval Institute Proceedings* 113, no. 9 (1987): 66–72.

Rayfuse, Rosemary. "Warm Waters and Cold Shoulders: Jostling for Jurisdiction in Polar Oceans." *University of New South Wales Faculty of Law Research Series.* No. 56 (2008). Accessed 28 May 2009. http://law.bepress.com/cgi/view content.cgi ?article=1131&context=unswwps.

Revkin, Andrew C.. "Experts Urge U.S. to Increase Icebreaker Fleet in the Arctic." *New York Times,* 17 August 2008, 6.

Roland, Floyd. "Arctic Energy Resources Will Be Needed." *Embassy,* 6 November 2008, 22.

Rompkey, William (Bill). "Russian Flags Aren't the Real Threat to Arctic Sovereignty." *Ottawa Citizen,* 17 July 2008, A13.

————. Press release, "Time to Control Our Arctic Waters." 18 February 2010. Accessed 15 May 2010. http://www.liberalsenateforum.ca/In-The-Senate/Publication/8731 _Time-to-control-our-Arctic-waters.

Rothwell, Donald. *Maritime Boundaries and Resource Development: Options for the Beaufort Sea.* Calgary: Canadian Institute of Resources Law, 1988.

Rowe, Elana Wilson. "Arctic Unity, Arctic Difference: Mapping the Reach of Northern Discourses." *Polar Record* 43, no. 2 (2007): 125–33.

————. 2009. "Russian Regional Multilateralism: The Case of the Arctic Council." In *The Multilateral Dimension in Russian Foreign Policy.* Edited by Elana Wilson Rowe and Stina Torjesen. London: Routledge, 2009.

Royal Canadian Mounted Police (RCMP), Marine and Ports Branch Great Lakes and St. Lawrence Seaway Interim Marine Security Operation Centre (GLSLS

MSOC). "Frequently Asked Questions." 2008. Accessed 28 May 2009. http://www
.rcmp-grc.gc.ca/mari-port/faq-eng.htm.

Rudd, David. "Northern Europe's Arctic Defence Agenda." *Journal of Military and
Strategic Studies* 12, no. 3 (2010). Accessed 18 November 2010. http://www.jmss
.org/jmss/index.php/jmss/article/view/311/332.

Runnalls, David. "Arctic Sovereignty and Security in a Climate-Changing World." In
Securing Canada's Future in a Climate-Changing World. Ottawa: National Round
Table on the Environment and the Economy, 2008. 75–88.

Russian Federal Ministry of Defence. "Russian Navy Resumes Presence in Arctic Area."
News Details. 14 July 2008. Accessed 5 June 2009. http://www.mil.ru/eng/
1866/12078/details/index.shtml?id=47433.

Russian Federation. Security Council. "Press-reliz po Osnovam gosudarstvennoi politiki Rossiiskoi Federatsii v Arktike na period do 2020 goda i dalneishuyu per-
spekrivy" [Press Release on the Foundations of the State Policy of the Russian
Federation in the Arctic for the Period to 2020 and Long Term]. 27 March 2009.
Accessed 30 March 2009. http://www.scrf.gov.ru/news/421.html.

"Russian Navy Promised New Nuclear Subs with New Strategic Missiles." *Bellona.*
6 October 2008. Accessed 5 June 2009. http://www.bellona.org/news/news
_2008/new_nuke_subs.

"Russia Restarts Cold War Patrols." *BBC News,* 17 August 2007. Accessed 5 June 2009.
http://news.bbc.co.uk/2/hi/europe/6950986.stm.

"Russia Sends Naval Vessels to Spitsbergen." *Barents Observer,* 15 July 2007. Accessed
5 June 2009. http://www.barentsobserver.com/russia-sends-navy-vessels-to
-spitsbergen.4497720-58932.html.

Scarborough, Rowan. "Russian Flights Smack of Cold War." *Washington Times,* 26 June
2008, A1.

Schubert, Captain Conrad. Letter to Commander Joint Task Force North. 22 October
2007. DND file 1920-1 (DCO).

Scott, Norval. "'U.S., Canada Chart Path for Arctic Future.'" *Globe and Mail,* 2 July
2008, A7.

Seguin, Rheal. "Scientists Predict Seasonal Ice-Free Arctic by 2015." *Globe and Mail,*
12 December 2008, A7.

Seidler, Christoph. "Politicians Censor Report on Dangers of Arctic Drilling." *Spiegel
Online International.* 23 January 2008. Accessed 5 June 2009. http://www.spiegel
.de/international/world/0,1518,530454-2,00.html.

Shaw, Richard. "Oil Predictions and Break-Even Prices." *Seeking Alpha,* 25 December
2007. Accessed 5 June 2009. http://seekingalpha.com/article/58322-oil-price
-predictions-and-break-even-prices.

Sieff, Martin. "Russia Upgrades Bomber-ALCM Force for the 21st Century." *UPI.com.*
5 January 2009. Accessed 5 June 2009. http://www.upi.com/Security_Industry/
2009/01/05/Russia_upgrades_bomber-ALCM_force_for_21st_century/UPI-399
51231177215.

Simon, Mary. "Does Ottawa's Northern Focus Look Backwards?" *Nunatsiaq News*, 11 April 2008. Accessed 21 June 2011. http://www.nunatsiaqonline.ca/archives/2008/804/80425/opinionEditorial/opinions.html.

———. "Inuit: The Bedrock of Arctic Sovereignty." *Globe and Mail*, 26 July 2007, A15.

———. "Inuit Say Budget Falls Far Short of Throne Speech Promises." ITK press release. 27 February 2008.

———. "The Militarization of the Arctic." ITK blog. 5 October 2010. Accessed 6 October 2010. http://www.itk.ca/blog/mary-simon/oct-05-2010-militarization-arctic.

———. Speech to the Canadian Club of Victoria. 25 September 2008. Accessed 18 April 2009. http://www.itk.ca/presidents-speaking-tour#1.

———. Speech to Canada–UK Colloquium. "The Arctic and Northern Dimensions of World Issues." Iqaluit, 4 November 2010.

Simpson, Jeffrey. "What's a Canadian to Do When There's No Bush to Beat Around?" *Globe and Mail*, 28 October 2008, A21.

Smith, Gordon W. "Sovereignty in the North: The Canadian Aspect of an International Problem." In *The Arctic Frontier*. Edited by R. St. J. MacDonald. Toronto: University of Toronto Press, 1966. 194–255.

———. "The Transfer of Arctic Territories from Great Britain to Canada in 1880, and Some Related Matters, as Seen in Official Correspondence." *Arctic* 14, no. 1 (1961): 53–73.

———. "Weather Stations in the Canadian North and Sovereignty." *Journal of Military and Strategic Studies* 11, no. 3 (Spring 2009). Accessed 28 May 2009. http://www.jmss.org/jmss/index.php/jmss/article/view/69.

"SSN-774 Virginia-Class New Attack Submarine [NSSN] Centurion." Globalsecurity.org. 5 September 2008. Accessed 5 June 2009. http://www.globalsecurity.org/military/systems/ship/ssn-774.htm.

Standing Senate Committee on Fisheries and Oceans (SSCFO). Committee Proceedings, 39th Parl., 2nd session (16 October 2007—7 September 2008). Accessed 28 May 2009. http://www.parl.gc.ca/common/Committee_SenProceed.asp?Language=E&parl=39&Ses=2&comm_id=7.

———. *The Coast Guard in Canada's Arctic: Interim Report*. June. Ottawa: 2008.

———. *Controlling Canada's Arctic Waters: Role of the Canadian Coast Guard*. 15 April. Ottawa: 2010.

———. *The Management of Fisheries and Oceans in Canada's Western Arctic*. May. Ottawa: 2010.

———. *Nunavut Fisheries: Quota Allocations and Benefits*. April. Ottawa: 2004.

Standing Senate Committee on National Security and Defence (SSCNSD). *Canadian Security Guide Book—Coasts*. March. Ottawa: 2007.

———. *Canada's Coastlines: The Longest Under-Defended Borders in the World*. October. Ottawa: 2003.

———. *Emergency Preparedness in Canada: How the Fine Arts of Bafflegab and Procrastination Hobble the People Who Will Be Trying to Save You When Things Get Really Bad …* September. Ottawa: 2008.

Standing Committee on Public Accounts (SCPA). *Managing the Coast Guard Fleet and Marine Navigation Services—Fisheries and Oceans.* April. Ottawa: 2008.

Statistics Canada. "Inuit Regions." 2006. Accessed 28 May 2009. http://www12.stat can.ca/english/census06/analysis/aboriginal/maps/Inuit/InuitRegionsAboriginal _Reference_ec.pdf.

Stauch, James. "Sovereignty for Whom? A Closer Look at Use and Occupancy in the Canadian Arctic." Presentation to the Canada in the World Conference, University of Toronto International Relations Society. 18 January 2008.

Stewart, E.J., S.E.L. Howell, D. Draper, J. Yackel. and A. Tivy. "Sea Ice in Canada's Arctic: Implications for Cruise Tourism." *Arctic* 60, no. 4 (2007): 370–80.

Stoffer, Peter. House of Commons *Debates*, 31 October 2006. 1015.

Stokke, Olav Schram. "Radioactive Waste in the Barents and Kara Seas: Russian Implementation of the Global Dumping Regime." In *Protecting the Polar Marine Environment: Law and Policy for Pollution Prevention,* ed. Davor Vidas. Cambridge: Cambridge University Press, 2000. 200–220.

———. "Sub-Regional Cooperation and Protection of the Arctic Marine Environment in the Barents Sea." In *Protecting the Polar Marine Environment: Law and Policy for Pollution Prevention.* Edited by Davor Vidas. Cambridge: Cambridge University Press, 2000. 124–48.

Stokke, Olav Schram, and Geir Hønneland, eds. *International Cooperation and Arctic Governance: Regime Effectiveness and Northern Region Building.* London: Routledge, 2007.

Struck, Doug. "Russia's Deep-Sea Flag-Planting at North Pole Strikes a Chill in Canada." *Washington Post*, 7 August 2007. Accessed 5 June 2009. http://www.washington post.com/wpdyn/content/article/2007/08/06/AR2007080601369.html.

Struzik, Ed. "As the Far North Melts, Calls Grow for Arctic Treaty." *Yale Environment 360*, 14 June 2010. Accessed 21 June 2011. http://e360.yale.edu/content/feature .msp?id=2281.

———. "Canada Urged to Take Lead in Polar Research." *Edmonton Journal*, 25 February 2009, A3.

———. "The True North Strong and Free but Not Cheap." *Toronto Star*, 1 December 2007, ID 01.

Sutherland, R.J. "The Strategic Significance of the Canadian Arctic." In *The Arctic Frontier*. Edited by R. St. J. MacDonald. Toronto: University of Toronto Press, 1966. 256–78.

Taylor, Paul. "A Hawkeyed Addition to Canada's Arctic Arsenal," *Globe and Mail*, 10 December 2007, A7.

Thatcher, Chris. "MSOCs: A Pan-Government Approach to Marine Security." *Vanguard* (October–November 2006). Accessed 28 May 2009. http://www.vanguard canada.com/MSOCThatcher.

Thompson, John. "Ottawa Clears Path for Devolution Talks." *Nunatsiaq News*, 14 March 2008. Accessed 21 June 2011. http://www.nunatsiaqonline.ca/archives/2008/ 803/80314/news/ nunavut/80314_1007.html.

Transport Canada. *Guidelines for Operation of Passenger Vessels in Canadian Arctic Waters.* TP 13670E. Winnipeg: Transport Canada, Prairie and Northern Region, Marine, 2005.

———. News Release H078/10. "Government of Canada Takes Action to Protect Canadian Arctic Waters." 22 June 2010. Accessed 23 June 2010. http://www.tc.gc.ca/eng/mediaroom/releases-2010-h078e-6019.htm.

Turner, Michael. "A Job for the Coast Guard: It's Too Bad That the Harper Government's Preoccupation with the Military Has Caused It to Overlook a More Sensible Solution to Arctic Sovereignty." *Ottawa Citizen,* 13 July 2007, A13.

United Nations Convention on the Law of the Sea (UNCLOS). 10 December 1982. Accessed 28 May 2009. http://www.un.org/Depts/los/convention_agreements/texts/unclos/unclos_e.pdf.

United Nations Environment Programme (UNEP). "Revised Draft Decision on Sustainable Development of the Arctic Region." 1 February 2008. Accessed 10 March 2009. http://www.unep.org/civil_society/GCSF9/pdfs/draft-dec-ARCTIC-1feb08.pdf.

UN Oceans and Law of the Sea. Division for Ocean Affairs and Law of the Sea. "Chronological Lists of Ratifications of, Accessions, and Successions to the Convention and the Related Agreements as at 31 December 2008." Updated 31 December 2008. Accessed 5 June 2009. http://www.un.org/Depts/los/reference_files/chronological _lists_of_ ratifications.htm.

———. "Commission on the Limits of the Continental Shelf (CLCS)," (2007). Accessed 5 June 2009. http://www.un.org/Depts/los/clcs_new/clcs_home.htm.

———. "Commission on the Limits of the Continental Shelf (CLCS): Outer Limits of the Continental Shelf Beyond 200 Nautical Miles from the Baselines: Submissions to the Commission: Submission by the Russian Federation." 18 November 2008. Accessed 5 June 2009. http://www.un.org/Depts/los/clcs_new/submissions _files/submission_rus.htm.

———. *Report of the Secretary General.* 62nd session. UN Doc A/62/67/Add.1. 31 August 2007. Accessed 21 June 2011. http://daccess-dds-ny.un.org/doc/UNDOC/GEN/N07/494/09/PDF/N0749409.pdf?OpenElement.

United States Geological Survey. *Circum-Arctic Resource Appraisal: Estimates of Undiscovered Oil and Gas North of the Arctic Circle.* Fact Sheet 2008-2049. Washington: 2008.

VanderZwaag, David L. "Land-Based Marine Pollution and the Arctic: Polarities Between Principles and Practice." In *Protecting the Polar Marine Environment: Law and Policy for Pollution Prevention.* Edited by Davor Vidas. Cambridge: Cambridge University Press, 2000.

VanderZwaag, David, and J.A. Hutchings. "Canada's Marine Species at Risk: Science and Law at the Helm, but a Sea of Uncertainty." *Ocean Development and International Law* 36 (2005): 219–59.

Verhoef, Jacob, and Dick MacDougall. "Delineating Canada's Continental Shelf According to the United Nations Convention on the Law of the Sea." *Ocean Sovereignty* 3, no. 1 (2008): 1–6.

Victor, David G., et al. "The Geoengineering Option." *Foreign Affairs* 88, no. 2 (March–April 2009): 64–76.

Viorst, Milton. "Arctic Waters Must Be Free." *Toronto Star*, 20 September 1969, A16.

Wallace, Ron, and P. Whitney Lackenbauer. "Unstoppable Momentum: The Real Meaning and Value Behind *Operation Nunalivut 10*." Canadian Defence and Foreign Affairs Institute Policy Update Paper. May 2010. http://www.cdfai.org/PDF/Unstoppable%20Momentum.pdf.

Walter and Duncan Gordon Foundation (WDGF). *The Arctic and Canada's Foreign Policy*. Report and Recommendations from a workshop sponsored by the WDGF. 4–5 October 2006. Accessed 28 May 2009. http://www.gordonfn.org/resfiles/ForeignArcticPolicyWorkshop_Nov%202006.pdf.

Wang, E.B. "Canadian Forces Activities in the North: Sovereignty." Memorandum to Mr. Cameron, External Affairs. 25 November 1970. LAC, RG 25, vol. 10322, file 27-10-2-2, pt. 2. Acquired under Access to Information.

———. "Canadian Sovereignty in the Arctic." *Canadian Yearbook of International Law 1976*. Vancouver: UBC Press, 1976. 307–12.

———. "The Dew Line and Canadian Sovereignty." 26 May 1969. LAC, RG 25, file 27-10-2-2, pt. 1. Acquired under Access to Information.

———. "The Role of Canadian Armed Forces in Defending Sovereignty." 30 April 1969. LAC, RG 25, vol. 10322, file 27-10-2-2, pt. 1. Acquired under Access to Information.

———. "The Role of Canadian Armed Forces in Defending Sovereignty: A Paper by E.B. Wang, 30 April 1969." *Journal of Military and Strategic Studies* 11, no. 3 (2009): 1–23. Issue edited by P. Whitney Lackenbauer.

Watt-Cloutier, Sheila. "Connectivity: The Arctic—The Planet." Speech at Oslo Sophie Prize Ceremony. 15 June 2005. Accessed 28 May 2009. http://www.sophieprize.org/Articles/23.html.

Weber, Bob. "Arctic Needs Health Towns, Economy, Not Just a Military Presence: Northern Leaders." *Canadian Press*, 11 July 2007.

White House. *National Security Presidential Directive/NSPD 66. Homeland Security Presidential Directive/HSPD 25—Arctic Region Policy*. 9 January 2009. Washington.

"Who Owns the Arctic?" Episode of *The Agenda* with Steve Paikin. TV Ontario. 29 September 2008. Accessed 10 October 2008. http://www.tvo.org/TVO/WebObjects/TVO.woa? video?TAWSP _Dbt_20080929_779336_0.

Wilson, Gary N. "Inuit Diplomacy in the Circumpolar North." *Canadian Foreign Policy* 13, no. 3 (2007): 65–80.

Windeyer, Chris. "Tories Praised for Helping Nunavut with Housing." *Nunatsiaq News*, 27 February 2009. Accessed 21 June 2011. http://www.nunatsiaqonline.ca/archives/2009/902/90227/news/nunavut/90227_1949.html.

———. "Tories Put Three Places on Short List for Research Centre." *Nunatsiaq News*, 27 February 2009. Accessed 21 June 2011. http://www.nunatsiaqonline.ca/archives/2009/902/90227/news/nunavut/90227_1939.html.

Wingrove, Josh. "Want to Do Business in Nunavut? You'd Better Talk with Us First. Josh Wingrove Explains How a Group of Inuit Took on the Feds and Won." *Globe and Mail*, 14 August 2010, F5.

Wolfers, Arnold. *Discord and Collaboration: Essays on International Politics*. Baltimore: Johns Hopkins University Press, 1962.

Woods, Allan, and Tonda MacCharles. "PM, Obama Begin 'Green' Talks: Say They Want to Work to Tackle Shared Goals of Cutting Emissions from Dirty Energy Sources.'" *Toronto Star*, 20 February 2009, A6.

Worm, Boris, and David Vanderzwaag. "High Seas Fisheries: Troubled Waters, Tangled Governance, and Recovery Prospects." *Behind the Headlines* 64, no. 5 (2007): 1–32.

Young, Oran R. "Arctic Governance: The Next Phase." Paper commissioned by the Standing Committee of Parliamentarians of the Arctic Region. June 2002. Accessed 26 February 2009. http://www.arcticparl.org/_res/site/File/static/conf5_scpar 2002.pdf.

———. "Governing the Arctic: From Cold War Theatre to Mosaic of Cooperation." *Global Governance* 11 (2005): 9–15.

———. "Whither the Arctic? Conflict or Cooperation in the Circumpolar North." *Polar Record* 45, no. 1 (2009): 73–82.

———. "Whither the Arctic 2009? Further Developments." *Polar Record* 45, no. 2 (2009): 179–81.

Young, Oran R., and Neils Einarsson. "Introduction: Human Development in the Arctic." In *Arctic Human Development Report*. Akureyri: Steffanson Institute, 2004.

Yukon, Northwest Territories, and Nunavut Governments. *A Northern Vision: A Stronger North and a Better Canada*. Yellowknife, 2007. Accessed 28 May 2009. http://www.anorthernvision.ca.

Zarate, Gabriel. "Arctic Bay Opposes Seismic Testing in Lancaster Sound." *Nunatsiaq News*, 6 June 2010. Accessed 6 June 2010. http://www.nunatsiaqonline.ca/stories/article/98789_arctic_bay_opposes_seismic_testing_in_lancaster_sound.

Zysk, Katarzyna. "Russia and the High North: Security and Defence Perspectives." In *Security Prospects in the High North: Geostrategic Thaw or Freeze?* Rome: NATO College, 2009. 102–29.

———. "Russia's Arctic Strategy: Ambitions and Constraints." *Joint Force Quarterly* 57, no. 2 (2010): 103–10.

Index

A

a mari ad mare ad mare, 161–62

Advisory Committee on Northern Development, 160

Advisory Committee on Northern Security and Stewardship, 12

aegis combat system, 56

Aglukkaq, Leona, 158

agree-to-disagree approach, 8, 9, 80, 105, 106, 116, 117, 120, 126

air independent propulsion system, 105

Airoldi, Adele, 143

Alaska, 125, 158, 187, 160, 170n256, 187, 193

Alert, xix–xx, 105, 229

Aleut International Association, 199

Alvarez, Pierre, 149

Antarctic, 15, 139, 140, 183–84, 242

anti-satellite attack technology, 190

Arctic-5, 139, 191, 194, 240, 241–45, 261

Arctic-8, 181, 184, 186, 187, 189, 191, 193, 195, 197–98, 200, 201, 203, 206, 208, 210–11, 218, 219, 242

arctic "arms race," 8, 232

Arctic Athabaskan Council, xviii, 86, 87, 138, 141, 199, 243

Arctic Basic Principle Agreement, 197–99, 204, 219

Arctic Canada Council, 12, 86, 141, 157

Arctic Capabilities Study, 83, 104

Arctic Climate Impact Assessment, 4, 26, 193

Arctic Cooperation Agreement, 78, 79, 128

Arctic Council, xvii, 5, 6, 7, 10, 11, 24, 25, 26, 36, 63, 65n10, 82–83, 87, 92, 118, 131, 136–39, 146, 154, 174n228, 176n244, 186, 192, 193–94, 195–211, 217, 224n35, 237, 239–40, 241–45, 247, 261, 267, 271, 272; *Arctic Human Development Report*, 264; Arctic Monitoring and assessment Program, 26, 144, 149–50, 159; Conservation of Arctic Flora and Fauna, 26; formation of, 36, 193; observer states, 199–203, 240, 244; 210, 220; offshore Oil and Gas Guidelines, 263; Oil and Gas Assessment, 2007, 263; Permanent Secretariat for, 11; proposed Arctic fund, 201–3; Protection of the Arctic Marine Environment, 90; Search and Rescue Agreement, xi, 244, 261; Sustainable Development Working Group, 138, 158–59, 264–65

Arctic Council Advisory Committee, 176n244, 271

Arctic Council Core Group, 176n244

Arctic Environmental Protection Strategy, 36, 242

Arctic governance, 184, 193, 196–97, 203, 237–45
arctic identity network, 218
Arctic Indigenous Languages Symposium, 265
Arctic Marine Shipping Assessment, 238, 247, 263–64
Arctic (Polar) Saga, 6, 12, 93–94, 145, 147, 162
Arctic Regional Hydrographic Commission, 264
Arctic Security Intergovernmental Working Group, 52, 109, 161
Arctic Treaty, 7, 24, 138–39, 174n227, 183–84, 242–43
Arctic Waters Pollution Prevention Act, 34, 77–78, 114, 238, 265
Assistant Deputy Ministers' Committee on the Arctic, 109
Association of World Reindeer Herders, 199
Axworthy, Lloyd, 122, 137
azipod propulsion system, 32

B
Bagnell, Larry, 126
Baird, John, 247
Baker, Betsy, 242
Bancroft-Hinchey, Timothy, 234
Barber, David, 25
Barents Euro-Arctic Region (BEAR), 220n2
Barents Sea, 10, 184, 191, 194, 209, 220n2, 238, 245
Bartels, General Knud, 236
Beaufort Sea, 31, 35, 42, 45, 63, 77, 123, 235–36, 237, 238, 246, 253n65, 266, 271; boundary dispute, 9, 12, 19, 21, 45, 125–27, 205, 259; 1825 Treaty and, 44–45, 125
Beesley, Alan, xviii
Berger, Thomas, 146, 154
Bering subregion, 132, 184, 191, 194
Borgerson, Scott, 126
Briggs, Philip, 128
Brigham, Lawson, 232–33, 242, 251n32
Britain, 44, 45, 73, 121, 125. *See also* United Kingdom
British Petroleum, 30

Bush administration, xvii, 47, 57, 58, 127; National Security Objective of; xvii. *See also* United States
Byers, Michael, 238, 245

C
Canada: alarmism, 213–14; Arctic Council and, 136–39, 214–15, 264–65; Arctic Council chairmanship, 11, 12, 183, 217, 219, 272; Arctic Environmental Protection Strategy, 36; climate change, 143; continental shelf, 41–42, 46, 121–24, 213, 257, 259; cooperation with United States, 105, 117, 123–24, 185, 204–7, 219–29, 228; Denmark and, 119–21, 235–37; development, 146–55; education, 160; European Union and, 131–32; formation of Arctic Council, 36; environment and, 265–69; Global Commerce Strategy, 188; health, 158–59; human development, 154–57; icebreakers, 32; *Northern Strategy*, 1, 86, 131, 145, 148, 156, 160, 214, 217, 227–28, 229, 232, 248, 256–57; research, 157–58; Russia and, 10, 44–45, 62, 82, 92–93, 121–23, 132–36, 173n206, 173n214, 195, 228, 234–35; stewardship, 211–18; United States and, 9, 45, 62–63, 125–31, 194–96, 204–5, 214, 218
Canada and the Circumpolar World, xv, 81
Canada Border Services Agency, 110, 113
Canada First Defence Strategy, 85, 94, 102, 118, 229, 258
Canada Revenue Agency, 113
Canada–Russia Economic Cooperation and Memorandum of Understanding, 134, 173n214
Canada–Russia Northern Development Partnership Program, 136
Canada Shipping Act, 116
Canada's Northern Strategy, 1, 227–28
Canadian Arctic Marine Environment Working Group, 12, 63
Canadian Arctic Research Initiative, 157–58
Canadian Association of Petroleum Producers, 149
Canadian Coast Guard, 60, 87, 94, 101–3, 106, 107, 110, 116, 123, 172n185, 229

Canadian High Arctic Research Station, 248
Canadian International Council, 4–5
Canadian International Development Agency, 136
Canadian Forces, 7, 8, 52–53, 94–106, 113, 228–29; ACC-117 Globemaster, 106, 230; *Arctic Capabilities Study*, 83, 104; Arctic Littoral, Surveillance, and Reconnaissance Experiment, 104; Arctic offshore patrol vessels, 38, 54, 99, 101–3, 230; Aurora maritime patrol aircraft, 106; CF Arctic Training Centre Resolute, 54, 68, 103–4, 231, 258; CH-47F Chinook, 231; F-35 aircraft, 230; Joint Task Force North, 109, 117; long-range patrol aircraft, 38; Loyal Edmonton Regiment, 232; Maritime Coastal Defence Vessels, 102; NORPLOYS, 52; nuclear-powered submarines, 36; replenishment vessels, 38, 105, 116; sovereignty and, 78, 94–98; UAV surveillance in Arctic, 104–5. *See also* surveillance and Department of National Defence
Canadian Northern Economic Development Agency, 246
Canadian Polar Commission, 89, 122
Canadian Rangers, xix, 3, 37–38, 52, 81, 87, 94, 98, 99–101, 104, 231, 232, 258
Cannon, Lawrence, 133, 162, 173n206, 217, 228, 237, 241, 243, 250n24
Cellucci, Paul, 47, 129
China, xviii, xvii, xviii, 5, 10, 25, 139, 199, 202, 208–9, 220, 239, 240; demand for oil, 31
China Prepares for an Ice-Free Arctic, 240
Chrétien, Jean, xviii
Chrétien government, 36, 81
Churchill (Manitoba), 264
Circumpolar Ambassador, 60, 83, 86, 88, 141
Circumpolar Inuit Declaration on Arctic Sovereignty, 145, 244
Circumpolar Inuit Health Action Plan, 159
Citizenship and Immigration Canada, 113
Clarkson, Adrienne, xvi
climate change, xii, xvi, 1, 2, 3, 4, 5, 6, 10, 12, 17, 18, 23, 25–29, 44, 51, 55, 69, 70, 78, 80, 82, 83–84, 87–89, 92, 131, 137–38, 139, 141–45, 149–50, 158, 181, 187, 189, 194, 196, 198, 201, 204–5, 210, 211, 213, 215, 216, 220, 227, 230, 235, 247–48, 257, 265–79
Clinton, Hillary, 239, 241–42
Cold War, 5, 17, 19, 34, 62, 74–75, 134, 189, 234
continental shelf (seabed), xvi, xviii, 5, 9, 12, 14–15, 20, 94, 119, 121–24, 129, 185, 191, 214, 227, 237–38, 242, 248, 257, 259, 260, 261
Commission on Limits of the Continental Shelf, 39, 43, 123, 260, 261
Conference on Security and Cooperation in Europe, 207–8, 209
Convention for the Protection of the Marine Environment of the Northeast Atlantic, 195
cooperative stewardship, 181, 182, 186–87, 189–90, 201, 204–5, 206, 207, 209, 248
Cotter, Captain Jamie, 102

D

Deepwater Horizon oil spill, 246, 263
Defence Research and Development Canada, 104, 229
Denmark, xx, 10, 24, 70, 119–20, 131, 191, 222n15, 232, 235–37, 238, 241, 271; continental shelf and, 41, 121–24
Department of External Affairs, 96–98
Department of Fisheries and Oceans, 106, 110, 113, 141, 237, 253n66; Nunavut Small Craft Harbours Report, 152
Department of Foreign Affairs and International Trade, xvii, 81, 83, 94, 121, 122, 141, 145–46, 160, 214, 216, 217, 219, 228, 237, 245; Arctic sovereignty and, 93–98; Inspector General's report, 83; *Statement on Canada's Arctic Foreign Policy*, 245–48, 255–74
Department of Indian and Northern Affairs, 84, 134, 141, 160, 214, 219
Department of Justice, 113
Department of National Defence, xix, xx, 52–53, 60–61, 75, 83, 96–97, 103, 107, 110, 141, 229; *Canada's International Policy Statement*, 53; roles and responsibilities, xviii, 51–53, 60, 83, 96–98, 110

Diefenbaker, John, xi, 69, 162, 274; northern vision of, 69
Distant Early Warning Line, xix, 34, 75–76

E

Ellesmere Island, 119, 120, 123, 159, 236
environment, xvi, 2, 5, 10, 11, 12, 18, 21, 25–29, 49, 63, 81, 82, 83, 84, 87, 88, 129, 132, 141–45, 146, 152, 153–54, 157, 183, 184–86, 189, 190, 192–93, 196–97, 200, 204, 205, 210, 214, 217, 233, 238, 246–47, 260–65, 265–70
Environment Canada, 113, 141
Esau, Warren, 232
European Commission, 131
European Free Trade Association, 264
European Union, xvii, 10, 11, 82, 87–88, 131–32, 139, 142, 143, 158, 191, 199, 201, 206–8, 220, 240, 242; Arctic policy, 47, 225n42; Northern Dimension Policy, 131, 220n2; Northwest Passage and, xvii, 10, 21, 48, 131–32
Eyre, Kenneth, 99
Exclusive Economic Zone, 14, 39, 102, 119, 121, 122, 152
Exxon, 31

F

Federal Contaminated Sites Action Plan, 269
Finland, 10, 271; Arctic Environmental Protection Strategy (AEPS), 36; icebreaker construction, 31
Fort Greely, ballistic missile interceptor base, 52
France, 199

G

gas hydrates, 29
Gazprom, 209
Germany, 199
Gibraltar, Strait of, 48
Goose Bay, 104
Graham, Bill, 4, 81, 119
Greenland, 6, 24, 35, 41, 43, 78, 110, 119, 120, 124, 131, 149, 184, 191, 206–7, 221, 224n41, 236, 244, 246, 252n49, 263
Griffiths, Franklyn, 2, 3, 7–12, 70, 89–90, 129, 152 , 239

Guidelines for Operation of Passenger Vessels in Canadian Arctic Waters, 153
Gwich'in Council International, 86, 141, 145, 243

H

Hans Island, xx, 4, 119–20, 236, 238, 259; domino theory, 4, 119
Hanson, Udloriak, 247
Harper, Stephen, xii, xxi, 4, 69, 85, 93–94, 95, 98–99, 122, 127, 141, 153, 154, 161, 162–63, 247, 256, 266, 274; Throne Speech of 2007, 54, 88; 148; use-it-or-lose-it message, 5, 85, 95–96, 154, 195, 228, 232
Hells Angels, 22
historical bays, 16
Holtsmark, Sven, 132–34
Homer-Dixon, Thomas, 142
Hormuz, Straits of, 129
House of Commons Standing Committee on Foreign Affairs and International Trade, 81, 132
Huebert, Rob, 2, 3, 5–12, 89, 120, 130, 138, 227, 232, 242
Humble Oil, 77

I

Iceland, 10, 131, 242, 264, 271
Ilulissat Declaration, 9, 41, 138, 139, 146, 170n160, 191, 194, 222n15
incrementalism, 10, 184, 185, 189, 203
India, 21, 31, 139, 202
Indonesia, 76
Institutional Building for Northern Aboriginal Peoples in Russia, 136
internal waters, definition of, 16
International Arctic Science Committee, 199
International Court of Justice, 41
International Dimension to the Inuit Action Plan, 140
International Maritime Organization, 21, 114, 116, 139–40, 154, 195, 239, 247, 263–64; *Guidelines for Ships Operating in Ice-Covered Waters*, 140
International Polar Year, 157, 159, 257, 265, 269–70
International Policy Statement, 4, 83–84
International Strait, definition of, 16

International Tribunal for the Law of the Sea, 41
International Union for Circumpolar Health, 159
International Whaling Commission, 131
Inuit Action Plan, 159–60
Inuit Circumpolar Council, 86, 88, 137, 140, 141, 158, 159, 207, 215, 241, 243, 244, 265
Inuit Nunaat, 71, 72, 88
Inuit Tapiriit Kanatami (ITK), xviii, 88–89, 101, 118, 140, 141, 154, 215, 244; *An Integrated Arctic Strategy*, 88–89, 118
Inuvialuit, 71, 72, 157
Inuvialuit Final Agreement, 126
Iqaluit, 110
Italy, 199

J

Japan, 5, 10, 25, 202; gas hydrates and, 29
Jean, Michaëlle, xvi
Joint Arctic Weather Stations, 75
Joint Rescue Coordination Centres, 107
Jones, David, 122, 128

K

Kessel, Alan, 122–23
King, William Lyon Mackenzie, 74
Klondike Gold Rush, 73
Koivurova, Timo, 138, 242
Kraska, Captain James, 233–34, 239

L

Lackenbauer, P. Whitney, 3, 5–12, 227, 228, 236
Lalonde, Suzanne, 5, 120, 238
land claims, 71, 83, 89, 140, 156, 216, 219, 241, 244, 268, 270
Lavrov, Sergey Viktorovich, 133, 134, 238, 241
Layton, Jack, 102
Legault, Len, 97–98
Lincoln Sea, xvi, 20, 21, 124, 259
Linklater, Joe, 145, 243
Lomonosov Ridge, 43, 123

M

MacEachern, Allan, xviii
MacKay, Peter, 43, 108, 122, 234

Mackenzie Gas Project, 33, 150, 156
Mackenzie Valley Pipeline Inquiry, 154
Malacca Strait, xvii, 48, 129
Manhattan, 34, 77, 78, 94
Marine Security Operations Centres (MSOCs), 109–10
Martin, Paul, xviii
Martin government, xx, 53–54, 60, 84–85; Defence Policy Statement, 98; *International Policy Statement*, 4; Northern Strategy of, 54. *See also Northern Dimension of Canada's Foreign Policy*
Mary River Iron Ore Mine, 31
McFadden, Vice Admiral Dean, 230
McNab, Ron, 122
McRae, Donald, 129
Medvedev, Dmitry, 92, 240
Ministry of Regional Development of the Russian Federation, 134
MS *Bremen*, 169n133
MS *Hanseatic*, 169n113
Mulroney, Brian, 36, 78

N

Nanisivik, 38, 54, 103, 105, 230
National Energy Board, 246, 263
Natural Resources Canada, 143, 150, 231, 237
Natural Sciences and Engineering Research Council, 157, 158, 160
Natynczyk, General Walter, 236
Netherlands, 199
Noble, John, 130
Nordic Council of Ministers, 199
NORDREG (Arctic marine traffic system), 113–16, 238, 251n34
North American Aerospace Defence Command (NORAD), 116–17, 206, 222n18, 235, 258
North Atlantic Fisheries Organization, 150
North Atlantic Treaty Organization (NATO), 75, 76, 122, 132–33, 189–90, 191, 208, 235–37
North Pole, 43, 44, 45, 121, 204, 220, 234
North Slope, xx
northern deployments (NORPLOYs), 52
The Northern Dimension of Canada's Foreign Policy, 81–84, 86, 134, 245
Northern Forum, 190

Northern Project Management Office, 246
Northern Sea Route, 47, 58, 136
Northern Vision, 85, 147
Northern Watch, 37, 104, 229
Northwest Passage, xvii, 2, 3, 4, 5, 9, 21, 28,
    32–35, 46–50, 58, 63, 71, 76, 77, 78, 80,
    89, 90, 94, 103, 105, 113, 118, 121,
    126–31, 142, 205, 213, 219, 234, 235,
    238, 239, 244, 263–64; European Union
    and, 47–49; United States and, 47–49
Northwest Territories, 14, 72, 87, 147, 150,
    156, 157, 255
Norway, 10, 24, 131, 132, 184, 188, 194,
    209–10, 224n39, 238, 241, 264, 271;
    Arctic Council and, xvii; defence pol-
    icy, 55, 232
nuclear-powered floating natural-gas ter-
    minal, 33
Nunatsiavut, 71, 72, 140, 157
Nunavik, 71, 72, 140, 157
Nunavut, 71, 72, 152, 156, 157, 220, 253n65
Nunavut Land Claims Agreement, 89, 216
Nunavut Marine Council, 89, 157, 216,
    220, 253n65
Nunavut Resources Corporation, 246

O

Obama, Barack, 142–43, 203–4, 206,
    224n35
oil and gas development, 6, 23–25, 27,
    29–33, 39, 43–44, 62, 132, 146–47,
    149–51, 207, 208, 210, 219–20, 246,
    262
Okalik, Paul, 156
Operation Nanook, xix, 107, 231–32, 237,
    258–59
Operation Narwhal, xx
Operation Nunalivut, 231, 236

P

Pangnirtung, 152
Pearson, Lester B. (Mike), xi
Permanent Participants, 83, 86, 138–39,
    199–200, 201–2, 206, 208, 215, 241, 244,
    246, 270–71. *See also* Aleut Interna-
    tional Association; Arctic Athabaskan
    Council; Gwich'in Council Interna-
    tional; Inuit Circumpolar Council
persistent organic pollutants, 138, 143–44,
    269

Pettigrew, Pierre, 119
Pharand, Donat, 43, 73
Philippines, 76
Poland, 199, 202
Polar Bear Treaty, 184, 266
Polar Code, 10, 61, 63, 140, 154, 175n237,
    247, 263–64
Polar Continental Shelf Project, 231, 248
Polar (Arctic) Race, 1, 6, 12, 39, 70, 88,
    92–93, 119, 149, 162
Polar Sea, 2, 35–36, 69, 70, 77–78, 94
Porcupine caribou herd, 205
Prime Minister's Office, 12, 197, 216, 218,
    219–20
Privy Council Office, 113, 168n110
Project Polar Epsilon, 104
Public Safety, 106, 109
Pullen, Captain Thomas, 128
Putin, Vladimir, 54

Q

Qikiqtani Inuit Association, 244

R

Radarsat, xix, xxi, 37, 99, 104–5, 116, 189
Ralston Saul, John, xvi
Rasmussen, Anders Fogh, 235
Reagan, Ronald, 78
resource development, 29–33, 181, 187,
    245, 261; fisheries, 150–52, 247,
    253n64; impact on communities, 22;
    uncertainty of, 33
Roland, Floyd, 147
Rompkey, William (Bill), 241–42
Royal Canadian Mounted Police, 60, 73, 94,
    106, 110, 113, 141
Royal Danish Navy, 237
Runnals, David, 146
Russia, 7, 24, 42, 50, 55, 62, 70, 92–93, 131,
    132–36, 184, 187, 188, 192–93, 194,
    197, 206, 207–8, 209, 220n2, 225n49,
    230, 234–35, 237, 238, 240, 241, 242,
    271; Arctic Strategy, 134, 235; conti-
    nental shelf, xvii, xviii, 41, 43, 92,
    121–24; icebreaker construction, 31;
    nuclear-powered icebreaking drill
    ships, 44; nuclear submarines, xvii, 51,
    54–55, 234
Russian Association of Indigenous Peoples
    of the North (RAIPON), 136, 199

Russian Foreign Ministry, 92–93, 192, 198
Russian–Georgian Crisis, 189

S
Saami Council, 199
Samsung Heavy Industry, 32
Saunders, Allison, 124
Scott, Andy, xx
seal ban, 207, 240, 265
search and rescue, xviii, xix, 10, 61, 94, 102,
    104, 106–7, 112, 114, 140, 185, 194,
    205, 220, 230, 244, 256, 261, 264, 272
Secretary of State for the Arctic, 11, 218–20
sector theory, 43
security, 7, 17, 18, 20, 141–42, 205–6, 228–34,
    245; definition of, 17, 18, 81; human
    security, 2, 17, 81–82; relationship
    between security and sovereignty, 19–22
Shell, 31
shipping, 2, 3, 10, 16, 21, 33, 34, 35, 46,
    48–49, 57, 63, 113–14, 127–28, 129,
    139–40, 149, 186, 201, 205, 207, 210,
    238, 244, 247, 263–64
Simon, Mary, 143, 144, 148, 154, 244–45,
    246
Small Island Developing States, 138
Smith, Duane, 241, 243
Social Sciences and Humanities Research
    Council, 157, 160
South Korea, 5, 10, 25, 139, 199, 239; ice-
    breaker construction, 31; natural gas
    carriers, 33
Spain, 199, 202
Spitsbergen, 42
Standing Committee on Foreign Affairs
    and International Trade, xv, xvi, 81,
    132
Standing Senate Committee on Fisheries
    and Oceans, 112, 113, 114, 172n185,
    229
Standing Senate Committee on National
    Security and Defence, 107, 116
Statement on Canada's Arctic Foreign Policy,
    6, 245–48
StatoilHydro, 209
Stauch, James, 162
Steel, James, 128
Stockholm International Peace Research
    Institute, 240
Støre, Jonas Gahr, 238

Straight Baselines, 16, 36, 76, 78
Struzik, Ed, 242
submarines, 16, 34, 36, 43, 51, 54–55, 56,
    76, 78, 98, 105, 106, 121, 234
surveillance, 8, 37, 51, 60, 104–7, 116, 190;
    sovereignty and, 96–98. *See also* Cana-
    dian Forces
Sustained Arctic Observing Network, 158
Svalbard, 208
Sweden, 10, 220, 271

T
territorial governments, 59, 86–87, 146,
    213, 215, 270, 271; *A Northern Vision:
    A Stronger North and a Better Canada*,
    87, 147, 154–56
territorial sea, 14
Territorial Sea and Fishing Zone Act, 77
"thinning ice" thesis, 2, 3, 118
tourism, 10, 63, 134, 152–54, 188, 195–96,
    260, 267
transboundary pollutants, 21, 83
Transport Canada, 107, 110, 113, 116
Trofimov, Dmitry, 122
Trudeau, Pierre Elliott, 76; functional
    approach to sovereignty, 77–78
Tuktoyaktuk, 110, 143, 153
Turbot War, 4, 119

U
United Kingdom, 199, 202
United Nations Convention on the Law of
    the Sea (UNCLOS), xviii, 9, 11, 14–16,
    18, 23–24, 31, 33, 39, 41–42, 45, 47, 90,
    114, 121, 123, 136, 139, 146, 152, 238,
    242–43, 259–60; Article 76, 23, 39, 41;
    Article 234, 77, 136, 152; International
    Strait, 164n24
United Nations Declaration on the Rights
    of Indigenous Peoples, 145, 247
United Nations Economic Commission for
    Europe's Long Range Transport of Air-
    borne Pollutants Process, 144
United Nations Environment Program,
    141, 247
United Nations Framework Convention on
    Climate Change, 142, 247
United States, xvii, xix, 6, 7, 9, 19, 20, 21,
    24, 33, 34, 39, 41–42, 43, 45, 50, 52, 54,
    56, 62, 63, 73, 74, 75, 77, 78, 80, 82, 90,

94, 105, 110, 114, 116, 125–31, 140, 191, 193, 196, 197, 204–7; 24, 232, 241, 242, 271; Arctic Council and, 24, 36; continental shelf, 41–42, 121–24, 237; defence policy of, 55–58; on international straits, 76; nuclear submarines, 54–55, 105; Presidential Directive 66, 57–58, 169n141, 171n173, 174n228, 223n23; UNCLOS, 41, 45–46
United States Coast Guard, 57, 77, 117, 123, 237
United States Geological Survey, 23, 29, 30, 146
United States Navy, xvii, 48, 54, 76, 105, 128, 193, 233, 237
University of the Arctic, 82, 131, 160, 164n33
unmanned aerial vehicles (UAVs), xix, xxi, 84, 104

V
Vancouver Olympics, 161
Vanderzwaag, David, 138
Vasilyev, Anton, 92

W
Wallace, Ron, 236
Walter and Duncan Gordon Foundation, 86, 162
Wang, Erik, 75, 96, 97
Watt-Cloutier, Sheila, 93, 141
Wilkins, David, 127
whole of government, 8, 11, 59, 83, 94, 98, 106–9, 116, 161, 258
World War II, 228; Arctic and, 34, 73–74
World Wildlife Federation, 199

Y
Young, Oran, 136–37, 152, 174n227, 220n5, 242–43

Z
Zysk, Katarzyna, 235